Cairo
PRACTICAL
Guide

"Marvelous and maddening,
full of secrets and surprises,
peopled with the whole spectrum
of humanity. . . .
This is Cairo, my home.
Please come in and enjoy it."

Omar Sharif

Cairo
PRACTICAL
Guide

New Fully Revised Edition

Lesley Lababidi

Eighteenth Edition
Original 1975 Edition
edited by Deborah Cowley and Aleya Serour

The American University in Cairo Press
Cairo   New York

First Edition 1975   Compiled & Edited by D. Cowley & A. Serour
Second Edition 1977   Revised & Edited by Aleya Serour
Third Edition 1981   Revised & Edited by S. Arulantham & J. O'Hanlon
Fourth Edition 1984   Revised & Edited by Arunkumar Pabari
Fifth Edition 1986   Revised & Edited by Marianne Pearson
Sixth Edition 1988   Compiled & Edited by Cassandra Vivian
Seventh Edition 1997   Compiled & Edited by Claire Francy
Eighth Edition 1998   With updated directory
Ninth Edition 1999   Revised by Michael McCain
Tenth Edition 2000   With updated directory
Eleventh Edition 2001   Revised by Mandy McClure
Twelfth Edition 2001   With updated directory
Thirteenth Edition 2002 Revised by Alex Dessouky
Fourteenth Edition 2004 Revised by Abigail Ulman
Fifteenth Edition 2006 Revised and edited by Lesley Lababidi
Sixteenth Edition 2008 Revised and edited by Lesley Lababidi
Seventeenth Edition 2010 Updated and edited by Lesley Lababidi

Eighteenth Edition © 2011 by
The American University in Cairo Press
113 Sharia Kasr el Aini, Cairo, Egypt
420 Fifth Avenue, New York, NY 10018
www.aucpress.com

Dar el Kutub No. 22440/11
ISBN 978 977 416 467 5

Dar el Kutub Cataloging-in-Publication Data

Lababidi, Lesley
    Cairo: The Practical Guide/ Lesley Lababidi. —Cairo: The American
  University in Cairo Press, 2011
        p.   cm.
        ISBN 978 977 416 467 5
        1. Cairo (Egypt)—Description and Travels   I. Title
        916.216

1 2 3 4   13 12 11

Designed by Andrea El-Akshar
Printed in Egypt

Contents

Contents

Acknowledgments

The first edition of *Cairo: The Practical Guide* came out in 1975. Over the past thirty-six years this book has informed, advised, and demystified the process of settling into Egypt. Many people shared their knowledge and experiences to provide the best and most up-to-date information. This 2011 edition is no exception. As always, I am grateful to the entire staff of the American University in Cairo Press, particularly Neil Hewison and Nadia Naqib. I am grateful to Caitlin Hawkins and Johanna Baboukis, editors, whose suggestions, clarifications, and corrections have been invaluable. Thank you to Andrea el-Akshar for the cover design. Thanks to Gihan Dakkak for her help in researching subjects in chapters 3, 4, and 6. Lisa Sabbahy revised the information in chapter 1 on ancient Egyptian history. I am grateful to Shaimaa Ashour, Ahmed Dorghamy, and Yahia Shawkat for their contributions to "Recycling in Cairo" in chapter 4. Bruce Lohof of the Fulbright Commission provided a list of institutions for "Scholarly Research" in chapter 6. Many thanks go to Gertrud Simmert-Genedy for sharing her in-depth knowledge and experience in "Having a Baby in Egypt" in chapter 5. I am grateful to all who have taken the time to answer my e-mails and telephone calls, to explain systems and schedules, and to provide information and directions. Thank you.

Preface

You've just received word that you are moving to Egypt. Pharaohs, pyramids, deserts, and the Nile swirl through your thoughts, as well as concerns about safety. Your friends and family have more questions than you have answers. Where do you look? The Internet is your first choice, but *Cairo: The Practical Guide* is where you will find the answers or the right information source. You and your family may be 'seasoned' expatriates and understand what it takes to move from one country to another, or this may be your first overseas experience. Whatever the case, anticipating the many logistical and financial changes can ensure a smooth start. Take time to plan and organize, get a grasp of the logistical ramifications, consider expectations, and seek out pertinent information. *Cairo: The Practical Guide* is here to help.

This book provides the insights needed to make the right decisions for a smooth transition and to settle quickly into the Egyptian community. *The Practical Guide* is your starting point. You will devour the information and depend on the suggestions while finding your own way, meeting new people, and settling in. Consider this book your portable reference—the Internet without a server. Then, one day, this *Practical Guide* will sit on a bookshelf to be referred to from time to time or to be passed along, its service completed because Egypt is now your home.

Accuracy in providing the best and most up-to-date information has been our goal. However, as in all aspects of life, things change. Since the Revolution of 25 January 2011, change has been significant. All information has been checked and rechecked to reflect the upheaval in the country, but statistics, places, times, and events change without notice. Some suggestions are through word of mouth or personal experience and are passed on to you with our best intentions. Nevertheless, we cannot guarantee quality, times, or hours.

In chapters 2 through 10, telephone numbers are given. All Cairo and Giza landline telephone numbers given in this book comprise only the eight-digit local number. All mobile numbers are prefixed by '0' and landline numbers outside Cairo/Giza include the area code. If calling a Cairo/Giza number from a mobile or from outside of Cairo, the eight-digit local number needs to be prefixed by the '02' Cairo area code. When calling any Egyptian number internationally, the '+(00) 20' international code needs to be used, omitting the first '0' from the area code or the mobile number.

Welcome to your new home!

1

Welcome to Egypt

Egypt. If there is one word that signifies the span of time and the footsteps of civilization, it is 'Egypt.' There are five thousand years of documented history, yet well before those records began, dinosaurs roamed this land. At the Geology Museum you can view a 99-million-year-old skeleton of *Paralititan stromeri* that lived in mangroves near the shores of the Tethys Sea, which was discovered near Bahariya Oasis. In the Fayoum, you can walk through an outdoor museum, the Valley of the Whales, and see skeletons of the giant ancient whale, *Basilosaurus isis*, in the position in which it died over 31 million years ago. Today, a desert wanderer comes across the flint tools, grinding stones, and rock paintings of prehistoric man: ten-thousand-year-old relics that defined human existence. Compared to such a history, the name 'Egypt' is an infant. 'Egypt' is derived from the ancient Greek 'Aigyptos,' which found its roots in the ancient Egyptian word 'Hwt-ka-Ptah' (meaning 'Temple of the soul of the god Ptah'). From 'Aigyptos' comes the word 'Copt,' meaning 'Egyptian.' In Arabic, Egypt is 'Misr'—the name that refers to both Cairo and the entire country.

Language

Egypt's population in 2000 was 68 million; in 2010 it reached 79 million, making Egypt the most populous country in the Middle East and the second most populous country in Africa. Yet the population is relatively homogenous. Arabic is spoken by nearly 98 percent of the nation. Nubians in southern Egypt make up a small linguistic minority speaking two dialects, Fadija and Kenuzi. Berber is spoken in the Siwa Oasis, and a tiny population of Beja near Aswan speaks Beja. English and French are widely spoken as second languages.

Before the Arab conquest in AD 640, the Coptic language evolved from the language spoken by the ancient Egyptians, and its alphabet evolved from Greek script. Letters of the Greek alphabet were used to represent Coptic sounds, and these, plus seven more characters derived ultimately from hieroglyphic script, were the origins of Coptic script. Coptic was recognized as the official language of Egypt as far back as the second century BC. Under the Arab rulers, the language of government work and texts shifted to Arabic. By the twelfth century, Arabic had become the official language of Egypt, while Coptic survived only in liturgical use in the Coptic Orthodox Church. Today, Arabic is the everyday language of both Egyptian Christians and Muslims.

Arabic is considered a complex language to learn and ranks with Korean, Japanese, and Chinese as one of the most difficult for westerners. There are three types of Arabic. Classical Arabic is the language of the Qur'an. Modern Standard Arabic *(fosha)* is a formal language used for books, newspapers, speeches, and television news reporting. The first two types are used throughout the Middle East. The third type is colloquial Arabic *(ammiyya)*, spoken in regional dialects. A person from Egypt may find it difficult to understand someone from Algeria or Lebanon. However, the reverse is not necessarily true: thanks to Egyptian cinema, which dominated the Arab world from the 1940s to the 1980s, most Arabic speakers understand Egyptian colloquial. Today, with satellite and cable, Arabic-speaking programs from every country are available and the dialect gap narrows.

Geography

Egypt is an astonishingly diverse and beautiful country, boasting the Nile River, lush farmland, the Red Sea and Mediterranean coastline, and vast, windswept deserts, massifs, and depressions. Egypt—or, more precisely, the Arab Republic of Egypt—covers an area of approximately 1,000,000 square kilometers in the northeastern corner

Distances between Cairo and Other Major Egyptian Cities in Kilometers

Abu Simbel	1,235
al-Alamein	293
Alexandria	217
Aswan	929
Asyut	386
Damietta	295
Fayoum	100
Heliopolis	24
Helwan	26
Hurghada	510
Ismailiya	135
Kharga	578
Luxor	679
Marsa Matruh	473
Port Said	212
Saint Catherine's	378
Sharm al-Sheikh	350
Siwa	700
Suez	129

of Africa and the Sinai Peninsula, which extends into southwestern Asia. It is twice the size of France and more than half the size of the state of Alaska. To the west, Egypt borders Libya; to the south, Sudan; to the east, the Red Sea, the Gaza Strip, and Israel; to the north, the Mediterranean Sea. The Nile River runs from south (Upper Egypt) to north (Lower Egypt). As it flows past Cairo, its waters branch out into the Delta region to form an area of rich farmland. Beyond the Nile Valley, 93 percent of

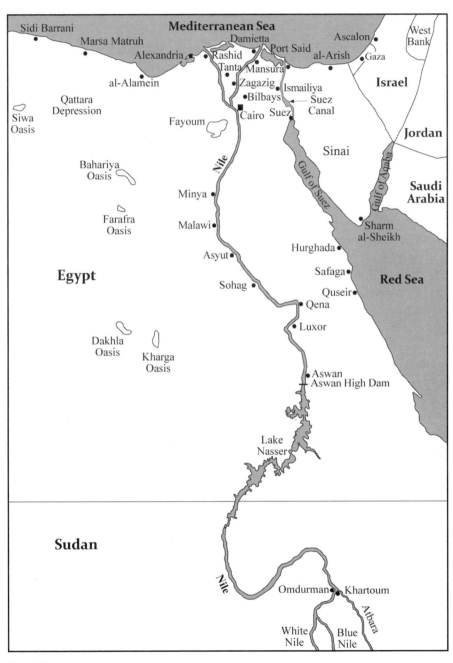

Map of Egypt

Egypt is covered by dry deserts, the Eastern and Western Deserts, which are part of the Sahara.

Each part of the country has distinguishing characteristics. The Nile Valley is a narrow strip of fertile land where 98 percent of Egypt's population lives. The names 'Upper Egypt' and 'Lower Egypt' refer to the flow of the Nile River, with Upper Egypt, in the south, being the land upstream, and Lower Egypt, in the north, the land downstream. The Nile River, the world's longest, flows from south to north and empties into the Mediterranean Sea. The Western Desert is the largest geographical area, nearly 500,000 square kilometers. Vast areas are below sea level in the Qattara Depression, Gilf al-Kabir is a plateau the size of Switzerland, and the Great Sand Sea spreads as far as the eye can see with 72,000 square kilometers of dune fields. Within this arid landscape are five major oases: Bahariya, Farafra, Dakhla, Kharga, and Siwa. The Fayoum is a fertile depression in the Western Desert. The Eastern Desert is a rocky and mountainous land that stretches for nearly 2,500 kilometers from the Suez Canal along the Red Sea to Sudan. Farther east is the Sinai Peninsula, with majestic mountains, the highest being Mount Sinai where Moses is said to have received the Ten Commandments, and coral-rich beaches.

Climate

In Egypt the days are commonly warm or hot, and the nights are cool. It has a mild winter from November to April, a hot summer from May to October, and fluctuating temperatures in the spring and fall. Temperatures vary widely in the inland desert areas, especially in summer, when they may range from 7°C (44°F) at night to 50°C (122°F) during the day, and in the winter the temperature fluctuates from 0°C (32°F) at night to 18°C (64°F) during the day. Cairo receives a little more than twenty-five to fifty-five millimeters (one to two inches) of precipitation each year. The city reports humidity as high as 77 percent during the summer. But during the rest of the year humidity is low. The summer months, May to October, are hot, with daytime temperatures averaging between 35° and 38°C (95° and 100°F). In the winter months, November to April, the daytime temperature range is between 10° and 18°C (50° and 65°F).

The areas south of Cairo receive only traces of rainfall. Some places will go for years without rain and then experience sudden downpours that result in flash floods. A phenomenon of Egypt's climate are the hot spring winds that blow across the country. The winds, known as the *khamasin*, usually occur from March to May and bring sand and dust from the desert. The winds blow intermittently from eight hours to two days at a time and raise temperatures by as much as twenty degrees.

What does this all mean for your wardrobe? Summer is hot and humid, and the sun is harsh. This may be 'shorts and sleeveless' weather in other parts of the world, but, for the most part, it is best to dress conservatively when in public places in Egypt. Cairo and Alexandria host tourists from around the world and are tolerant. However, for peace of mind and protection of the body from the sun, the dress code is comfortable cotton clothing: shirts with sleeves, and pants or skirt hems that are below the knee. A cap or hat with a good brim and polarized-lens sunglasses are necessary items throughout the year. If sleeveless blouses and tank tops are a fashion must, carry a shawl and jacket to cover flesh in public areas. Summer nights are often cooler than expected, particularly if you go into the desert, so pack a sweater or jacket.

Winter is cool and brisk. A warm winter coat may only be needed a few times a year, but having it available will make the day and evening much more comfortable. In the winter it is best to layer clothing: mornings and nights are cool, but it often turns quite warm in the middle of the day.

Everyone loves sandals, but they are not a good choice for Cairo streets. Dirt, sand, and pebbles get trapped under feet. It is a constant battle to walk in comfort. Closed-toe shoes are better. Also, beware of uneven sidewalks or no sidewalks at all! Flat shoes are a safe choice and prevent heels getting caught and ankles twisted. Rain is almost nonexistent, but due to poor street drainage, flooding of the streets occurs when it does rain. Be careful.

In Egypt, we dust every day and by nighttime there is already a layer of dust! The dust and pollution in Cairo are a major cause of allergy and skin sensitivities, particularly in *khamasin* season. Be prepared with sunscreen, moisturizers, and eyedrops.

Economy

The Revolution of 25 January 2011 has had some negative effects on the Egyptian economy. In addition, in the last thirty years the population has doubled to over 80 million, increasing by a million every nine months. Although the standard of living has improved, the country is still considered 'developing.' Due to a more liberal economic policy easing currency restrictions and controls on private capital, a significant rise in foreign investment, and an increase in international trade between 2004 and 2009, the Egyptian economy has high performance marks.

About 49.2 percent of the gross domestic product (GDP) comes from services— the majority from tourism—37.7 percent from industry, and about 17 percent from agriculture. The Suez Canal provides revenues which were expected to exceed $5 billion in 2010 (*The Economist*, 17 July 2010). There is also a major construction industry, an extensive network of banks, and a successful stock exchange. *Business Today Egypt* (April 2010) states, "After a mediocre 2009, the economy is finally bouncing back, and the construction industry is poised to lead the way. . . . Experts are optimistic about construction growth, centered on new infrastructure, housing and tourist developments."

The backbone of Egypt's social and economic development through the centuries has been agriculture. In the Nile Delta farmers plant crops two to three times a year, producing high yields of cotton, sugarcane, wheat, maize, rice, citrus fruits, and vegetables. Today, agriculture employs 34 percent of the labor force and provides 30 percent of commodity exports, giving $2 billion worth of revenue. However, predictions of a future population increase in a massive urban expansion, increased unemployment, and a limited water supply have prompted the government to venture into reclaiming the desert for farming. High-tech desert farming is planned for the future, with such undertakings as the Sahara Forest Project, which combines salt water, sunlight, and carbon dioxide with various technologies to produce electricity, water, biofuel, and food.

With the desert making up as much as 95 percent of the country, Egypt has begun taking advantage of the great wealth under its sands. Minerals such as manganese, phosphates, tantalum, tin, gold, and iron ore; stone such as granite and marble; oil and gas are all resources that the world hungers after.

In 2005, Goldman Sachs identified the Next 11 (N11) countries, which "share the characteristics of rapidly growing populations combined with significant industrial capacity or potential. The factors indicate a growing consumer market with increased earning potential,

creating business opportunities for both local and international firms." Egypt is one of the eleven.

Currency

The local currency is the Egyptian pound, *gineeh* (LE). Notes are in denominations of LE5, LE10, LE20, LE50, LE100, and LE200. There are one hundred piasters, *'irsh*, to a pound; they come in notes and coins in dominations of 25 piasters and 50 piasters. There is also a one-pound coin. Coins are in the process of replacing 25-piaster, 50-piaster, and LE1 notes. Many stores still price items with 5 piasters or 10 piasters but rarely have correct change. Expect your bill to be rounded up to the change that the store has available. Tip: If you are in need of change, go to the nearest gasoline (petrol) station or sidewalk food kiosk.

Time

The local time is two hours ahead of Greenwich Mean Time. In 2011 the government discontinued the practice of changing to Daylight Saving Time in the summer.

Business Hours

Banks, government offices, and most businesses are closed on public holidays. Banking hours are 8:30 a.m. to 2:00 p.m., Sunday to Thursday; some hotel banks are open twenty-four hours. Government offices are open approximately from 8:00 a.m. to 4:00 p.m. from Saturday to Thursday. Friday and Saturday are days when banks, foreign embassies and consulates, private businesses, and some schools close. Stores and shops can be open seven days a week, or take either Friday or Sunday off. Store hours are usually between 10:00 a.m. and 8:00 p.m., with great variations. Many stores are closed during Friday noon prayers. It is best to inquire. In the summer months and in Ramadan store hours change.

Electrical Current

The electrical current in Egypt is AC 220/380 volt, 50Hz. Round, two-pronged,

Type C plugs are standard. Number of phases is 1.3. Check the power ratings on appliances and equipment. Appliances and equipment that have AC 110/220 volt, 50/60 Hz are safe to use in Egypt. Laptops' and cameras' power supply is usually 100/240 volts, 50/60 Hz, which can be used in Egypt. To convert the current from 110V to 220V you will need a voltage transformer. Voltage stabilizers protect equipment from voltage fluctuations. These are available in Egypt. Please note that a 'power strip' is not a transformer or a stabilizer.

Warning: an electrical grounding system is not built into the electrical wiring of buildings. Consider an earth fault leakage detector (sometimes referred to as a residual current circuit breaker), which is a safety device installed in the main fuse box.

Government and Political System

Egypt's last monarch was ousted in a military coup led by Gamal Abdel Nasser in 1952, replacing a constitutional monarchy in 1953 with one-party rule. The Constitution of the Arab Republic of Egypt was adopted in 1971 and set in place a political system as follows.

♦ The executive branch, headed by a president elected for a six-year term and who could be re-elected for subsequent six-year terms. The president appointed a prime minister and a cabinet of ministers.

♦ The legislative branch, composed of two legislative bodies: Maglis al-Sha'b, or the People's Assembly (Upper House of Parlia-

---

Egypt: Population Facts and Figures

Population Clock, 23 August 2011:
80,701,110
Fertility rate:
3 children per woman (2008)
Life expectancy:
72.2 years

source: CAPMAS

Religions:

Muslim (mostly Sunni)	90%
Coptic	9%
other Christian	1%

source: 2010 CIA World Factbook

Literacy
(definition: age 15 and over and can read and write):
male 83%
female 59.4%

source: 2010 CIA World Factbook

8

Government Directory

Egyptian Cabinet website:
http://www.cabinet.gov.eg/

Egyptian Ministry Directory website:
http://www.egypt.gov.eg/english/guide/directory.aspx

At the time of going to press, the following websites were closed until after parliamentary elections scheduled to take place by November 2011, after which they may be reinstated:

Egyptian People's Assembly website:
http://www.parliament.gov.eg/English/default.htm

Egyptian Shura Council website:
http://www.elshoura.gov.eg/shoura_en/index.asp

ment), and Maglis al-Shura, or Advisory Council (Lower House of Parliament). Four hundred and forty-four seats in the People's Assembly were elected every five years. An additional ten seats were filled by presidential appointment. The Advisory Council consisted of 140 members, half of which were appointed by the president.

♦ The judicial branch, based on English common law, shari'a law, and Ottoman and Napoleonic codes, exercised through four categories of courts of justice.

♦ Local government leaders were appointed through the minister of the interior; the president also named governors for the twenty-seven governorates. In towns and villages, councils were elected to work with local representatives to deal with issues such as garbage collection and zoning.

However, all this was turned upside down by the Revolution of 25 January 2011. Until 11 February 2011 President Muhammad Hosni Mubarak was serving his fifth six-year term (thirty years in office), and was the head of the ruling National Democratic Party (NDP). There were seventeen legal parties, the two strongest opposition parties to the NDP being the Wafd Party (center-right) and the Tagammu' Party (leftist). More influential in some ways was the outlawed Muslim Brotherhood. Muslim or Christian religious parties were prohibited. In an unexpected show of electoral success, the 2005 parliamentary election candidates affiliated with the Brotherhood ran as independents and won 88 out of the 444 contested seats.

In the elections of November 2010, however, all but a few candidates from parties other than the NDP were booted out. The outlawed Muslim Brotherhood, running under an independent banner, lost most of its seats, as did legal opposition parties. The NDP won a sweeping victory, but within months the Mubarak regime and the NDP leadership met their downfall.

On 11 February Mubarak stepped down and handed over his powers to the Supreme Council of the Armed Forces. Egypt's legislative branches were dissolved with the cancellation of the constitution. The Supreme Council of the Armed Forces, consisting of twenty members and headed by Field Marshal Muhammad Hussein Tantawi, took over the country. On 19 March 2011 Egyptians went to the polls to vote on a referendum on the constitution, which, among other things, limited the president to two four-year terms in office and proposed drafting a new constitution following parliamentary elections. As a result of this referendum, one of the responsibilities of the next parliament will be to revise or rewrite the constitution. The parliamentary elections were scheduled to take place by November 2011, giving new and old political parties a chance to organize. As of the time of writing, the presidential election was due to follow the parliamentary elections.

Symbols of Egypt

Flag: The current flag of Egypt came into existence at the Revolution of 1952 and consists of three horizontal strips of red, white, and black. Egypt's national emblem, the Eagle of Saladin, is in the center of the white band. The red band is a symbol for the revolution, the white band symbolizes that the revolution was bloodless, and the black band is a symbol for the end of the monarchy. The Eagle of Saladin symbolizes beauty, power, and independence. The national name, Jumhuriyat Misr al-Arabiya (Arab Republic of Egypt), is written in Arabic on the pedestal.

National Anthem: *Biladi, Biladi, Biladi* (My Country, My Country, My Country). The music and lyrics were composed by Sayed Darwish and adopted in 1979.

More Symbols of Egypt

National sport: football (soccer). The most popular clubs and rivals are al-Ahly and al-Zamalek.

National language: Arabic.

Other languages: English and French are popular.

National flower: Egyptian lotus.

National airline: EgyptAir. Its symbol is Horus.

Ancient Egypt: three Giza pyramids and the Sphinx.

Islamic heritage: nineteenth-century Muhammad Ali Mosque.

Egypt's geography: the Nile River.

Calendar

In Egypt there are three calendars used for secular and religious purposes. The Gregorian calendar is in everyday use for all secular purposes. The Islamic (Hijra) calendar follows the lunar cycle, with twelve months of twenty-nine to thirty days, based traditionally on the sighting of the new moon each month. The Islamic calendar is ten to eleven days shorter than the Gregorian calendar. It passes through all the seasons every thirty-three years, needing periodic adjustment. Islamic religious events past and present are dated using this calendar. Islamic years are identified by the abbreviation AH (Anno Hegirae, 'in the Year of the Flight'). The Coptic calendar is the descendant of the ancient Egyptian calendar. It is a solar calendar with thirty days per month for twelve months and five days in the thirteenth month. The Coptic calendar is used by farmers in the Delta region and by the Coptic Church.

Holidays

Please note: the 2011 Revolution began on 25 January, then known as Police Day. It is possible that this day will be renamed to celebrate the anniversary of the Revolution. This holiday remains on the list, but be aware that the date may change as well as the name of the event.

Religion

While the constitution officially guarantees freedom of religion, Islam is constitutionally recognized as the official faith of Egypt. The terms 'Copt' and 'Coptic' apply to the Egyptian Christians and their culture. Egyptians tend to be devout without being fanatical. No village, however small, is without its mosque or church. Egyptians frequently invoke the notion of God as all-powerful. Any statement about the future is likely to contain *insha'allah* (God willing), which professes that though the intention is human, God has the ultimate determination of the outcome. The expression *il-Hamdulillah* (thanks be to God) is often interjected into a conversation.

Islam appeared in Arabia in the seventh century, proclaimed by Muhammad, the messenger of God. Muhammad was born around AD 570 in Mecca. In 612 he received a series of divine revelations through the Archangel Gabriel. The collected revelations became known as the Qur'an, which is the holy book of the religion. Literally, Qur'an means 'recitation'; the language is Arabic. Great care is taken never to change a single letter or punctuation mark in the Holy Qur'an, as it is considered the word of God.

Islam is the declared religion of about 90 percent of Egypt's population. This fact is not likely to go unnoticed. Whether you stay in the city or travel through the countryside, you will notice the religious fervor of city-dwellers going to the mosque at the muezzin's call to prayer or peasants in their fields facing Mecca to pray.

The central belief of Islam is the oneness of God, whose truths were revealed through the Prophet Muhammad in the Qur'an.

FIXED HOLIDAYS

New Year	1 January (some government offices remain open)
Coptic Christmas	7 January
Police Day	25 January
Taba Day	19 March; commemorates return of Taba to Egypt from Israeli occupation
Sinai Liberation Day	25 April; commemorates the withdrawal of Israeli troops from the Sinai
Labor Day	1 May
Revolution Day	23 July; commemorates the 1952 Revolution
Armed Forces Day	6 October; commemorates the crossing of the Suez Canal by Egyptian forces during the October War of 1973

MOVABLE HOLIDAYS

Eid al-Adha (Great Feast)	Feast of the Sacrifice marking the day after Arafat. The Day of Arafat is the most important day of the Hajj. (Four-day holiday)
Eid al-Fitr (Small Feast)	Celebration after the fasting month of Ramadan. (Three-day holiday)
Islamic New Year	al-Hijra, meaning 'migration.' Marks the migration of the Prophet Muhammad and his followers from Mecca to Medina.
Mulid al-Nabi	Prophet Muhammad's Birthday
Shamm al-Nisim	Celebrates spring

HOLIDAY CALENDAR FOR 2011

1 January	New Year's Day
25 January	Police Day
15 February	Mulid al-Nabi (Birthday of Prophet Muhammad)*
19 March	Taba Day
25 April	Shamm al-Nisim (Spring Festival)
25 April	Sinai Liberation Day
1 May	Labor Day
23 July	Revolution Day
30 August	Eid al-Fitr*
6 October	Armed Forces Day
6 November	Eid-al Adha*

HOLIDAY CALENDAR FOR 2012

1 January	New Year's Day
25 January	Police Day
4 February	Mulid al-Nabi (Birthday of Prophet Muhammad)*
19 March	Taba Day
16 April	Shamm al-Nisim (Spring Festival)
25 April	Sinai Liberation Day
1 May	Labor Day
23 July	Revolution Day
19 August	Eid al-Fitr*
6 October	Armed Forces Day
26 October	Eid al-Adha*
15 November	Islamic New Year (al-Hijra)*

HOLIDAY CALENDAR FOR 2013

1 January	New Year's Day
24 January	Mulid al-Nabi (Birthday of Prophet Muhammad)*
25 January	Police Day
19 March	Taba Day
25 April	Sinai Liberation Day
1 May	Labor Day
6 May	Shamm al Nisim (Spring Festival)
23 July	Revolution Day
8 August	Eid al-Fitr*
6 October	Armed Forces Day
15 October:	Eid al-Adha*
4 November:	Islamic New Year (al-Hijra)*

HOLIDAY CALENDAR FOR 2014

1 January	New Year's Day
14 January	Mulid al-Nabi (Birthday of Prophet Muhammad)*
25 January	Police Day
19 March	Taba Day
21 April	Shamm al-Nisim (Spring Festival)
25 April	Sinai Liberation Day
1 May	Labor Day
23 July	Revolution Day
29 July	Eid al-Fitr*
5 October	Eid al-Adha*
6 October	Armed Forces Day
25 October	Islamic New Year (al-Hijra)*

EASTER

Coptic Orthodox Easter (Eastern Easter) is not a public holiday; however, Shamm al-Nisim is a public holiday and is always celebrated the day after Coptic Easter.

Dates for Coptic Easter
24 April 2011
15 April 2012
5 May 2013
20 April 2014

RAMADAN

Ramadan is a holy month of fasting for Muslims. Fasting lasts for twenty-nine to thirty days.

Dates for the first day of Ramadan
1 August 2011*
20 July 2012*
9 July 2013*
28 June 2014*

* Dates of Islamic holidays are approximate

The following holidays are celebrated across the country, but government offices are open:

21 March	Mother's Day
18 June	Evacuation Day
15 August	Wafaa al-Nil (Flooding of the Nile)
21 October	Naval Day
24 October	Suez Day
23 December	Victory Day

Prayer, or rather the five daily prayers, is one of the five pillars of Islam, together with the *shahaada*, or declaration of faith, the *zakaat*, or giving of alms, fasting during Ramadan, and the pilgrimage *(hajj)* to Mecca. The act of saying the *shahaada*, which is to proclaim publicly that "There is no god but God and Muhammad is His Prophet," is the sign of one's commitment to the Islamic community *('umma)*.

It is not uncommon for Egyptians to visit shrines of individuals who are believed to be saints and to seek intercession with God, in order to invoke God's help for illnesses or problems. One such shrine is in the al-Rifa'i Mosque, where petitioners visit the shrine of Sheikh Abd Allah al-Ansari and Sheikh Ali Abu Shibak, grandsons of the Sufi Sheikh Ali al-Rifa'i, who was considered a saint and was head of the cult of snake charmers. Sufi brotherhoods are male-dominated groups of mystics who devote themselves to collective rituals called *zikr* to attain a mystical experience of union with God.

Current mainstream practice in Egypt focuses on the core beliefs of Islam, and the 'law' of Islam (shari'a). Friday is the day of prayer. The leader of Friday prayers is the imam and the sermon is said by a *khaaTib*, a religious scholar. The debate on whether women can be accepted into this role has begun, but the idea is not popular. Egyptian Islamic jurisprudence is headed by two religious leaders, the Sheikh al-Azhar, who heads the religious bureaucracy, and the Grand Mufti, who issues fatwas, or religious edicts.

Christians make up 10 percent of the Egyptian population, with about 9 percent belonging to the Coptic Orthodox Church and 1 percent to other Christian churches. Christianity came to Egypt in AD 60 through Alexandria; traditionally, Saint Mark is regarded as the first to introduce the new religion to Egypt. The Coptic Church is one of the Oriental Orthodox family of churches that was associated with the early Christian Patriarchate of Alexandria. In AD 451, the Church of Alexandria, along with other Eastern Christian communities, broke away from the main church. The Coptic Church is headed by a patriarch, supported by bishops and priests. Monasticism is central to the Coptic Church, and the patriarch comes

Sunni and Shia

After the death of Muhammad in AD 632, a split arose over who should succeed him. Two men, Abu Bakr (the father of Muhammad's wife Aisha) and Ali (Muhammad's son-in-law), contended for the leadership. Abu Bakr was named the first caliph. However, Ali's supporters believed that Ali was the natural successor and those followers later grew in number and became known as Shia, or the party of Ali. The Sunni (meaning 'practice') faction followed the belief that the successor of the Prophet should be appointed by the elders after a process of election and consensus among the community, as was the tradition in the desert. Ali was assassinated by his opponents, as was Husayn, the Prophet's grandson, and both men are regarded as martyrs by the Shia. The head of Husayn was interred in the al-Husayn Mosque in Cairo in 1131.

from the ranks of the monks. Most sources ascribe the origins of monasticism to Saint Anthony (ca. 251–356), who adopted a solitary, pious life of austerity in the Eastern Desert of Egypt. The principal aims of the monastic life are celibacy, education, devotion, and labor. The current Coptic Orthodox pope (patriarch) of Alexandria is Pope Shenouda III, who took office in 1971.

The two main Christian holidays are Easter and Christmas. Minor holidays include some that are extensions of these seasons, such as Eid al-Ghutas (Epiphany, or the baptism of Christ), Palm Sunday (Hadd al Za'f, which begins Passion Week or Holy Week, Usbu' al-Alam, before Easter), and Pentecost, which falls on the fiftieth day after Easter. The Apostles' Feast (12 July) commemorates the martyrdom of the apostles Peter and Paul; the Feast of the Virgin Mary, Eid al-Sayyida al-Azraa (22 August), commemorates the death and ascension of the Virgin Mary.

Although Egyptian Jews were at one time influential and an integral part of society, the Jewish community in Egypt today is very small. After the Revolution of 1952 and the nationalization of many businesses, many ethnic and national groups left Egypt, including most of the Jewish community. There are still twelve synagogues in Cairo.

Feasts and Fasting
Ramadan, Eid al-Fitr, and Eid al-Adha
Fasting during the holy month of Ramadan is one of the five pillars of Islam. Ramadan is the ninth month of the Islamic calendar. Muslims fast from sunrise to sunset and abstain from food, drink, smoking, sex, and anger. During fasting hours it is respectful not to eat or drink in public other than at restaurants that remain open for business. Pregnant women, the ill and elderly, and women in menses are exempt from fasting. Normal working hours change during

Mosque Etiquette

Dress is conservative. All parts of a woman's body must be covered except the face, hands, and feet. (Often mosques have *abaaya*s available to cover one's clothing.) Men should wear long trousers, no shorts. Shoes must be removed before entering. Shoes can be checked, or carried with the soles together. When setting shoes on a rug, do not place the soles on the rug; place them on their sides with the soles pressed together. It is not advisable to leave shoes at the entrance without being checked as sometimes they do disappear. Do not enter a mosque during prayer time unless you intend to pray. Often there is a separate entrance for women, who pray at the back of the mosque or in a different area, such as on a mezzanine. Do not take photographs within a mosque unless it is clearly permissible. The mosque, like any place of worship, is for meditation and prayer, so do not carry on a conversation or use a cell phone. Be aware that according to Egyptian law it is forbidden to proselytize and deportation is immediate.

Ramadan to accommodate the *ifTaar* (breakfast), which is eaten at sunset, and a late meal called *suhuur*, taken before sunrise. Both meals are usually shared with family and friends and consist of many delicacies. Traditionally, a meal might consist of dates, juices, lentil soup, squash stuffed with rice and meat, and *kunaafa*, a sugary pastry. If you are invited to *ifTaar*, be prompt. It is appropriate to bring a gift of oriental sweets to the household. The Ministry of Culture arranges musical programs in Ramadan at historical sites, beginning in the second week. These programs are free and usually begin at 9:30 p.m. Consult *al-Ahram Weekly* newspaper or http://cairoliveeventsguide.blogspot.com/

The two main Muslim religious holidays are Eid al-Fitr, which follows Ramadan, and Eid al-Adha, which corresponds to the Muslim pilgrimage to Mecca. The Ramadan holiday comes after a month of fasting. The Eid al-Adha celebrates Abraham's willingness to obey God's command to sacrifice his son, who then was replaced miraculously by a ram—hence the tradition to sacrifice sheep on this day and give the meat to the poor. *Fatta* is one of the traditional meat dishes served during the celebration of Eid al-Adha. Other religious holidays include Mulid al-Nabi, commemorating the birth of the Prophet Muhammad, and Islamic New Year. Sugary nut and date sweets called *ka'k* are served to visitors at these holidays.

Christmas and Easter

Christmas (Eid al-Milad) is the celebration of Jesus Christ's birth on 7 January. Copts fast for forty-three days before Christmas, abstaining from all meat and animal products. On Christmas Eve the fast is broken, usually with a feast that includes eggs, liver, grilled meat, and *fatta*, a dish of lamb, rice, and yogurt. On Christmas Day, sweets of *ka'k*, cookies filled with date or nuts, and *ghorayyeba*, sugar cookies topped with an almond, welcome family and guests to the celebration. Though trees are decorated, Coptic Christmas is less commercial than its western counterpart. Gifts of money, new clothes, or sweets are customary from adults to children. The day is spent visiting family and friends, going to the movies, or eating at a favorite restaurant where the children can enjoy themselves. Soon after the end of the Christmas celebrations, preparation gets underway for the major Coptic feast, Easter.

Easter (Eid al-Qiyama) concludes a fifty-five-day fast. Passion Week begins on Palm Sunday. Prayers and chants mourning the death of Jesus Christ are performed during morning and evening services. On Holy Thursday, a priest re-enacts the Last Supper and Jesus's washing of his disciples' feet. On Good Friday, prayers mark the crucifixion event. The Easter service is held on Holy Saturday evening from about 8:00 p.m. until midnight. The joyful service to commemorate Jesus's resurrection ends at midnight, as does the fasting. Tip: If you are invited to a church service, dress conservatively. Men and women are segregated. Be sure to arrive at the church before 10:00 p.m.

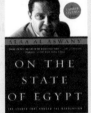

MIDDLE EAST

Critical Studies from
The American University in Cairo Press

For 50 years the AUC Press has been publishing the best of modern
scholarship on Egypt and the Middle East in a wide range of disciplines,
from history to politics, from economics to social issues.

A History of Egypt
From Earliest Times
to the Present
By Jason Thompson
New paperback edition,
updated to 2011
LE150 / $29.95
ISBN: 978 977 416 527 6

**Egypt, the Arabs,
and the World**
Reflections at the Turn
of the Twenty-first Century
By Hani Shukrallah
Hardbound
LE120 / $27.95
ISBN: 978 977 416 486 6

**Revolutionary
Womanhood**
Feminisms, Modernity,
and the State
in Nasser's Egypt
By Laura Bier
Paperback
LE120 / $22.95
ISBN: 978 977 416 519 1

**Islamic
Fundamentalism**
The Theological and
Ideological Basis of
al-Qa'ida's Political Tactics
By Sayed Khatab
Hardbound
LE150 / $29.95
ISBN: 978 977 416 499 6

**Mapping Arab
Women's Movements**
A Century of Transformations
from Within
**Edited by Pernille Arenfeldt
and Nawar Al-Hassan Golley**
Hardbound
LE180 / $34.50
ISBN: 978 977 416 498 9

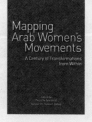

Connected in Cairo
Growing Up
Cosmopolitan in the
Modern Middle East
By Mark Allen Peterson
Paperback
LE120 / $22.95
ISBN: 978 977 416 522 1

**A Convergence
of Civilizations**
The Transformation of Muslim
Societies around the World
**By Yousef Courbage
and Emmanuel Todd**
Hardbound
LE120 / $22.95
ISBN: 978 977 416 518 4

**Toward More Efficient
Services in Egypt**
Reforming Tourism, Construction,
Information Technology,
Wholesale and Retail, Roads, and
Banking Services
**Edited by Hanaa Kheir-El-Din and
Naglaa El Ehwany**
Paperback, LE150 / $29.50
ISBN: 978 977 416 494 1

www.aucpress.com

Egypt Past

To delve into Egypt's 5,000 years of civilization there are bookstores galore to find the perfect history book. For an excellent read, look for Jason Thompson's *A History of Egypt: From Earliest Times to the Present* (Cairo: American University in Cairo Press, 2011). In the meantime, here is a summary:

♦ **ca. 5000 BC**

Predynastic cultures relying on agriculture and domesticated animals settle in both Upper and Lower Egypt.

♦ **ca. 3300 BC**

Upper and Lower Egypt share a single, unified culture under early kings, and the earliest hieroglyphic writing appears.

♦ **ca. 3100 BC**

Pharaonic history begins with Dynasty I under the rule of King Menes, and Memphis is founded as Egypt's capital. The three main periods of ancient Egyptian civilization are referred to as kingdoms. These were times when Upper and Lower Egypt were united under one king. The periods that come between the kingdoms are times of instability and political disunity. Kings are divided into dynasties, which for the most part indicate a family bloodline.

♦ **ca. 2696–2181 BC**

Old Kingdom (Dynasties 3–6). A highly centralized state centered on the king, who rules from Memphis and is buried in a pyramid nearby at Giza, Saqqara, Abu Sir,

History

5000 BC	Predynastic cultures
3300 BC	Upper and Lower Egypt share unified culture
3100 BC	Pharaonic history begins with Dynasty I
2696–2181 BC	Old Kingdom (Dynasties 3–6)
2041–1786 BC	Middle Kingdom (Dynasties 11–13)
1552–1069 BC	New Kingdom (Dynasties 18–20)
323–30 BC	Ptolemaic period
30 BC–AD 641	Roman and Byzantine periods
640–1805	Arrival of Arabs and successive dynasties
1805–1952	Egyptian royal family
1952–70	President Gamal Abdel Nasser
1970–81	President Anwar Sadat
1981–2011	President Hosni Mubarak

or Dahshur. This kingdom is often referred to as the 'Pyramid Age.' By the end of the Old Kingdom, provincial officials rival the power of the king, and climate change brings about drought and famine.

♦ **ca. 2041–1786 BC**

Middle Kingdom (Dynasties 11–13). A Theban king, Nebhepetre Mentuhotep, reunites Egypt by military force. Under the Twelfth

Dynasty, art and literature flourish, and Egypt expands to the south, colonizing Nubia. Toward the end of the Middle Kingdom, nomads from Syro-Palestine, called the Hyksos, begin settling in the Delta. The kings of the Middle Kingdom still build pyramids. They can be seen at Dahshur, and farther south at Lisht, Lahun, and Hawara.

♦ ca. 1552–1069 BC

New Kingdom (Dynasties 18–20). This is the best-documented period of ancient Egyptian history, and the time when Egypt ruled a great empire in the Near East, extending from northern Syria south to Sudan. The New Kingdom begins with the expulsion of Hyksos invaders by King Ahmose. The kings who follow in the Eighteenth Dynasty include: Hatshepsut, the queen who became pharaoh; Tuthmose III, the great builder of the empire; Amenhotep III, the great temple builder; Akhenaten, who moved to Tell al-Amarna to worship his deity the Aten; and Tutankhamun, famous for his tomb. The best-known king of the later New Kingdom is the great Ramesses II of the Nineteenth Dynasty. Thebes becomes an important religious center, with the temple of Amun at Karnak on the east bank of the river at Thebes, and the royal burials and funeral temples on the west. By the end of the New Kingdom the empire has been lost, civil war rages in Thebes, and the High Priest of Amun eclipses the power of the king.

Following the New Kingdom are seven hundred years of political instability, as well as foreign invasions and warfare.

Egypt is invaded by Libyans, Sudanese, Assyrians, Persians, and finally Greeks, when Alexander the Great is victorious in 323 BC. Alexander spends about a year in Egypt, during which time he designs his city, Alexandria, and consults the oracle in Siwa Oasis.

♦ 332–30 BC

Ptolemaic period. Upon the death of Alexander the Great, his general Ptolemy takes Egypt and rules as Ptolemy I. He and Ptolemy II are responsible for the building of Alexandria, famous for its lighthouse and library. Cleopatra VII rules as the last of the Ptolemies, and struggles to retain her rule with the support, first of Caesar, and then of Mark Antony.

♦ 30 BC–AD 641

Roman and Byzantine periods. Emperor Augustus seizes Egypt after the deaths of Cleopatra and Mark Antony. Egypt is heavily taxed by the Romans, and supplies the grain for Roman bread. There are rebellions against Roman rule, particularly in Upper Egypt, and the Roman emperors add to the great temples of Upper Egypt begun by the Ptolemies, portraying themselves as traditional pharaohs of Egypt. In AD 395 Egypt becomes part of the Eastern Roman, or Byzantine, Empire.

♦ 640–1798

The arrival of the Arabs, and their successive dynasties. The Arabs, camped at Fustat, besiege and take the fortress of Babylon in 640.

Egypt is ruled by a succession of caliphates: Umayyad (658–750), Abbasid (750–868), Tulunid (868–905), Abbasid (905–935), Ikhshidid (935–969), Fatimid (969–1171), Ayyubid (1171–1250), Bahri Mamluk (1250–1382), Burgi Mamluk (1382–1517), and Ottoman (1517–1805).

◆ **1798–1805**

Napoleon Bonaparte. In 1798, Napoleon Bonaparte and his army arrive on Egyptian soil to close British routes to India. Egypt's Isthmus of Suez is where Africa, Asia, and the Mediterranean meet and Napoleon knows this is a key point to control trade, which would strengthen the French against their British foe. However, advancing Ottoman troops weaken Napoleon's resolve, and he hands command over to General Kléber. The French army cannot hold on, and the British oust the French. In 1801 Napoleon's legacy is the *Description de l'Egypte*, compiled by a team of scholars, the Commission of Arts and Sciences, who explore the Nile Valley during the French occupation, collecting a wealth of material.

◆ **1805–1952**

The Egyptian royal family. Muhammad Ali (born in Kavalla, Macedonia) becomes governor of Egypt under the Ottoman Turks in 1805. Later, Egypt becomes independent of the Ottomans, and descendants of Muhammad Ali take the title 'sultan,' and then the title 'king.' The British occupy Egypt militarily in 1882, and in 1914 Egypt becomes a British protectorate. The country

again becomes nominally independent in 1922, but Britain maintains military control. From that time on there are three main forces engaged in a political struggle: the British, the king, and an Egyptian nationalistic movement. The monarchy ends with a coup d'état, the Egyptian revolution of 1952, led by the Free Officers.

◆ **1952–present**

The Republic. The 1950s are turbulent times. A weak king, British dominance, and disunity among Egyptian leaders culminate in the Free Officers seizing the Abdin Palace in Cairo and forcing King Farouk to abdicate. He is put on his royal yacht in Alexandria, never to see Egypt again. King Farouk's infant son, Ahmad Fuad, is ruler of the country for six months. Gamal Abdel Nasser introduces massive industrialization policies and experiments with socialism. In the early 1960s most Egyptian industry and business is nationalized. The High Dam in Aswan is built under Russian supervision. Russian influence lasts only one year after Nasser's death in 1970. His successor, Anwar Sadat, takes over leadership. Sadat's policy of the 1970s is a shift to economic and political liberalism. He signs a peace agreement with Israel. In 1981, Sadat is assassinated and Hosni Mubarak is sworn in as president. During the next twenty-eight years, Egypt witnesses massive public-works projects of road and highway expansion and the Cairo Metro. Hosni Mubarak is forced from office by a popular revolution in early 2011.

Future Outlook

A major change swept the Middle East in 2011. Populations in Tunisia, Bahrain, Yemen, Libya, Syria, Jordan, and, of course, Egypt have demanded a change in their politics and their governments. People want change and they want a voice in their future. Though the Egyptian 25 January Revolution only lasted eighteen days and was primarily led by youth, the revolt against the Mubarak regime changed Egypt significantly. The popular demand for free parliamentary and presidential elections and a new constitution has been overseen by the Egyptian Supreme Council of the Armed Forces. Who will lead the country forward is the question in everyone's mind.

Egypt's rapidly growing population is a major concern, as it has an impact on every policy decision; it is a drain on resources and the environment, places pressure on the education system and the country's infrastructure, and creates high unemployment.

Egypt's most important natural resource is water. The Nile and Egypt have been synonymous for millennia; however, the future of the flow of waters into Egypt is politically fragile. Since 1929 Egypt has held a monopoly over the water flow, but in 2011 Burundi, Ethiopia, Kenya, Rwanda, Tanzania, and Uganda signed the Entebbe Treaty. Neither Sudan nor Egypt recognized the treaty, which states that the source countries of the Nile no longer have to ask Egypt's permission for water diversion. Protection of the Nile water, natural resources, and agriculture are major concerns.

Only wise leadership, navigating with the cooperation of diverse voices, will be able to steer the country through its post-revolution challenges.

2

Travel to and in Egypt

Relocating overseas means an entirely different set of circumstances to consider. Here are some suggestions to help you take the first steps to a successful transfer to your new country.

✦ Finances

Contact your bank and credit card companies and let them know you are moving, so that when you use your credit card in Egypt, the charges will be accepted. Know the regulations on taxation of income in your home country and in Egypt.

✦ Documentation

Gather birth certificates, health records, and educational degrees. You may never need them, but if you do and they are in a security box in Kansas it will be an expensive trip. Collect all documents that pertain to applications for permits for each member of the family. Get duplicates and have them notarized. You may not plan to drive, but having an international driver's license may come in handy. It may cause less stress to arrange for one in your home country.

✦ Health

Check with your company about health insurance and coverage in Egypt or, if you are on your own, check your current policy as to whether it covers doctors and hospitals overseas. Look into an international health insurance policy. Vaccinations should be up to date; take the time to browse the website of the Centers for Disease Control and Prevention at http://wwwnc.cdc.gov/travel/content/vaccinations.aspx. If you need prescription drugs, find out whether the same medication is available in Egypt; if it isn't, have your doctor prescribe enough for your stay.

✦ Language

It never hurts to learn a little Arabic before you arrive. Simple greetings are always well received. Find out as much as you can about Egypt before you come, via exhibitions, concerts, TV documentaries, books, and classes.

✦ Become familiar with **Arabic numbers.** For buses, trains, and the metro, knowing Arabic numbers will facilitate your travel.

♦ **Accommodation**

If your company does not take care of housing, look at your finances and determine how much you can spend on rent. Rent varies significantly depending on where you live. Evaluate the different areas of Cairo in terms of proximity to your job, your interests, and your finances.

♦ **Education**

If you have children who are school age, research the plethora of schools in Cairo. In other areas of Egypt there are fewer choices. Ultimately, consider the educational needs of your child. Tuition is often costly for expatriates, so if your company does not offer tuition fees as a perk it is essential to be aware of the cost, quality, and distance of travel when choosing a school.

♦ **Pets**

Consider whether your housing has space for an animal; think of the climate; look into the availability of veterinarian services; and, most importantly, figure out who will take care of your pet when you travel.

♦ **Children**

Involve your children and teenagers sufficiently and in advance. Ask them to research Egypt. Give them plenty of opportunities to ask questions and answer them with honesty. Let them make decisions on what they will take and what they will leave behind. Create a sense of adventure, research extracurricular activities, and listen to them. On www.you-tube.com

there are short videos made by teenagers about their third-culture experiences. Buy the book *Third Culture Kids: The Experience of Growing Up among Worlds* by David Pollock and Ruth Van Reken. Your kids will now and forever be TCKs—Third Culture Kids!

If you feel you need some help with your move and settling in to Cairo, you might want to consider contacting a moving consultancy. Some based in Cairo are:

Crown Logistics. Relocation services: Tel: 2704-2297/98, 2704-6360. E-mail: cairo@crownrelo.com.Website: www.crownrms.com

Expat Services. Provides nanny and housekeeper recruitment, real-estate services, and support for newcomers. Hours: Sunday–Thursday 10:00 a.m.–8:00 p.m., Saturday 12:00 p.m.–6:00 p.m. Address: 51 Road 9, Maadi. Tel (mobile): 0111-209-0902. E-mail: info@expat-service.net. Website: www.expat-service.net

Global Relocation Consultants. Experts in relocation services, real estate, and immigration services, and provide a settling-in program. They help organize electricity, telephone, TV, and Internet services, with personalized service according to your needs, to get settled in Cairo. Address: 19 Road 151, Maadi. Tel: 2525-5755/5618. Mobile: 0100-233-9025. E-mail: monaradwan@link.net. Website: www.grconsultants.org

For more information on relocating: Community Service Association—New to Egypt Orientation. Website: www.livinginegypt.org

Arrival in Egypt
Quarantine
Egypt requires a yellow fever vaccination certificate for travelers arriving from certain African countries, as well as for travelers over one year of age coming from infected areas. Those arriving in transit from such areas without a certificate will be detained at the airport until their onward flight departs. The following countries and areas are regarded by the Egyptian health authorities as being infected with yellow fever: all countries in mainland Africa south of the Sahara, Sudan, Belize, Bolivia, Brazil, Colombia, Costa Rica, Ecuador, French Guiana, Guyana, Panama, Peru, Surinam, Trinidad and Tobago, and Venezuela. See http://egypt.visahq.com/customs/

Duty Free
Duty-free items that an adult can bring into Egypt are one liter of alcohol and two cartons of cigarettes. If the quantity is more, duty must be paid or the goods will be confiscated. There are duty-free stores in areas of Cairo—Downtown, Mohandiseen, Maadi—where three liters of alcohol (or a case of beer) and four cartons of cigarettes can be purchased duty-free within forty-eight hours of your arrival in Cairo. (If you want to take advantage of this, take your passport with you, so the store personnel

can check the date on your entry stamp.) Exemptions from duty include personal effects, photographic equipment, calculators, radios, video cameras, computers, and personal jewelry which accompany tourists, residents, or immigrants for their own use.

Arrival by Air
International and domestic flights arrive at and depart from Cairo International Airport, which is twenty kilometers northeast of Cairo. There are international airports at Alexandria, Hurghada, Luxor, and Sharm al-Sheikh as well. Most international carriers fly to Egypt from Asia, Africa, Europe, the Middle East, and North America. The national airline, EgyptAir, www.egyptair.com, provides air service all over the world and to all cities in Egypt. Airfares vary according to season. There are always good fares to be had. Be sure to compare airline websites and travel agents to discount sites. One site that consolidates airlines and several discount sites is www.yapta.com

Cairo International Airport
The newly renovated Cairo International Airport is a far cry from its former self. In 2009 Terminal 3 opened to serve EgyptAir international and domestic flights as well as airlines that are members of the Star Alliance (Lufthansa, Singapore Air, Turkish Air, Austrian Air, Swiss Air, bmi, and United). Terminal 1 and Terminal 2 are located three kilometers from Terminal 3. A free shuttle bus service that runs every thirty minutes,

Airlines (Cairo Offices):

Air France	Tel: 2770-6250
Alitalia	Tel: 3333-0612; Call Center 3333-0613
Austrian Airlines	Tel: 19404
Algerian Airlines	Tel: 2574-0688; 2291-0409
American Airlines	Tel: 3337-3495
bmi	Tel: 2269-0971/2
British Airways	Tel: 2690-1690
China Airlines	Tel: 2393-0395/0416
Delta	Tel: 2736-2030/9
EgyptAir Call Center	Tel: 0900-700000; 1717 (from a mobile, within Egypt)
Emirates	Tel: 19899
Gulf Air	Tel: 3748-7781, 3761-1119
Japan Airlines	Tel: 2738-1422/33
KLM	Tel: 2580-5747/57
Korean Airlines	Tel: 2576-8255/488
Lufthansa	Tel: 19380
Middle East Airlines (MEA)	Tel: 2574-3422, 2575-0984
Royal Jordanian Airlines	Tel: 3344-3114
Saudi Arabian Airlines	Tel: 19898
Singapore Airlines	Tel: 2575-0276, 2578-8777
Smart Air (private jet)	Tel: 2267-0870
Swiss International Airlines	Tel: 2739-8500, 2737-7739

twenty-four hours a day, connects the terminals. A shuttle train will connect all three terminals by 2012. Be sure to ask the travel agent or airline agent your departure and arrival terminal. To inquire about flight arrivals or departures at Cairo International Airport, call from a mobile: 2777; from a landline: 0900-77777; or log onto www.cairo-airport.com. The main telephone numbers for Cairo International Airport are: 2265-2222/5000/2436/2825.

For private jet services, Smart Air (for business, pleasure, or Air Ambulance) is located at the Business Jet terminal, next to Hall 4. Tel: 2267-0870. Website: http://www.smartaviation.com.eg/

Cairo International Airport has come a long way in the past decade. In 2009 it opened the Air Mall, which has a Segafredo café and oriental restaurant, Kenoz. On the other side of the mall, you can sit outside and wait for your guests at Chez Eddy. On the Uruba Street exit, across from the Air Mall, there is Internet and a photocopy machine available at Quattro Pizza. A car mechanic and Ragab and Sons supermarket are next door; in case your car breaks down you can buy groceries, too!

In the departure hall of Terminal 1, you can find your favorite café: Coffee Bean & Tea Leaf, Beano's, and Starbucks. In Terminal 3, you can snack at Burger King, Hippopotamus, or Café Puro.

Buy the latest AUC Press book at the new Hudson's News or Diwan in Terminal 3. Newspapers are available in Arabic, English, and French. All terminals have duty-free shops with favorite foreign and local products. Money exchange is available throughout the airport and Banque du Caire has a small branch next to Ragab and Sons supermarket.

The nearest hotel, within the airport, is the Novotel Cairo Airport, located between Terminal 1 and Terminal 3. The Iberotel Le Passage is next to the airport and the Fairmont Heliopolis is ten minutes away on Salah Salim Road.

Meet and Assist

Getting through immigration and customs and into Cairo on your own is straightforward, but if you need assistance, there are meet-and-assist services.

◆ American Express

Contact: Mr. M. Elshabrawy, vice chairman and managing partner, or Mr. Ahmed Askalani, general manager. Address: 33 Nabil al-Waqqad St., Ard al-Golf, Heliopolis, Egypt. Tel: 2418-3222/2144. E-mail: Mohamed.elshabrawy@amexfranchise.com, ahmed.askalani@amexfranchise.com. Website: http://www.amexfranchise.com

◆ Cairo Airport Exclusive Service

Their 'Meet and Assist' service provides a speedy clearance through all arrival and departure formalities (Terminals 1, 2, and 3), at a cost of $50. They also offer use of a VIP lounge. For further information call: Terminal 1—2265-5647/3160/3120/3215; Terminal 2—2265-2030/2412/2417; Terminal 3—2267-7305.

◆ Paradisio Travel

Contact: Manar Saada. Address: 28 Ali Amin St., 1st Zone, Nasr City. Tel: 0100-668-8426. Fax: 2401-4363. E-mail: tourism@paradisiotravel.com. Website: http://www.paradisiotravel.com

Transportation into the City

There are several choices of transportation from Cairo International Airport. Taxis are safe and plentiful. There are two types of taxi service, metered (white taxis) and non-metered (black-and-white taxis). A trip in a non-metered taxi is about LE50–80 to central Cairo. It is best to settle on a price before getting in. If you choose a metered taxi, check if the meter is working before setting off. (At the time of going to press, black-and-white non-metered taxis are fighting to remain licensed. January 2011 was the deadline for the conversion; however, there has been widespread dispute between the government and black-and-white taxis, and since the Revolution of 25 January 2011 this issue remains unresolved.)

Limousine company stands are located conveniently in all arrival halls. The price is around LE80–100 to central Cairo. A tip to the driver is expected.

There are private taxi firms to call and reserve a vehicle:

◆ Cairo International Taxi

Tel: 19155. (Women-only taxi service available by reservation.)

◆ **City Cab**
Tel: 16516.

◆ **Sixt London Cab**
Tel: 19670.

Sixt London Cab is located in Terminal 3. Passengers can book ahead and from outside of Egypt. The cabs operate on a fixed price, with journeys from the airport to Heliopolis LE85; to Downtown LE125; to Maadi LE155. This price is for the cab, not per person. The cab holds five people and is equipped with ramps and swivel seats for the disabled or elderly. For round-trip service there is a 25 percent discount for the first booking and a 50 percent discount for the second booking.

Cairo Airport Shuttle operates private, air-conditioned vans to and from Cairo International Airport for individuals and groups. The service includes destinations outside of Cairo. A service desk is located in all arrival halls. Advance reservations are available but not required. For prices and reservations contact the twenty-four-hour customer service center at 2265-3937/8 or 19970. The shuttle accommodates up to seven persons. The price is for the bus, not per person. Prices vary according to area: Heliopolis LE30–50; Downtown LE50–80; Maadi LE90–120.

Public Airport Bus Service, with and without air conditioning, operates from Terminal 1. There are several stops at bus stations: at Tahrir Square in downtown Cairo, in Mohandiseen, and along Pyramids Road in Giza. Prices and bus numbers are as follows:

From Cairo Airport to Tahrir,
with a/c, Bus #356, LE3

From Cairo Airport to Shubra–Ramsis,
with a/c, Bus #799, LE3

From Cairo Airport to
Roxy–Ramsis–Tahrir,
no a/c, Bus #400, LE0.50

From Cairo Airport to Ramsis–Tahrir–Giza,
no a/c, Bus #949, LE0.50

From Cairo Airport to Alexandria,
take Super Jet or Western Delta. Both are air-conditioned and leave every half hour from the bus terminal at Terminal 1. The price is LE25 until 3:00 p.m. and LE28 after 3:00 p.m. There is also a limousine service to Alexandria.

For buses to Alexandria, Hurghada, and Sharm al-Sheikh from the airport call 2266-0212. The airport also offers a shuttle bus service (Tel: 2265-3937). The shuttle bus leaves every half hour with set prices that can be booked for a whole group.

Arrival and Departure Overland and by Boat and Ferry

All information concerning international travel on bus, train, and ferry was accurate before the widespread uprisings and unrest through Libya, Egypt, and other countries.

Since February 2011, all schedules have been subject to this fast-changing situation. The following provides information on the possibilities of overland travel. Please check ahead as situations change rapidly. The schedules and prices quoted below can change without prior notification.

Buses and taxis are available for travel to Egypt from Israel, Jordan, and Libya. There is a ferry from Jordan and a Nile steamer from Sudan to Aswan. There is now a weekly ferry service from Venice, Italy, to Egypt. For extensive information on how to travel by bus and ferry from Egypt to Jordan, Syria, Turkey, Libya, and Sudan, go to http://www.seat61.com/Egypt.htm, to the section titled "International Buses and Ferries from Egypt."

To and from Israel

The Israel–Taba border is open twenty-four hours a day, but the best time to cross is between 7:00 a.m. and 9:00 p.m. On Friday night and Saturday, due to the Jewish Sabbath, immigration into Israel is closed. Bus services linking the two countries are run by Misr Travel. Address: 1 Tal'at Harb St., P.O. Box 1000, Cairo. Tel: 2393-0010. Fax: 2392-4440. Website: www.misr-travel.net. Be sure to have the Israeli visa stamped on your entry card rather than in your passport, as many Arab countries will not allow entry into their country if your passport contains an Israeli stamp. You can take a taxi into Egypt or Israel after the border crossing.

To and from Italy

If you don't like flying, there is now a way to travel from Europe to Egypt via Tartous, Syria. The Visemar Line service from Venice, Italy, to Egypt opens up a long-ignored route. The new vessel is furnished with spacious passenger cabins, entertainment facilities (cinema, satellite TV), shopping, and several dining options (bar, à la carte, and self-service restaurants). A round-trip ticket for two is approximately 850 euros. Make your bookings online at www.visemarline.com. The contact in Egypt is at 1 al-Mushir Ahmad Ismail St., behind Fairmont Hotel, Challenger Building, Heliopolis. Tel: 2268-3852/4/6. Fax: 2268-3850. E-mail: iss.egypt@iss-shipping. com. Or contact: Karim El Senousy, Karim.El Senousyl@iss-shipping.com. Direct line: 2268-3852. Mobile: 0122-312-5553, 0106-880-7644.

To and from Jordan

Amman to Cairo: An air-conditioned bus leaves Amman (JETT terminal) on Tuesdays, Thursdays, Saturdays, and Sundays at 2:00 p.m., taking about twenty hours to reach Cairo. The fare is $102. It is run by Jordan Express Tourist Transportation (JETT). Tel: Amman 662722. Fax: 601507. Website: www.jett.com.jo. This bus crosses Israel— remember that you won't be able to re-enter Syria with any sign of a visit to Israel in your passport. To avoid Israel, go by ferry: travel from Amman or Petra to Aqaba by bus or service taxi. There is a daily fast ferry (departing noon, taking one hour) and a daily slow ferry (departing 3:00 p.m., taking three to four hours) from Aqaba to Nuweiba. The fare is about $60 for the slow ferry or $90 for the fast ferry. There are direct buses from Nuweiba to both Cairo and Sharm al-Sheikh. The fare must be paid in cash, local currency.

Cairo to Amman: a bus runs four times a week, fare around $100, run by JETT of Jordan (www.jett.com.jo) and taking twenty hours. Take notice that this bus crosses Israel, and you will be refused entry to Syria later on if you have any sign of a visit to Israel in your passport. To buy JETT tickets e-mail their Egyptian agents, super-jet@post.com. Tel: 2290-9013. To avoid Israel go by bus and ferry. Take a bus, run by East Delta Bus Company, from Cairo to Nuweiba from Cairo Gateway station. It leaves at 8:00 a.m., and it is a six-hour drive. Take either the fast ferry (departing at 3:30 p.m., taking one hour) or the slow ferry (departing 2:00 p.m., taking three to four hours) from Nuweiba to Aqaba. The fare is about $60 for the slow ferry and $90 for the fast ferry. The fare must be paid in cash in U.S. dollars. There is a $10 Egyptian exit tax as well. Visas to Jordan are issued on the ferry according to nationality, so it is best to check first with the Jordanian Embassy in Egypt. Address: 6 al-Juhayni St., Dokki, Cairo. Tel: 3749-9912, 3748-6169.

To and from Libya

At the al-Bardia–Sallum crossing, taxis and local buses are available on either side to provide transport to larger cities, either Marsa Matruh or Benghazi. No visas are issued at the border. If you are in a private car, make sure you have all necessary papers for the car and an entry visa. Please note that, at the time of going to press, Libya was still in a state of civil unrest and visas were not being issued to individual tourists.

To and from Sudan
Khartoum to Cairo

Tickets and information are available at Wadi Nil Halfa Company. Tel: 097-230-3348. According to www.seat61.com/Sudan, here is how to travel from Khartoum to Cairo:

1. Travel from Khartoum to Wadi Halfa by train. The weekly train leaves Khartoum Bahri station at 8:40 a.m. on Mondays, At-bara at 7:00 p.m. on Mondays, and arrives at Wadi Halfa at 10:45 p.m. on Tuesdays.
2. Travel from Wadi Halfa to the Aswan High Dam (al-Sadd al-Ali) by ferry, sailing from Wadi Halfa on Wednesdays around 4:00 p.m., arriving in Aswan at lunchtime on Thursday. The northbound ferry fare is around $20, first class. There is a Sudan exit tax when leaving Sudan.
3. Travel from Aswan to Cairo by overnight air-conditioned sleeper train.

Cairo to Khartoum

1. Travel from Cairo to Aswan by overnight air-conditioned sleeper train.
2. A weekly Nile steamer, run by Nile Valley River Transport, sails every Monday at noon from Aswan High Dam (al-Sadd al-Ali) to

Wadi Halfa in Sudan, arriving on Tuesday. The first-class fare (with cabin) costs about LE131, meal included; the second-class fare (deck place) is around LE78. Call 2578-9256 for information and reservations. You'll need to spend the night in Wadi Halfa.

3. A weekly train connects with the Nile steamer, leaving Wadi Halfa at 8:45 p.m. every Thursday (earlier reports have said Wednesday; please check locally), arriving in Atbara at 2:00 a.m. on Saturday morning and Khartoum (Bahri station in the north) at 12:30 p.m. on Saturday. It has first-class sleepers and first-, second-, and third-class seats. The train is slow, old, and basic, but should get you there, give or take the odd breakdown. It's not air-conditioned, so bring plenty of water, as it can get very hot as the train crosses the desert. The Wadi Halfa–Khartoum first-class fare is reportedly around $18.

4. For visa information contact the Embassy of the Republic of Sudan. Address: 3 Ibrahim St., Garden City, Cairo. Tel: 2355-7705.

Travel in Egypt
Train
The main train station in Cairo is Ramsis Station (maHaTTat ramsis), accessible from al-Shuhadaa (formerly Mubarak) metro station. Also, al-Giza train station near Giza Square receives trains mainly from Upper Egypt. Traveling by train in Egypt is easy. Egyptian railways run between Cairo, Alexandria, Port Said, Luxor, Aswan, Suez, and many other cities. The best website for rail travel in Egypt is www.seat61.com/Egypt.

For train times, go to the Egyptian National Railways website, www.egyptrail.gov.eg, or go to the railway station in Ramsis Square. The offices are open every day from 8:00 a.m. to 4:00 p.m. and tickets are available for all trains throughout Egypt. For information about overnight sleeper trains to Luxor and Aswan, go to www.sleeping-trains.com. (Tip: making inquires by fax is best: 2574-9074, or call them on 2574-9474/9274.) Also, if you are planning to see Egypt by rail, it is a good idea to invest in *Thomas Cook Overseas Timetables*, an international book of timetables published every two months. It can be purchased online at www.thomascooktimetables.com.

How to Buy Tickets
There are three kinds of train travel: first, second, and third class. First- and second-class cars are air-conditioned, but second class is half the price. Third class has no a/c and can be crowded and dirty. Also take note of the type of train for speed: 'ordinary' is slow and stops often.

Purchase tickets at Ramsis Train Station, or through travel agents such as www.safariegypt.com, www.osoris.com, www.paradisetravelegypt.com (expect a booking fee). The concierges at most high-end hotels provide this service, but expect an extra fee added onto the ticket price. As of yet, tickets can be bought online only by using an Egyptian credit card through the Egyptian Railways website, www.egyptrail.gov.eg (however, sometimes the charging system does not work). To buy tickets for the

Cairo–Luxor–Aswan sleeper, call 2574-9474 or fax 2574-9074, or call a travel agent. Also, for information from Ramsis Station about trains to Alexandria, Luxor, and Aswan, call 2575-3555.

Bus

The new Cairo bus station, Cairo Gateway (Miina al-Qaahira), at the Turguman Garage, is next to al-Gala' Hospital, only three hundred meters from Urabi metro station. Most long-distance bus services originate from Cairo Gateway. To book bus tickets, you need to go to the terminal for schedules and tickets. It is best to go one to two days before travel. Other, smaller, bus services to the Delta and Fayoum operate from Abbud bus station in Shubra. The Munib bus station in Giza is located under the Munib flyover on the Giza corniche, just north of Munib metro station. Buses and service taxis operate from here.

The only bus schedules available online are at www.ask-aladdin.com; however, they may not be updated regularly. Your best bet is to go to Cairo Gateway for the most current information.

There are no trains to Sharm al-Sheikh, Hurghada, or Siwa Oasis. The bus service to Sharm, stopping at Ras Sidr, is provided by East Delta Bus Company and Super Jet Bus. It is a seven-hour ride, departing eight times daily and costing about LE60. The bus service to Hurghada is run by Super Jet or al-Gouna. It is also a seven-hour trip, departing four times daily and costing about LE55. To Siwa Oasis there is a direct bus once a week

Bus Companies

◆ **Central Delta Bus Company:** Buses to Mahalla, Tanta, Kafr al-Sheikh. Located at Abbud Station. Tel: 2431-2868.

◆ **East Delta Bus Company:** Buses to Sharm al-Sheikh, Dahab, Ismailiya, Suez, Saint Catherine's, Taba, and Ras Sidr. Located in Almaza (Heliopolis) and Cairo Gateway (Turguman). Tel: 2577-8347, 2419-8533.

◆ **Go Buses:** Buses to Sharm al-Sheikh, Hurghada, and Alexandria. Tel: 19567.

◆ **Super Jet:** Buses to Alexandria, Port Said, Hurghada, and Sharm al-Sheikh (Summer—North Coast). Located in Almaza (Heliopolis), Cairo Gateway (Turguman), Giza (Munib), and Cairo International Airport. Tel: 2266-0212, 2290-9013/8.

◆ **Upper Egypt Bus Company:** Buses to Luxor, Aswan, Bahariya, Farafra, Dakhla, and Kharga. Located at Cairo Gateway (Turguman) and Giza (Munib). Tel: 2576-0261, 2431-6723.

◆ **West Delta Bus Company:** Buses to Alexandria and Marsa Matruh. Located in Almaza (Heliopolis), Cairo Gateway (Turguman), and Giza (Munib). Tel: 2576-5582, 2415-6597.

on Wednesday nights operated by West Delta Bus Company. It is about a ten-hour trip costing approximately LE80.

Ferry

A ferry connects Sharm al-Sheikh to Hurghada, crossing the Red Sea. There are fast and slow ferries between these two cities each week. Please check current schedules and arrive at least one hour early, but be prepared for delays. The crossing takes just ninety minutes for the fast ferry and six hours for the slow ferry. The cost for foreign residents and Egyptian adults is the same, with a round trip on the fast ferry costing LE335 (children LE190), and for foreigners costing LE475 (children LE285). The slow-ferry cost is LE100 per adult, one way. The boats leave from the main harbor in Sharm al-Sheikh. Times are as follows:

Hurghada to Sharm
Saturday 8:00 a.m.; Monday 4:00 a.m.; Tuesday 8:00 a.m.; Thursday 8:00 a.m.

Sharm to Hurghada
Saturday 6:00 p.m.; Monday 6:00 p.m.; Tuesday 6:00 p.m.; Thursday 6:00 p.m.

The ferry can transport twelve cars. Sedan and hatchback cars are LE245; minivans, 4x4 cars, and microbuses are LE345; motorcycles are LE125; bicycles are LE50.

Tickets can be purchased from tour operators and travel agencies all over Egypt (although you may be charged a commis-sion), or alternatively through the Red Sea Jet offices in Hurghada and Sharm al-Sheikh. Telephone numbers to call to confirm information are: Sharm al-Sheikh, 069-360-0936; Hurghada, 065-344-9481/2; Dahab, 069-364-0886.

Service Taxi or Microbus

Long-distance service taxis depart Cairo for cities throughout Egypt from different stations. The main depot is near Ramsis Station. This is a cheap way to get around Egypt. The taxi is shared between five to seven people. There is a fixed fare per seat. You can buy the seat next to you or hire the entire taxi. The fare is the same or slightly more than a bus fare. This service goes where buses and trains do not, but the drivers have a notorious reputation for being reckless as they drive fast and furiously to get to their destination so as to collect more fares to the next destination.

Car Rental

If you arrive at Cairo International Airport for the first time and decide to rent a car and drive, you might be warned that it is better to be driven for your first time to get used to the traffic, roads, and street system. After your initial visit, you will have a better understanding of Cairo and the mode of driving. Driving in Egypt, not to mention Cairo itself, can be a life-threatening experience with the continual weaving of cars, lack of traffic lights, and the particular care one must take about pedestrians, who cross at all places and directions on streets and highways. There are cars that are driven at night with no headlights and one must also be vigilant of motorcycles (often laden with an entire family) that swerve in and out through the traffic. If you are determined to risk life and limb, cars for rent are available from Cairo International Airport and also locally. An international driver's license is required and you must be at least twenty-five years of age. You will need your passport, driver's license, and pre-payment. Credit cards are accepted. Petrol (92 percent octane or super) is about LE1.95 per litre. Street signs are in Arabic and English in major areas, otherwise only in Arabic. Egypt uses International Road Signs and speed limits are posted in kilometers per hour.

Contact information for car rental agencies:

◆ **Avis**
Address: 16 Ma'mal al-Sukkar St., Garden City. Tel: 2354-8698. Website: www.avis.com.

◆ **Budget**
Zamalek branch address: 5 al-Maqrizi St. Tel: 2340-0070, 2340-9474. Maadi branch: 85 Road 9. Tel: 2350-2724. Heliopolis branch: 1 Muhammad Ebeid St. Tel: 2291-8244. Website: www.budget.com.

◆ **Digital Group**
Contact Mr. Khalid Hassan, General Manager. Address: 1 al-Nasr St., Sheraton Bldgs., Heliopolis. Tel: 2266-1652; mobile:

0122-225-3066. Fax: 2266-1652. E-mail: KH_DigitalGroup@hotmail.com.

◆ **Europcar**
Address: Cairo International Airport, Terminal 1, Hall 3, 2nd floor. Tel: 0106-661-1027. Opening hours, Monday–Saturday 9:00 a.m.–10:00 p.m.

◆ **First Limousine**
Address: 28a New Nirco Buildings, Zahra' al-Maadi. Tel: 2516-5408; Mobile: 0100-610-6701.

◆ **Green Gear**
Car rental company with high environmental awareness. Limousine service, airport pick up and drop off, self-drive and chauffeur-driven cars. Address: 27 Giza St., Giza. Tel: 3571-6400, 0127-716-4400. E-mail: afathi@greengearegypt.com. Website: www.greengearegypt.com

◆ **Gulf Limousine**
Contact Ayman Ezz, General Manager. Address: 7 al-Nadi al-Gidid St., New Maadi. Tel: 3303-5674. Fax: 3303-5669. E-mail: Gulf_limousine@yahoo.com

◆ **Hertz**
Contact Ms. Renata Al-Mughrabi, General Manager. Address: Km. 28 Cairo–Alexandria Desert Road, Dandy Mall. Tel: 3539-1380/1/2/3. E-mail: renata@hertzegypt.com. Website: http://www.hertzegypt.com

◆ **Al-Salam International Limousine**
Contact Mr. Ahmed El-Hadedy, Chairman. Address: 2 Bahgat Ali St., Tower C, Zamalek. Tel: 2736-3551/2. Fax: 2736-3551. E-mail: alsalamint@link.com.eg

◆ **Smart Limousine**
Contact Ms. Aziza Abousteit, Business Development Manager. Address: 151 Corniche al-Nil, Maadi. Tel: 2524-3006. Fax: 2524-3009. E-mail: aziza.abousteit@smartlimo.com. Website: http://www.smartlimo.com

◆ **Tourist Car Rental**
Address: 60 Muhammad Muqallid St., off Mustafa al-Nahhas St., Nasr City. Tel: 0100-342-7436, 0111-910-8231. Fax: 2654-4983.

Travel Agents

If you are an independent traveler but want the advice of a local, go to www.couch surfer.org. Otherwise, for more traditional travel advice, there are travel agencies galore in Cairo that offer different services from car rentals to safaris, Nile cruises, business travel, and, of course, airline reservations and ticketing. Below are a few suggestions to get you started.

◆ **American Express Travel**
Head Office address: 33 Nabil al-Waqqad St., Ard al-Golf, Heliopolis. Tel: 2418-3222/2144. Maadi office: Tel: 2751-3930/10. Website: http://www.amexfranchise.com

◆ **Egypt Panorama Tours**
(Ted Cookson). Address: 4 Road 79, Maadi.

Tel: 2359-0200 (multiple lines), 2358-5880. Fax: 2359-1199. E-mail: ept@link.net. Website: http://www.eptours.com/.

◆ **Paradisio Travel**
Contact Manar Saada. Address: 28 Ali Amin St., First Zone, Nasr City. Tel: 0100-668-8426. Fax: 2401-4363. E-mail: Tourism@paradisiotravel.com. Website: http://www.paradisiotravel.com.

◆ **Thomas Cook Overseas Ltd**
Address: 3 Abu al-Fida St., Zamalek (plus multiple other locations). Tel: 16119; 2735-9223/4. Website: http://www.thomascook egypt.com

◆ **Travco Group**
Address: Travco Center, 26th July Corridor, al-Sheikh Zayed City, 6th October. Tel: 16161; 3852-0852. Website: www.travco-eg.com

Travel Restrictions

The Egyptian government is concerned for the well-being of its foreign guests. To protect them, certain restrictions on travel are in place.

Train to Middle and Upper Egypt: There are specific trains guarded by police that non-Egyptians are allowed to take.

Bus to Upper Egypt: If there are more than four non-Egyptian passengers on a bus, the bus must travel in a convoy.

Car to Middle and Upper Egypt and Oases: There are police checkpoints along paved roads and you will be asked to register, so it is imperative that Egyptian citizens carry their Egyptian ID and foreigners carry their passport. Registration may be all that is necessary, but sometimes a police escort will follow your car. If an officer wants to ride in the car, you can decline, but be prepared for delays. Service taxis in Upper Egypt usually will not take foreigners as they are required to have an escort if they do so.

Desert travel: To travel off-road, you will need police permission and registration. As of September 2010 the Ministry of Interior has levied a tax on desert travelers, particularly in the Western Desert and including Siwa (see http://hebdo.ahram.org.eg/arab/ahram/2010/9/1/voyp1.htm). The tax charge is LE100 per hour per traveler. Therefore a ten-day trip would rack up a government fee of LE24,000. It is still too early to know how this will affect the price that travel agents charge individuals who drive into the desert. Do consult travel agents and the Ministry of Interior. The Travel Permits Department at the Ministry of Interior is on Sheikh Rihan Street (near Abdin Palace), Tel: 2354-8661; 2355-6301; hours: daily 9:00 a.m.–2:00 p.m. except Friday. Take two photographs and current Egyptian ID or your passport, plus two photocopies of the passport information page and your visa. The permission takes from one to seven days. If you are traveling with an organized tour, the tour leader is responsible, but make sure that this step has been completed before travel. Misr Travel can help with these arrangements. Address: 1 Tal'at Harb St., Downtown. Tel: 2393-0010. Fax: 2392-4440. Website: www.misrtravel.net.

Visas, Immigration, and Residency Permits

At the time of going to press, the rules governing entry visas and extensions are being reviewed by the Egyptian government. Please check the latest situation with your nearest Egyptian consulate or the website of the Ministry of Foreign Affairs (MFA): www.mfa.gov.eg/english/ConsularServices/Pages/ConsularServiceDetails.aspx?ID=Visa%20Application

Visas and Passports

Non-Egyptian visitors arriving in Egypt are required to have a valid passport, which should remain valid for at least six months beyond the period of your intended stay in Egypt. Entry visas may be obtained from Egyptian diplomatic and consular missions abroad. Fees vary according to nationality, and for some categories of visitor (such as holders of diplomatic passports) visas are issued free of charge. It has until recently been possible for most tourists and visitors to obtain a visa at any of the major ports of entry, and this arrangement may yet be reinstated. Please check with your nearest Egyptian consular mission for more details concerning visa regulations that apply to your citizenship.

Those in possession of a residency permit in Egypt are not required to obtain an entry visa if they leave the country and return to it within the validity of their residency permit or within six months, whichever period is less.

Arrival at All Egyptian International Airports

Until August 2011 it was usual for most travelers to obtain their visas upon entry to Egypt. However, as this book goes to press, new rules are contemplated that would require all travelers to obtain their visas in advance from an Egyptian consulate abroad. It is not clear whether these changes will be permanent, so you should check well in advance of your trip with your nearest Egyptian consulate or at the MFA website cited above.

Arrival cards are passed out by the airlines prior to landing or are available before you reach immigration. (If visas are once again issued at the airport, official banks stationed before the immigration line will take the visa fee and issue a stamp to be stuck in your passport. You will then proceed through immigration.)

Arrival at Taba

Visitors entering Egypt at the overland border post at Taba to visit the Gulf of Aqaba coast or St. Catherine's can be exempted from a visa and granted a free permit for fourteen days to visit the area. This is a Sinai-only visa. Be aware that Sinai-only visas are not valid for Ras Muhammad or hiking in central Sinai.

Arrival by Boat

Foreigners arriving in Egypt on board ships are granted permission to visit the port of arrival for twenty-four hours and to catch their ship again at the same port. They can also be granted permission to enter the country for a visit not exceeding a period of three days before boarding their ship at the port of arrival or at any other port.

Types of Visa

There are three types of Egyptian visa:

♦ **Tourist visa**

Usually valid for a period of one month, with extension not exceeding three months, and granted on either a single- or multiple-entry basis. As of the time of printing, Egypt has frozen all new multiple-entry applications.

♦ **Entry visa**

Required for any foreigner arriving in Egypt for purposes other than tourism, such as work, study, and so on. A valid entry visa is needed to complete the Egyptian residency procedure.

♦ **Transit visa**

Air passengers transiting in Egyptian airports are allowed entry for a visit not exceeding a period of twenty-four hours. In the event of an emergency landing, passengers are entitled to enter Egypt for a period of twenty-four hours in the case of poor weather conditions, or forty-eight hours in the case of technical problems with the aircraft.

Visa Exemptions

Nationals of the following countries are currently exempt from visa requirements: Bahrain, Jordan, Kuwait, Libya, Oman, Saudi Arabia, Syria, and the United Arab Emirates.

Residency Permits for Foreign Nationals

Egypt grants legitimate foreign nationals the right of temporary residency in the country for one, three, or five years, depending on personal circumstances. The most common residence permit (valid for one year) is the one given to holders of work permits (see below) and their spouses and minor children. This permit, like its associated work permit, is normally arranged by the employer. For other kinds of residence permits (for example, for spouses of Egyptian nationals, investors, or property owners), see the MFA website cited above, or inquire at the Mugamma' on Tahrir Square.

At the end of your residency in Egypt, you may leave within fifteen days following the expiration date of your visa directly through the country's outlets. You may be permitted to renew your residency for another period by applying to the proper Egyptian authority or its branches.

Obtaining Permits, Extending Visas, and Paying Fines

For any of these, go to the first floor of the Mugamma' on Tahrir Square, Downtown. If your company or institution has a facilitator that can help obtain permits, by all means, use the service. If you feel you need help, there are relocation experts who have facilitators to take care of permits—for a fee, of course. Otherwise, you can head for the Mugamma', which is open from 8:00 a.m. to 3:30 p.m., except Fridays. Go early to avoid crowds. In Ramadan, work ends between 1:00 p.m. and 2:00 p.m. To obtain the correct application, go to the window marked 'Forms.' The cost, with stamps, is about LE20. For renewal you will need your passport (validity must be six months beyond the visa you are seeking), three photographs, a photocopy of the identity page, and a bank receipt showing a recent change of hard currency of at least $200. Visa extensions are completed on the same day. Currently, a one-year tourist visa extension costs LE53. (In summer 2011, tourist visa extensions were cancelled until further notice.) A one-year, no-work residency visa is LE83.10. For a three-year residency visa for an applicant with an Egyptian spouse, the fee is LE143. A five-year residency visa is LE203.10. The most common fine is LE153 for overstay (there is a fifteen-day grace period).

For the same service in Luxor, go to Khalid ibn al-Walid St. In Alexandria, go to to 28 Tal'at Harb St. Other cities in Egypt that have a visa extension service are Ismailiya, Aswan, Marsa Matruh, and Suez.

Note: If you have had your passport renewed, you must go to the Mugamma' to have your visa or residency permit transferred into your new passport.

Work Permits

In order to obtain a work permit you need to be hired by a company or have a sponsor. The company will facilitate the work permit. You will need to provide a valid passport (for members of your family as well) with a six-month validity beyond the amount of time applied for. You need copies of your educational degrees, birth and marriage certificates, and a valid driver's license. These documents must be certified at your embassy and translated into Arabic, and then certified at the Ministry of Foreign Affairs. Once in Egypt, before a work permit can be issued, you must take a blood test for HIV. Each time the permit is to be renewed, a blood test for HIV is required. If you leave the country before the results are submitted you will need to take the blood test again.

Moving Your Personal Effects
Pets

Moving your pet can be a worry for all members of the family. Well ahead of the move, and at least two months prior to travel, select the most direct route to Egypt. You will have to meet the entry requirements of each country you pass through. The websites www.pettravel.com and htttp://cairopets.com are good places for excellent information. Egypt is pet-friendly and, with proper paperwork, your pet will enter Egypt easily. Call your veterinarian to make a photocopy of your pet's records, have a microchip inserted, and make sure all vaccinations are up-to-date and the animal is free of parasites. Once your vet knows your travel plan, if you are in the U.S., ask for the U.S. Department of Agriculture APHIS International Health Certificate. Some other countries have specific animal passports. You must have a standard International Veterinarian Health Certificate issued and signed in ink by a licensed vet-

The Mugamma'

The Mugamma', meaning 'compound,' is a hub of government offices, one of which is the office for immigration, visas, and permits. The building was commissioned by King Farouk in 1951 and completed in 1952. The architect Kamal Ismail describes the neo-Islamic architecture as "a simplified form of the Islamic style." The thirteen-story building became a symbol representing Gamal Abdel Nasser's socialist government and a well-known emblem of bureaucracy at its worst. Today, some government offices have moved to satellite areas of Cairo in an attempt to decentralize government offices and reduce the stress of traffic, parking, and pollution in the downtown area.

erinarian not more than fourteen days before your arrival to Egypt. The certificate must confirm the pet is healthy, free of parasites, and vaccinated for distemper, rabies (not less than thirty days and not more than eleven months before travel), hepatitis, parvovirus, canine parainfluenza, and leptospirosis. Egypt requires a pet to have the ISO 11784/11785 microchip. Forty-eight hours before you travel, your pet must go to the quarantine office at the airport to obtain another health certificate. There is a fee upon arrival to clear the animal, which might include tipping. Refer to http://cairopets.com, Pet Shipping, for further details. All pets must be in your possession for a period of the first three months in Egypt. All the information above as well as information about traveling with pets from all countries, forms, and how to buy a microchip is available at http://www.pettravelstore.com/store-pet-immigration-forms1.html

Check with airlines for regulations and price for carrying your pet; each airline is slightly different. **Here are a few tips:**

◆ Check with airlines about accompanied and unaccompanied animals.

◆ Different rules apply according to the size of the animal. That is, a large animal will travel in the cargo hold whereas a small animal may be allowed as carry-on luggage.

◆ Check prices.

◆ Take the most direct route to Egypt.

◆ Each country that you land in has pet regulations and quarantine rules that must be observed. Remember, some countries such as the UK have strict quarantine regulations; also, be aware that some breeds of dogs are banned in certain countries.

◆ Practice having your animal stay in a crate for long periods of time so they can get used to the confinement.

◆ When buying a crate, make sure it is airline-approved for international travel (different than domestic). One such crate with approval for domestic and international travel is Sky Kennels; see http://www.skykennelsupply.com/skykennel-en.htm. Make sure the crate is the right size, so the animal can stand up and turn around.

◆ Buy a water bottle and food bowl that are attached to the crate. Provide a pad for the animal to lie on.

◆ If the animal travels in the cargo hold, ask about the temperature conditions.

Cars

Importing a Car

All private vehicles entering Egypt must have a triptych or *Carnet de Passage en Douane* (meaning 'notebook for passing through customs') from an automobile club in the country of registration or pay customs duty, which can be as high as 250 percent of the car's original value. Emergency triptychs are available at the port of entry via the Automobile and Touring Club of Egypt. This permits a car to enter Egypt for three months with one extension. The extension is available from the Automobile and Touring Club of Egypt, Qasr al-Nil, Cairo (details below). All persons traveling in the vehicle must have a valid passport and the driver must have an international driver's license. The latter is also available via an automobile club in the country of registration. For more information about triptych or *Carnet de Passage en Douane* go to http://www.go-over land.com/indy/articles/carnet.php.

◆ **Automobile and Touring Club of Egypt (ATCE)**

Working hours from 9:30 a.m. till 2:00 p.m. Address: 10 Qasr al-Nil St., Downtown, Cairo (two blocks away from the Egyptian Central Bank). Tel.: 2574-3355/48. You can also obtain an international driver's license here.

If you wish to import your car into Egypt there are two categories:

* Foreigners who work for an embassy or on a project related to the government (gas and oil companies, for example) do not pay taxes to import a car. The first-time fee is approximately LE2,000 and thereafter a yearly fee of LE1,000. At the end of the contract you can sell your car to another expatriate.

* If your work is not government related, then you can either bring the car in on a triptych for six months and then export it for another six months, or pay full taxes for the car. The imported car must be new. Taxation is determined by original value, size, weight, and so on, and is from 220 to 250 percent of the original value.

Buying a Car in Egypt

An alternative to importing your car is to buy one. To buy a car in Egypt you must have a tourist visa or residency permit and an international driver's license. You will need to register the car in your name and obtain a vehicle license from the *muroor*, the Department of Vehicles Licensing, which has an office in each governorate. Dealers can do this paperwork for you. There are no customs to pay as taxes are included in the price of the car.

To register a car, buy insurance, pay fines, get new license plates, and renew registration, as well as apply for an Egyptian driver's license, foreigners who live in the governorate of Cairo go to the *muroor* behind Arkadia Mall (burnt during the Revolution), behind Wakalat al-Balah. In Giza governorate the *muroor* location is in Bayn al-Sarayat in Dokki. For more information on buying a car, go to chapter 4, "Living in Cairo."

Moving Agents

It is best to call several moving agents to get an estimate of shipping prices in order to decide whether it is best to send your belongings by air, which is calculated in kilograms, or by sea, which is calculated in cubic meters. Insurance is optional, but is usually 3–5 percent of the total declared value. Most importantly, it is essential to feel secure in your choice of movers as they will be handling your treasures.

A website service called One Entry, www.oneentry.com, allows you to enter your moving information and get free quotes from a number of companies in your area for national and international moving needs.

Here are details of some agents with offices in Egypt:

* **AGS Frasers Egypt**
Address: Road 248, Partition 5 and 6, Factory Zone Zahra' al-Maadi, Cairo. Tel: 2813-6465. Fax: 6668-0163. E-mail: manager@agsegypt.com. Website: http://www.ags-worldwide-movers.com

* **Four Winds Egypt**
International door-to-door services; packing and crating; local office and household moves; customs clearance; warehousing

and trucking; insurance. Address: 11A Corniche al-Nil, Corniche al-Maadi, Maadi. Tel: 2358-3608; Mobile: 0106-664-4810. E-mail: fw@fourwinds-eg. com. Website: www.fourwinds-eg.com

♦ **United Sons Moving Services**

International door-to-door service; local office and household moves; packing and crating; customs clearance; transportation; warehouse storage. (This group comes highly recommended by several expatriates who commented on excellence in personal attention and thoroughness.) Address: 18c Road 198, Maadi, Cairo, Egypt. Tel: 2754-4974/94; Mobile 0100-, or 0111-, or 0106-, or 0127-, or 0128-210-1998. E-mail: unitedsons@hotmail.com. Website: www.unitedsons.org

Customs Clearance

It is highly recommended that you confirm that the moving company will clear your goods at customs. If your employer is managing your move, they usually have their own clearing agents who do this work. However, if you are on your own, check with your moving company, as customs clearance is your responsibility. If you find that you need to clear your goods yourself, it is advisable to hire a clearing agent to deal with the paperwork and any problems that might arise.

Antiques (Import and Export)

Keep in mind that genuine antiques (that is, anything over one hundred years old) cannot be exported out of Egypt without approval. If you bring antiques into Egypt in your shipment, be sure to register them so you can take them out again upon leaving the country. If you buy antiques during your stay in Egypt, you need to contact the Supreme Council of Antiquities for approval. Moving companies do have facilitators who can handle this paperwork. Contact the Supreme Council of Antiquities at 3 al-Adil Abu Bakr St., Zamalek. Tel: 2735-8749. It is strictly forbidden to remove from Egypt items such as coral from the Red Sea, antiquities, and prehistoric tools.

What to Bring

Cairo is a city where everything is available, from furniture to electronic goods to underwear; you have your choice of quality and quantity. The difficulty might be where to find these items. For more information on this, see chapter 10, "Shopping." However, if you have personal effects that you can't live without, then bring them. Christmas decorations are available, but they are expensive. For North Americans, remember the electrical current is 220 volts, so don't bring Christmas lights unless you also bring a transformer. Don't forget that the local traditional crafts, artwork, and handmade and carved furniture are beautiful and unique. You may return home with more than you brought. Of course, bring any specific medication you need and check with your pharmacy as to whether it is available in Egypt. Most food items from Europe and North America, or the equivalent, are sold in Cairo. There are shoes galore here, but if you have difficult-to-fit feet, wide or long, be sure to bring shoes and sneakers. You might have to look around a bit, but you will no doubt find what you need.

If you are living outside of Cairo, your choices are more limited. If your company is moving you, then bring what you need. If not, a shopping trip to Cairo is an alternative. There are cars for hire that will transport small or large items.

Here are a few items that, if you are coming from the United States, are unavailable here:

♦ Mattress sizes here are not the same as in the U.S., so if you bring your mattress with you from the U.S., bring sheets and mattress covers as well.

♦ Measuring cups and spoons for U.S. recipes

♦ Pie and cake pans

3

Welcome to Cairo

Cairo is a city of over 20 million people! It is the most populous city in Africa and the Middle East. This city, for all its confusion and complexities, is vibrant and exciting. Yes, there are new systems to figure out, frustrations, and annoyances, but the good news is that, when it all works, there is satisfaction in taking on new challenges and reaping the rewards for doing so. Ask for help if you are overwhelmed, and there will be days that you are! But be comforted that so many people have gone through the same feelings before you. There are ways to contend with difficulties and to ease the first months of settling in. Each day you will learn and grow with each experience. Soon you will be telling folks back home all about those stories. They will be proud of your resilience and perseverance, and envious of your adventure. Welcome to Cairo!

Culture Shock—Cultural Adaptation

Moving to Cairo requires adjustment from all family members. Everyone adapts to a new environment in different ways. The adjustment period ranges from six months to a year. Recognizing the transitions and

Stages of Culture Shock

Early Stage

An initial sense of adventure and excitement accompanies your arrival in the host country. Discovering a new culture, the hustle and bustle of moving into a new home, and getting settled creates a flurry of activity and eagerness.

Frustration Stage

The honeymoon is over and the initial thrill of a new country begins to wane. You miss your familiar surroundings and family you left back home. You feel frustrated and are judgmental of the people, the new culture, and the new language. To get through this stage, stay positive and active, and write a journal or blog.

Adjustment Stage

You become familiar with Egyptian culture, the people, and its food, and have taken Arabic lessons. You have made friends and laugh about the things that are frustrating. You find yourself accepting and appreciating differences.

being sensitive to individual needs will help you deal with the difficult decisions on education, housing, or just getting around.

There are many opportunities to meet people. Join expatriate groups, visit the Community Service Association in Maadi, and if you have children, participate in parents' groups. Support systems at work, schools, churches, and organizations welcome newcomers. Although many Egyptians speak English and French, it is best to learn some Arabic, not only to get around the city but also to integrate into the community. Definitely learn Arabic numbers, both written and spoken: it will ease your daily life in innumerable ways.

A key to enjoying your time in Egypt is to be patient. *Ma'lish* (never mind) and *bukra* (tomorrow) often frustrate newcomers, as these concepts diminish quality and expectations, and put off promises and work for another day. Everything requires patience; everything will get done at its own pace.

There are ways to be at home in your new environment: read about Egypt and Cairo, do not be afraid to ask when you don't understand a cultural difference, be flexible and open to new experiences, try not to be judgmental, mix with people with similar interests and backgrounds, join an online expat group, learn Arabic, be active in sports or hobbies, set aside a special day just for yourself. Invest in a little book that might make a big difference: *Egypt: The Culture Smart Guide to Customs and Etiquette* by Jailan Zayan (AUC Press 2007).

Until then, here are some things that you need to know.

What You Need to Know

Addressing people by their given name is preceded by some kind of title, such as *'amm* (uncle for men), *umm* + name of the first-born son (for an older woman), *madame* or *mademoiselle* to formally greet a woman, *duktuur* for a person with a doctorate, *muhandis* for an engineer, *hajj* for an older man or one who has gone to Mecca. *Pasha* and *bey* were official titles used before 1952 and still are used today out of respect for authority, age, or position. Among friends, simply place *ya* before the given name.

Adoption is forbidden by Islamic religious law and is illegal in Egypt.

Alcohol is available in Egypt, but excessive indulgence is not acceptable. Never bring a bottle of alcohol as a present to a Muslim family. Devout Muslims do not drink alcohol.

Animals are wild in the streets. They may have rabies or be diseased. Do not try to approach an animal and keep children away. For the most part these animals fear humans and will run away, but never corner a street cat or dog.

Balcony safety may be a lifesaving exercise as most Cairo residents live in high-rise buildings. Every apartment has one or more balconies, usually attached to a living room, kitchen, or one bedroom. Beware of the danger that a child might pull a chair up against the railing to look over. Also, do not lean out over the railing trying to clean outside glass, as the head is heavier than the legs and it is easy to slip over the railing. (This author has personally seen three accidents.)

Illegal use and sale of drugs carry a severe punishment under Egyptian law for anyone found guilty. Smuggling drugs, trafficking, or dealing with drugs can carry a death sentence. Foreigners are subject to Egyptian law when in Egypt. Parents should be aware that prescriptions are not needed and prescription drugs are sold over the counter.

Egypt's emergency law was one of the contentious issues that gave rise to Egypt's Revolution of 25 January 2011. Prior to the Revolution, the Emergency Law had been renewed every three years since the assassination of President Anwar Sadat in October 1981. The Emergency Law "[which] gives police wide powers of arrest, suspends constitutional rights and curbs non-governmental political activity, was backed by a majority of MPs in Egypt's 454-member parliament [in May 2010]" (http://news.egypt.com/en/the-emergency-law-in-egypt.html). However, after the Revolution, the Egyptian Armed Forces stated that the Emergency Law would be removed before the parliamentary elections due to take place in November 2011.

Explicit sexual material—magazines, photos, and any recorded material, video or audio—is illegal and subject to confiscation.

Flirting and overt displays of affection are frowned upon. Lovers often sit in cars or on park benches holding hands, which is becoming more acceptable. Men often hold hands and kiss cheeks upon greeting one another. This show of affection is considered appropriate. A woman should not be too friendly to a man as it gives the wrong impression. Foreign men should not flirt with Egyptian women. Egyptian women go out to clubs in groups and socialize only with those they know; strangers are not welcome in the group, nor should they try to flirt.

Gifts are customary for a dinner invitation. A small present for the hostess—flowers, chocolate, a book, or a small decoration—is appropriate. The gift will be put away to open after the guests leave. It is not usual to send a note of thanks. Florists will deliver flowers directly to the house on the day of the invitation. If a plate of food is sent to your home and you are to return the plate, it is a custom, old-fashioned but still lovely, to return it with goodies from your kitchen.

Greetings are an important form of communication, either by a daily greeting like good morning, *Sabaah il-kheir*, or *salam 'aleekum*, meaning 'peace upon you.' Shaking hands is acceptable. Usually a woman will offer her hand first to a man for a handshake; do not expect a man to offer his hand first. Sometimes, a pious individual (of either sex) will refuse a handshake from the opposite sex; do not be offended as this is not about you, but about their beliefs. Kissing on the cheeks is acceptable between the same sex. The typical European or Lebanese cheek-kissing ritual is not a greeting commonly observed between opposite sexes in Egypt. Upon greeting an Egyptian, ask about their health and family first before launching into the business at hand.

Harassment, mostly by young Egyptian men, is not uncommon. All unescorted women, young and old, Egyptian and foreign, complain about the overt and sometimes rude attention by Egyptian men. It is best to ignore any comments. Modest dress might ward off attention, but even women who wear scarves complain about being pestered and verbally abused. Be aware of your surroundings, walk with confidence, and do not go alone anywhere with a stranger. If you feel threatened, shout *Haraam* (forbidden [by God]) or *'eeb* (shame). There is an anti-harassment initiative to provide women with a way to report incidents of sexual harassment via SMS messages. This system, called Harassmap (www.harassmap.org, in Arabic, English, and French), maps harassment online via reports sent in by victims. Women can look at the map on the website to see where attacks take place. The list of offenses ranges from ogling, groping, and indecent exposure to rape. Send a message via SMS: 0106-987-0900; E-mail: report@harassmap. org; Twitter: By sending a tweet with the hashtag/s #harassmap; Website: www. harassmap.org

Homosexuality is considered debauchery and, though not illegal in Egypt, it is forbidden. It is assumed that bisexuality and homosexuality do not exist. Exercise extreme caution if you are gay. However, it is not uncommon to see men holding hands and this is not an indication of being gay. Holding hands and kissing on the cheek are acceptable expressions of friendship between men.

An invitation to an Egyptian's home is more formal than in western cultures. Dropping over for a cup of coffee is not typical except among family members. An invitation is necessary. Never enter a home uninvited. A lone man should not enter a home when only a woman is at home; an exception to this is a man who is working with the family.

Photographing Egyptians has recently become a more sensitive issue than in past years. It is best to ask before snapping a shot, but if you ask, expect 'no' for an answer. Photography is banned in museums; permission must be obtained from the Ministry of Culture or the Supreme Council of Antiquities. There are restrictions on photographing military personnel and sites, bridges, and canals, including the Suez Canal. Egyptian authorities may broadly interpret these restrictions to include other potentially sensitive structures, such as embassies, banks, other public buildings with international associations, and some religious edifices. Visitors should also refrain from taking photographs of any uniformed personnel.

Proselytizing is illegal. There is personal religious freedom in Egypt, and you have the right to worship in established religious institutions, but it is illegal to try to convert an Egyptian to other religious beliefs.

Security and personal safety have been one of Cairo's strong points. Even during and after the 2011 Egyptian Revolution, the city is still probably one of the safest in the world.

Violent crimes such as rape and murder are rare. As these violent crimes are often associated with poverty and overcrowding, one might wonder why in Egypt they are so infrequent. Though not confirmed by sociological data, a possible explanation is that Egypt is a deeply religious country and respect and fear of the afterlife are strong influences that keep the Egyptian psyche less violent. Also, problems are shared. The family, extended family, and community play a strong role in an individual's choices and development. All of this is not to say that common sense should be thrown to the wind. Women should not walk alone beyond crowded areas at night. Petty crime, such as purse snatching and picking pockets, does exist, particularly in crowded areas. Protect against snatchers by holding your bag close to your body and carrying it on your side next to a wall, away from the road, so a motorcyclist or bicyclist cannot snatch it from the road. If there is such an incident, contact the tourist police or go to a police station near where the incident occurred, and also contact your embassy. Tourist police are recognizable by their arm bands that say 'Tourist Police.' If your Arabic is poor, ask for an officer, who probably speaks English. Complaints can be filed for investigation at the Tourist Police Headquarters. The emergency line in Egypt is 122.

Soles of the feet should stay on the ground. You should never point them at or put them near someone's face.

The superstition that someone might put the evil eye (curse) on you is a paranoia that is guarded against by an 'eye' or the 'hand of Fatima.' Do not be overtly complimentary about another's possession. The superstition is that to admire something attracts the evil eye and so the owner will then offer the possession to you. This brings on an awkward conversation of decline, insistence, and explanation. Also, avoid gushing over the cuteness of a baby or child. This is believed to bring an evil eye and so it is best to say nothing about the beauty of a child.

Terrorist attacks in Egypt have occurred sporadically. Be vigilant in crowded tourist areas and be alert to security warnings of demonstrations or of areas to avoid. Egypt is very concerned for its foreign residents and tourists. Before the Revolution there was high security around all hotels, resulting in no parking around the perimeter. However, since February 2011 there has been less of a security presence due to a lack of police and security guards, meaning that cars around hotels are not being as closely scrutinized as before. The army maintains a security presence at embassies and some government buildings.

Ticket lines are often segregated by sex. Bus drivers may ask a woman to sit with other women. On the metro, cars 4 and 5 are reserved for women.

Traffic in Cairo is heavy and slow, but weaves aggressively. Pedestrians do not have the right of way. Furthermore, pedestrians cross streets at any point, which makes driving difficult and dangerous. Traffic police are easily recognizable by their white uniforms in the summer and black in the winter months, and are seen at intersections and roundabouts. They regulate the traffic and stop those who break the law.

Women are not required to wear a *higab* (headscarf) or a robe. However, be sensible and conservative in your wardrobe choices in public (and when at home if a workman is expected). At a minimum, keep your legs, breasts, and stomach covered. Put something over your exercise clothes to wear to and from the gym. It's okay to wear a bathing suit at the pool or on a beach frequented by foreigners, but please don't go topless.

Customs and Traditions

Over generations, customs and traditions have developed in families, social networks, and religious communities. If you have an Egyptian friend, ask about the appropriate etiquette for special occasions.

Muslims and Christians speak a common language and share a common culture in Egypt. Other than a higab or a cross tattooed on the wrist, there is no visible distinction. Christians and Muslims live in the same areas. Both Muslim and Christians are deeply rooted in their beliefs, but they

do share areas of religious practice. All Egyptians celebrate the arrival of a child one week after the birth with a naming ceremony. Boys are circumcised. It is customary for friends to visit the baby and mother.

Marriage is a major event in the life of Egyptians. For Copts, the sacraments bind the marriage in the church followed by family celebrations; for Muslims, marriage is the signing of a contract followed by family celebrations. To get married in the Muslim tradition, the man goes to the male guardian of the woman and asks for her hand in marriage. If the guardian accepts, the man buys a *shabka*, an engagement gift of gold and/or diamond jewels according to his financial capabilities. The *fatha* is read, which legalizes the engagement. An engagement celebration might be a small gathering in the house of the man or a massive party. The wedding is when the formal contract, *katb al-kitab*—writing in the book—is signed in front of an imam by the male guardian of the woman and the husband. The marriage is now legal; however, the newlyweds live apart until suitable living accommodations are obtained. There is usually a party or reception that follows the *katb al-kitab*. The path to Coptic matrimony begins with asking permission from the elder of the household and presenting the *shabka*. The engagement and wedding ceremony are held in church. A wedding gift for both Copts and Muslims should be a household item. It may be sent to the house of the bride, but more often it is presented in person when you go to

LOCAL KNOWLEDGE

Guides to Egypt from
The American University in Cairo Press

With more than 50 years experience, we know Egypt inside-out and can guide you from one end of the country to the other, show you the culture, and reveal the secrets of the Egyptian kitchen along the way.

Cairo
The Family Guide
By Lesley Lababidi
Paperback
LE100 / $18.95
ISBN: 978 977 416 402 6

Alexandria and the Egyptian Mediterranean
A Traveler's Guide
By Jenny Jobbins and Mary Megalli
Paperback
LE90 / $22.95
ISBN: 978 977 416 989 1

Islamic Monuments in Cairo
The Practical Guide
By Caroline Williams
Paperback
LE100 / $24.95
ISBN: 978 977 416 205 3

The Illustrated Guide to the Coptic Museum
By Gawdat Gabra and Marriane Eaton-Krauss
Flexibound
LE150 / $29.95
ISBN: 978 977 416 007 3

Egyptian Customs and Festivals
By Samia Abdennour
Paperback
LE75 / $16.95
ISBN: 978 977 416 060 8

Cairo's Street Stories
Exploring the City's Statues, Squares, Bridges, Gardens, and Sidewalk Cafés
By Lesley Lababidi
Paperback
LE120 / $24.95
ISBN: 978 977 416 153 7

Inside the Egyptian Museum
With Zahi Hawass
Paperback
LE180 / $39.95
ISBN: 978 977 416 372 2

My Egyptian Grandmother's Kitchen
Traditional Dishes Savory and Sweet
By Magda Mehdawy
Paperback
LE150 / $29.95
ISBN: 978 977 424 927 3

Celebrating 100 Years of Egypt's Nobel Laureate

The Naguib Mahfouz Centennial Library

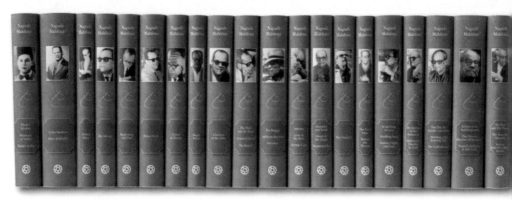

The definitive collection of all the translated works in 20 volumes

In Praise of Nobel Laureate Naguib Mahfouz

"One of the greatest creative talents in the realm of the novel in the world."
—Nadine Gordimer

"Mahfouz's work is freshly nuanced and hauntingly lyrical. The Nobel Prize acknowledges the universal significance of his fiction."
—*Los Angeles Times*

20-Volume Set. 8000 pages. Limited Hardbound Edition.
978-977-416-503-0   LE3,000 / $600   December 2011

The American University in Cairo Press
www.aucpress.com

congratulate the couple at their home after the honeymoon.

After a death, both Muslims and Copts rush to bury the body the same day. Condolences are paid immediately, and again after forty days and after a year. The Islamic condolence sessions are often marked by Qur'an reading. On the first day, both Muslims and Copts may receive male guests in a tent or an 'occasion hall,' while women go to the home of the deceased. Men and women are segregated. Condolences are received at the church as well. The first three days are for formal receiving of condolences, after which there is a forty-day mourning period. The last day of the forty days is an important observance. The phrase for condolence is *al-ba'iyya fi Hayaatak/tik* (roughly translated: "May his/her remaining years be added to yours").

Legal Matters
Marriage in Egypt
Marrying a person outside of your culture, religion, nationality, and ethnicity is a risk that must not be taken lightly. The more you know about your partner and the similarities and differences between you, your commitment will have a better chance of survival. If a woman plans to marry a Muslim Egyptian man, there are three types of marriage in Egypt:

♦ An *'urfi* marriage is legalized at a lawyer's office with two male witnesses and can be registered in court. This type of marriage gives the husband the right to divorce by terminating the contract. If there are children involved, there may be paternity issues raised.

♦ A court-registered marriage is a fully legal marriage within Egyptian law, giving marriage benefits of residence. If you are a second wife you qualify for a court-registered marriage. There are contractual clauses similar to a pre-nuptial agreement that can be inserted at this time, such as the freedom to travel without a husband's permission.

♦ An internationally recognized marriage must take place at the Ministry of Justice in Cairo. If you are a second wife and your husband is not divorced legally from his first wife, you cannot obtain an internationally registered marriage license.

Note: IAF is a nonprofit organization that provides information for women who wish to marry or are married to Egyptian men. IAF answers questions on family rights, visas, working permits, marriage contracts, and so on. Address: 2–4 Ludofusstrasse, 60487, Frankfurt, Germany. Tel: 049-707-5087/8.

Americans who wish to marry in Egypt must follow these steps (see http://egypt.usembassy.gov/consular/acs12.html) for an internationally recognized marriage. Citizens of other countries wishing to marrying Egyptians should first consult their embassy. Step 1: Visit the American Citizen Services, U.S. Embassy. Address: 5 Tawfiq Diyab St. (formerly Latin America Street), Garden City. Appointments: http://egypt.usembassy.gov/consular/appntmnt.html

At American Citizen Services you will sign a marriage affidavit that will be notarized by the U.S. embassy. This affidavit includes your biographical data and your religion. Interfaith marriages are permitted by Egyptian law, except in the case of a Muslim woman and a non-Muslim man. The affidavit also affirms that you are free to marry and that the embassy has no objection to the marriage. Bring your valid American passport and proof of termination of your last marriage, if you were married before. An original or certified copy of the last divorce decree or death certificate must be submitted. There is no need to get this document authenticated or translated into Arabic for the purpose of marriage. Authentication and translation by the Egyptian embassy or an Egyptian consulate in the U.S. may be required later for other purposes. Please note that if you are a female American citizen previously married, you may only remarry in Egypt at least ninety days after your divorce or 130 days after the death of your former spouse. If you are pregnant from your former marriage, you can only remarry after the birth of the baby.

♦ If your fiancé(e) is an Egyptian citizen, it is mandatory that he or she accompany you with their Egyptian ID and/or passport as well as a copy of his/her telephone, electricity, or gas bill showing his/her place of residency as indicated on their Egyptian national ID.

♦ If you are a female of Egyptian origin under the age of twenty-one, you are required either to be accompanied by your father, a guardian, or a person *in loco parentis*, or to present written consent from any of the above. The consent should be in

English and Arabic. It should be notarized by the Egyptian embassy or an Egyptian consulate in the U.S. and by the Egyptian Ministry of Foreign Affairs in Egypt.

♦ The fee is $50 or LE283.

Note: If two American citizens are getting married, each one of them needs a separate statement.

Step 2: After obtaining the notarized statement from the U.S. embassy, you must visit one of the Egyptian Ministry of Foreign Affairs authentication offices. Addresses: Mohandiseen (5 Ahmad Urabi St.); Abbasiya (Ahmad Said St.); or Sabak St. next to the Merryland Gardens in Heliopolis. The office hours are Saturday through Thursday from 9:00 a.m. to 3:00 p.m. The Ministry of Foreign Affairs will certify the statement for a fee of LE11.

Step 3: After obtaining the certification from the Egyptian Ministry of Foreign Affairs, you must visit the Egyptian Ministry of Justice. Address: Egyptian Ministry of Justice Annex (Office of Marriage of Foreigners), fourth floor, Lazughli Square, Abdin. Open Saturday through Wednesday from 9:00 a.m. to 1:00 p.m. and from 3:00 p.m. to 5:00 p.m.; Thursday from 9:00 a.m. to 1:00 p.m.

The Ministry of Justice will register your marriage. Forms to be completed at the marriage court can only be obtained on the wedding day or the day before. The following are required:

♦ Proof of identity (a passport) for both parties, a photocopy of the passport data page, the Egyptian entry visa, and the residency stamp if you have obtained one

♦ Egyptian ID (Egyptian passport or national ID card) and a photocopy of it if one of the parties is Egyptian

♦ Five passport photos for each party

♦ An LE50 *ta'meen igtimaa'i* (social insurance) stamp (purchased at any Egyptian post office)

♦ Two male witnesses with identification documents (passport or ID card) must be present to sign the marriage documents. It is preferable to bring your own witnesses, such as friends or travel agents.

♦ Original proof of termination of a previous marriage if you were married before. No authentication or translation is required. A routine physical exam performed by an Egyptian doctor is sometimes required if the person appears unhealthy.

It will take at least ten business days for a marriage certificate to be issued by the Ministry of Justice. The marriage certificate must be picked up by one of the parties.

Fees to complete the marriage at the Ministry of Justice:

If both parties are Muslim, the fee is 2 percent of the dowry (a minimum of LE40).

If both parties are Christians, a dowry is not required and the fee is LE35.

In order to be able to use the marriage certificate in the U.S., it should be translated into English by the Egyptian Ministry of Justice translation office (LE40). It takes four to seven days to receive the translation, which must then be authenticated by both the Egyptian Ministry of Foreign Affairs (LE11) and the American Citizen Services Unit at the U.S. Embassy in Cairo

($50). The Ministry of Justice translation office is located at the Ministry of Justice building, 13th floor, Lazughli Square, Abdin.

Please note: If you do obtain a marriage certificate in English from the Egyptian Ministry of Justice translation office, you DO NOT need to have it authenticated at the American embassy to use for immigration in the U.S. If you have any questions, send an e-mail to the U.S. embassy at consular cairoacs@state.gov or call 2797-2301.

Birth in Egypt

If you decide to give birth to your child in Egypt, check with your embassy on the procedure to obtain citizenship for the newborn. Be sure to do this well before the baby is due in order to have all the required documents ready in time. An appointment to visit the U.S. Embassy American Services Counselor office is necessary before submitting papers. The following are required by the U.S. government for citizenship. Consult http://cairo.usembassy.gov/consular/acs2.htm.

1. A photocopy of the child's Egyptian birth certificate and an English translation.

Note: the birth must be registered at the Egyptian health office in the district where the child was born within seven days of the child's birth. Upon registration, the Egyptian health office will issue an Egyptian birth certificate for any child born in Egypt. Failure to register the birth within the first seven days will result in a prolonged registration process that usually takes months.

2. A letter from the hospital where the birth took place, if the name of the hospital is not

written on the Egyptian birth certificate. If you delivered at home or in a clinic, you will need a letter from the doctor or midwife who handled the delivery, including a photocopy of the midwife's practice license.

3. A photocopy of the legal marriage certificate and an English translation if the certificate is not in English.

4. If you do not have a civil marriage certificate or if you got married after the birth of the child, the child is considered to have been born out of wedlock. In this case, if the U.S. father is the applying parent, he must fill out an Affidavit of Parentage, an Affidavit of Support, and submit proof of five years of physical presence in the U.S. If the U.S. mother is the applying parent, she must submit proof of one year of physical presence in the U.S. (See number 11 below for an explanation of proof of physical presence.)

5. A photocopy of the divorce or death certificate(s) if the parent(s) was married before. An English translation if the certificate(s) is not in English.

6. Photocopies of all pages of all passport(s) of the American citizen parent(s).

7. A photocopy of all pages of the non-American parent's passport or photo ID.

8. Two photos of the child, 5x5 centimeters, white background, front view, small face.

9. A photocopy of the U.S. Consular Report of Birth Abroad (CRBA) issued by the American embassy in Cairo to your previous child(ren), if you were issued one.

10. A fee of $65, or the equivalent in Egyptian pounds, must be paid for the CRBA when the application is submitted. The fee

for the passport is $85 or the equivalent in Egyptian pounds.

11. Proof of five years of physical presence in the U.S. before the child's birth, at least two of which were after the age of fourteen. The five years need not be continuous and can be before or after naturalization. The following documents are examples of evidence of physical presence in the U.S.:

a. Transcripts from college or school in a sealed envelope

b. Original W-2s

c. Original Social Security statements

d. Government or military service records

e. Entry and exit stamps on passports, supported by a 'Movement Certificate' if the American citizen parent is of Egyptian origin

12. You do not need to submit requirement number 11, if:

a. You have a Consular Report of Birth Abroad for a previous child issued by the U.S. embassy in Cairo, or

b. Both parents are U.S. citizens (either of them have any period of physical presence in the U.S.). If you did not physically live in the U.S. for five years, or if you know that you do not have proof of the required physical presence, please inform the embassy about this in a statement written in English on a white sheet of paper.

13. If the U.S. parent will not be in Egypt and present for an appointment at the embassy, the following are required from him/her:

a. Statement of Consent form DS-3053,

notarized by a notary public in the U.S., or by a U.S. Consular Officer at a U.S. embassy or consulate. The form is available at www.travel.state.gov and at the American Citizen Services Unit in Cairo and other U.S. embassies and consulates.

b. Affidavit of Physical Presence notarized by a notary public in the U.S., or by a U.S. consular officer at a U.S. embassy or consulate

c. Notarized copy of all the pages of the American citizen's passports.

Death in Egypt

All deaths must be registered in the country where the death occurs. The local police or embassy can advise you how to go about this.

Make sure you have as much documentation as possible about the deceased and yourself. This should include: full name, date of birth, passport number, and where and when the passport was issued. If you are not the closest relative, find out who the next of kin of the deceased person is. If the deceased was known to be suffering from an infectious condition, for example hepatitis or HIV, it is essential that the authorities be told so that they can take precautions against infection. Consult: http://travel. state. gov/travel/tips/emergencies/emergen cies_1191.html

According to the U.S. State Department, a death should be immediately reported to the embassy or consulate. The consulate officer will confirm the death, identity, and U.S. citizenship of the deceased; make notification to the next of kin if they do not already know about the death, providing information about disposition of the remains and the effects of the deceased; and provide guidance on forwarding funds to cover costs.

Upon completion of all formalities, the 'Report of the Death of an American Citizen,' based upon the local death certificate, is prepared by the Consular Section and forwarded to the next of kin or legal representative for use in U.S. courts to settle estate matters. This document is an administrative report that provides essential facts concerning the death of the U.S. citizen and the custody of the personal estate of the deceased. If the deceased passed away due to unnatural causes (murder, car accident, and so on), the local police and law officials will probably become involved in the matter and cause delays in transporting the remains. Local officials may need to issue a coroner's report (that can take days or weeks to complete), and may not release the remains to next of kin until all procedures are completed. Muslim countries forgo embalming because they traditionally bury their dead within twenty-four hours.

Comprehensive travel insurance, particularly plans that cover accidents, injuries, or death, can offset expensive fees and travel costs in an emergency. Interglobal (http://www.interglobalpmi.com/interna tionalhealthinsurance/aboutus/default.aspx) and International SOS (http://www.interna tionalsos.com/en/) are just two companies

3 Welcome to Cairo

that offer assistance as well as individual and corporate travel insurance. Most airlines offer cargo service for transporting remains. Contact a travel agent or visit a specific airline's website for quotes.

Getting around Cairo

Cairo is congested. Think of one million cars on Cairo's streets, two million people a day using the metro, two million people in minivans, and four million on buses. The best time to get around the city without heavy congestion is on the weekend. One must allow extra time for any appointment because of the chance of an unexpected traffic jam. Some notorious roads for congestion during morning and evening rush hours are 26th July Corridor, 6th October Bridge, Salah Salim Street, Ramsis Street, the Corniche, and Murad Street. Zamalek is gridlocked from 2:00 p.m. until 6:00 p.m. when schools are dismissed. Here are ways to get around the city:

Walking. This is the best, yet not without its perils. Uneven sidewalks, or no sidewalks at all, and crossing the street require concentration and vigilance. Crossing the street is all about timing: do not expect that a car will stop for you just because you are in its path! Ask a policeman to help or walk with another person who is crossing the street. Be very careful when pushing baby carriages or strollers. A driver may not be able to see the stroller or may be reckless, so exercise extreme caution.

The Metro. What a deal—for only LE1 you can traverse the city! The Cairo Metro is the only subway system in all of Africa and is one of the most important projects undertaken in the capital. There are two lines: Line 1 from New al-Marg to Helwan and Line 2 from Shubra to Munib. Line 3 is under construction and will run from Imbaba to Cairo International Airport. Although women may ride in any car, on all Metro trains the fourth and fifth cars are for women only. The cars are labeled and their positions are marked on the platform. Each car has 'entrance' and 'exit' doors, but the signage is rarely observed. The Metro stations are open from 5:30 a.m. to midnight. The trains run every eight to ten minutes in normal hours and every five to six minutes during peak rush hours. In the summer, the service extends till 1:00 a.m. Keep your ticket as, upon exiting, you must insert it into a turnstile. If you do not have a ticket, there is an LE15 fine.

Buses. The government has eased, slightly, the transportation problem by introducing a new fleet of red, fifty-seat buses. These Cairo Transport Authority (CTA) red buses replace the old green ones and also increase the price from LE0.50 to LE1.

Minibuses, microbuses, and service taxis. Tickets for microbuses operated by the private Greater Cairo Bus Company are from LE0.50 to LE1 depending on the distance. The fares, routes, and stops for these are fixed. The government-licensed, privately

Tourism by Metro

Line 1 New al-Marg to Helwan:
Helwan: Japanese Garden
Maadi: Road 9
Mar Girgis: Roman fortress, ancient churches and synagogue, Mosque of Amr ibn al-'As, ancient site of Fustat, Darb 1718, Civilization Museum (opens in 2012), Coptic Museum
Sa'd Zaghloul: Sa'd Zaghloul Mausoleum and House, Education Museum, MAKAN —Egyptian Center for Culture and Art
Sadat (Lines 1 and 2): Egyptian National Museum, American University in Cairo (Downtown campus), Mugamma', Downtown
Nasser: Entomology Institute, Arab Music Institute
al-Shuhadaa (formerly Mubarak) (Lines 1 and 2): Ramsis Train Station, Railway Museum
Demerdash: Ahmad Mahir Mausoleum
Ghamra: Mosque of Baybars, Sakakini Palace (closed)
Saraya al-Qubba: Saad El-Khadem and Effat Naghi Museum, Science Center
al-Matariya: Virgin's Tree and Obelisk of Senusret I

Line 2 Shubra to Munib:
Ataba: Post Office Museum, Puppet Theater
Naguib: Abdin Palace

Opera: Cairo Opera House, Mahmud Mukhtar Museum, Hurriya Garden, Andalusya Garden, Cairo Tower
Dokki: Agriculture Museum (15-minute walk)
Cairo University: Cairo University, Giza Zoo (20-minute walk)

owned vans and Peugeots have no fixed stops; you can get on and off where you want. Prices vary, but because the ride is shared the price starts at just LE1. Microbus drivers drive recklessly, often stopping abruptly in the middle of the road. The drivers are for the most part inexperienced youths without a proper driving license. The accident rate is high. However, the microbus is the most popular form of transportation because of its speed and availability.

Nile bus ferries. They are yellow and green, and are usually parked by the river in front of the Radio and Television Union building. The ticket for this public transport is still very cheap: LE0.25 from Abu al-Fida to Imbaba, and LE2 from Tahrir to Giza. The trip is far more comfortable than its counterpart—a small and crowded microbus—and the scenery is obviously better.

Taxis. Taxis are safe and plentiful in Cairo. There are two types of taxi service hailed on the streets—metered white taxis and non-metered black-and-white taxis. The white taxis start at LE2.50. Usually they are

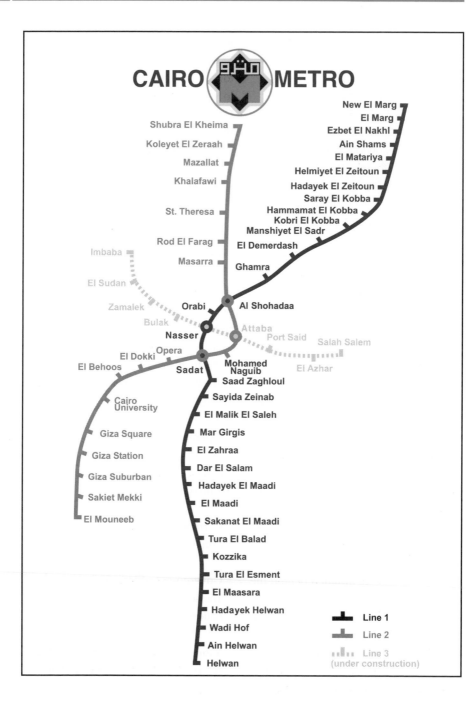

Useful Bus Routes

Number 400 from the airport to Downtown
Number 66 from the station in front of Ramsis Hilton to Khan al-Khalili
Number 72 from the station at Ramsis Hilton to the Citadel
Numbers 800 and 900 from the Mugamma' in Tahrir Square to the Pyramids
Numbers 951 and 154 from Tahrir Square to the Citadel/Ibn Tulun
Number 82 from Tahrir Square to the Pyramids

air-conditioned; however, you might need to ask the driver to turn on the a/c. The advantage of taking a white cab is that there is no bargaining! There have been some grumblings of rigged meters, which would be difficult to prove unless you are positive of the fare cost from point to point. A taxi ride in a white cab from 26th July in Zamalek to the Giza Zoo, in traffic, is approximately LE7–8, while a black-and-white will always expect LE10. If you are lucky, you might get into one of the fifty white taxicabs that have small libraries installed behind the driver's seat. Brainchild of Alef Books, it is an initiative called 'The Taxi of Knowledge' or Taxi al-Ma'rifa, which encourages the rider to spend time reading.

Black-and-white taxis have no meters, so it is best to settle on a price before getting

in. A rough guide to pay for a taxi within the Dokki–Mohandiseen–Zamalek–Downtown area is normally LE10–12; Downtown to Maadi or Heliopolis LE25–30; Zamalek to Carrefour LE50; Downtown to Cairo International Airport LE50–80. Hotel taxis charge a lot more than a taxi hailed on the street.

Yellow taxis can be hailed from the street, but are mainly taken from a taxi stand or reserved by phone (City Cab: 16516, and Cairo International Taxi: 19155, operators speak Arabic and English). They are metered: LE3.50 base fare and LE1.25 per kilometer. The Blue Cab service (3760-9717/616) is for booking a taxi in advance, as is Alo Taxi (2525-2181, 0100-530-0576). The price is fixed depending on distance. For example, for a return trip from Zamalek to Carrefour in Qattamiya the fare is LE50 each way and LE20 an hour to wait. Sixt London Taxi (19670) serves the airport for Egyptians

Opening Hours

Banks: Sunday–Thursday 8:30 a.m.–2:00 p.m.; closed national holidays

Currency exchange banks at major hotels: open twenty-four hours, daily

Government offices: Saturday–Thursday 9:00 a.m.–2:00 p.m.; closed national holidays

Shops: vary by religion, tradition, and season. Check with individual shops.

and foreigners, but provides a limousine service for foreigners only (not residents and Egyptians). Sixt charges LE550 for an eight-hour day and 100 kilometers, with an additional charge for extra hours and/or kilometers.

In a metered taxi, check that the meter is working before setting off. If not, get out and take the next taxi.

Flying Taxi. Smart Aviation, partially owned by EgyptAir, announced that five turbo helicopters will soon be turned into flying taxis that will transfer people from governorates as well as communities on the outskirts of Cairo. Two helicopters will be used as air ambulances. According to the article in Al Arabiya (http://www.alarabiya.net/articles/2010/08/10/116236.html), "the new flying taxis will be affordable to all people."

Private Car. In chapter 4 there is extensive information about buying, driving, and licensing a private car. Take into consideration carpooling! See www.egyptcarpoolers. com. You have to be registered to use the website, and you must be at least eighteen to register. The website includes:
* A detailed user profile (optional)
* A carpool ratings and reviews system

Limousines. Limousine service is expensive, but to be driven hassle-free is sometimes worth the cost. Here are a few to call when those occasions arise:

Tips For Taxi Rides:

* Dress appropriately.
* Hail new cabs.
* Check if the meter is working and get out if it is not.
* At night, take a taxi from a busy area where there are people around.
* Greet the taxi driver with "*salaamu 'aleekum.*"
* Sit in the back, never in the front seat.
* Know the landmarks of where you are going; if you don't, have a friend call and tell the taxi driver the directions.
* Have change and small notes to pay.
* If you feel uncomfortable, call your friends from the taxi or just get out.
* Do not start a conversation with the driver.
* Get out and pay or pay as you are getting out; do not linger.
* Keep possessions close to your body at all times.
* Before closing the door, check for any possessions that might have fallen on the seat or floor.

* **Alex Limousine**
Caters to businessmen. Tel: 3305-9759, 3302-0159. Website: http://www.limoegypt.com.

* **First Limousine**
Address: 28A New Nirco Buildings, Zahra' al-Maadi. Tel: 2516-5408; Mobile: 0100-610-6701.

Landmarks:

With no street names or numbers, use landmarks to navigate. To give and get directions, learn landmarks by their Arabic names.

Abbas Bridge	kubri 'abbas	كوبرى عباس
Abdin Palace	'aSr 'abdiin	قصر عابدين
American University	il-gam'a il-amrikiya	الجامعة الأمريكية
	(specify Tahrir, Qattamiya,	
	or Zamalek)	
al-Azhar Park	Hadiiqat il-azhar	حديقة الأزهر
Botanical Garden	gineent il-urmaan	جنينة الأورمان
Cairo Tower	burg il-qaahira	برج القاهرة
Cairo University	gam'at il-qaahira	جامعة القاهرة
Camel Market	suu' il-gimaal	سوق الجمال
Citadel	il-'al'a	القلعة
City of the Dead	il-'araafa	القرافة
Coptic Cairo	maSr il-'adiima	مصر القديمة
Downtown	wust al-balad	وسط البلد
Duty-free shop	il-suu' il-Hurra	السوق الحرة
Egyptian Museum	il-matHaf il-maSri	المتحف المصرى
Fish Garden	gineent il-asmaak	جنينة الاسماك
Gezira Club	naadi il-giziira	نادى الجزيرة
Heliopolis	maSr il-gidiida	مصر الجديدة
International Gardens	il-hadiqa il-dawliya	الحديقة الدولية
Islamic Cairo	il-Huseen	الحسين
Islamic Museum	il-matHaf il-islaami	المتحف الإسلامي
Manial Palace Museum	matHaf 'aSr il-manyal	متحف قصر المنيل
Ministry of Foreign Affairs	wizarit il-khargiyya	وزارة الخارجية
Mugamma'	il-mugamma'	المجمع
Old Cairo	maSr il-'adiima	مصر القديمة
Opera Complex	daar il-ubra (fi-l-giziira)	دار الأوبرا
Pyramids	il-haram	الهرم
Qasr al-Nil Bridge	kubri 'aSr il-nil	كوبرى قصر النيل
Ramsis Train Station	maHattit ramsiis	محطة رمسيس

Ring Road	id-da'iri	الطريق الدائرى
Roxy	ruksi	روكسى
Shooting Club	nadi iS-Seed	نادى الصيد
Swissair Building	mabna swiseer (fi-l-giiza)	مبنى سويس أير
Tahrir Square	midan it-taHriir	ميدان التحرير
Television Building (Maspero area)	mabna it-tilivizyoon	مبنى التليفزيون
World Trade Center	markaz it-tigaara	مركز التجارة
Zoo	gineent il-Hayawanaat	جنينة الحيوانات

♦ **Green Gear**

Car rental company with high environmental awareness. Limousine service, airport pick up and drop off, self-driven and chauffeur-driven cars. Address: 27 Giza St., Giza. Tel: 3571-6400; Mobile: 0127-716-4400. E-mail: afathi@greengearegypt.com. Website: www.greengearegypt.com

♦ **Gulf Limousine**

Contact: Ayman Ezz, General Manager. Address: 7 al-Nadi al-Gidid St., New Maadi. Tel: 3303-5674. Fax: 3303-5669. E-mail: Gulflimousine@yahoo.com

For very special occasions:
♦ **Stretch Limousine Cars**
Tel: 2205-8018, 2268-8020, 2267-8336.

Baksheesh, Begging, and Bargaining

Baksheesh (from a Persian root meaning 'to give' or 'to distribute') is a part of the society, woven into every transaction and street corner. From the parking attendant to the garbage collector, a tip is expected. Grocery and vegetable-bag carriers expect LE2. At hotels, bellhops expect LE5–20 per piece depending on the quality of the hotel. Deliverymen are tipped LE5–10. Restaurant bills sometimes include a service charge, but usually a 10–12 percent tip is added on top. Parking attendants expect at least LE1, and if a policeman allows you to wait in your car there is an expectation of at least LE5. If you are a guest it is a tradition to tip domestic help. If you are on a tour, unless the tip is clearly stated in the price of the tour, the tour guide and driver expect a tip. Please do not offer tips to professionals, businessmen, or others who would be considered to be your equal. You may seriously offend them.

Beggars are on all streets. The majority of people are poor and, with no state welfare, many find begging is their only source of income. However, there are families who make a career out of street begging. It is difficult to draw a line as to who receives and who does not. You will find that some days you will feel more generous than others. Do think about donating clothes, shoes, and toys to those in need.

Bargaining is alive and well in Cairo and in Egypt in general. The rule of thumb is to appear uninterested in the object you want, casually ask about the price, then, when quoted a figure, offer 25 percent off it and bargain upward. Walk away, and if you are called back you have your price. If not, the price is too low and you can make another offer or just leave. Usually the final price agreed upon will be between a 15 and 5 percent discount. Remember the seller won't sell unless they are happy with the price and making a profit. Small stores, not department stores with fixed prices, will sometimes give discounts when asked.

Banks

Cash is king in Cairo, although credit cards are gaining popularity. Checks are rarely used except for companies to issue salaries and payments. ATMs are located throughout the city to dispense Egyptian pounds, allowing direct withdrawals from your Visa and MasterCard credit and debit cards. There are ATM machines in every mall, in hotels, and on major streets.

There are numerous international banks with branches throughout the city. Foreigners may open a foreign currency current account and saving account as well as an Egyptian pound bank account. Banks require a copy of your passport and proof of residency, with a minimum deposit for each account. For example HSBC requires an LE5,000 deposit to open an Egyptian

pound account and a $2,000 deposit for an account in dollars. The policy varies from bank to bank, so go to the bank you wish to deal with and ask about the particulars. Bank personnel usually speak English. Once an account is open you can transfer money and receive transfers as well as have checks issued. Checks, however, are not a typical form of payment between individuals, although companies do pay salaries and give refunds with checks. To cash a check you can deposit the check in your bank and, for a fee, your bank will eventually clear the check, or you can go to the bank of the issuer and receive the cash.

Credit cards in Egyptian currency can be secured by a certificate of deposit. For example, HSBC requires a deposit of a minimum of $2,000, which is the credit limit. Actually, you can never overspend as the credit card companies have the right to collect from your deposit if you do not pay your bill on time. However, in the next year or two all this will change and the banks will no longer require a time deposit. Credit lines will be extended by banks approving the amount of credit that can be extended to you, like in the U.S. or Europe. In the near future and in Egypt, credit and debit cards will used from your mobile phones. You will receive a one-time number for each purchase.

Banks are open from 8:30 a.m. to 2:00 p.m. (some international banks, like HSBC, are open until 5:00 p.m.) from Sunday through Thursday. Most branches give out numbers upon entrance. You will take a seat and when your number is called you

3333333333333

Main Banks in Egypt

Arab African International Bank
Tel: 19555, 2794-5096
Arab International Bank
Tel: 19100, 3301-2555
Bank Audi
Tel: 16555, 3336-2516
Bank of Alexandria
Tel: 19033, 2391-6369
Banque du Caire
Tel: 2391-6915/63/66
Banque Misr
Tel: 19888, 2391-2015/25
Barclays Bank
Tel: 16222, 2366-2600
Blom Bank
Tel: 19233, 3332-2770
CIB
Tel: 19666/19843
Citibank
Tel: 16644/16677
Crédit Agricole
Tel: 19077/19191, 2728-0126/0114/2661
Faisal
Tel: 3762-1285/6/7/9
HSBC
Tel: 19007, 2739-6001
National Bank of Egypt
Tel: 19623
NSGB
Tel: 19700, 2770-7000

proceed to the teller with the corresponding number. Go early to avoid crowds; expect

Credit Card Emergencies

American Express
Tel: 19327, 2480-1500. Toll free: 0800-4444
Diners Club International Card
Tel: 2578-3355
Visa Card and MasterCard (Bank Misr)
Tel: 2391-2015
**Visa Card and MasterCard
(National Bank of Egypt)**
Tel: 2391-4458

long waits prior to holidays. Remember that the branch where you open your account is the branch where you will bank, except with international banks where you can make transactions at any branch.

Bank and Wire Transfers in Egypt

If you have an Egyptian bank account, you will be able to transfer money to and from your overseas account. Fees vary from bank to bank. Western Union is in Egypt and is the fastest way to send and receive money. Western Union transfers must be in U.S. dollars. Take your passport and the cash to the Western Union office, and a clerk will provide you with the proper paperwork. Specify the recipient of the funds and the wire service will provide you with a reference number. To obtain the funds, the recipient must go to a Western Union branch in his own country and present the clerk with the correct reference number. Never wire money to a stranger.

Post Office
Transfer money within Egypt for low rates at post offices throughout the country. Open until 9:00 p.m. For more information go to www.egyptpost.org or call 0800-800-2800.

Western Union
There are numerous branches throughout Cairo. Hotline: 19190. Tel: 2755-5165; toll-free number 0800-88-000-88.

Insurance
Look into insurance plans before you come to Egypt. Does your company provide coverage for your health and that of your family? Is emergency evacuation provided? Life insurance is a personal option. Check what circumstances it covers, that is, does it cover traveling in areas of unrest? Though property insurance is not common in Egypt, if you have valuables that are irreplaceable you might look into insuring them while here. Always invest in moving insurance. Travel insurance is usually provided by the airlines or travel agency. Car insurance is discussed in the next chapter. Here is a brief list of insurers in Cairo.

Private Sector Companies
(all types of insurance):

Al Chark Insurance Company
Established in 1931. Address: 15 Qasr al-Nil St., Downtown. Tel: 2575-3265

Delta Insurance Company
Established in 1980. Address: 10 Tal'at Harb St., Downtown. Tel: 3335-2045 (10 lines). Website: www.deltains.org

MISR Insurance Company
Established in 1934. Address: 44a al-Dokki St., Dokki. Tel: 3335-5350 (10 lines)

Mohandes Insurance Company
Established in 1980. Address: 3 al-Misaha St., Dokki. Tel: 3336-8101/3/7

National Insurance Company
Established in 1900. Address: 33 al-Nabi Danyal St., Alexandria. Tel: 19446. Website: www.ahlya.com

Suez Canal Insurance Company
Established in 1979. Address: 31 Muhammad Kamil Mursi St., Mohandiseen. Tel: 3360-1053/1052/1051/6868

Private Sector Companies
(property and liability insurance):

AIG Egypt Insurance Company
Address: Nile City, North Tower, Corniche al-Nil St., 26th floor, Cairo. Tel: 2302-9838

Allianz Insurance Company
Address: Saridar Building, 92 Tahrir St., 8th floor, Dokki. Tel: 19909; Customer service center: 3333-5208

BUPA Egypt Insurance Company
Address: 48 al-Thawra St., Dokki. Tel: 16816, 3762-8685

◆ **Egyptian Saudi Insurance House**
Address: 15 Musaddiq St., Dokki. Tel: 3337-7997 (10 lines); Direct: 3762-9906

Private Sector Companies (life insurance):
◆ **Allianz Life Insurance Company**
(same as above)

◆ **NSGB Life Insurance Company**
Head Office Address: Ever Green Building, 10 Tal'at Harb St., Downtown. Tel: 2770-8104/05/60; Call Center: 19753. Website: www.nsgblife.com

Temporary Accommodations
When you don't want to stay in a hotel and are not yet into your home, there are options in Cairo for temporary accommodations that provide small kitchens or short-term leases. Below are a few suggestions. Be careful, however, if renting an apartment for a short time. Look for hidden expenses like a month's extra rent as down payment. Also inquire about damage and repair, building maintenance fees, and utility bills. Make sure all is written in a contract.

◆ **Airbnb**
An online marketplace allowing anyone from private residents to commercial properties to rent out their extra space. This is how it works: The open platform allows users to post listings of their space. Prospective travelers can search by city or by country. Travelers contact hosts directly through the website; payment is by credit card or PayPal account. Dates are con-firmed through onsite messaging. Hosts receive a reservation request which they can accept or decline. Both parties then receive an itinerary on accepted reservations. http://www.airbnb.com

◆ **Conrad Cairo**
Features: kitchenette, family rooms, fitness center, dry cleaning/laundry. Address: 1191 Corniche al-Nil, Cairo. Tel: 2580-8000

◆ **Horus House**
Egyptologists like to stay here. There are refrigerators in the rooms. Address: 21 Ismail Muhammad St., Zamalek. Tel: 2735-3634/3034/3977, 2736-0694/2937. Website: http://www.horushousehotel.4t.com

◆ **Longchamps Hotel**
No refrigerator in room, but lovely and comfortable, good recommendations. Address: 21 Ismail Muhammad St., Zamalek. Tel: 2735-2311/12. Website: http://hotellongchamps.com

Egypt Communication Statistics

Telephone landlines in use:
9.6 million (2009)

Mobile telephones in use:
55.4 million (2010)

Internet hosts:
187,197

Internet users:
11.5 million (2008)

◆ **Maadi International Center
and Apartments**

Situated a thirty-minute drive from the airport, this property offers self-catering and spacious accommodation. Each room has a balcony, kitchen, and seating area. Twelve rooms. Address: 18a Road 11, Maadi. Website: www.letsbookhotel.com/en/egypt/cairo

◆ **Mayfair Hotel**

Under Canadian management. Address: 9 Aziz Osman St., Zamalek. Tel: 2735-7315. E-mail: mayfaircairo@yahoo.com. Website: www.mayfaircairo.com

◆ **Residence Hotel Suites
and Apartments**

Offers spacious suites with private balconies and kitchens. Twenty-eight rooms. Address: 11 Road 18, Maadi. Website: http://www.agoda.com/africa/egypt/cairo/residence_hotel_suites_apartments.html

◆ **Staybridge Suites, Cairo CityStars**

New hotel (opened in 2008) in Africa's largest shopping and entertainment center. Extended-stay studios, one-, two- and three-bedroom serviced apartments with full kitchen, free Wi-Fi Internet, and balcony. Free breakfast and evening reception. Onsite: business center, convenience store, fitness room, guest laundry. Address: Extension of Makram Ebeid St., Nasr City. Hotel front desk: 2480-3333.

◆ **Zamalek Residence Cairo**

Address: 21 Muhammad Mazhar St., Zamalek. Tel: 2737-0055.

Communication

Technology, the Internet, and mobile phones have radically altered how we communicate. No longer does it takes weeks to get news from home through the post office. Mobile phones and messaging, not to mention Skype, provide inexpensive ways to stay in touch with friends and loved ones moment by moment.

Postal services and landline telephone companies throughout the world are struggling to keep their services afloat with the Internet and mobile phones offering instant and inexpensive communication. Whereas twenty years ago it was necessary to have a postal address and a landline telephone, today it is an extra hassle and expense. Egypt Post, www.egyptpost.com, and Egypt Telecom, www.telecomegypt.com.eg/english, have diversified into many areas to compete in global communication. They no longer just deal with packages and letters or local and long-distance calls; they now offer courier, insurance, and e-government services as well as telecommunications and Internet.

Postal Services

Egypt Post's modern history dates back to 1831 when some foreign countries established post offices throughout the country. However, postal communication can be traced back to the pharaohs, who organ-

International Courier Services

Aramex
Tel: 16996, 3338-8466
DHL
Tel: 16345
Egypt Express
Tel: 2268-7888
EMS
Tel: 3393-9630
Fedex
Tel: 19985, 2268-7888/9999
Middle East Courier
Tel: 2241-3033
TNT Express Worldwide
Tel: 16667, 2749-9851
UPS
Tel: 16004, 2414-1456

ized the post internally by following the Nile, and externally by taking advantage of trading caravans or armies.

Today, letters, though derided as 'snail mail,' are still considered by millions of Egyptians the best way to communicate with relatives or for formal notifications. Regular mail to Europe takes three to four days, and to the U.S. five to seven days. Over twenty years of using the Egyptian postal service attest that it is competent and reliable. At least there is no junk mail! Overseas stamps are available at some hotel newsstands and receptions, some souvenir shops, and the post office. Print addresses clearly with ink, do not use black felt pens,

and be sure to write the country to which the letter is going. For example, write "New York City, NY, USA." The mailboxes are color-coded: blue is for international mail; red is for internal mail; green is for express mail. Post offices are open 8:30 a.m. to 3:00 p.m. from Saturday to Thursday. To guarantee delivery, send your mail registered or, for faster service, use Express Mail Service (EMS), which is the same as a courier service but less expensive and just as reliable. Poste Restante, or mail to hold, is available at post offices, sometimes for a small fee: be sure to have the clerk carefully check your name as well as the title before the name.

Parcels and packages by air or sea are inspected by customs officials and sometimes the items are broken. Do not close a package before going to the main post office to send it. Forms must be completed. CDs and DVDs will be checked carefully. To send and receive these articles it is better to use an international courier service. Some shopkeepers offer shipping service to the buyer's country for purchased goods.

Telecommunications
Egypt's telecommunication industry began in 1854. The first telegraph line connecting Cairo and Alexandria was inaugurated early that year, by the company that was later to become Telecom Egypt. In 2005, Egypt's fixed-line telecommunication monopoly, Telecom Egypt (TE), was deregulated. The National Telecommunication Regulatory Authority (NTRA) has not issued licenses

for a second fixed line, although it has plans to do so. When this happens, TE will no longer be a monopoly and international calling rates will decrease significantly. Nevertheless, Egypt's telecommunications infrastructure is excellent (http://www.tele comegypt.com.eg/English).

Telecom Egypt's service has come into the twenty-first century by providing an informative website in Arabic and English, with information about prepaid cards, installation of telephone lines (local and international), directory assistance, and the Internet. For assistance, dial 10 or 140.

In the spring of 2007, we woke up to discover telephone numbers had been changed in Cairo. All numbers are now eight digits. The number '2' is the prefix for telephone exchanges on the east side of the Nile, including Gezira and Zamalek, while the number '3' is the prefix for telephone exchanges on the west side of the Nile. If you come upon a telephone number that does not begin with either a '2' or '3,' call information on 140 (English-speaking operators are available). If after dialing eight digits you still get the wrong-number message, the telephone number is no longer working or has been changed.

Landlines

To acquire a fixed line in your home:
1. Take official documents detailing the address where you want the telephone to be installed (the property contract, utility bills, electricity, gas, or water receipt) to your nearest telephone centrale.

Useful Numbers

Emergency numbers
Ambulance: 123
Fire Brigade: 180
Police: 122
Railway Police: 145
Tourism Police: 126
U.S. embassy emergency numbers: 2792-3000/2200/3300
Your embassy's emergency number:

Communication:
International Operator: 120
International Directory: 144
Local Directory: 140/141/142
Speaking Clock: 150
Telecom Egypt Call Center: 111
Telephone Bill Inquiries: 177
Telephone Complaints and Repair: 188 or call your centrale (telephone exchange) directly
Trunk Operator: 00

Other useful numbers:
Electricity Information: 121
Ministry of Health: 2795-1821
Petrogas: 129
Railway Information: 2575-3555

2. Fill out the telephone subscription form and submit it with a copy of your identification card or passport, and take your numbered receipt after payment.

3 Welcome to Cairo

68

Telecom Egypt Cairo Branches:

Abbasiya Centrale
Ahmad Said St.

Almaza Centrale
al-Thawra St.

Dokki Centrale
1 Musaddiq St., next to the Ministry
of Agriculture

Giza Communications Center
Murad St., Giza Square

Heliopolis Centrale
Gisr al-Suez St.

Maadi Communications Center
Next to Satellite St.

Mohandiseen Centrale
Ahmad Urabi St., next to Omar Effendi

October 2 Centrale
Laylat al-Qadr Square, 6th October

Qubba Centrale
Sarai al-Qubba Square

Ramsis Centrale
Ramsis St.

Sheikh Zayed Centrale
6th October

Sheraton Centrale
next to al-Sidiq Mosque

Shubra Centrale
Shubra St., near the College of Engineering

All centrales are open every day, except
Friday, from 8:00 a.m. to 4:00 p.m.

3. Purchase of a telephone set from the
centrale is optional.
4. Fees: contracting and installation:
LE564.61 with telephone set, LE389.61 without telephone set. Administration fees: LE55,
sales taxes LE5, stamps LE2.

Long-distance and International Calls
Long-distance calls within Egypt and overseas calls can be made from any hotel, but
remember there is always a hefty surcharge
added to the cost of the call. Most people
use their mobile phones when traveling or
purchase prepaid cards, such as Marhaba
Cards. From a residential landline that has
an international line, there is a special rate
of LE0.90 a minute to North America,
Puerto Rico, the Virgin Islands, Turkey, and
some European countries between 11:00
p.m. and 7:00 a.m. Dial 101 plus country
and city code and the telephone number.
For example, to call a number in the U.S.,
dial 101-1-area code-telephone number.
There is no need to include '00' before
101. Calls can be made from the centrales,
or telephone exchanges. Telephone time is
purchased in advance. The cost is about
LE15 for the first three minutes to the U.S.

Normal international rates (per minute):
U.S.
8:00 a.m. to 8:00 p.m.: LE3
8:00 p.m. to 8:00 a.m.: LE2.25

France
8:00 a.m. to 8:00 p.m.: LE3.50
8:00 p.m. to 8:00 a.m.: LE3

Telephone City Codes

10th of Ramadan	015
Alexandria	03
Aswan	097
Asyut	088
Beni Suef	082
Cairo	02
Dakhla	050
Damietta	057
Fayoum	084
Ismailiya	064
Luxor	095
Marsa Matrouh	046
Minya	086
Munufiya	048
North Sinai	069
Port Said	066
Red Sea	065
Sharqiya	055
Siwa	046
Sohag	093
South Sinai	068
Suez	062

Lebanon
8:00 a.m. to 8:00 p.m.: LE3
8:00 p.m. to 8:00 a.m.: LE2.25

Australia
8:00 a.m. to 8:00 p.m.: LE4.50
8:00 p.m. to 8:00 a.m.: LE3.50

Satellite Phones
Calling via satellite means you can be in the middle of the desert and call home . . . anywhere in the world! But it is expensive. In the Middle East the satellite service is called Al Thuraya. Al Thuraya covers the world except the Atlantic Ocean, South Africa, and northeast Asia. It requires a special handset.

There are two ways to use Al Thuraya:
♦ Purchase the Al Thuraya SIM card and receive a number starting with +882-16. This method incurs international phone rates.

♦ Purchase a GSM SIM card from Etisalat, Mobinil, or Vodafone. With this method, the caller calls a local Egyptian number, incurring local rates.

To buy phones and inquire about services, the Al Thuraya agent is Alkan Telecoms in Maadi. Address: 8 al-Gazayir St., New Maadi. Tel: 2516-9722, 2754-6027. E-mail: info@alkantelecom.com. Website: www.alkantelecom.com. Radio Shack sells charge cards.

For more extensive information, see "How to Use Satellite Phones in Egypt" at http://saharasafaris.org/how-to-use-satellite-phones-egypt

Trunk Calls, Prepaid Cards, and Call-back Services
Trunk calls are in-country calls that begin with a '0,' including mobile phones. Make sure your local phone can call numbers that

Welcome to Cairo 3

begin with '0.' If not, you will need to go to the nearest centrale first to pay a deposit.

Prepaid calling cards are available under the name of Ringo, NileTel, and MenaTel. Buy a prepaid card for LE10, 20, or 30 from any kiosk. Ringo has purple telephone cabins, NileTel has red cabins, and MenaTel has yellow and green cabins. Marhaba prepaid cards can be used from residential telephones. They are very easy to use and allow you to make local, national, mobile, and international calls from any landline without adding charges to the phone bill.

Call-back services are not as common or necessary, but for a list of worldwide call-back services go to www.escapeartist.com/internet/callback.htm. Another option is calling computer to computer via a program such as Skype: www.skype.com.

Fax Services

If you don't have a fax machine and need to use one, you can go to Xerox business centers or any post office. Most five-star hotels have business centers with fax machines.

Telephone Boutiques

Telecom Egypt has smaller offices in addition to the major centrales and you can carry out most of your telephone needs at one of these phone boutiques. You can:

1. Purchase a subscription to a new telephone line.

2. Organize a line transfer, line(s) ownership transfer, change the telephone number, and add Call Waiting, Conference Call, Follow Me, Caller ID, Hot Line, Do Not Disturb, Wake-up Call, Call Barring, Automatic Transfer, and ISDN.

3. Pay your bill.

4. Purchase prepaid telephone cards (Marhaba and Marhaba Plus).

5. Receive a PIN code free of charge, which can be used to facilitate subscription to services through calling 111, or using the company website.

6. Repair equipment and resolve complaints. To speed up all procedures, do not forget to bring a copy of your personal ID and a gas or an electricity receipt showing your address. Boutique working hours are from 8:00 a.m. till 8:00 p.m. (Smart Village and Sharm al-Sheikh from 8:00 a.m. till 4:00 p.m.).

Boutique telephone offices:

♦ al-Abbasiya

Abbasiya Centrale, Ahmad Said St. Tel: 2674-9420 to 2674-9428

♦ Almaza Centrale

Heliopolis. Tel: 2415-1580, 2690-8568

♦ al-Giza Street

2 Zakariya ibn Bakhnas St., off Murad St. Tel: 3776-8218/6/7

♦ al-Qubba Centrale

Saraya al-Qubba Square. Tel: 2258-5806, 2256-3571

♦ Sakanat al-Maadi

Road 9, in front of Sakanat al-Maadi metro station. Tel: 2380-0493/0187/0277

♦ **Satellite al-Maadi**
Next to al-Maadi Centrale. Tel: 2519-4042/3883/3973

♦ **Smart Village**
Km 28, Cairo–Alexandria Desert Road. Tel: 3537-0021/3

♦ **Fayoum**
al-Hurriya Street, al-Horiyya Square. Tel: 084-631-1737, 084-630-7363, 084-251-4000

♦ **Hurghada**
Dahar Square. Tel: 065-355-9455/9456/9558

♦ **Manshiya, Sa'd Zaghloul**
al-Manshiya Centrale, Alexandria. Tel: 03-486-5151, 03-486-5044, 03-486-5066.

Tips when you are traveling

1. Ask your service provider for the best international tariff.
2. Get a prepaid currency MasterCard from Caxton FX. Save on ATM charges. The currency card is available in euros and dollars. Website: http://www.caxtonfxcard.com
3. Get an international SIM card. Mobile phones can cost a fortune to use when traveling. Buy a global SIM card for your mobile phone from a company such as www.Go-Sim.com and you can slash the cost by up to 85 percent. It cuts call costs in 175 countries worldwide.

♦ **Sharm al-Sheikh Centrale**
Sharm al-Sheikh. Tel: 069-360-1601, 069-360-5555.

Subscribing to an International Line
You will need to go to a major centrale Telecom Egypt office in Korba, Mohandiseen, Giza, or Ramsis. You will need to bring: personal ID, passport, or driving license; your property contract (rental or ownership); a recent document proving residency at the address, such as an electricity, gas, or water bill. After paying the fees, you should have an international line in one week.

Paying Telecom Egypt Bills
Every three months—in January, April, July, and October—a bill for local telephone charges is sent out. International telephone bills are monthly, with the local charges included quarterly. The bills are delivered to your home free of charge. View your bill at http://www.telecomegypt.com.eg/English/ You can pay at any Telecom Egypt phone boutique or centrale and at all post offices. If you have an Egyptian credit card, you can pay online or through ATM machines for CIB bank and Banque Misr.

Mobile Phones
There are three mobile phone companies in Egypt: Vodafone, Mobinil, and Etisalat. Competition and the introduction of 3G technology-expanded network capacity has lowered prepaid phone rates significantly. Each company offers all solutions for communication needs, from simple

phone calls to Internet and e-mail with USB modem. Each company has special rates for particular services. All offer pre-paid and postpaid options. One tip is that if you travel outside Cairo, particularly to the desert, Mobinil has the best coverage. Check out their websites or visit one of the mobile shops for up-to-date information and services.

Mobile telecommunication companies in Egypt

♦ **Etisalat Telecom Egypt**
Tel: Etisalat line 333, landline 02-3534-6333, any mobile 0111-123-4333, international +20-11123-4333. Website: www.etisalat.com.eg. The international tariff is called 'World Tariff' *(Kull il-dunya)*, with calls to any country at LE1.99 per minute.

♦ **Mobinil**
Tel: 'Customer Service' option from any Mobinil mobile phone or 16110 from any landline. Website: http://www.mobinil.com. Mobinil has a communication package called Star Max with unlimited local calls, SMS, free BlackBerry Service, unlimited Internet, and international calls for LE1.99 per minute.

♦ **Vodafone Egypt**
Tel: 16888. Website: http://www.vodafone.com.eg/en/Home/index.htm.
Tip: Vodafone users who have the international access service can now call North America, Puerto Rico, the Virgin Islands,

Turkey, and Europe between 11:00 p.m. and 7:00 a.m. for LE0.90 per minute plus the Vodafone local off-peak landline minute rate according to your rate plan. Dial 101 instead of 00 when making an international call: 101-country code-local telephone number. The international tariff is 'The World in Your Hands,' with calls to any country around the world at anytime for LE1.99 per minute.

Directory Assistance
Each mobile phone company has a directory assistance number to call, for which there is a charge. From a landline, the International Directory is 144; the Local Directory is 140/141/142; there are English-speaking operators available. On the Internet there are many directories; however, they can be out-of-date. Check if the Cairo telephone numbers have eight digits; if not, the site has not been updated since 2007. The Cairo Yellow Pages site, www.yellow-pages.com.eg, is excellent and includes a virtual map to the destination as well as information in Arabic and English. (You can pick up a free Yellow Pages directory from their offices in Maadi, across from Miriam Market. Address: Plot 6a/18, Intersection of 253 Road and 205 Road, Digla, Maadi; Tel: 19345.) For businesses, the American Chamber of Commerce in Egypt's Membership Directory is useful. These sites provide directory information about companies and businesses in Egypt: Egypt Trade at http://www.egtrade.com/index.html and https://www.buyusa.gov/egypt/en/admin/bsp.html

Internet and E-mail

People who move from country to country are, by now, dependent on e-mail and the Internet, and have the knowledge and information to connect with an Internet provider. All three mobile telephone companies—Vodafone, Mobinil, Etisalat—offer Internet and e-mail, sometimes free of charge at certain times. However, there are many Internet providers with even more of a variety of services to choose from in Egypt. In Egypt there are two types of Internet providers. Class A carriers are directly connected to international service providers; two are LinkDotNet and TE Data. It is wise to use the services of a Class A provider rather than going through an intermediary such as the Class B Internet providers. There are more than two hundred Class B providers in Egypt, including Yalla Online, MenaNet, and Raya Telecom.

DSL, ADSL, and Wi-Fi are all available, at varying costs. Research your options. There is still 'free' Internet, using landline dial-up, but it is painfully slow. (The service is not totally free as a small charge of LE1.20 per hour for usage is billed to the landline.) All dial-up numbers begin with 0777 or 0707. The number for TE Data is 0777-7777. The number for LinkDotNet is 0777-0777.

Internet Providers

♦ LinkDotNet

Address: 77 Misr–Helwan Agricultural Road, Maadi. Tel: 2768-6500 or 16333. E-mail: info@link.net. Website: http://www.link. net/english

♦ MenaNet

Address: MenaNet Communications SAE, 51 Beirut St., Heliopolis. Tel: 2416-6200, Home Sales 2416-6214. E-mail: info@mena net.net. Website: http://www.menanet.net. Free dial-up Internet: 0707-0808.

♦ Raya Egypt

Raya provides businesses with IT solutions specifically tailored to the companies' needs. Address: Block 7A, al-Hayy al-Mutamayyiz, Atlas Zone, 6th October City, Giza. Tel: 3827-8900. Website: http://www.ray acorp.com

♦ TE Data

Address: TE Data Company, Building (A11–B90), Smart Village Cairo, Km 28, Cairo–Alexandria Desert Road, 6th October. Tel: 3332-0700 or 19777. Website: http://www.tedata.net/web/eg/en/

♦ Yalla Online

Address: 72 al-Nuzha St., al-Safadi Bldg, 3rd floor, Nasr City. Tel: 2416-1700/99 or 19210. E-mail: info@yalla.com. Website: www.yalla.com. Free dial-up Internet: 0777-4444.

Cyber Cafés

Cyber cafés are located in many places throughout Cairo. Ask at a shop or hotel for the closest one to you. The cost per hour is LE10–20. Operating hours are usually from 9:00 a.m. to 11:00 p.m. Wi-Fi is often available at coffee shops, many restaurants, Cairo International Airport, and hotels. Some are free.

Online Periodicals

(Sites are in Arabic unless noted.)

Al-Ahaly	http://www.al-ahaly.com/
AhlyNews.com	(Arabic and English) http://www.ahlynews.com/
Ahram	http://www.ahram.org.eg/
	(English) http://english.ahram.org.eg/Index.aspx
Al-Ahram Hebdo	(French) http://hebdo.ahram.org.eg/
Al-Ahram Weekly	(English) http://weekly.ahram.org.eg/
El Akhbar	http://elakhbar.akhbarway.com/
Akhbar El Yom	http://www.akhbarelyom.org.eg/
Arab Net 5	(TV) http://www.arabnet5.com/
Business Today	(English) http://www.businesstodayegypt.com/
Community Times	(English) www.communitytimesmagazine.com/
Daily News Egypt	(English) http://www.thedailynewsegypt.com/
Democraticfront	http://www.democraticfront.org/
Egypt Daily News	(English and Arabic) http://www.egyptdailynews.com/
Egyptian Gazette	http://213.158.162.45/~egyptian/
Egypt Today	(English) http://www.egypttoday.com/
Ertu	http://www.egynews.net/wps/portal/home
al-Gomhuriah	http://www.algomhuria.net.eg/
International Herald Tribune	http://global.nytimes.com/?iht
Islam Online	(Arabic and English) http://www.islamonline.net/ar/Page/Home/
Masrawy	http://www.masrawy.com/new/
Al Masry Al Youm	http://www.almasryalyoum.com/
	(English) http://www.almasryalyoum.com/en
Al Mesryoon	http://www.almesryoon.com/
Al-Messa	(English: *The Egyptian Gazette*; French: *Le Progrès Égyptien*) http://www.almessa.net.eg/
Middle East News Agency	(English and French) http://www.mena.org.eg/
MisrNews.com	http://www.misrnews.com/index.html
Nahdet Masr	http://www.gn4me.com/nahda/index.jsp
Al Nilin	http://www.alnilin.com/
Le Progrès Égyptien	http://213.158.162.45/~progres/
Rosalyousef	http://www.rosaonline.net/default.asp

Al-Shaab	http://www.alshaab.com/
Al-Shorouk	http://www.shorouknews.com/
El-Wasat	http://www.el-wasat.com/portal/index.html
Watani	http://www.wataninet.com/
Yallakora	(For sports in English) www.yallakora.com
Al-Youm Al-Sabe'a	(Radio) http://www.youm7.com/

Follow your favorite newspaper on Twitter!

Media

Newspapers and Magazines

English newspapers and magazines are abundant in Cairo, considering Arabic is the national language. With the Internet taking control of information, newspapers are slowly disappearing. However, in Egypt there are enough people who do not have access to the Internet that Arabic-language newspapers still do a brisk business. International daily newspapers arrive daily (sometimes a day late) and magazines from around the world are sold at newsstands, although they are expensive. There are several local newspapers in English online, including *Daily News Egypt* and *al-Masry al-Yom*.

Al-Ahram has two weekly foreign-language papers: *Al-Ahram Weekly* in English and *Al-Ahram Hebdo* in French. *The Egyptian Gazette* is also printed in French under the name *Le Progrès Égyptien*. *Obelisque Magazine* is dedicated to Egypt's culture, traditions, and travel, and writes about Egypt's unique style in architecture and interior decorating.

The English-language local magazine market produces what seems like a new magazine every month. However, they often don't last longer than a few issues. The magazines that have stayed for a long run are *Egypt Today, Community Times, Insight,* and *Business Today*. Well-written and mildly provocative, each has in-depth human interest articles. *Enigma* and *Cleo* are society and fashion magazines. *Teen Stuff* is for teens and is about music, movies, fashion, and self-improvement. *The Employer* is a monthly publication that provides information for improving professional skills through listings of educational and training opportunities. *The Trainer* is a quarterly publication that gives an overview of training courses in Egypt and the Middle East. *Magez Design* is a modern design and architecture/interior decorating magazine in English and Arabic.

Business Monthly, the publication of the American Chamber of Commerce, is free. It covers the Egyptian business and economic scene. For subscription details contact the American Chamber of Commerce: Tel: 3338-1050; Direct: 3338-9890. E-mail: publications@amcham.org.eg

Television and Radio

Egypt has a mix of state-run and private television and radio stations. A large number of Arabic satellite channels are also available via subscription.

FM 95 carries Cairo's European service radio and features news and stories in various languages. Nile FM 104.2 is an English-language rock station. For easy listening that varies between Arabic and western music, there is FM 98.8. Of course, through the Internet there are hundreds of choices from around the world.

The new Radio Ta7rir is an online interactive radio station that was established as a result of the Egyptian Revolution and features voices of youth. Visit: www.radio ta7rir. com. Facebook: Radio Ta7rir. E-mail: info@radiota7rir.com

Sound of Sakia is an online radio station launched by El Sawy Culture Wheel in 2009. Its mission is to enrich the cultural scene in Egypt by making local artists, workshops, and speakers accessible to a broader audience in Egypt and worldwide. Sound of Sakia is run and managed by young Egyptian talents who volunteer and contribute to the success of the radio station. Website:http://www. soundofsakia. com/en/home.html.

A word to the wise: if you arrive from North America with your television, bring a transformer. The electricity here is 220V. There are all kinds of televisions sold in Cairo. It is better to buy one here, if you can.

Satellite and cable are available from a number of different companies. Apartments rented to expatriates usually include connection to a satellite dish. Orbit Showtime Network (OSN) packages are available through any Cable Network Egypt (CNE) office. Here are a few companies to check with for available services:

♦ **Cable Network Egypt (CNE)**
Addresses: 175 Sudan St., Mohandiseen. Tel: 3303-5419, 3345-2858, 3345-9350; 3 Road 262, Maadi. Tel: 2519-0122, 2519-2668; 6th October Road, Free Zone, 6th October, Giza. Tel: 3855-5555.

♦ **The Orbit Satellite Television and Radio Network**
Customer Care: 3827-4444.

♦ **Orbit Showtime Network (OSN—Egypt)**
Address: Media City, Nilesat Compound, 6th October, Cairo. Tel: 3827-9100.

There are many companies that offer receivers at a reasonable price. These are some satellite companies:

♦ **Abo el Azm**
Tel: 2392-4677 (Downtown)

♦ **Connect**
Tel: 2271-4223 (Nasr City)

♦ **Digital Com**
Tel: 2272-6151 (Nasr City)

♦ **Electronic Center**
Tel: 2257-7137 (Roxy)

♦ **Global Sat**
Tel: 2518-2917 (New Maadi)

◆ **Queen Satellite**
Tel: 2519-6938 (Maadi)

◆ **Techno Sat**
Tel: 2639-7757 (Heliopolis)

◆ **Zein**
Tel: 2291-0775 (Nasr City)

Internet is another way to watch television. Today there are many services, paid and free, for watching television programs from your home country. For U.S. free television, go to http://www.ustvnow.com. For those who miss U.K. channels, check out My Private Network at https://my-private-network.co.uk/

4

Living in Cairo

Connect

As soon as you arrive, get connected. Look for lists of organizations in magazines, newspapers, and newsletters. There is no one publication that has it all. If you are looking for an organization to join, visit the Community Service Association (CSA) in Maadi. Their monthly publication, *Oasis*, has a good list of various organizations to join, as does *Egypt Today*. Within the *Practical Guide* you will find many suggestions and a comprehensive list of organizations and activities at the end of this chapter. You need never be alone in Cairo, unless it is your choice.

Children

Egyptians are family-oriented and love children. They have untold patience with kids and are not annoyed if they're running around a restaurant or if a baby is noisy. (It is usually the foreigner who becomes annoyed first!) Moving to a new country with children means decisions will revolve around a child's priorities. As you go through the next few chapters, you will find information about neighborhoods, living accommodations, health, education, and activities. The school that your child(ren) attends will be the first source of activities and level of adjustment to Cairo. Children might be frustrated because apartment buildings do not have playgrounds or gardens. It is worth investing in *Cairo: The Family Guide* (AUC Press 2010), designed to encourage familiarity with the city through its culture and history. There are age-appropriate suggestions for visiting historical sites as well as just having fun. The appendix is full of suggestions for entertainment, sports, art, music, drama, and theater.

Cairo: The Family Guide also offers suggestions for summer entertainment and academic opportunities. Contact Cairo American College or the Community Service Association, and check with local universities for their summer programs for youth. For example, Cairo University has offered summer programs for young people interested in architecture. However, be sure to check the language of instruction before registering for any program.

Birthday celebrations for children are always important. If you need help putting together a party, here is a group that plans and organizes birthday parties for kids.

Online Sites for Information

Tip: subscribe to the newsletters. Most sites listed below also provide newsletters with daily, weekly, or event notifications.

The best blog:
Cairo Live Events Guide, http://cairoliveeventsguide.blogspot.com

The best all-round guide to restaurants, places, and events:
Cairo 360, www.cairo360.com. Twitter: @Cairo360

Ticket delivery to your door:
Ticketsmarche. Website: www.ticketsmarche.com. Tickets may be purchased online through their guaranteed safe and secure website. Call 0100-TICKETS (0100-842-5387).

Cairo Yellow Pages for numbers, addresses, and map location:
www.yellowpages.com.eg

Music and movies at Yallabina:
www.yallabina.com

Monthly conferences at Egypt Calendar:
http://www.egycalendar.com

American Research Center in Egypt (ARCE) schedule of events:
send e-mail to programs@arce.org

Al Ahram Weekly:
a newspaper on stands every Thursday morning, http://weekly.ahram.org.eg/; Ahramonline: http://english.ahram.org.eg/; and on Twitter: @ahramonline

American University in Cairo schedule of events:
http://www.aucegypt.edu/Pages/default.aspx.

BCA Cairo Chronicle:
send e-mail to: magazine@bcaegypt.com (free)

Community Times, monthly publication:
http://www.communitytimesmagazine.com

Egypt Today, monthly publication:
http://www.egypttoday.com

Egypt Exploration Society schedule of events:
send an e-mail to EES.Cairo@britishcouncil.org.eg

Oasis, Community Service Association publication:
www.livinginegypt.com

Check Twitter, too.

♦ Kids' Birthday Parties

Tel (mobile): Sherine Kharma on 0122-735-1200 or Marwa Sharaf on 0122-760-7603. E-mail: sherinekh@hotmail.com

♦ **Mother and Child Magazine.** This magazine has extensive listings for children's classes, summer activities, family outings, baby showers, and birthday-party services. Available at Diwan or through the magazine's website: http://mother-and-child.net

Choosing a Neighborhood

Most foreigners live and work in Cairo or Alexandria. Take time to look around the city you will live in, ask a friend about the 'feeling' of a neighborhood. Choosing an accommodation depends on the budget and needs of an individual or family. Individuals might like to live in the center of the city while those with children usually prefer living near the school their children attend.

There is no shortage of available rentals in Cairo. Depending on the area, expect to pay a monthly rent of $4,000 for a villa and $2,000 for a modern furnished apartment in Maadi. If you shop around (resist taking the first offer), you can find a two-bedroom apartment for $1000 a month in Dokki or Mohandiseen. Apart from cost, here are a few things to think about when looking at a neighborhood:

♦ Consider public transportation, schools, and shopping for groceries.

♦ Consider whether you want your experience in Egypt to be near expatriates or if

Neighborhoods

Agouza is a crowded neighborhood that is less expensive than the other areas on this list. Some foreigners live in apartments along the Nile, but otherwise it is not a popular area for expatriates. Houseboats float inconspicuously along the banks of the Nile. Mostly for rent, these houseboats are the favorite homes for students and artists.

Dokki is centrally located. The streets were once lined with villas, but many of them are now dilapidated or abandoned, surrounded by looming highrise buildings. However, there are still squares and green gardens among the apartment blocks. It is popular with lower-middle to middle-class families and professionals. Parking is dreadful as the streets are quite narrow.

Downtown is noisy and polluted, particularly from 10:00 a.m. until midnight. There are no green areas, but the historical Downtown attracts students, artists, and intellectuals even though the neighborhood is struggling against urban decay. Downtown boasts a wide variety of European architecture, known as *belle époque*, including baroque, neoclassical, and art deco, and investors are buying up real estate to salvage this neglected heritage (for profit, of course). Restaurants are still reminiscent of the 'good ol' days' and that is their charm. Authentic *baladi* food, coffeehouses, and markets in alleys are the heart of Cairo.

Garden City was once filled with gardens, but is now a maze of streets and buildings that were designed by the British in colonial days to protect the embassy. Hotels, banks, embassies, consulates, and even schools have taken over this labyrinth of curved streets. There are few residences left to rent, which is just as well as parking is a nightmare!

Giza ranges from luxurious high-rises along the Nile to gated communities near the Pyramids, and in between there is every choice of area from poor to middle class. Beyond Giza, on the Cairo–Alexandria Desert Road, there are residential areas known for their mansions and resorts. Between the Pyramids and Wadi Natrun, gated communities of weekend houses are being developed at an astounding speed. Transportation in and out of the city is a problem. With the largest business center, Smart Village, plus Dandy Mall and Designopolis pulling Egyptians to move beyond Cairo, these areas are growing quickly. The highway is notoriously dangerous, particularly at night, but once you're home, the desert air is reviving.

Heliopolis was built in the early twentieth century for Egyptian aristocrats and wealthy foreigners, and was a significant distance from Downtown Cairo, but now both have grown to overlap each other. Once a posh district, Heliopolis can only reminisce about its heyday, as the historical suburb is now in real danger of further succumbing to concrete high-rises. Heliopolis is still the home of the Egyptian affluent, although the trend is to move out to the new suburbs.

Maadi is a tranquil suburb away from chaotic Cairo. Until ten years ago, Maadi seemed mentally separated from the city, but no longer. Known for its quiet tree-lined streets, manicured lawns, and beautiful villas, the secret got out and the suburb is changing rapidly. Still, expatriates prefer Maadi as the air quality seems better, the environment is serene, and there still is a feeling of getting away from the hustle and bustle of Cairo.

Mohandiseen grew out of the villa- and tree-lined streets of Dokki into a mass of cement-block architecture to house the growing upper-class population of the 1960s. This is the area for shopaholics and a popular area for Gulf Arabs, particularly in the summer months. A plethora of restaurants, fast-food joints, and upscale boutiques keep a steady flow of young people on the streets into the wee hours of the night.

Nasr City was established to take the overflow of population out of Heliopolis. It has more malls than any other area, including the Egyptian favorite—the mega-mall CityStars. Because of all the government buildings and company offices, traffic is terrible. There are few villas, and the streets are lined with commercial and apartment buildings.

New Cairo, and particularly **Qattamiya,** is a new area popular with expatriates and affluent Egyptians. In the gated communities, children can play in the streets and backyards. For many people, the greenness, the quiet, and the reduced pollution outweigh the daily drive. (Public transportation is nearly nonexistent and taxi fares are high from the city.) A number of international and private schools and universities are located here as the air is cleaner and there is more space for sports and recreation.

6th October is officially part of Cairo. It is filled with cookie-cutter villas enclosed by manicured lawns. People from the city are moving in, and in the past five years the shopping and infrastructure for living in this area have flourished (though public transportation remains poor).

Zamalek is the posh district of Cairo, a haven for Europeans and affluent Egyptians. The Opera House and green gardens give breathing space. Zamalek houses embassies, schools, and excellent cafés and restaurants, as well as offering unique shopping experiences.

you want to live in a diverse setting. For example, Maadi is a haven for expatriates, which might isolate you from broader Cairo experiences.

♦ Check the proximity of the local mosque's loudspeakers as you do not want them to face directly onto the bedroom.

♦ No matter what the landlord or real estate agent says, never rent an unfinished property.

♦ If you have to walk your dog morning and night, pay attention to the surrounding area.

♦ Pay attention to the condition and safety of the building's elevator: can you walk up five flights of stairs if the elevator is out of order? Check the state of the stairs themselves.

♦ One word of caution: There are always monthly building fees for garbage collection, *bawwaab* services, and building maintenance. Be clear and write into your contract who is responsible for these fees.

♦ If you have school-age children, check the roads at the times your child will go to and return from school. Will you drive, or does the school provide transportation? How long does the journey take? Even if the actual drive is only twenty minutes from home to school, during regular traffic the ride might take an hour. There will be extra fees for bus transportation.

♦ If you intend to drive a car, does the rent for your apartment cover a space for the car if there is a garage? If there is no garage, how difficult will it be to park?

♦ Single men and women, traditionally, live in their parents' home until they marry. If you are single, be aware that neighbors and landlords do not approve of visitors of the opposite sex, particularly if you are considering a conservative neighborhood.

Finding Accommodations

Once you have decided where you want to live, the best procedure is to get in touch with a building's *bawwaab* (doorman/ concierge). If you do not have a working knowledge of Arabic, take an Arabic-speaking friend with you. *Bawwaab*s have first-hand knowledge of which apartments are for rent or for sale and can contact the landlord. Or go to a real estate agent who will show you properties. Real estate agents will take a commission equivalent to one month's rent on your property. This fee is applicable only if you rent a property. Don't expect a real estate agent to negotiate. Negotiation is between the prospective tenant and the landlord. There are a few well-known agents listed at the end of this section. When dealing with a broker, landlord, or *bawwaab*, be

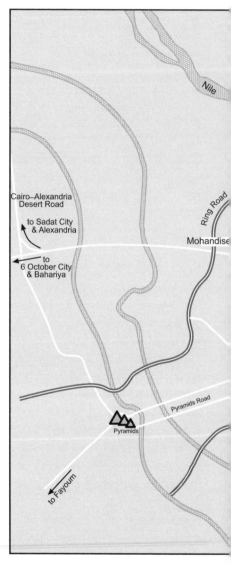

polite but firm and clear about what you want; it is easy to be taken in by sweet words and promises. No longer is a handshake a seal of honoring a deal; get everything in writing with signatures and two witnesses.

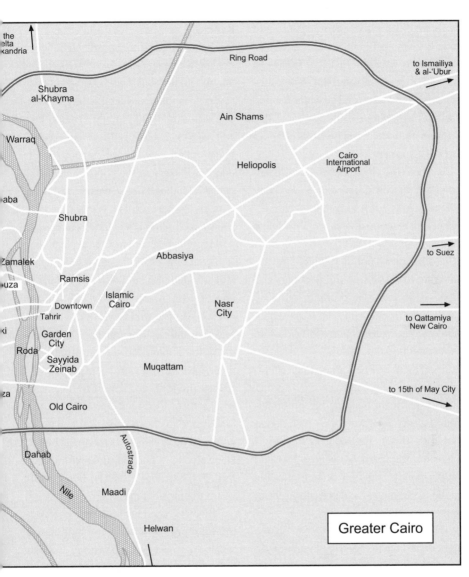

the
elta
xandria

Ring Road

to Ismailiya
& al-'Ubur

Shubra
al-Khayma

Ain Shams

Warraq

Cairo
International
Airport

Heliopolis

aba

Shubra

Zamalek

Abbasiya

to Suez

uza

Ramsis

Islamic
Cairo

Downtown

Nasr
City

Tahrir

to Qattamiya
New Cairo

ki

Garden
City

Roda

Sayyida
Zeinab

Muqattam

za

to 15th of May City

Old Cairo

Dahab

Autostrade

Nile

Maadi

Greater Cairo

Helwan

Things to check when viewing an apartment

♦ Inquire about the telephone line: Is it local with trunk capabilities (any number in Egypt beginning with zero)? Is it an international line? Can Internet be installed?

Physically check the line and use the telephone to call and have someone call you.

♦ Look for leaks around the walls of sinks and toilets. Look at the ceilings for leaks as there is a huge problem with water damage coming from neighbors' apartments. Flush the toilets. Check the water pressure and water heaters.

♦ Are there enough electrical outlets in strategic places? Ask about the voltage current, circuit breakers, and grounding. Is the electrical wiring two- or three-phase? This is important if you bring heavy appliances into the apartment.

♦ Ask where the electric meter is, as every month a man from the electricity company will enter your home to read the meter.

♦ Check all air conditioners and TV satellite connections.

♦ Cairo is a dusty, polluted, noisy city. You will want to make sure the windows and doors are sealed. Make sure there are no cracks in the window and door frames that let in dust. You will be happy you did when the *khamasin* season arrives.

♦ Check the sturdiness of railings on all balconies.

♦ If the apartment building has an underground garage, check if this is included in your rent. If not, the monthly rate for a place in a garage is between LE350 and LE400 a month. Confirm who is responsible for taking this money and prepare a receipt for their signature.

♦ It is always a wonderful feeling to open a window and have a breeze blow through. Check if your window is northern-facing *(bahari)*, the direction from which the prevailing winds blow.

♦ A final piece of advice: it is a good idea to fumigate before you move your possessions into the apartment.

Renting

It is better to be cautious and careful when dealing with a landlord. Most landlords are fair and honest, but there have been horror stories of landlords who raise the rent without notice, or rent to another person who will pay more, or terminate the lease prematurely, or find a way not to return the security deposit. Make sure the contract covers all details including the rent, the period the rent remains in effect before it is raised, responsibility for building fees and repairs, and parking space in a garage (if applicable). It is in your best interest to specify any repairs and whether the landlord will reimburse you. Have an Arabic speaker with you and put everything in writing with two witnesses. Make several duplicates of the original contract. If a landlord objects to all this, you might have the first warning of problems to come, and it could be best to look elsewhere. Also, if you have problems with a landlord who cheats, steals, or evicts you without reason, threaten to go to the police. Filing a police report may unnerve the landlord. You can hire a lawyer, but it is not worth the hassle, time, and money.

The lease contract is a simple one-page form. Be precise about the rental period, repairs, payment for the *bawwaab*, building fees, security, and pre-existing damage. Do not move in until all repairs are completed. The lease, and any addendum, is signed by tenant and landlord, and should be in Arabic and English and certified. The rental period is negotiable and, unless pre-agreed, there is usually a 10 percent raise

List of Real Estate Brokers

♦ Amlak for Real Estate Investment and Marketing
For properties in 6th October City and the North Coast. Address: 1 Bur'i Plaza Towers, 6th October, Giza. Tel: 3837-0770, 0122-779-9846, 0122-779-8711, 0128-160-0646. Website: http://www. amlakegypt.com/Default.aspx

♦ Coldwell Banker Egypt–Betna Investment and Real Estate
Deals with residential and commercial real estate brokerage and property management. Address: 66 Corniche al-Nil, Zahra' al-Maadi Tower, Maadi. Tel: 16223, 2528-6578/83. Website: http:// www.cb-egypt.com

♦ Damac Properties
Deals with luxury projects as well as residential and commercial projects. Customer Service: Heliopolis, Cairo. Tel: 16696. Web-site: http://www.damac properties.com

♦ Edar Real Estate Experts
Deals in real estate and property management. Address: 57 City Light Tower, Makram Ebaid St., 2nd floor (beside Starbucks Café), Nasr City. Tel: 2273-5237/5303, 0100-110-1162. Website: http://www.e-dar.com

♦ Edar First Class Real Estate
Investment opportunities, real estate consultancy, selling, buying, renting, property appraisal, market studies, portfolio management, mortgage facilities, relocation, property management. Tel: 3335-0928, 3762-1986, 3761-7378. E-mail: info@aclass egypt.com. Website: www.aclassegypt.com

♦ ERA (Egypt Real Estate)
Offers guidance for buying and selling homes, and is a residential brokerage. Address: 5 Port Said Square, beside Maadi Police Station, Maadi. Tel: 16372, 2380-7563, 2750-7530/1. Address: 22 Ramsis St., Heliopolis. Tel: 16372, 2690-6732, 0100-855-9710, 2415-4620. Website: http://www.era-egypt.com/Pages/index.aspx

♦ Landmark Egypt
Real estate and property management. Address: 1 al-Mahatta Square, Maadi Palace, Road 9, Office 28, 1st floor, Maadi. Tel: 2380-8845. E-mail: land mark@landmark-eg.net. Website: www. landmark-eg.net

♦ Memaar Al Morshedy: Degla Group for Investment
Sells residential projects. Website: http://www. deglagroup.com/main.php

in rent every year. Electricity and gas readings should be taken before moving in and signed by the landlord so no prior bills will show up on your doorstep.

Buying

Any investment requires serious consideration; however, if you are an expatriate and want to buy property to make Cairo your permanent home, take time to analyze all the pros and cons. There are advantages: no landlord to deal with; ownership qualifies for a yearly residency permit; and all decisions about the property are yours alone. The disadvantages are that if you have made a mistake in location or decide not to remain permanently in Cairo, moving and selling can both be a hassle. Before you buy, rent in the area of your choice and note the negatives and positives of the district. If you decide to buy, here are some basics you need to know:

♦ Always hire an English-speaking Egyptian lawyer to sift through the forms and formalities. Ask friends for recommendations for a reputable lawyer. You might interview several lawyers, and it is important to ask about their fees from the start.

♦ Deal directly with the owner to settle on an all-inclusive price (that is, including any parking garage space). Record all agreements on paper with two witnesses. Have a lawyer draw up the preliminary contract with a deposit of 5–10 percent.

♦ The lawyer needs to acquire copies of all documents of ownership from the seller, which include building permission, floor plan, and ownership history that provides proof of the property's record of sale and by whom it was built.

♦ The lawyer will confirm the authenticity of these documents at the registration office, and will go to the electricity company to check if the bills are paid.

♦ When the final contract is finalized, make sure it has the same conditions as the preliminary contract before the buyer and seller sign it. After signature, it is very difficult to make changes. Absolutely have an expert lawyer check all documents.

♦ The seller then goes to the registration office (al-shahr al-'aqaari) and will provide the buyer with a power of attorney (tawkiil). It is important that neither party be able to cancel the power of attorney without the other's knowledge and confirmation.

♦ Do not pay the final payment until the seller provides the contract and the power of attorney to the buyer.

♦ The buyer must register the property and pay a land registration tax. There is a tax office in each area: go to the tax office and fill out the tax registration. You will need to go every year to this office to pay property tax. The receipt will qualify you for a residency permit.

Driving in Egypt

Driving in Egypt is not for the faint of heart. Unlike western countries where traffic lights keep the flow of traffic moving, here policemen do the job. Staying in lanes is not possible for the Egyptian driver: a two-lane street will become four lanes and weaving is continuous. Driving at night is particularly hazardous as some drivers do not use their headlights. Donkey carts have no reflector lights and may be difficult to see. There are always pedestrians crossing the street. If you decide to drive, here are a few tips:

♦ Road signs are in Arabic and English.

♦ Road signs are international road signs.

♦ Driving is on the right-hand side of the road.

♦ The speed limit is 60 kph (36 mph) in the city and 90 kph (56 mph) on highways. On desert highways the speed limit is 100 kph (62 mph).

♦ Radar is used and fines are high if you are caught speeding, plus your driver's license is confiscated. If the police keep your license, you will receive a receipt for it.

There are two websites that rely on the input of drivers or passengers via iPhones, BlackBerries, and Nokia phones to provide traffic information. The websites are interesting, but bear in mind that the information may be unreliable.

♦ Bey2ollak: http://www.bey2ollak.com

♦ Wasalny: http://www.wasalny.com

There is a list of the new traffic laws at the Egypt State Information Service website: http://www.sis.gov.eg/En/LastPage.aspx? Category_ID=803. It is worth reading up on these laws and penalties carefully as the police are serious about enforcing the law. Because traffic is getting out of control, the police are not lenient.

♦ Failing to buckle your seat belt doubles your risk of being injured in an accident and subjects you to a fine of LE100–300.

♦ Hand-holding your cell phone distracts your attention from driving and subjects you to a fine of LE100–300.

♦ Besides putting you and other people in danger, driving in the wrong direction will get you fined from LE1,000 to 3,000.

♦ Parking in the wrong place causes traffic jams and could subject you to having your license suspended for a period of no less than thirty days.

♦ You could be imprisoned for a period of no less than six months and fined from LE200 to LE1,000, if caught removing your car clampers.

♦ You could be imprisoned for a period of no less than six months and fined LE300 for allowing acts of public indecency to take place in your car.

♦ Driving at night without head or tail lights, and at any time without side mirrors, could result in your license being suspended for a period of no less than six months.

♦ Driving in unauthorized processions subjects you to having your license suspended for a period of no less than thirty days.

♦ Use of a triangle warning sign prevents road accidents when stopping at night. If it is absent your license could be suspended for a period of no less than thirty days.

♦ A first-aid kit will help you take care of your injuries until the ambulance arrives. Failing to have a first-aid kit inside your car could subject you to having your license suspended for a period of no less than thirty days.

♦ Using projector headlights at night endangers other people's lives. Your license could be suspended for a period of no less than thirty days.

♦ Failing to wear your protective headgear when riding your motorcycle could subject you to a fine of no less than LE100.

Egyptian Driver's License

If you are in Egypt for one year or less, you can use your foreign driver's license for three months and an international driver's license for one year. After that time, you will need to acquire an Egyptian driver's license. You must be eighteen years old to apply for an Egyptian driver's license. To begin the process, collect a certificate from an Egyptian ophthalmologist and take a lab test to verify blood type. Bring your valid driver's license from your home country, two photographs, your passport with residency stamp, a document that states your name and address (this could be rental lease, property papers, phone bill, electricity bill) and LE60. Take all these documents to the *muroor* (Vehicle Department). Cairo residents go to al-Gezira, located behind Arkadia (burnt during the Revolution) Mall after Wakalat al-Balah. Giza residents go to Bayn al-Sarayat in Dokki. You will be given an oral test on international road signs (study Google: international road signs). You will need to bring your own car, which will be used for a very simple driver's test that may only be to back up. Be sure to have a first-aid kit and emergency triangle in the trunk. If your driver's license is lost or stolen, you need to report it to the nearest police station to have

a report issued. The driver's license is valid for ten years and renewable at that time.

Owning a Car

To buy a car, you need a valid Egyptian visa and an international driver's license. You can own a car without a driver's license, but you cannot drive it. In this case, you will need to employ a driver. After you buy the car, the agency will take care of licensing the car for a fee. The car license is called the *rukhsa*. The *rukhsa* is issued at the *muroor* or vehicle registration office in your governorate. It is valid for one to three years, depending on the taxes you want to pay in advance. The expiry date has a grace period of one month, after which you will be fined. An expired *rukhsa* cannot be renewed, which is complicated, so just renew on time! You cannot sell your car without the *rukhsa*. If you are buying a secondhand car, you will need to have the existing *rukhsa* and apply for a new one, and you will need to get the change of ownership registered as well.

All cars must carry third-party personal liability insurance. This insurance is issued when applying for the *rukhsa*.

CAUTION: Carry your driver's license, registration, and insurance papers at all times in your car.

Finding a Driver

You have a car and a driver's license, but realize that parking is impossible and that it is such a help to be able to send a driver to pay bills and take the children to all their lessons. In the western world, this is the job of the wife/mother, but for LE1,400–1,800 a month you can have a full-time driver who will make your life easier. However, there are some things to consider. You will be putting your car and your life in someone else's hands, so you want to be confident that the driver does not speed and takes the greatest care possible. Of course, accidents will happen in Cairo. Invest in insurance and keep a watchful eye on the driver and his habits. Make sure the driver presents himself well (there are no female drivers), looks fresh and healthy, and is attentive. If you need to have a driver with a particular language skill, the salary and benefits will come at a higher price. The monthly LE1,400–1800 quoted above is fairly typical for an English-speaking driver, and would include his own transportation to and from work.

The best way to find a driver is by word of mouth, recommendations from your company, or through a friend. A *bawwaab* or another driver whom you respect are good sources. Placing an ad in *Al-Ahram* (Arabic-language newspaper) is an option (Tel: 2290-0160 or 2644-4372), but be aware that it would be difficult to sort through the applicants. Make sure to take a photocopy of the driver's ID and driver's license, in case, heaven forbid, something happens.

A driver has one of two types of driver's license. The first is a regular Egyptian driver's license, called *mallaaki*, which allows him to chauffeur a car. This license is good for ten years. Another type of license is called *mihaneyya*. There are three levels of this: the first is for private cars; the second and third are to drive taxis, buses, and trucks. A first-class *mahaneeya* license must be renewed every one to three years. One year's cost is between LE400 and LE500. (A driver might ask you to pay the fee while he is in your employment.) All licenses are applied for at the *muroor*. If you decide to dismiss the driver, you are expected to pay a month's salary for every year that the driver was in your employment; however, this is only an expectation, not a law.

Car Insurance

Car insurance is optional except for the mandatory third-party personal liability insurance issued when registering and licensing a car. It is best to have additional automobile insurance. Premiums vary according to size, horsepower, and value of the vehicle. Here are some suggestions of companies to approach for a quote:

✦ **AIG Egypt Insurance Company**
Address: 2005 Corniche al-Nil, Nile City Buildings, North Tower, 26th floor, Ramlit Bulaq, Cairo. Tel: 2461-7000. Website: www.aigegypt.com

✦ **Allianz Insurance—Egypt**
Address: 92 Tahrir St., Saridar Bldg., Dokki. Tel: 19909, 3760-5445. Website: http://www.allianz.com.eg/

✦ **Arab Misr Insurance Group**
Address: 13 al-Ma'had al-Ishtiraki St.,

Merryland, Heliopolis. Tel: 19901, 2451-7620, 2451-7622, 2451-7624. Website: http://www.amig.com.eg/

Systems You Need to Know About
Utilities

Water, garbage disposal, and electricity are utilities provided by the Egyptian government. You do not have a choice of provider. All accommodations come with utilities prearranged. If, for some reason, you must organize your own, ask the *bawwaab* or landlord for help in contacting the right office. Usually, the garbage is collected directly from your door on a daily basis. (Garbage disposal has undergone a tremendous change in the past few years, and not always for the better. . . . Read the following section on recycling in Cairo.) A man will collect between LE5 and LE10 a month for garbage services, and will not give a receipt. Electricity, water, and gas bills do have a receipt. There are three ways to pay these bills: give the bill and money to the *bawwaab* (ask for the receipt back), pay the collectors directly (get the receipt), or go to the utility office and pay yourself (get the receipt). It is of the utmost importance to keep your receipts to prove payment and as a form of identification of your residence when you apply for a visa, driver's license, car license, and so on.

Each month a man will come to read the electricity meter, which is located inside your apartment. The time he comes is inconsistent, so if you are not at home he will calculate your bill from the usage of the prior month. You will continue to pay accordingly until a proper reading can be made and then the bill will be adjusted—at which time you may pay nothing or a huge sum. If bills are not paid, the electricity is disconnected until payment is made. So if you are traveling it is necessary to arrange for the bill to be paid even if the meter is not read. Your utility bill will probably be between LE100 and LE700 a month, depending on usage and the season. The Egyptian Electric Utility and Consumer Protection Regulatory Agency maintains a website in English that explains usage, tariffs, and electricity consumption: http:// www.egyptera.com/en/Bill_Calculation.htm.

Your electricity is calculated in kWh (kilowatts per hour) and the amount you pay depends on how much you consume. The cost per kilowatt is calculated in bands, so the more you consume, the greater the cost per kilowatt becomes. You can get the scale of charges at your local electricity office. Here are the basics; as the usage progresses through the bands, the cost is accumulative:

Band 1: the first 50 kilowatts @ LE0.05
Band 2: 51–200 kilowatts @ LE0.11
Band 3: 201–350 kilowatts @ LE0.16
Band 4: 351–650 kilowatts @ LE0.24
Band 5: 651–1,000 kilowatts @ LE0.39
Band 6: over 1,000 kilowatts @ LE0.48

Services and Household Help

Once you have your house, maintenance and cleanliness are a constant battle. Finding reliable people for house repairs is a challenge, and the same is true of domestic help. Landlords should bring good workmen, but price usually trumps quality and the repairs may not be up to your expectations. Again, word of mouth is your best guide to finding electricians, plumbers, carpenters, and so on. Ask friends, the *bawwaab*, or an interior decorator. Most workmen do not speak English. Finding a repair person is as important as supervision. Do not take anything for granted, not even the time of the appointment. Be specific and clear about punctuality and workmanship.

Utility Emergency Numbers	
Electricity	121
Natural Gas	129
Water	125

Domestic Help

With unemployment high, one might think that finding domestic help would not be difficult, but it is. Whether you need full-time, live-in, or part-time help, you will eventually be able to find what you are looking for at a reasonable price (compared to the U.S.). Recommendations from a friend or the *bawwaab*, or checking the notices posted at CSA, are good ways to begin your search. Once you bring the person into your house as a maid, driver, or nanny, ask for references that can be

checked and photocopy their passport, ID, and medical clearance.

The average monthly salary for a part-time maid can vary greatly, depending on her nationality (Egyptian or other), the number of days and hours, and whether you hire her directly or through an employment service. In some parts of the city, maids charge expatriates more than they would charge an Egyptian employer. A typical amount might be LE600–800 per month for two to three days' work per week.

The rate for a full-time maid depends on her qualifications and your requirements. Do you want to hire an Egyptian or a foreigner? (Remember to check whether a foreign worker is in Cairo legally.) Is there a language requirement? Will she live in or come to your home every day? How big is your house? For an Egyptian with little or no English to work six to eight hours a day, five days a week, budget LE1,000–1,400 per month.

There are also cleaning companies that bring a group of cleaners into your home. The service might be convenient, but it is usually expensive. Be sure to watch them carefully.

Gardeners can be recommended through flower shops or the landlord. If the house or apartment building is fortunate enough to have a garden, you will probably inherit a gardener, who, like the *bawwaab*, stays with the building.

Not so long ago, a *makwagi* (ironer) would come to your home to do the ironing, but this is rare these days. You can arrange with the *bawwab* to have someone come and pick up your clothes and deliver them ironed to your door. Dry cleaners usually have ironers or can direct you to their shop. There is nothing more luxurious than ironed sheets, and for LE20 a week you can have an entire basket of sheets ironed!

The Bawwaab

The *bawwaab* is an Egyptian-style doorman, like a concierge without the glamour. (*Bawwaab*s are never women.) They are your best friend or can be your worst nightmare. They rarely leave the block, usually live in the building, and know everything about the surrounding neighborhood. The *bawwaab* is the custodian of the building: he maintains it, cleans the interior, runs nearby errands, and acts as security guard and general busybody. The residents in the building pay a small monthly fee for his services, usually LE20–50. If he does special jobs for you, such as buy vegetables, pay the electricity bill, or run any small errand, he expects a tip for this service. Of course, you are happy to give the tip, which ranges from LE5 to LE10. Remember the *bawwaab* was in the building before you arrived and will no doubt be there after you leave, so it is best to develop an amicable relationship during your time in Egypt.

Recycling in Cairo

As people all over the world become more worried about the environment and are individually concerned with recycling, one may wonder why there are few initiatives available for an individual to recycle personal waste in Cairo. The sad answer to this query is that Cairenes have been spoiled by generations of *zabbaaliin* (garbage people), who developed an entire way of life around gathering rubbish and recycling it throughout the city. In the Muqattam Hills, there is an area known as Manshiyat Nasser. Therein is *zabbaaliin* city, home of 60,000 people whose livelihood depended on keeping Cairo clean . . . until recently. A few years ago the government stepped in and introduced foreign waste-management companies as the new trash collectors. Not only did this action put thousands of people out of work, but the foreign companies sent all our garbage to the desert for landfill, thus ending the recycling expertise of the *zabbaaliin*.

Watch the award-winning movie, *Garbage Dreams* (www.garbagedreams. com), which documents the way of life of three teenage boys growing up in the largest garbage city in the world. Also watch Dr. Laila Iskander talk about her work with the *zabbaaliin* (http://www. youtube.com/watch?v=Umeic3b70kE). Visit Spirit of Youth Association for Environmental Service. Address: 7 Girgis Isa St., Manshiyet Nasser. Tel: 2343-4851.

There is now an NGO, The Spirit of Youth for Environmental Services, which works with the *zabbaaliin* in Manshiyat Nasser and has started a project for electronic-waste management. The hazardous materials in electronic devices are detrimental to the environment if not disposed of properly. Women from the *zabbaaliin* community have been trained to dismantle and reassemble computers. Parts of mobile phones and computers can be recycled, so if you have a computer or mobile phone that you no longer need and want to dispose of, call 2343-4851/5920, 0122-660-5322, or 0100-364-3660, or e-mail spirit.ofyouth@yahoo.com. They will also pick up any donation free of charge.

There are several paper recycling projects in Cairo. Both of the following groups will come to your home or business and collect the paper.

♦ Al Boraq Charity Group. Address: 11 Kabul St., behind al-Sallag and parallel to Makram Ebeid St., Nasr City. Contact person: Ahmed Saied. Tel: 0100-503-8388.

♦ Resala Charity Organization. Address: 24 al-Madina al-Munawwara St., off Muhyi al-Din Abu al-Izz St., Mohandiseen. Tel: 19450, 3337-3658/7714, 3336-0064. E-mail: raselna@resala.org. Website: http://www.resala.org

Yahia Shawkat is an architect and heritage planner with the Tarek Waly Center, as well as an environmental activist. For an excellent overview of the dilemma, read his article in *Al Masry Al Youm*, "Our Local Green Agenda" (http://www.almasry alyoum.com/en/opinion/our-local-green-agenda).

Environmental Issues

It is sad to say that Cairo's air pollution levels are between ten and one hundred times higher than the WHO standards, which makes Cairo the third most polluted city in the world. For over 20 million people these levels are the equivalent of smoking one pack of cigarettes a day. The news is not good and it will take courageous government officials and dedicated citizens to make changes to clean up the city for our children and to protect their rich heritage from pollution damage.

Earth Day in Egypt is observed by schools and environmental groups. One such NGO, Hurghada Environmental Protection and Conservation Association (HEPCA), organizes diving centers and resorts that operate along the Red Sea coast from Hurghada to Marsa Alam to collect garbage along the beaches. HEPCA's mission is the conservation and protection of land and marine life in the Red Sea. You can report a violation to the environment through their website. Address: B2-Marina Boulevard, Hurghada. Tel: 065-344-5035. E-mail: info@hepca.com. Website: http://www.hepca.com

Many countries are becoming more dependent on imports rather than being self-sufficient. This trend creates many long-term problems, one of which is the fuel it takes to deliver these products (in some cases, overnight). You can help cut down on exhaust pollution by shopping in your local area. Buy local products rather than imports that use millions of metric tons of fuel by being transported all over the world. Take public transport or carpool. An initiative began several years ago to organize people and cars. Check out the website at www.egyptcarpoolers.com. You will need to be over eighteen to register

**FAQs on recycling
and the environment:
An interview with Ahmed
El-Dorghamy, environmentalist with
the NGO Nahdet El-Mahrousa:**

Are there recycle points?
Resala, a nonprofit organization, recently began a campaign to recycle paper from offices and households. They even bought ad space on the streets where they posted their hotline (19450) to encourage people to either drop in and donate their used paper (and old clothes), or call for pickup.

What, if anything, is being done to curb use of plastic bags?
Although little is being done, read about what HEPCA is doing in Hurghada. Their campaign eventually persuaded the governor to ban plastic bags (http://www.hepca.com/red-sea-plastic-bags.aspx).

What about glass and aluminum?
Recyclables, in general, in Egypt are scavenged in the streets and by the collectors, so they are recycled as a livelihood. Unfortunately, this informal system causes littering, yet it is important income for many people.

Foreigners are buying second homes in Egypt. What are environmentally-friendly building materials and/or energy-saving suggestions that can be incorporated into building or upgrading an apartment or home?
Traditional houses and buildings in Egypt were built to be climate sensitive, using shade, light, wind, heat, and cold to the advantage of the dweller. Modern buildings and construction materials have destroyed these ancient techniques. There are eco-lodges being built for tourism from Dahab to Siwa, which use local and natural building materials. Egyptian architect Hassan Fathy spent fifty years working with natural thermodynamics and local materials that incorporated vernacular architectural elements of a desert climate. Solar Cities helped build biogas digesters from kitchen waste to produce clean energy for households in the slum area of Manshiyat Nasser. Solar Cities are also producing water heaters using solar power.

Can Cairo be a bicycle-friendly city?
There is rapidly growing interest in cycling in the city. On Facebook, there are several groups: CCC (Cairo Cycler's Club)—E-mail: cairocyclersclub@gmail.com; Alexandria Cycling (several groups); Cairo Night Cyclists; MTB Egypt (and MTBEgypt.com); Cycling Tours; Cycle Egypt Club (www.cycle-egypt.com). Nahdet El-Mahrousa's Green Arm is also working to convert Cairo into a bicycle-friendly city.

and use the website, submit a profile, and rate and review the carpool system.

Websites about Egypt and the environment:

♦ **http://www.350.org**
An international campaign that's building a movement to unite the world around solutions to the climate crisis—the solutions that science and social justice demand. Egyptian groups and schools are participating.

♦ **http://www.ape.org.eg**
The Association for the Protection of the Environment (APE) is a nonprofit organization serving the communities of garbage collectors in Cairo, Hurghada, Tora, and Wadi Natrun in Egypt. This group collects rags and recycles them to produce rugs.

♦ **http://www.ecooptionsegypt.com**
Omnia Amr, a member of the NGO Nahdet El-Mahrousa's Green Arm, has a comprehensive website about projects, events, and activities to conserve energy, ecolodges in Egypt, and recycling.

♦ **http://www.egyptcarpoolers.com**
Carpooling in Cairo.

♦ **http://www.goumbook.com**
Keep up with 'green' initiatives throughout the Middle East.

♦ **http://www.greenprophet.com**
An environment news site reporting on the Middle East.

♦ **http://www.nahdetmasr.org**
Has projects and groups that work on various environmental issues.

♦ **Keep Egypt Clean Facebook Group**
An informal group on Facebook.
Nature Conservation Egypt (NCE) is an NGO that seeks to preserve Egypt's biodiversity. E-mail: info@ncegypt.org

Articles about Egypt and the environment:
♦ **"Cairo's Climate Art of Epic Proportions"**
by Arwa Aburawa. http://www.greenprophet.com/2010/11/cairos-climate-art/

♦ **"It's Easy Being Green"**
by Ali El-Bahnasawy. *Egypt Today*. http://www.egypttoday.com/article.aspx?ArticleID=7806

♦ **"Maadi Environmental Rangers"**
by Nadia Salem. *Al-Ahram*, 22–28 October 2009. http://weekly.ahram.org.eg/2009/969/sc72.htm

♦ **"Save the Earth . . . Become an Armchair Environmentalist"**
by Sankalita Shome. *Community Times.* http://www.communitytimesmagazine.com/component/content/article/44-green-community/113-save-the-earth-become-an-armchair-environmentalist

♦ **"Solar Cities: Cairo's Green Project"**
www.cairo360.com

♦ **"Stop It"**
by John Harris. *Al-Ahram* 22–28 October

Living in Cairo 4

2009. http://weekly.ahram.org.eg/2009/969/sc53.htm

♦ "Trash Talk"
by Passant Rabie. *Egypt Today*. http://www.egypttoday.com/article.aspx?ArticleID=8648

Recycling Tips

♦ Avoid plastics so that chemicals like BPA do not leak into food.

♦ Rather than using strong commercial household cleaners that are imported, simply use a solution of water and vinegar.

♦ Buy local products.

♦ Anything that enters the house, use twice. For example, print both sides of paper and reuse plastic shopping bags for garbage rather than buying garbage bags.

♦ Minimize the use of plastic bags at shopping centers by carrying your own cloth bags or making sure the bagger fills the bags sufficiently.

♦ Turn off electricity in unoccupied rooms, and computers and printers when they are not in use.

♦ Have dripping faucets and running toilets fixed immediately.

♦ Separate garbage for the collector into 'organic waste' and 'non-organic items.'

♦ Take the metro, walk, bicycle, or carpool.

♦ REDUCE, REUSE, RECYCLE

Pets in Cairo

Pet owners know the love and care required to keep a pet. The biggest challenge voiced is to find veterinary services in Cairo. Luckily for owners of any type of pet, there is an excellent website, http://cairopets.com, that provides thorough information on veterinary services, grooming, pet stores, kennels, dog training, horses, and much more. Animal food is available in most grocery stores. Imported animal food is exorbitantly expensive. Snappy Toms cat food is locally made and is essentially whole fish mashed in a can with jelly. If you have pets, keep animal hair off the carpets and furniture by wiping down cats and dogs with a microfiber dusting cloth. This cuts down on the amount of hair and dander. The electrostatic properties of microfiber cloths attract the hair, dander, and dust.

If you travel and leave your animal, the next challenge is to find someone to 'pet sit' while you are away. There are horror stories, so you need to be confident in the person who is looking after your pet. Remember that some Egyptians consider neutering to be barbaric and a violation of the animal's right to 'marry' and have babies.

For more information about pets in Egypt, visit www.petsmarche.com and http://cairopets.com.

Vets and Animal Clinics

Here is a list of contacts you may find useful when searching for veterinary services:

♦ **American Veterinary Center**
Dr. Salah Hassan. Maadi branch address: 3 Khalid ibn al-Walid St., Road 262. Tel: 2517-7266, 0111-080-3803. Zayed branch address: In front of Zayed Sports Club. Tel: 3852-4260, 0111-080-2802. Zamalek branch address: 30 al-Gezira al-Wusta St. Tel: 2737-6664/8, 0111-080-1801.

♦ **Dr. Farouk Bahgat**
Head of Cairo Veterinary Association, Veterinary Consultant to the Egyptian Society for Animal Friends (ESAF) and has his own clinic in Maadi. Address: 14/3 al-Shatre al-Sabeh St., Apt. 2, off Uruba St., New Maadi. Tel: 2704-4225, 0122-219-8733. Map on website: http://faroukbahgat.com

♦ **Dr. Rafik Nashed Helmy**
Address: 7 Shafiq Mansur St., off Hasan Sabri St., Zamalek, and 50 Qasr al-Nil St., Downtown. Tel: 2391-4314, 0122-310-2401. E-mail: Boxer8@hotmail.com

♦ **I Vet For Pet Animal Hospital**
Mohandiseen branch address (Dr. Ahmed Hesham El Nabrawy): 42 Adnan St., off Shihab St., next to al-Safa Medical Tower, Mohandiseen. Tel: 0100-634-4025, 3762-6883. Maadi branch address (Dr. Mohamed Shehata): Road 219, Bldg. 22b, Apt. 2, Digla, Maadi. Tel: 0100-689-5894. Dr. Ahmed Hesham comes with top recommendations from cat lovers.

♦ **Dr. Rania Kashif**
Comes recommended by several animal owners. She has clinics in Maadi and 6th October City. Maadi branch address: 24 Shukri Abd al-Halim St., New Maadi. Tel: 2516-4428, 0100-620-5694. 6th October branch address: District 8, al-Tahrir St. (approx. 5 minutes' drive from Hosary Mosque). Tel: 3837-8336, 0100-900-8736.

♦ **Dr. Amir Mikhail**
Prior to opening his own clinic, Dr. Mikhail worked at the Egyptian Society for Animal Friends (ESAF). Address: 5/1 Small al-Lasilki St., New Maadi. Tel: 0100-345-8080 (SMS only), 2520-3267 (12:00–4:00 p.m. only). Website: ourpetclinic.com. He also gives free online advice: http://www.ourpet-clinic.com/clinic_contacts.html

♦ **Pet Vet Clinic**
Address: 20 al-Hurriya St., Heliopolis. Tel: 2417-0494. E-mail: info@petvetclinic.net. Website: http://www.petvetclinic.net/www.vetpetclinic.net

♦ **Facebook Group:**
Vets in Practice Facebook Group.

♦ **Facebook Group:**
Dr. Ahmed Hesham Facebook Group. E-mail: dr.ahmed@vetforpet.net

24-hour Emergency Service:
♦ **Dr. Ahmed Hesham**
Mohandiseen. Tel: 0100-634-4025, 3762-6883.

♦ **Dr. Mohamed Sheheta**
Maadi. Tel: 0100-689-5894.

Pet Food and Pet Accessories

Amin
Address: 76 Road 9, Maadi. Tel: 2358-2857, 2359-6182.
Al Fares Shop
Address: 18 Sherif St., in front of Hurriya Mall, Heliopolis. Tel: 2455-4995, 0100-512-1407.
Pet Planet
Address: 166 26th July St., Sphinx Square, Mohandiseen. Tel: 0100-170-3866.
Samy's Farm
Agents for import and export of birds, tropical fish, and pets; pet food for all kinds of pets; cages, travel carriers. Address: 134 26 July St., Zamalek. Tel: 2735-5173/2140. E-mail: samys_farm@hotmail.com

Other Groups Concerned with Animal Welfare

♦ **Egyptian Society for Animal Friends**
To report abuse issues for all animals and to help abandoned animals. Website: www.esaf.info.

♦ **Egyptian Society for Mercy to Animals (ESMA)**
Volunteers are most welcome to donate time or money, or to sponsor an animal. ESMA is a nonprofit association, operating on the principle of 'no kill' animal welfare that offers aid and shelter to stray and abused animals. Call Mona Khalil. Tel: 0122-218-8823. E-mail: mona@esmaegypt.org. Website: www.esmaegypt.org. On Facebook search for ESMA.

♦ **The Egyptian Mau Rescue Organization (EMRO)**
A nonprofit animal organization that rescues the indigenous Mau cat. EMRO office and veterinarian clinic address: Villa 11, al-Tugariyyin City, Muqattam. Tel: 2507-6946 or 0106-0122-8821. E-mail: info@emaurescue.org. Website: www. emaurescue.org.

♦ **The Middle East Network for Animal Welfare**
Promotes the exchange of news, ideas, and lessons learned and provides a networking forum among animal welfare societies in the Middle East. Website: www.menaw.net/client/index.html.

♦ **Society for the Protection of Animal Rights in Egypt (SPARE)**
Its shelter houses up to forty dogs, and has an animal adoption program. It needs volunteers to help with animals. Tel: 3381-3855, 3819-0575, 0122-316-2912. Website: www.sparelife.org.

Making Your Acquaintance

The best times you have in Egypt are when you share your life, talents, and experiences with others. There are so many groups to join and things to learn. Here are a few:

◆ **Afro-Asian Women's Group**
Tel: 0100-190-0965

◆ **Association of Cairo Expatriates (ACE) Club**
Tel: 2519-4594. Website: http://theace club-maadi.com

◆ **British Community Association, Heliopolis**
Tel: 2291-8533. Website: www.bca egypt.com

◆ **British Community Association, Maadi**
Tel: 2358-0889. Website: www.bca egypt.com

◆ **British Community Association, Mohandiseen**
Tel: 3749-8870. Website: www.bca egypt.com

◆ **Cairo American Softball League**
Tel: 0122-724-8961

◆ **Cairo Aussie Girls**
E-mail: misell_emma@hotmail.com

◆ **Cairo Cyclers Club**
Website: http://www.facebook.com/group. php?gid=7873950427

◆ **Cairo Hash House Harriers**
Website: www.cairohash.com

◆ **Cairo Rugby Club**
Website: www.cairorugby.com

◆ **Cairo Toastmasters Club**
Website: http://www.cairotoastmasters.com

◆ **Community Services Association (CSA)**
Website: www.livinginegypt.org

◆ **Cycle Egypt Club**
Tel: 0109-914-4142 or 0122-574-5034. Website: www.cycle-egypt.com; Facebook: cycle egypt; E-mail: Cec@cycle-egypt.com

◆ **Gruppo Italiano Egitto (Italian Women's Club)**
Tel (mobile): 0100-077-0285. Website: www.giegypt.net

◆ **Indian Women's Association, Annapoorna**
E-mail: annapoorna@googlegroups.com

◆ **Pharoahz Riders of Egypt: Harley Davidson**
Website: www.harley-davidsonegypt.com

◆ **Women's Association of Cairo**
Tel: 2736-4187. E-mail: WAC@intouch.com

◆ **WOW Women of the World**
E-mail: wowcairo@yahoo.com

Living in Cairo

4

Foreign Embassies in Cairo

Argentina. 8 al-Salih Ayyub, 1st floor, Room 2, Zamalek. Tel: 2735-1501/5234.

Australia. World Trade Center, 11th floor, Corniche al-Nil, Bulaq. Tel: 2575-0444. http://www.egypt.embassy.gov.au/caro/home.html

Austria. Wissa Wassef St. (corner of al-Nil St.), 5th floor, Riyadh Tower, Giza. Tel: 3570-2975. www.austriaegypt.org

Belgium. 20 Kamil al-Shinnawi St., Garden City. Tel: 2792-5966, 2794-7494. www.diplomatie.be

Brazil. Corniche al-Nil, Avenue Maspero, Cairo. Tel: 2576-1466, 2577-3013. http://www.brazilembcairo.org/about.htm

Bulgaria. 6 al-Malik al-Afdal St., Zamalek. Tel: 2341-3025/ 6077. www.mfa.bg/en

Canada. 26 Kamil al-Shinnawi St., Garden City. Tel: 2791-8700. http://www.canada international.gc.ca/egypt-egypte/index.aspx

China. 14 Bahgat Ali St., Zamalek. Tel: 2324-5738, 2315-9176. www.china embassy.org.eg

Colombia. 6 Gezira St., Zamalek. Tel: 2342-3711.

Cuba. 10 Kamil Muhammad St., 13th floor, Apt. 1, Zamalek. Tel: 2736-0651, 2736-0657.

Czech Republic. 4 Dokki St., Giza. Tel: 3333-9700/1. www.mzv.cz/cairo

France. 29 Avenue Charles de Gaulle, Giza. Tel: 3567-3200, 3570-3917. Consulate: 5 al-Fadi St.. Downtown. Tel: 2393-4316. www.ambafrance-eg.org

Germany. 8b Hasan Sabri St., Zamalek. Tel: 2728-2177. www.german-embassy.org.eg

Greece. 18 Aisha al-Taymuriya St., Garden City. Tel: 2795-0443/5915.

Hungary. 29 Muhammad Mazhar St., Zamalek. Tel: 2735-6478/8659.

India. 5 Aziz Abaza St., Zamalek. Tel: 2736-3051, 2735-6053. Consulate: 37 Tal'at Harb St., Downtown. Tel: 2392-5162. www.indembcairo.com

Indonesia. 13 Aisha al-Taymuriya St., Garden City. Tel: 2794-7200/9.

Italy. 15 Abdel Rahman Fahmi St., Garden City. Tel: 2794-7541. Consulate: 24 al-Gala' St., Downtown. Tel: 2773-0110/9. http://www.ambilcairo.esteri.it/Ambasciata_Ilcairo

Japan. 8 Corniche al-Nil, Maadi. Tel: 2528-5910. www.eg.emb-japan.go.jp.

Malaysia. 21 al-Anba St., Mohandiseen. Tel: 3761-0013/68/73.

Mexico. 7 Port Said St., Maadi. Tel: 2358-0256/58/59. www.sre.gob.mx/egipto

Morocco. 10 Salah al-Din St., Zamalek. Tel: 2735-9677, 2736-4718.

Netherlands. 18 Hassan Sabri St., Zamalek. Tel: 2739-5500. http://egypt.nlembassy.org

Portugal. 1 al-Salih Ayyub St., Zamalek. Tel: 2735-0779/81.

Russian Federation. 95 Giza St., Giza. Tel: 3748-9353/4.

South Africa. 55 Road 18, Maadi. Tel: 2359-4365.

Spain. 41 Ismail Muhammad, Zamalek. Tel: 2735-5813/3652.

Sudan. 3 al-Ibrahimi St., Garden City. Tel: 2794-0364.

Syria. 18 Abdel Rahim Sabri St., Dokki. Tel: 3749-4560/5210.

Thailand. 9 Tiba St., Dokki. Tel: 3760-3553.

Turkey. 25 al-Falaki St., Bab al-Luq, Downtown. Tel: 2794-8364.

United Kingdom. 7 Ahmad Raghib St., Garden City. Tel: 2794-0850/2/8. http://ukin egypt.fco.gov.uk/en/

United States. 8 Kamal al-Din Salah St., Garden City. Tel: 2797-3300. http://cairo.usem bassy.gov

5

Staying Healthy

Traveling away from our normal routine
and home country may bring on
stress or ill-health that manifests itself
in a variety of physical discomforts. New
environments always have 'bugs' that your
system has not encountered before.

The following chapter provides health
information, from common ailments to how
to choose a doctor. The point is for you to
take the lead in your own health care.

Before You Arrive
In Egypt, there are common ailments that
may cause discomfort and others that are
more dangerous. Although Egypt does not
require any proof of vaccinations (except
yellow fever, in certain circumstances; see
chapter 2, "Travel to and in Egypt," "Arrival
in Egypt," and "Yellow Fever Vaccination in
Cairo," below), it is prudent to arrive with
vaccinations that are up to date for you and
your family members. To find the best travel
vaccine recommendations and to find information about risk of disease and out-
breaks in any country, check the Centers for
Disease Control and Prevention website,
www.cdc.gov/travel/, and the World Health
Organization website, www.who.int/en/.

Clinics that give vaccinations for international travel provide the International Certificate of Vaccination (yellow booklet). As
you acquire vaccinations, each will be
recorded in the booklet, which is regarded
as an official register. It might be prudent to
register with the International Association
for Medical Assistance to Travelers (IAMAT;
www.iamat.org). This is a free service that
helps travelers find a doctor.

Medical Checklist

♦ All vaccinations up to date for adults
  and children
♦ Valid medical insurance
♦ All medical records
♦ Supply of medications, if necessary

Common Ailments
Gastrointestinal Upsets and Parasites
As a newcomer, it is normal to be afflicted
with a bout of diarrhea and a stomach upset
for a few days, sometimes jokingly referred
to as 'Pharaoh's revenge.' Of course, it's no
laughing matter! Culprits of such discomfort

can be drinking tap water or eating leafy vegetables and fruits with the peel, or under-cooked meats. Eating food from the streets is not advisable. If seafood or alcohol tastes bad, spit it out! When enjoying a buffet table at restaurants, make sure the hot foods are hot and the cold foods are cold. If the food looks as if it has been out for hours, don't eat it. Although the water supply is heavily chlorinated at the water stations, pipes carrying the water are old and can have breaks or cracks that allow bacteria to seep into the water supply. Until you and your family are acclimated, it is advisable to drink bottled water or boiled and filtered water (water filters systems are available). Also, avoid ice cubes.

Home remedies for diarrhea are to drink plenty of liquids—that is, water or weak black tea—and eat plain food such as yogurt, boiled potatoes, and rice. There is also oral rehydration therapy (ORT). The packets are available at all pharmacies and replace body electrolytes with a solution of oral rehydration salts (ORS), or, if a pharmacy is not near, you can make a mixture of sugar, salt, and water. If the diarrhea lasts more than a few days or if you pass bloody stools, consult a doctor immediately. For children or the elderly, diarrhea can turn from a minor problem to a dangerous situation. Consult a doctor immediately.

Giardiasis and schistosomiasis (bilharzia) are caused by parasites that are found in untreated water and the Nile river. Do not drink from or swim in the Nile, slow-running rivers, or freshwater lakes.

Giardiasis is caused by a parasite that infects the small intestine. Schistosomiasis is caused by a parasite that is spread by a freshwater snail. It causes bleeding in the bowels and bladder. These parasites are difficult to diagnose and you'll need potent medication to be rid of them.

Common Food-borne Illnesses

Salmonellosis is caused by *Salmonella* bacteria. It is found in food like eggs, undercooked poultry and meat, or unpasteurized milk. Symptoms include nausea, vomiting, and diarrhea. Cholera is caused by the bacterium *Vibrio cholera* and is transmitted through contaminated drinking water. *Clostridium botulinum* causes botulinum poisoning; it is a bacterium that survives without oxygen and is found in canned foods. Beware of *fesikh*, a smoked fish that is popular with Egyptians during Shamm al-Nisim. Shigellosis is caused by contaminated raw foods like vegetables in salads. Foods should be washed and cooked properly. The viral infection hepatitis A can be contracted from food contaminated by an infected person.

Heat Rash, Heat Exhaustion, and Heatstroke

Parts of Egypt are hot twelve months of the year. Cairo has up to five intensely hot and sometimes humid months. If you arrive during the summer months, try to keep outdoor activities to a minimum between 11:00 a.m. and 5:00 p.m. Carry a water bottle to hydrate while in a traffic jam or shopping. Wear loose clothing made out of natural fibers, a hat, and sunglasses. Use sunscreen with an SPF of fifteen and avoid strenuous physical activity. If you are over-exposed to the sun and heat, there is a risk of developing sunburn, heat rash, or even heatstroke (sometimes called sunstroke).

Sunburns and heat rash can be allevi-ated with calamine lotion and by keeping the skin cool with compresses or showers. Heat cramps, heat exhaustion, and the more severe heatstroke are all forms of hyperther-mia—overheating of the body. Heat cramps are caused by sweating, which depletes the body of salt and water. To relieve the pain, stop the activity and sit in the shade. Drink water, juice, or a sports drink. If there is no relief within an hour, seek medical atten-tion. Heat exhaustion symptoms include heavy sweating, paleness, muscle cramps, dizziness, headache, and nausea; the skin is moist and cool. Heat exhaustion without treatment can lead to heatstroke. Heatstroke is a medical emergency that can be fatal. Signs are high body temperature, absence of sweating, red and dry skin, rapid pulse, difficult breathing, and confusion. Seek medical attention immediately.

Allergies

Pollution and dust levels are high in Cairo and are a serious concern. Dangerous levels of lead, carbon dioxide, and sulfur dioxide have been reported. From September to November a black cloud settles over the city. Some experts blame this particular pollution on Nile Delta farmers burning rice chaff. During this time there is a sig-nificant rise in respiratory diseases and eye irritations. Asthma and allergic reactions are common. If you are prone to either, it is prudent to have a complete checkup before you live for any length of time in Cairo. If you wear contact lenses, it is a good idea to have a spare pair of glasses, as dust par-ticles are particularly irritating when caught between the eye and a lens. If allergies are worsened due to pollution and dust (not plant allergies), consider using plants to help purify the air. See the section "Gardens and Shade" in chapter 9, "Making a House Your Home," for information on the best indoor plants to filter the air.

Less Common Ailments
Malaria

Malaria is caused by a plasmodium para-site that is transmitted by the female *Anopheles* mosquito. The mosquito feeds on blood. When it bites an infected person it ingests a small amount of blood that con-tains the malaria parasites. The parasites develop within the mosquito so when it takes its next meal the mosquito injects the parasite into the human through its saliva. The parasite lodges itself in the liver and begins to multiply within red blood cells, causing a fever and headache, and possibly death. Malaria is present in Egypt, particu-larly in the Nile Delta and oases in the Western Desert. Precautions such as bed nets, use of mosquito spray with DEET, staying inside at dusk, and wearing light-colored clothing all help in deterring bites.

Staying Healthy

5

However, if you have high fever and a headache, consult a doctor and ask for a malaria test.

H1N1 (Swine) Flu and Avian (H5N1) Flu

Both of these types of influenza have been found in Egypt. When H1N1 became a pandemic, Egypt took an aggressive defense against transmission. However, avian influenza, or 'bird flu,' has been more tricky to deal with. Raising chickens and ducks is an important agricultural activity and handling the animals is quite common, particularly in rural areas. Avian flu is a contagious disease of animals caused by viruses that normally infect only birds. This virus is highly aggressive and causes rapid deterioration, with a high fatality rate in humans. It can be prevented by not touching a dead bird or handling birds.

To protect yourself and your family from any type of influenza, take a few precautions to stay healthy:

♦ Wash your hands often with soap and water. Use an antibacterial hand wash if water is not available.

♦ When you sneeze or cough, cover your nose and mouth with a tissue and then throw it in the trash.

♦ Don't touch and rub your eyes, mouth, and nose.

♦ Stay at home when sick. Don't infect others.

♦ If you suffer symptoms that include fatigue, fever, chills, and vomiting, consult a doctor immediately.

Rabies

Wild cats and dogs roam the streets of Cairo. Do not touch them and make sure your children know to never approach a wild animal, corral it, or try to touch it or pick it up. Rabies is prevalent in Egypt and is spread by a bite or even a lick from an infected animal. Rabies is fatal.

It is recommended to have a rabies vaccination if you are handling animals. This vaccine can cause a reaction. Have a professional administer it. The vaccine does not provide immunity; it only gives you time to get medical attention.

Hepatitis C (HCV)

Egypt has the highest incidence of hepatitis C virus in the world and it is considered a public health emergency. The overall percentage of Egyptians who test positive for HCV antibody is 14.7 percent, which means that, out of the current population of 78–80 million, the number of Egyptians thought to be infected with HCV is over 11 million. Today, it is estimated that over 500,000 Egyptians become infected with HCV every year through person-to-person transmission, by sharing body fluids, through unhygienic medical and dental procedures, by sharing needles, and by barbers or manicurists using shared razors and unsterile instruments. The most common causes for the spread of the virus in Egypt are unhygienic medical or dental treatments and blood transfusions during surgery.

From the 1960s through the 1980s, mass campaigns were carried out to treat hepatitis C and schistosomiasis. Research suggests that unsterilized syringes were a major cause of HCV transmission during these campaigns. There is no vaccine against HCV.

HIV/AIDS
The prevalence of HIV and AIDS in Egypt is low. The United Nations Program (UN-AIDS) estimates the HIV infection rate in Egypt is less than 0.1 percent. The reported cases have been transmitted through unprotected heterosexual sex. If you are working in Egypt, you will need to show proof of a negative AIDS test. Though the chances of contracting HIV are low, avoid high-risk behavior such as unprotected sex and sharing needles.

Yellow Fever Vaccination in Cairo
Yellow fever vaccination is not required for Egypt, nor is the disease endemic in Egypt. However, travelers arriving from or going to countries infected with yellow fever are required to present proof of the vaccination. (See chapter 2, "Travel to and in Egypt," "Arrival in Egypt," for a list of countries where yellow fever is present.) Without the proper immunization, new arrivals will be quarantined at Cairo International Airport for thirty-six hours. Be sure to have the immunization recorded in your International Certificate of Vaccination (yellow booklet).

Here is a list of clinics in Cairo that provide yellow fever vaccination. Call before going, as yellow fever immunizations are usually carried out on specific days.

♦ Terminal 1 at Cairo International Airport, costing about LE60.
♦ Shaalan Surgicenter. Address: 10 Abdel Hamid Lutfi St., Mohandiseen. Tel: 3760-3920, 3338-7648, 0122-226-3535.
♦ Ghaly's Medical Group. Address: No. 32, 33 Golf St., Maadi. Tel: 2380-9247/995/997, 2359-2593.

Health Care
Health care in Egypt varies significantly, according to where you live. Throughout Egypt there is an extensive network of public hospitals. In every village there are

---

Recommended Vaccines

Hepatitis B
Hepatitis B virus is transmitted via body fluids or blood. In Egypt 2–7 percent of the population are carriers.

Hepatitis A
Hepatitis A is transmitted person-to-person by ingestion of contaminated food or water, or by direct contact with an infected person.

Rabies
Recommended if there is a risk of exposure to stray dogs and cats.

Typhoid
Infection occurs through food and water.

clinics that offer basic medical services, though the standards may vary. More affluent Egyptians seek treatment in private hospitals and clinics. Cairo is considered to have the best healthcare, with over fifty hospitals and hundreds of clinics. For Egyptians, the main government bodies for healthcare are the Ministry of Health and the Health Insurance Organization (HIO). The Ministry of Health runs the majority of government medical facilities that range from urban hospitals to rural clinics. Care at Ministry of Health facilities is free to Egyptian citizens. University hospitals are administered by the Ministry of Education and military hospitals by the Ministry of Defense.

Egypt has two government-supervised insurance providers: the Health Insurance Organization, whose services cover nearly 57 percent of Egypt's population, and the Curative Care Organization. The HIO operates a network of hospitals and covers employed persons, students, and widows through premiums deducted from employee salaries and employer payrolls. The Curative Care Organization contracts with individuals, private companies, and government agencies for healthcare needs, and tallies premiums accordingly. For an overview of the health system in Egypt, go to http://www.measuredhs.com/pubs/pdf/SPA5/02chapter02.pdf.

Many mosques in Cairo and Alexandria provide clinics. They are funded by the community and often offer a better quality of health care than government-run hospitals. In villages, traditional practices and modern healthcare are combined. For example, the midwife plays a key role in women's health, childbirth, and ceremonial activities. Homeopathic cures and traditional remedies are practiced in rural areas; even in Cairo and Alexandria there are specialized herbal stores. Traditional health practitioners in villages do not necessarily diagnose and prescribe for a 'disease,' but have a system of personalizing the need of the patient by overcoming whatever manifestations of imbalance he or she may be experiencing. For example, the *zaar* ceremony marks an intervention to cure or alleviate an affliction by contact with the spirits possessing the person.

If they are financially able, Egyptians prefer to go to a private clinic. These clinics employ staff who speak English and maintain a high standard of care compared to public hospitals. At private clinics and hospitals, out-of-pocket payments for medical services are collected before medical services are rendered.

Expatriates may be used to paying for medical services after the service is rendered or to the insurance being billed before the patient receives a bill, but in Egypt charges for services are collected before seeing a doctor or having a procedure. If further charges are required, the bill must be settled before leaving the clinic or hospital, after which the patient is responsible for collecting from their local or international insurance company. Private hospitals and clinics accept cash and major credit cards. International insurance providers offer a variety of plans ranging from comprehensive packages to catastrophic emergency insurance; prices vary. Insurance packages can be purchased specifically for the length of stay in Egypt and can be renewed if the stay is extended.

In Cairo the level of routine medical services can be excellent. Nevertheless, expatriates often decide to have surgery outside of Egypt. The concern is due to post-surgery care that is below western standards. Many expatriates obtain medical evacuation insurance that covers the cost of transporting the patient out of Egypt for surgery in their home country.

Within the following paragraphs are suggestions of where to look for hospitals and doctors in Egypt. (The author and publisher assume no responsibility for the professional ability or integrity of the persons or hospitals whose names appear in the following lists.)

♦ Community Service Association lists hospitals, doctors, dentists, specialists, and laboratories in the Maadi area at www.livinginegypt.org/portal/Portals/0/Online%20Resources/Factsheets/13%20Doctors%20 color.pdf, or ask at the CSA front desk for a list of providers. Tel: 2358-5284/0754.

♦ International Association for Medical Assistance to Travelers, at www.iamat.org. Provides free advice in finding a doctor and health advice, and assists travelers in need of emergency medical care.

♦ For a list of HIO hospitals and doctors, go to http://hioegypt.org/english.aspx (there is even a telephone number for hospital complaints).

♦ A list of government hospitals in Cairo can be found at www.egypt.alloexpat.com/egypt_information/government_hospitals_in_egypt.php

♦ For a list of private hospitals and medical centers that have English-speaking staff, visit http://cairo.usembassy.gov/consular/hospitallist.pdf

♦ Egypt's National Cancer Institute is also located in Cairo: http://www.nci.edu.eg/

♦ You can find a fairly comprehensive listing of Egyptian hospitals and medical clinics at www.hospitalsworldwide.com

♦ Pacific Prime lists hospitals with English-speaking staff at http://www.pacificprime.com/countries/egypt/hospitals.php

♦ Theodor Bilharz Research Institute (http://www.tbri.sci.eg/) in Cairo is dedicated to the diagnosis, treatment, and research of schistosomiasis parasites.

♦ The International Medical Center in Cairo is one of the preferred medical facilities for expatriates. The center provides consulting and surgical services reflecting a wide range of specialties, including dentistry, radiology, pediatrics, obstetrics, cardiology, and gastroenterology. It has eight hundred beds and a sixty-three-bed intensive care unit for serious illnesses and injuries. Both Egyptian and American doctors are on staff to diagnose and treat illnesses and injuries, and it has an international standard of care. The center is located at Km 42, Cairo–Ismailiya Road, and can be contacted via telephone at 2477-5902/3/4. For a list of medical services and doctors, and information about the on-site hotel, go to http://imceg.com

Choosing a Physician

It is difficult enough to find a family physician in your own country, but finding one in Egypt is a worry and can be stressful, particularly where children are concerned. Egyptian medical training to become a doctor involves six years of medical school, a one-year internship in public hospitals, and, depending on the specialization, two to four years as a resident. Many continue to specialize outside of Egypt or qualify through medical bodies in Europe, the U.K., and the U.S. There are a few general practitioners, but most doctors are specialists. A large number are associated with hospitals and/or have their own clinics.

Most doctors speak English, but language may be a barrier, as receptionists and nurses usually do not. Many doctors' office hours are in the afternoon or evening. In the past, the system to secure an appointment with a doctor was on a first-come, first-served basis within the doctor's office hours. This remains the case outside of Cairo. In recent years, this system in Cairo changed to making appointments a day or two in advance by calling the doctor's office for an exact time (but don't be surprised if, even with an appointment, there is still a system of first-come, first served of those sitting in the waiting room). Payment for an office visit is made prior to seeing the doctor. Charges for foreigners are usually higher than for an Egyptian. If you are submitting a claim for insurance, ask for a receipt but do not assume it will be readily available.

Here are a few things to consider when choosing a doctor in Cairo:

♦ Ask friends, your company, or the school nurse for recommendations. Embassies often have lists of recommended physicians. There is a list of English-speaking doctors at http://cairo.usembassy.gov/consular/acslist1.htm

♦ On arrival, it is a good idea to register with a physician or medical clinic to establish a medical record. This would be the first contact for any medical issues that might arise.

♦ Check qualifications and training.

♦ Finding a doctor and health care program that you are comfortable with is important. Look for another doctor if the one you are dealing with does not meet your expectations.

♦ If you do not feel comfortable with a particular health care provider, look for another.

♦ If you feel that a second opinion is necessary, do not be afraid to find another physician or specialist to consult.

Once you have found a physician or specialist, be sure to get his mobile number for any emergencies. Many doctors will make house calls. Most doctors and clinics do not keep laboratory, x-rays, and scan reports. You are given these results and will need to keep track of your medical record. Some doctors do keep medical updates on visits. It is important for you to make copies of all reports, results, and prescriptions. With the Internet, it is common for westerners to research medical information and come prepared to the doctors' office with information and questions. You might find that doctors in Egypt are used to giving a diagnosis without a great deal of explanation. Discuss your options politely, although there may be some resistance or impatience. Punctuality is not something that is observed with medical appointments, so be patient and give yourself plenty of time and take a book to read (often, when you are prepared to wait, you won't need to!). Hours change during the month of Ramadan. Ask for a weekend emergency number as most physicians to do not work from Thursday evening through Friday.

Emergency!

Dial 123 for ambulance services. Dial 140 for telephone numbers of pharmacies and medical services (ask for an English-speaking operator).

Ambulance services in Cairo may not be as well-equipped and staffed with qualified medics as you are used to in your country. When you call for an ambulance the service will send an ambulance from the public hospital nearest to your area. Consider traffic and the time of day, as cars do not pull over to allow ambulances to pass, which causes a wailing ambulance to be stuck in a traffic jam just like any other vehicle. Depending on the emergency, it might be better to take the patient by taxi

Main Hospitals in Cairo, Alexandria, and the Red Sea Area

6th October Central Hospital
Vodafone Square, 6th October City, Giza. Tel: 3832-2180.
Alexandria International Hospital
20 Baha' al-Din al-Ghatwari St., off Mustafa Kamil St., Smuha, Alexandria. Tel: 03-420-7243/4/6/7.
Alexandria Medical Center
14th May Road, Smuha, Alexandria. Tel: 03-420-2652.
Arab Contractors Medical Center
al-Gabal al-Akhdar, Nasr City. Tel: 19660, 2342-6000.
Cairo Medical Center
4 Abu Ubayda al-Bakri St., Roxy, Heliopolis. Tel: 2450-9800.
Capital Clinic
20 Syria St., Mohandiseen. Tel: 3761-7322/3.
Cleopatra Hospital
39 Cleopatra St., Salah al-Din Square, Heliopolis. Tel: 2414-3931.
Dar Al Fouad Hospital
26th July St., Touristic Zone, 6th October City, Giza. Tel: 12568; General: 3835-6040; Emergency Hotline: 2577-7300.
Egyptian British Hospital
25 Muhammad al-Ghatwari St., Smuha, Alexandria. Tel: 03-427-0355.
Family Health Care Medical Group
71 Road 9, Maadi. Tel: 2380-6766, 2359-2048; 24-hr. tel: 0100-602-3118.

Staying Healthy 5

The German Hospital
56 Abdel Salam Aref St., Saba Basha, Alexandria. Tel: 03-584-1717, 0122-350-6364.

Ghaly's Medical Group
No. 32, 33 Golf St., Maadi. Tel: 2380-9247/9995/9997, 2359-2593.

Golf Specialized Hospital
17 al-Rahala al-Baghdadi St., Heliopolis. Tel: 2415-2953/8550, 2417-1514.

al-Gouna Hospital
Downtown al-Gouna. Tel: 065-358-0011/2, 0122-799-5700, 0122-147-1015.

International Eye Hospital
14 Adel Hussein Rustum St., Dokki. Tel: 19650, 3338-1818.

Misr International Hospital
12 al-Saraya St., Dokki. Tel: 3360-8261, 3335-3345, 3760-8267.

al-Nil Badrawi Hospital
Corniche al-Nil, Maadi. Tel: 2524-0022.

Nile Hospital
Villages Road, beside Maritime Inspection, Hurghada. Tel: 065-355-0974/5/6.

al-Salam Hospital
3 Syria St., Mohandiseen. Tel: 3302-9091, 3303-0502, 3303-4780.

al-Salam International Hospital
Corniche al-Nil, Maadi. Tel: 19885, 2524-0250.

Shaalan Surgicenter
10 Abdel Hamid Lutfi St., Mohandiseen. Tel: 3760-3920, 3338-7648, 0122-226-3535.

al-Shourok Hospital
5 Bahr al-Ghazal, al-Sahafiyyin, Giza. Tel: 3304-4901.

Sinai Clinic
al-Bank St., Umm al-Sid Hill, Sharm al-Sheikh. Tel: 069-366-6850, 0100-555-4202.

yourself to a nearby hospital with which you are familiar. In rural areas there are probably no ambulances available. However, on highways there are medical outposts where there are ambulances that respond to highway accidents. If you are staying in a hotel, ask the receptionist or concierge, as they usually have a staff doctor available.

Labs and Scanning Centers
Physicians will send you to get your own laboratory work, x-rays, or scans needed for a diagnosis. Sometimes a doctor is associated with a particular laboratory or hospital, but you are free to go to any center. You will need to collect the results yourself and return to your physician with them. You'll have to make another appointment for this, but usually there is not a second charge.

Laboratory centers are:

♦ **Alfa Laboratories**
Call Center: 16191 for Mohandiseen, Hadayik al-Qubba, Nasr City, Downtown, Heliopolis, Shubra, Giza, Sayyida Zeinab, Hilmiyyit al-Zaytun, Maadi, Muqattam.

Ambulance Emergency Numbers
Dial 123

Heliopolis
Tel: 2634-4327
Maadi
Tel: 2359-5139
Dokki, Mohandiseen, Giza
Tel: 3572-0737
Air Ambulance (Smart Air, private jet)
Tel: 2267-0870

♦ **al-Borg Laboratory**
Call Center: 19911 for Mohandiseen, Downtown, Giza, Heliopolis, Nasr City, Pyramids, Alexandria.

♦ **Cairo Lab**
Call Center: 19962 for Mohandiseen, Downtown, Manial, Heliopolis, Nasr City, Giza, Beni Suef, Maadi, Muqattam.

Scan centers are:

♦ **Alfa Scan**
Call Center: 16171 for Mohandiseen, Heliopolis, Maadi.

♦ **Nile Scan**
Call Center: 19656 for Maadi, Bab al-Luq, Heliopolis, Dokki.

♦ **Women's and Fetal
   Imaging Center (WAFI)**
Address: 54 Manial St., Manial. Tel: 2368-1281, 2365-9488. Website: www.wafi-egypt.com

Pharmacies and Medicine
Pharmacies are abundant throughout cities in Egypt. They are well-stocked and the pharmacists are helpful, knowledgeable, and most speak English. Pharmacists are happy to help you find the correct medicine for your needs. Explain your condition in specific terms and they can suggest medications, but beware that pharmacists are not doctors and do not know about other conditions you may have. Medicating in this way makes you directly responsible for the treatment you choose to take. When doctor and hospital prescriptions are filled, the prescription is returned to you. If a medication is not available, the pharmacist will order it and deliver it to your door. Many medicines that normally need a prescription in other countries can be purchased over the counter. Read the insert instructions that come with each package of medicine carefully, particularly if you are self-medicating. A word of warning: teenagers have been known to buy powerful, easily available prescription drugs over the counter and abuse them.

Prices are extremely reasonable, as the government subsidizes medicines produced in Egypt. Brand-named medications are a fraction of their price in the U.S. and Europe. However, beware of generic drugs. Do *not* take anything that comes from an unmarked package. Generic medications may not be strong enough or may be too strong, so, if you are unsure, it might be a good idea to go to a doctor and ask their opinion.

24-hour pharmacies:

♦ **Africa Pharmacy**
Address: 45 Makram Ebeid St., Nasr City.
Tel: 2274-1413.

♦ **Eman Pharmacy**
43 al-Gazayir St., New Maadi. Tel: 2519-5688.

♦ **El-Ezaby Pharmacy**
Locations in Heliopolis, Mohandesin, Nasr City, Old Cairo, Giza, al-Korba, Maadi, Downtown, Abbasia, Manial. Tel: 19600.

♦ **al-Nadi Pharmacy**
Addresses: 40 al-Falah St., Mohandiseen; Hyper One, 6th October City; Dandy Mall, Cairo–Alexandria Road. Tel: 16196.

♦ **Seif Pharmacy**
Tel: 19199.

♦ **al-Zoghby Pharmacy**
Address: 65 Abbas al-Aqqad St., Nasr City. Tel: 2401-7650.

Other Medical Specialists
Dentists
Choosing a dentist is like choosing a physician. Ask for recommendations from friends, your child's school, or your company. Visit the dentist to make sure of the hygienic standards and inquire about how instruments are sterilized. Hepatitis B and C can be spread by unhygienic dental instruments. Inquire about the preventive dental care provided, x-rays, and equipment. Here are a few recommendations from *Oasis*, the Community Service Association magazine:

♦ **Laser-Cerec Dental Clinic**
Address: 73 Road 9, Maadi. Tel: 2359-0130/ 3393, 0100-660-9082. E-mail: info@tarek dental.net. Website: www.tarekdental.net

♦ **Maadi Dental Center**
Address: 4 Road 209, Digla, Maadi. Tel: 2519-8736. Website: www.maadidental.com

♦ **Maadi Dental and Implantology Clinic**
Dr. Mahmoud Shalash. Open seven days a week, Saturday–Thursday, Friday on request. Address: 85 Road 9, Maadi. Tel: 2359-6988, 0122-369-9967.

♦ **Osman Dental Clinic**
Mohandiseen branch address: 54 Abdel Mun'im Riyad St. (opposite the Cairo Medical Tower), 1st floor. Tel: 3347-5926. Maadi branch address: 19 Road 233, 4th floor, Apt. 42. Tel: 2754-5563. E-mail info@odcdentistry.com. Website: www.odc dentistry.com

Psychiatry and Therapists
We all have emotional issues and stress. If these become unmanageable, there are professional psychiatrists and therapists to talk with. Depending on the severity of the situation, you may wish to return to your home country. The following are some suggestions for clinics and professionals.

◆ Baraka Karin Maatwk

Family Constellation is a powerful technique in psychology to bring awareness about life's patterns. Its German founder, Bert Hellinger, developed a kind of role play where you can look at the hidden patterns inside yourself. You can interrupt unhealthy behavior effectively and open possibilities of changes even in traumatic or chronically tangled situations in your private life as well as in business relations. Group sessions or individual sittings are available. Tel: 0122-398-5748. E-mail: baraka.m@gmx.net. Website: Baraka-therapy.com

◆ Behman Hospital

The oldest and largest private psychiatric hospital in the Middle East. Outpatient services are available at the hospital in Helwan seven days per week, as well as at the outpatient centers listed below. Address: 32 al-Marsad St., Helwan. Tel: 2555-7551/9602/7894/9603. E-mail (administration): admin@behman.com; medical information: info@behman.com. Website: www.behman.com

Behman Hospital Outpatient Centers:

80 al-Gumhuriya St., Ramsis Square.
 Tel: 2591-9340.
55 Abdel Mun'im Riyad St., Mohandiseen.
 Tel: 3304-7453.
3 Hasan Sadiq St., Heliopolis. Tel: 2418-3572.
16 Urabi St., Maadi. Tel: 2359-2278.

◆ The Cairo Center for Sleep Disorders

Provides services for patients with all types of sleep disorders, including snoring, sleep apnea, and insomnia. Address: al-Borg Building (Clinic 909), 55 Abdel Mun'im Riyad St., Mohandiseen. Tel: 3345-4969. Fax: 3351-0906. For a full description of services, go to http://www.behman.com/ccsd.html

◆ The Learning Resource Center (LRC)

Provides diagnostic and educational services for children and adolescents who are experiencing learning difficulties and/or developmental problems. Address: 9 Road 278, New Maadi. Tel: 2516-3965/7, 0122-233-2809. E-mail: info@lrcegypt.com. Website: www.lrcegypt.com

◆ Maadi Psychology Center

Office hours 9:00 a.m.–7:00 p.m. Sunday–Thursday. Address: 16 Urabi St. (corner of Road 14), Old Maadi. Tel: 2359-2278, 0100-657-0691; 24-hours, call Behman Hospital: 2555-7551. E-mail: maadipc@yahoo.com

◆ Overeaters Anonymous

Tel: 2520-0567; Mobile: 0111-643-7500. E-mail: mego77@hotmail.com.

◆ Psychealth Team

Contact: Dina Soltan. Assessment and training for addictive behaviors, eating disorders, neurotic disorders. Address: Villa 13, Road 16, Maadi. Tel: 2358-5509, 0127-852-9814.

Staying Healthy

5

Psychiatric Health Resort

Address: 1 Prof. Ahmad Ukasha St., off Mihwar Anwar al-Sadat, al-Banafsig 2 District, behind Police Academy, First Settlement, New Cairo. Tel: 2920-0900/1/2/3/4/5/7/8, 0100-240-6998/9. E-mail: info@okashahospital.com. Website: www.okashahospital.com

Allergy Clinic

Vienna International Allergy Clinic (VIAC) has a branch in Cairo. They offer a package consisting of skin tests, lab tests, and treatment for allergies. VIAC is certified to European standards.

VIAC

Address: 1 Sphinx Square, Apt. 5, Mohandiseen. Tel 3302-9646/3225.

Alcohol and Drug Abuse

AA in Cairo

AA and Al-Anon meetings on Saturday and Sunday at 8:00 p.m. at Swiss Club, Kitkat, Imbaba. Monday, Wednesday, and Thursday at 8:00 p.m. at Qasr al-Maadi Hospital, Corniche al-Maadi.

Caritas—Egypt

Director Dr. Boshra Fahmmy. The 'Oasis of Hope' Center provides free counseling and rehabilitative services to drug addicts. Volunteers are welcome. Tel: 0100-522-1195. Headquarters: 1 Mahmoud Sedki St., Khouloussy, Cairo. Mailing address: P.O. Box 43, Shubra, 11231 Cairo. Tel: 2431-0201/0318. E-mail: cariteg@link.net,

caritas@idsc.net.eg. Website: http://www.caritasegypt.com

Freedom Drug Rehabilitation

Located in New Cairo. Tel: 0100-255-1717, 0122-393-3253.

Plastic Surgery

A word about plastic surgery in Cairo: all treatments are available and at more reasonable prices than in the U.S. As with any plastic surgery, please investigate the physician's qualifications and reputation thoroughly, as plastic surgery can deform and be life-threatening.

Alternative Medicine

Alternative, holistic, and homeopathic medicine are no strangers to the Cairo scene, but in recent years a wide choice of therapists and programs from acupuncture to yoga has become readily available.

Herbal therapy and remedies have been a part of Egypt's medical treatment ranging from embalming to cosmetics over the centuries. The most famous center is Harraz Herb Shop in Bab al-Khalq (Ahmad Mahir Street), but you can find herbal shops in every area of the city. (Note: Arabic is needed to know the particular herbs and recognize their properties. You will need to explain your ailment to one of the herbalists for them to prescribe the correct remedy.)

Aromatherapy is a popular alternative to medication that uses essentials oils to alter an individual's mood and for physical and psychological well-being. For example, lemon oil is considered an anti-stress remedy. In Hurghada, El Baraka Company specializes in the production of natural essential oils. They use a cold press to extract the oils from organically grown plants that include the leaves, stems, roots, seeds, and bark. Their product line is extensive, such as Egyptian black seed oil, jojoba oil, castor oil, almond oil, carrot oil, sesame oil, lettuce oil, rocket oil, aloe vera gel, marjoram oil, pumpkin oil, sage oil, and lemongrass oil. Warning: A rule of thumb when buying aromatherapy products is to look for a list of ingredients and products that contain pure essential oils and avoid words like 'fragrance.' Essential oils are extracted from the plant's roots, bark, seeds, petals, or berries. They contain nutrients and are expensive. (For example, it takes thirty rose petals to make one drop of rose oil.) Fragrant oils are less expensive, as they consist of oils that have been mixed with synthetic oils or other substances. Visitors are welcome at the shop and factory. Shop address: Villages Road, Marine Club, Grand Hotel, Hurghada. Tel: 065-346-3153. Factory Address: Industrial Area, behind al-Nil Hospital, beside El Tahanon Brothers, Hurghada. Tel: 065-920-0540, 0106-837-7101/2. E-mail: info@ el-baraka.net. Websites: www.el-baraka.net, www.elbarakafactory.com

Sand bathing is an ancient Egyptian remedy for the aches and pains of arthritis and other types of pain. Today there are five-star hotels that offer this specialty at a cost, or you can take a trip to Siwa Oasis, where you can be buried up to your neck in sand at Gabal Dakrur. Safaga is a well-known site for therapeutic tourism. It is said to be one of the best locations in the world for curing psoriasis and relieving joint pains and joint edema. The sea water is high in salt content. Surrounded by high mountains, Safaga is protected against wind and sand. The gravity is low which helps in treating some diseases such as vascular deficiency and a high flow of the blood to the limbs. The climate is moderate, and the concentration of sunlight and ultraviolet rays helps in the treatment of psoriasis. The black sand has three minerals—uranium, thorium, and potassium—that are at a safe level. The famous Karlov Vary Spa at Menaville Resort in Safaga is the place to go for this healing treatment.

The following are some suggestions if you are interested in alternative medicine:

♦ **Baraka Karin Maatwk**
German licensed physiotherapist for shoulder and neck pain, back syndrome, chronic pain management, headache and migraine, and post-surgery treatment. Tel: 0122-398-5748. E-mail: baraka.m@gmx.net. Website: Baraka-therapy.com

♦ **BodyFitCairo**
Address: 4 Road 21, Maadi. Tel: 0100-343-3111. Website: www.pilatesegypt.com

♦ **CSA Serenity Center**
Address: 4 Road 21, Maadi. BodyFitCairo,

Tel: 0100-343-3111. Website: www.pilates egypt.com. Bodyworx, physiotherapy. Tel: 0122-398-0237, 0100-310-3414. E-mail: noa manford@hotmail.com. Website: reached through www.livinginegypt.org

✦ **Egyptian Scientific Society of Homeopathy (ESSH)**
31 Ramy Tower, 9th floor, Zahra' al-Maadi. Lists names and addresses of certified homeopathy practitioners in Cairo. Website: www.egyptssh.com

✦ **Haiyan Chinese Health Center, Maadi**
Acupuncture, Chinese medical massage, pain relief, migraine, hypertension. Tel: 2753-9776, 0128-112-2518. E-mail: health518@yahoo.com

✦ **Health Care and Cure Clinic**
Physical therapy. Tel: 0114-157-8146, 0100-733-5459.

✦ **Ki Studio**
Dokki. Katriona Shawki is a British physiotherapist, a Trager practitioner and tutor, a color therapist, and a Reiki master. She offers physical therapy, Trager sessions, Trager training, family constellation groups and individual sessions, homeopathy consultations, reflexology, a chair exercise class for those less able, Reiki sessions, color and sound sessions, and general well-being sessions. Sessions by appointment. Tel: 3336-3930; Mobile: 0122-219-8131. E-mail: kshawki@googlemail.com

✦ **Strougo Academy for Fitness Education (SAFE)**
A wellness center that offers classes in nutrition, fitness, kinesiology, body dynamics, senior fitness, and prenatal and postpartum exercises. SAFE sponsors the annual ZEN Conference in Egypt. Address: 8 Dr. Hanim Muhammad St., Rimaya Square, behind Le Meridien Pyramids, Giza. Tel: 3376-7066/886, 0100-606-6181. Website: http://www.safeacademy.com

The practice of yoga in Cairo is spreading rapidly. There are private classes and yoga is also offered in various gyms. Yoga has a wide range of different practices and different levels, so inquire first and ask to take a complimentary class to see if it is the yoga for you. First look at http://www.yogafinder.com/, a website that lists yoga studios in Cairo, Alexandria, and Sinai.

✦ **Bodyworks**
Address: 29 al-Shahid Ishaq Ya'qub St., Heliopolis. Tel: 2291-6484.

✦ **The Breathing Room**
Address: 10 Road 216, Maadi. Tel: 0127-852-9798 for weekly schedule, 0100-629-2684 for general questions. Website: http://www.thebreathingroomcairo.blogspot.com

✦ **Egypt Yoga Art Studio**
Al-Nil St., Agouza, Dokki. Tel: 0122-222-9016. Website: http://www.egyptyogaart.com

♦ Ki Studio

Dokki. Yoga and Jin Shin Yitzu. Sessions by appointment. Tel: 3336-3930, 0122-219-8131. E-mail: kshawki@googlemail.com

♦ Maulana Azad Center

Address: Indian Cultural Center, 23 Tal'at Harb, Downtown. Tel: 2393-3396, 2396-0071. E-mail: macic@indembcairo.com. Website: www.indembcairo.com

♦ Mira Shihadeh

Teaches ashtanga yoga in Zamalek, behind Beanos on Sheikh al-Marsafi Sq., across from the Italian Cultural Center. Tel: 0122-275-8625.

♦ Reform Pilates Studio

Stott method of Pilates, as well as yoga classes. Open 8:00 a.m.–9:00 p.m. Address: 15 Taha Hussein St., 2nd floor. Zamalek. Tel: 0122-220-7669. Website: www.reform studio.info/contact-me

♦ STEP Center

Yoga, Pilates, fitness therapy, and wellness center. Managing director is Karim Strougo. Address: 8 Dr. Hanim Muhammad St., Rimaya Square, behind Le Meridien Pyramids Hotel, Giza. Tel: 0100-511-1752. Website: http://www.step-center.com

Having a Baby in Cairo

Expectant mothers and those with infants will be pleased to discover that there are practitioners with expertise in prenatal care, childbirth, and breastfeeding:

Interview with Gertrud Simmert-Genedy, founder of Cairo Birth House and first certified all-round doula (birth assistant) in Egypt:

Having a baby in Egypt is easy; every twenty-three seconds a baby is born here. Despite this fact, the question is how to deliver your baby here. There is no insurance system to cover delivery so all decisions regarding delivery, and even pre-pregnancy care and postnatal care, must be considered wisely and according to your budget. You can choose between five-star birth temples, reasonable birth clinics, standard hospitals with obstetric departments, and cheap governmental services.

On realizing you are pregnant, the first step is to find an obstetrician/gynecologist (Ob/Gyn). There is a vast choice of Ob/Gyns in Cairo, most of whom are male. Some doctors seem well-qualified, but may not do the important gynecological exam. From the start it is important to discuss the different birthing options and hospitals. Doctors practice in their particular hospitals, so if you have a hospital preference you will need to discuss this with your physician. Your budget will be one of the main factors in doctor and hospital choice. The best services are available to those who can

Staying Healthy

5

afford to pay. Well-known Ob/Gyns charge between LE2,000 and LE3,000 for prenatal care, LE4,000 for a natural birth, and LE6,000 for a Caesarean section. These fees are separate from the costs for a decent hospital stay, which is twenty-four hours for natural birth (between LE1,000 and 2,000 for food, bed, and standard medication) and two to three days after a Caesarean section. The choice of Ob/Gyns is vast in Cairo; good and skillful Egyptian male and some female doctors are located throughout all districts. They are well-educated and trained abroad, speaking fluently English, French, German, and other common languages. You will not be able to find a foreign doctor, as they are unable to be licensed here. Only embassy doctors are accredited here, but none of them is an obstetrician according to the latest information for this guide book. And, remember: Your gynecologist is always your obstetrician for delivering your baby.

◆ **Dr. Ashraf Sabry**
According to his website, he specializes in fertility issues. It contains a patient education library in the fields of fertility, prenatal care, and women's health in English and Arabic. Clinic: 22A Murad St., 9th floor, Giza (same street as zoo and Four Seasons Hotel). Tel: 0114-550-9290, 0111-276-

7776 (non-Arabic speakers). Clinic: 61 Nahda St., al-Mahatta Sq., Road 9, Maadi (beside CIB Bank, above Zahran Utensils). Tel: 0114-550-9291, 0111-276-7776 (non-Arabic speakers). Website: http://www.ashrafsabry.com.

◆ **Dr. Rania Hosny**
An assistant professor of pediatrics and neonatology at Cairo University, she is an international board-certified lactation consultant and gives breastfeeding classes. Tel: 0122-742-7104.

◆ **Egypt Yoga Art Studio**
Al-Nil St., Agouza, Dokki. Yoga for pregnant women. Tel: 0122-222-9016. Website: www.egyptyogaart.com.

◆ **Gertrud Simmert-Genedy**
Founder of Cairo Birth House, Simmert-Genedy is a certified doula. (A doula is a birth companion who stays with the pregnant woman through labor, birth, and the first hours after birth to help begin nursing. Birth doulas offer emotional support and encouragement. Postpartum doulas offer support for women and families after the baby is born.) Simmert-Genedy assists in your birthing, along with your doctor's treatment, with breathing techniques and body positioning during labor, sets up your birth plan, offers a birth course, German style, for natural birth, offers guidance in Caesarean section and epidural treatment, and develops a sensitive newborn care plan. Location: Dar al-Hikma Hospital,

Nasr City. Tel: 0100-502-7117. E-mail: birthcourse@yahoo.com. Website: www. freewebs.com/birthcoursegerman style/

◆ **Gohar Women's Health Clinic**
Dr. Hussein Sherif Gohar, Medical Director. In Manial and 6th October City. Address (Manial): 25 Abdel Aziz Sa'ud St.; (6th October): Central Corridor, Third District, Medical Tower. Tel: 0128-244-4060. Website: www.gohar-hospital.com.

◆ **Ki Studio**
Katriona Shawky, in Dokki, for active childbirth preparation lectures, conditioning for pregnancy, and delivery exercise classes; exercise for women, emphasizing awareness and fitness, including elements from yoga. Sessions by appointment. Tel: 3336-3930; Mobile: 0122-219-8131. E-mail: kshawki@googlemail.com.

◆ **Maha al-Zokm**
In Heliopolis. Gives classes in English and Arabic. Tel: 2267-2492, 0122-347-7821.

◆ **Mother and Child Magazine**
This magazine has extensive listings for pregnancy and parenting classes. Available at Diwan or through website: http://mother-and-child.net

◆ **Samia Allouba Creative Dance and Fitness Center**
Numerous locations in Maadi, Mohandiseen, Heliopolis, 6th October, and Smart Village; see "Health Clubs and Gyms," below, for addresses and telephone numbers. Fitness classes for pregnant and postpartum mothers. Website: www.samia allouba-center.com

◆ **Strougo Academy for Fitness Education (SAFE)**
Offers prenatal and postpartum exercises. Address: 8 Dr. Hanim Muhammad St., Rimaya Square, behind Le Meridien Pyramids, Giza. Tel: 3376-7886, 0100-606-6181. Website: http://www.safeacademy.com/

Babies' and Children's Health
Your child's health and well-being is a constant concern wherever in the world you live. Choosing the right pediatrician is most important. Interview several doctors, making sure the one you choose is accessible for emergencies during the night, weekends, and vacations. Check the nearest hospital for emergency facilities and consult your child's school as to the emergency policies and medical care provided for their students. Community Service Association is a good source for children's programs, support, and professional advice. Tel: 2358-5284. Website: www.livingin egypt.org. Pediatricians and pharmacists use Celsius for thermometer readings. When your child has a fever it is important to give professionals the thermometer reading in Celsius. See the box below for conversions from Fahrenheit to Celsius.

CAUTION: Walking, pushing strollers or baby carriages, and riding bicycles in Cairo

Temperature Conversion Chart

Fahrenheit		Celsius
96.8		36.0
97.7		36.5
98.6	normal	37.0
99.5		37.5
100.4		38.0
101.3		38.5
102.2		39.0
103.1		39.5
104.0		40.0
104.9		40.5

are extremely dangerous activities. Do not allow children onto the street unsupervised, particularly to ride a bike or scooter. Be very careful when pushing baby carriages or strollers. The sidewalks are either broken or nonexistent, forcing you to walk in the street. A driver may not be able to see the stroller or may be reckless. Exercise extreme caution.

Babies' and children's skin is sensitive and, in this dry, hot climate, susceptible to rashes. Nefertari is a local company that produces chemical-free shampoo, lotions, wipes, and powders for babies. All the soaps are 100 percent glycerin, which is tender on baby's skin. All Nefertari Baby Care products are 100 percent free of chemicals, preservatives, coloring agents, and artificial fragrances. The products contain no pesticides, parabens, propylene glycol, phthalates, sulfates, nuts, or animal

Vaccination Chart for Children

♦ **Diphtheria/pertussis (whooping cough)/tetanus (DTaP/Tdap):**
2, 4, 6, 15–18 months, 4–6 years, 11–12 years
♦ **Polio:**
2, 4, 6, 15–18 months, 4–6 years
♦ **Hepatitis B:**
birth, 1–2 months, 4 months, 6–18 months
♦ **Measles, mumps, rubella (MMR):**
12–15 months, 4–6 years
♦ **Haemophilus influenza type b (Hib):**
2, 4, 6 months, 12–15 months
♦ **Pneumococcal conjugate (PCV):**
2, 4, 6 months, 12–15 months
♦ **Rotavirus (RV):**
2, 4, 6 months
♦ **Varicella (chickenpox):**
12–15 months, 4–6 years.
♦ **Hepatitis A:**
6 months, 12–23 months
♦ **Human papillomavirus (HPV):**
11–12 years
♦ **Meningococcal conjugate (MCV):**
11–12 years (important for university students)
♦ **Influenza:**
fall and winter from 6 months onward (For further information, go to www.immunize.org or www.cdc.gov/vaccines/)

products. Shops are located throughout the city. Website: www.nefertaribodycare.com.

Nannies

Raising children with the help of a nanny is a real perk while living in Egypt, although hiring the perfect nanny is a different matter altogether. Be prepared to interview several candidates and always ask for references. Decide what is important for the nanny's duties, for example, language skills, working hours, education. Make it known from the start of the interview process that you require a 'clean bill of health' from YOUR doctor before final hiring takes place. You need to trust that this person will provide the utmost care and safety for your child. Nannies in Egypt might be Egyptian, but they are more likely to be Asian or from sub-Saharan Africa. There is no standard wage; the salary will depend on the hours, qualifications, and duties, and can range from $300 to $500 a month.

The Expat Service is a recruitment agency for nannies. Their office is located at 51 Road 9, Maadi. Hours: Sunday to Thursday 10:00 a.m.–8:00 p.m. and Saturday noon–6:00 p.m. Tel: 0111-209-0902. E-mail: info@expat-service.net. Website: www.expat-service.net. Also, for information on hiring a nanny, check the Community Service Association (CSA) website: www.livinginegypt.org

Exercise, Fitness, and Wellness

Stress can creep into our lives at any time and any place. There are many factors that contribute to stress, including external events, attitudes about life, emotional issues, poor social support, unhealthy lifestyles, and moving to a new country. The causes of stress vary from person to person. Everyone has a point at which they have difficulty and experience unpleasant symptoms of stress.

Good nutrition and exercise are the cornerstones of a healthy mind and body. Reaching your health and lifestyle goals is easier when you can reduce stress and cope with disturbing feelings such as anger and anxiety. In this section, you will discover places in Cairo that offer support and promote healthy choices through exercise, nutrition, and even spas for the little bit of pampering that we all need.

To begin, here are a few tips on choosing a health club:

♦ **Accessibility**

Locate a club close to home or work. If the club is difficult to get to, chances are you won't get to it.

♦ **Availability of equipment**

See if there are time limits on cardiorespiratory equipment. Look for a variety of equipment, such as bicycles, rowing machines, stair climbers, elliptical trainers, treadmills, and a swimming pool.

♦ Tour the facility at the time you will be going, to check out the crowds. You want to be able to spend your time working out, not waiting for equipment.

♦ **Atmosphere**

Different clubs cater to different populations. Some are geared for women only or have women-only classes.

♦ Price range

This varies widely. Some give a free first-time visit or month's subscription; others give bonus months or will 'freeze' months when you are traveling.

♦ Cleanliness

Inspect both the locker room and workout area to see if they are kept clean. Also check out the machines to see if they are free of dust and grime. Be aware of who is responsible for wiping off users' perspiration. Is it the user or are there cleaners?

♦ Extras

Check clubs for extras, like a towel service, child care, sauna, steam room, and massage services.

Personal trainers are available at all gyms. You pay a lot of money for an hour's session, so be sure to hire a trainer who gives you their full attention and is qualified. Here are a few tips for choosing a personal trainer:

♦ Educational background

A degree or certification in an exercise-related science is important.

♦ Experience

How long has the trainer been working?

♦ Expertise

Does the trainer specialize in an area that you are interested in, such as weights or aerobics? The trainer you choose should motivate you. Ideally, your attitude should be, "I look forward to my exercise sessions."

If you are keen to get in shape but do not want to hire a personal trainer, invest in a heart rate monitor to maximize performance and achieve fitness results faster. There are many brands, but Polar is the best. There is an authorized dealer in Cairo: 33 Gaza St., Mohandiseen. Tel: 3302-6848, 3305-4260. Website: www.polar.fi/eg-en

Health Clubs and Gyms

♦ Body Shapers Egypt

Kickboxing and customized personal training programs to suit individual needs. Address: 11 Ibrahim Osman St., off Shihab St., Mohandiseen. Tel: 3302-0217/312. E-mail: info@BodyShapersEgypt.com. Website: www.BodyShapersEgypt.com

♦ Body Vibe

Address: Villa 18, Road 214, Digla, Maadi. Tel: 0127-849-9988, 0127-849-9977. Website: www.yourbodyvibe.com

♦ Community Service Association

Address: 4 Road 21, Maadi. Tel: 2358-5284/0754. Website: www.livinginegypt.org

♦ Curves for Women

Ladies only. Gym, nutrition, and diet center. Open 9:00 a.m.–11:00 p.m. Nine gyms throughout Cairo; for locations, go to their website: www.curvesme.com

♦ **Gold's Gym**

Maadi address: al-Mahatta Square. Tel: 2380-3601/9817. Corniche al-Nil address: 121 al-Nile St., Giza. Tel: 3748-0003. 6th October address: MUST University, 26th July Corridor. Tel: 3837-2200/33/44. Zayed address: Hadayik Mohandiseen, Commercial Center, al-Sheikh Zayed. Tel: 3850-7872. Mohandiseen address: 18 Damascus St. Tel: 3303-6663. Lagoon Alex address: Alexandria International Garden Lagoon, Alexandria. Tel/Fax: 03-380-1600. Website: www.golds gymegypt.com

♦ **Oxygen**

Open twenty-four hours. Coed. Specializes in personalized fitness training. There is a private jacuzzi, sauna, steam room, massage, and Moroccan bath therapy. Address: 5 Amman Square, Dokki. Tel: 3336-5894.

♦ **Pro Center**

Affordable rates with good-quality equipment, nutrition and diet center, swimming pool, spa, rehabilitation, and physiotherapy. There are branches in Zamalek, Mohandiseen, and Nasr City. Tel: 19667. Zamalek address: Gezira Club. Tel: 0100-001-7142/3. Mohandiseen address: 6 Abdelaziz Selim St., off al-Thawra St., behind Shooting Club. Tel: 0100-001-7144/5/6. Nasr City addresses (2 locations): 5 al-Nasr St. Tel: 2260-4926; and al-Massah Hotel. Tel: 0100-001-7155. Website: www.pro center-eg.com

♦ **Reform Pilates Studio**

Stott method of Pilates, as well as yoga classes. Open 8:00 a.m.–9:00 p.m. Address: 15 Taha Hussein St., 2nd floor, Zamalek. Tel: 0122-220-7669.

♦ **Samia Allouba Gym, Dance, and Fitness Centers**

Samia Allouba is highly respected and considered *the* Egyptian exercise guru, as she was the first to open fitness centers in Cairo. Maadi addresses (2 branches): Shell Gym: 206 Shell Building, 40 Road 254, Digla. Tel: 2520-2599/2474, 0122-910-1914. Digla (includes a Ladies Only program): 13B Road 254, Digla. Tel: 2519-6575/8378. Mohandiseen address (includes a Ladies Only program): 3 Amr St., off Syria St., Mohandiseen. Tel: 3302-0571/2, 0100-538-2821. Heliopolis address: Smash Academy, behind Novotel Hotel, Cairo International Airport. Tel: 2267-0467/779; Mobile: 0122-809-9844. Website: www.samiaalloubacenter.com

♦ **Shake 'n' Shape**

Pilates, aerobics, dance, health, and fitness classes. Address: Heliopolis, 4 Mustafa Misharaha St., off Mirghani St. Tel: 2414-1521, 0100-628-1010. E-mail: info@shaken shapestudio.com. Website: http://www.shakenshapestudio.com

♦ **Smart Gym**

Open 24 hours. Women's programs offer postpartum fitness program, nutrition advice, aerobic classes, trainers, massage therapy, spa. Men's programs offer body building, aerobics classes, martial arts programs.

Gentlemen's branch addresses: 29 Muhammad Tawfiq Diyab St., Nasr City. Tel: 2287-7619; and 8 al-Nur St., behind Florida Mall, Masaken Sheraton, Cairo. Tel: 2267-2044. E-mail: men@smart-gym. com. Ladies' branch addresses: 13 al-Sayyid Afifi St., parallel to Nabil al-Waqqad St., Ard al-Golf. Tel: 2290-7921; and 5 Khalid ibn al-Walid St., next to al-Sidiq Mosque, Masaken Sheraton. Tel: 2268-7120. E-mail: ladies@smart-gym.com. Website: www.smart-gym.com

♦ **STEP Center**

Offers aerobics, personal training, fitness education classes, yoga, Pilates, and children's activities. The managing director is Karim Strougo. Address: 8 Dr. Hanim Muhammad St., Rimaya Square, behind Le Meridien Pyramids Hotel, Giza. Tel: 0100-511-1752. Website: http://www.step-center.com

Swimming Pools

Sporting clubs (see chapter 8) all have swimming pools, but if you do not want to join a club and only want to swim laps, most hotels in Cairo offer membership for use of swimming pool facilities. Memberships can be daily, monthly, or yearly. Inquire at the hotel of your choice and remember, proximity to your home or work will be more likely to guarantee motivation. Below is a list of hotels offering membership.

♦ **Cairo Marriott**

Zamalek. Tel: 2728-3000. Open 24 hours. Yearly membership.

♦ **Concorde El Salam**

Heliopolis. Tel: 2622-4000. Yearly membership.

♦ **Conrad Cairo**

Downtown. Tel: 2580-8000. Daily fee.

♦ **Fairmont Towers**

Heliopolis. Tel: 2696-0000. Daily fee.

♦ **Grand Hyatt**

Garden City. Tel: 2366-4885. Daily fee.

♦ **JW Marriott Hotel**

Mirage City, Ring Road, New Cairo. Tel: 2411-5588. Daily fee.

♦ **Le Meridien Heliopolis**

Tel: 2290-5055/18. Daily fee.

♦ **Le Meridien Pyramids**

Tel: 3377-7070. Daily fee.

♦ **Mohamed Ali Club**

al-Saeid Road, Giza. Tel: 0100-568-6000. Open 24 hours. Monthly membership.

♦ **Mövenpick Resort Cairo**

Pyramids. Tel: 3377-2555. Daily fee.

♦ **Ramses Hilton**

Downtown. Tel: 2577-7444. (Best bargain: 2 people at $100 for day use.)

♦ **Semiramis Inter-Continental**

Downtown. Tel: 2795-7171. Daily fee.

Staying Healthy

5

The Benefits of Massage

What exactly are the benefits of receiving massage or bodywork treatments? Massage can:

♦ Alleviate lower back pain and improve range of motion.

♦ Assist with shorter, easier labor for expectant mothers and shorten maternity hospital stays.

♦ Ease medication dependence.

♦ Enhance immunity by stimulating lymph flow—the body's natural defense system.

♦ Exercise and stretch weak, tight, or atrophied muscles.

♦ Help athletes of any level prepare for, and recover from, strenuous workouts.

♦ Improve the condition of the body's largest organ—the skin.

♦ Increase joint flexibility.

♦ Lessen depression and anxiety.

♦ Promote tissue regeneration, reducing scar tissue and stretch marks.

♦ Pump oxygen and nutrients into tissues and vital organs, improving circulation.

♦ Reduce post-surgery adhesions and swelling.

♦ Reduce spasms and cramping.

♦ Relax and soften injured, tired, and overused muscles.

♦ Release endorphins—amino acids that work as the body's natural painkiller.

♦ Relieve migraine pain.

(Source: http://www.massagetherapy. com/learnmore/benefits.php)

♦ **Solimer Hotel, Resort and Spa**
Cairo–Alexandria Desert Road. Tel: 3910-2000. Daily fee.

Support Groups for Nutrition and Weight

♦ **Choices**
A center for lifelong healthy eating, nutrition, and help in weight loss. Call Lynda at 0100-459-8283. E-mail: choicescenter@gmail.com

♦ **Overeaters Anonymous**
A support group for problems with eating too much or too little. Tel: 0111-643-7500. E-mail: Mego77@hotmail.com

Need Pampering?

Most of the five-star hotels in Cairo have a range of spa facilities that offer a variety of massages from Swedish to Thai, and even Moroccan baths. See advertisements in the magazines: *Oasis*, *Maadi Messenger*, or *BCA Cairo Chronicle*.

Hands and feet continually touch and feel the environment; here are a few places to pamper them.

♦ **Grooming Lounge**
For men. Address: 6 Building 1/2, al-Lasilki St., Maadi. Tel: 2519-3028, 014-022-1185.

◆ **Manuela Thai Spa**

Expensive, but worth an afternoon for deep-tissue massage. Address: 23 al-Mahruqi St., Aswan Square, Mohandiseen. Hours: 11:00 a.m.–9:00 p.m., daily. Tel: 3345-6999, 0100-900-1010. Website: http://www. manuelathaispa.com/site/manuela.html

◆ **The N Bar Hand and Foot Spa**

For women. Address: 1 Road 210, Digla, Maadi. Tel: 2519-8762, 0114-715-1504.

◆ **The Nail Spa**

Popular among both Egyptian and foreign women. Address: 21 al-Fawakih St., corner of Abdel Hamid Lutfi St., Mohandiseen. Tel: 3337-0354.

◆ **The Nail Studio**

Address: 35B Muhammad Mazhar St., Zamalek. Tel: 2735-6446.

For a quiet, meditative day, visit Anafora Retreat Center on the Cairo–Alexandria Road. To arrange a day visit, call Sister Sara at 0122-381-2604.

Disabilities in Egypt

Egypt is not organized to support people with disabilities. Cairo, in particular, is not a disabled-friendly city. Though there is progress, for example, the installation of ramps in government buildings and tourist sites, realistically, getting around Cairo on crutches or in a wheelchair is a superhuman feat! Sidewalks are often used as parking lots or are broken and dilapidated. Streets are not much better. At night, sidewalks are not lit properly. It is rare to see disabled tourists or residents venturing outside for a walk, or even in restaurants. If you or a member of your family is disabled, there are few avenues of support, so consider this point carefully if you are moving to Cairo. A word about guide dogs in Egypt and the Middle East in general: dogs are not accepted as in western countries. They are not allowed in restaurants, hotels, or other public places, and are considered unclean and dangerous.

There is a bright side, however. Egyptians are friendly and helpful, and that in itself is a great bonus. Most five-star hotels have special rooms with wide doors for wheelchairs and disabled-friendly bathrooms. There are ramps at major museums and Cairo International Airport has ramps and bathrooms for the disabled. Egypt for All is a tour group with the mission of providing specialized travel programs in Egypt for people with disabilities. You can find out more information at their web site: http://egyptforall.net/

Here are a few websites and organizations that may be of interest to those with various disabilities:

◆ **Autism Support Group**

Contact Reem Samy. Tel: 0100-636-9473. E-mail: rima_miro@hotmail.com

◆ **Deaf Unit**

Address: Under Anglican-Episcopal Church, 46 Amr ibn al-'As St., al-Malik al-Salih, Old Cairo. Tel: 2362-6022. E-mail: deafunit@gmail.com

◆ **Disability Organizations in Predominantly Muslim Countries**
Website: www.miusa.org. This site has many organizations that support travel for people with all types of disabilities. It has a 'Tip Sheet' that answers questions when planning an international trip: http://www.miusa.org/ncde/tipsheets

◆ **Egyptian Federation of Organizations for People with Special Needs**
Address: 32 Sabri Abu Alam St., Downtown. Tel: 2393-0300, 2390-0356. Fax: 2393-3077.

◆ **The Learning Resource Center (LRC)**
Provides diagnostic and educational services to children and adolescents who are experiencing learning difficulties and/or developmental problems. Address: 9 Road 278, New Maadi. Tel: 2516-3965/67, 0122-233-2809. E-mail: info@lrcegypt.com. Website: www.lrcegypt.com

◆ **Sixt London Taxi**
Vehicles have ramps for wheelchairs, but the taxi service is only for foreigners or Egyptians going to and from the airport as it is under license from the Ministry of Tourism. Tel: 19670.

◆ **Society for Accessible Travel and Hospitality**
Website: http://www.sath.org/index.php?sec=1170&id=10484

◆ **Special Olympics**
MENA is an international organization dedicated to empowering individuals with intellectual disabilities to become physically fit, productive, and respected members of society through sports training and competition. Special Olympics offers children eight years or older and adults with intellectual disabilities year-round training and competition in Olympic-type summer and winter sports. Special Olympics MENA serves twenty countries in the Middle East and North Africa. There is no charge to participate. Regional Headquarters address: 35 Gezirat al-Arab St., Mohandiseen. Tel: 2345-5510. Fax: 2345-5514. E-mail: info@somena.org. Website: http://www.somena.org/en/index.html

◆ **VSA Arts of Egypt**
An international affiliate of VSA Arts, an international nonprofit organization founded in 1974 to create a society where all people with disabilities learn through, participate in, and enjoy the arts. VSA Arts of Egypt is dedicated to the integration of people with disabilities into society through skills enhancement and equal access to opportunities in the arts. Address: 74 al-Thawra St., Heliopolis. Tel: 2368-2827. Fax: 2365-0429. E-mail: mbanna@starnet.com.eg. Website: http://www.vsarts.org/x364.xml

Volunteering
If you are interested in volunteering for a charitable group, Egyptian Initiatives (http://www.egyptianinitiatives.com) is a

Staying Healthy 5

website that provides an online awareness platform for the ideas of people driving positive change. Another such website is Eco OptionsEgypt (www.ecooptionsegypt.com), which is devoted to the environmental lifestyle options available in Egypt.

♦ **Académie Francophone Cairote des Arts (AFCA)**
An Egyptian cultural foundation that organizes art projects for Iraqi and African refugees. Their mission is to teach languages by using artistic activities such as performing arts, music, and cooking. Address: 27 Muhammad Yusuf al-Qadi St., al-Mirghani St., Heliopolis. Tel: 2415-6502, 0122-467-3435. E-mails: info@afca-arts.com and afca.direction@gmail.com. Website: http://www.afca-arts.com/en/index.php

♦ **Baby Wash**
A program of Caritas, a Catholic charity. It has a clinic near the pyramids for mothers to bring their newborn babies for a bath and general medical checkup. Volunteers bathe and weigh babies. Contact Community Service Association in Maadi for more information. Tel: 2358-5284/0754.

♦ **Breast Cancer Foundation of Egypt**
Egypt Race for Cure at the Giza pyramids. The pyramids of Giza and the Sphinx were witness to the second Egyptian Race for the Cure on Saturday 23 October 2010; 12,000 people joined in the race for hope and a cure for breast cancer. Website: www.bcfe.org

♦ **Deaf School**
Run by the Episcopal Church in Egypt. Needs volunteers to help deaf and hearing-impaired children with after-school activities. Tel: 2362-4836, 2736-4837.

♦ **Egyptian Food Bank**
Address: 6 Nafura St., Muqattam, Cairo. Tel: 16060, 2508-0000. E-mail: info@egyptianfoodbank.com. Website: http://egyptianfoodbank.com

♦ **Friends of Children with Cancer**
Friends of Children with Cancer and Care with Love have teamed up to create a care center in Wadi Natrun. The Health and Hope Oasis brings professionals in nutrition and recreation to provide programs for children with cancer.

Friends of Children with Cancer: 12 Mar'ashli St., Zamalek. Tel: 0122-216-4893. Website: http://www.hhoasis.org

Care with Love: 44B Tal'at Harb St., Downtown. Tel: 0122-2578-7594. Website: www.cwlegypt.org

For more information about Health and Hope Oasis: Dr. Magda Iskander, Friends of Children with Cancer, Tel: 0122-377-2307. E-mail: magda.iskander@gmail.com; or Faisa Khalick, Care with Love, Tel: 0122-216-4893. E-mail: fakhalick@yahoo.com

♦ **Al Ghad**
The Cairo office helps street children, and volunteers teach or prepare food. Contact Dr. Luciano Derdoscia, tel:

0122-778-235, e-mail: luder56@hotmail.com; or Shereen Tolba, e-mail: shereen_tolba@ hotmail.com

♦ **Hope Village Society**
Cares for street children. Address: 21 Ahmad al-Khashab St., behind EgyptAir offices, Nasr City. Tel: 2272-4563, 2274-5199. Website: www.egyhopevillage.com

♦ **Mother and Child Magazine**
This magazine has extensive listings for charitable organizations and special-needs services. Available at Diwan or http://mother-and-child.net

♦ **Mother Teresa's Orphanage**
In Muqattam. Sponsored by the Roman Catholic Church. Volunteers play with the children, feed and change them. Address: Missionaries of Charity, 43 Kamil Sidki St., Fagalah, Cairo. Tel: 2590-4326. For general information, see the website: www.motherteresa.org

♦ **Resala Charity Organization**
The first organization in Egypt based on volunteers. It serves children who live in orphanages. Address: 24 al-Madina al-Munawwara St., off Muhyi al-Din Abu al-Izz St., Mohandiseen. Tel: 19450, 3337-3658/7714, 3336-0064. E-mail: raselna@resala.org. Website: http://www.resala.org

♦ **Spirit of Giving**
Spirit of Giving Charity Gift Catalog presents a wonderful opportunity to contribute in a positive and tangible way toward relieving suffering and encouraging a brighter future for those facing tremendous challenges. Website: www.maadichurch.org/spiritofgiving

♦ **St. Andrew's Refugee Ministry Adult and Children's Education Program**
Needs volunteers to teach English and computers to adult refugees and the full English school curriculum to children. Tel: 2575-9451. E-mail: standrews.volunteer@gmail.com

The local free newsletter in Maadi, the *Maadi Messenger*, lists other opportunities to help as the need arises, as does the *Oasis* magazine from Community Service Association in Maadi.

Finally, you can volunteer to help out at your children's school and get to know other parents at the same time.

Staying Healthy 5

6
Working in Egypt

What brings people to Egypt? Tourism, mainly, and study, of course, but for thousands of expatriates it is work. Possibly you have come with a company, work at an embassy, or teach at one of the many schools or universities, or perhaps you are an entrepreneur. Whatever the reason for your sojourn in Egypt, this section will help you become familiar with the way that business is conducted, though it barely scratches the surface of all there is to know about working in Egypt. The most important point to remember is that you should always seek out professional advice.

Since the Egyptian Revolution on 25 January, 2011, change and uncertainty have been major concerns for businesses and the workforce. With the change of government, uncertainty in policy promotes sluggishness in the country's economy. Keep in mind that the economic and political environment in Egypt and the Middle East is fluid: businesses are struggling, job opportunities are not abundant, and security is an issue. Information can change without notice.

Investing in Egypt

It has become increasingly easier for foreigners to invest in Egypt over the past ten years. Although Egypt does not have the reputation of being as investor-friendly as some of the Gulf states, nevertheless there has been great progress in encouraging foreign and local business ventures. In 2007, Egypt was the fortieth country to ratify the Organisation for Economic Co-operation and Development (OECD) Declaration on International Investment and Multinational Enterprise. The Declaration is "a way for governments to commit to improving their investment climates, ensuring equal treatment for foreign and domestic investors and encouraging the positive contribtions that multinational companies bring to economic and social progress." Over the past several years the Egyptian government has overhauled the framework that governed investments. Establishing new businesses has become more streamlined and straightforward. Now, foreign investors can own 100 percent of companies, and mechanisms are in place for profit and dividend repatriation and dispute resolution. There are

Working in Egypt 6

transparency laws, consumer protection laws, and a new commercial court system.

The OECD provides a list of procedures for establishing an enterprise in Egypt and registering a foreign company:

♦ An application to the Head of Registration for Commercial Investment.

♦ A photocopy of the constitutive structure of the head office.

♦ A copy of the head company resolution to assign a manager for the branch in Egypt.

♦ A copy of the head company declaration of having no previous branch in Egypt.

♦ A bank certificate proving the transfer of an amount of hard currency equal to LE5,000 under the branch name.

♦ A copy of the possession or lease contract for the place of business, or the notarized and stamped contract.

♦ The approvals of the concerned ministry, according to the company's activity and the Ministry of Supply.

♦ An Arabic version of all documents should be endorsed by the Egyptian embassy.

(Source: "Egypt" by Michael Victor Gestrin, Organisation for Economic Co-operation and Development, www.oecd.org)

Registration of an enterprise or foreign company is done at the General Authority for Investment (GAFI) headquarters in Nasr City, Cairo, http://www.gafinet.org/english/Pages/default.aspx. The Commercial Registry Aurthority (CRA) Office at GAFI Cairo is at 3 Salah Salim Street, 2nd floor, Nasr City. Tel (CRA): 2263-3790. Tel (GAFI): 2405-5452/5604. CRA offices outside of Cairo can be found in Ismailiya at Cordoba Tower, before the Court Building. Tel: 064-335-3487; in Asyut at General Governorate Building, 4th floor. Tel: 088-229-3225/6; and in Alexandria at the Free Zone, al-Ameria. Tel: 03-449-3664/5.

Opening a Business

The first and most important step in opening a business in Egypt is hiring a local lawyer who is fluent in your language. A good lawyer will save you time and money in the long run, and help you navigate government regulations. Similarly, hiring an Egyptian business agent may seem to be an added expense, but it might save much more in the long run. A business agent can help make contacts and provide advice on business culture. No matter what kind of assistance you have, patience is the most important quality that you will need.

Business Etiquette

♦ The private business work week is from Sunday through Thursday. Arabic is the main language, but English and French are widely spoken. All written legal documents should be in Arabic, and if in another language, translated into Arabic and notarized at your embassy.

♦ Men and women should dress modestly in the office and for business meetings. A handshake is appropriate between men and between women. Greetings between men and women are more modest; to be on the safe side, if you are a man, it is bet-

How to Find Out and Networking

♦ **American Chamber of Commerce in Egypt** (AmCham). Publications include *Business Monthly*, *The Report Egypt*, and *Egypt Watch Bulletin*. Website, "Doing Business in Egypt": http://www.amcham. org.eg/resources_publications/trade_resources/dbe/

♦ *Business Monthly*: for more information, contact the Publications Department. Tel: 3338-1050; Direct: 3338-9890. E-mail: publications@amcham.org.eg

♦ *The Report Egypt 2010*: considered one of the most comprehensive economic, political, social, and business reviews on Egypt. To order a copy of *The Report: Egypt 2010*, contact Dina Nehad. E-mail: dnehad@amcham.org.eg

♦ *Egypt Watch Bulletin*: Bi-monthly bulletin on economic and business events in Egypt. The bulletin covers different sectors, including economy, IT and telecommunications, energy, finance, and industry. Website: http://www.am cham.org.eg/resources_publications/publications/

♦ *Business Today* magazine. Website: http://www.businesstodayegypt.com

♦ **Egypt 2010 MDG Report**, "Egypt's Progress Toward Achieving, 2010." Website: http://www.undp.org.eg/Portals/0/MDG/20 10%20MDGR_English_R5.pdf

♦ **Egypt Human Development Report 2010**. Website: http://www.undp.org.eg/

♦ **General Authority for Investment (GAFI)**. Website: http://www.gafinet.org/English/Pages/default.aspx

♦ **Governorates Directory**. Website: http://www.egypt.gov.eg/english/guide/governorsAll.aspx

♦ **Ministry Directory**. Website: http://www.egypt.gov.eg/english/guide/directory.aspx

♦ **Ministry of Investment**. For investment guide, laws and regulations, and economic indicators. Website: http://www.investment. gov.eg

♦ **Urbach Hacker Young International Limited (UHY)**. A business advisory, consulting, and accounting network. Website: http://www.uhy.com

♦ **U.S. Commercial Service in Egypt**. Website: http://www.buyusa.gov/egypt/en/ U.S. CommercialServiceEgypt

♦ *Your Legal Guide to Egypt: You and the Egyptian Law* by Eslam Danbel. Website: www.eslamdanbel.com

ter to not offer your hand to a woman. Wait for the hand to be offered; a greeting with a nod of the head is sufficient if not. When entering a meeting a common greeting is "Salam 'aleekum."

♦ When seated, do not sit with legs wide apart and do not show the soles of your shoes. This is considered rude. Pointing is considered rude, as well.

♦ Titles and status are important. *Duktuur,* or *Duktuura* for a female, is used for medical and academic titles, *Sheikh(a)* is for a religious person, and *Muhandis(a)* is for an engineer, followed by the surname. You will hear 'Basha' or 'Bey,' which are titles to elevate the status of a person and show respect, and are usually only used among Arabic speakers. If you do not know a person's professional title, address them with Mr. or Mrs. and their surname. Do not use a first name.

♦ At a meeting, business is not conducted immediately. There are a few social formalities that need to be recognized. Ask about the health and well-being of family members or comment on the weather. Tea and coffee will be offered. Accepting this offer will help the meeting begin smoothly.

♦ Expect interruptions during the meeting. Egyptians are accustomed to taking phone calls and dealing with other issues while conducting a meeting. Just be patient and calm, and the meeting will come back into focus.

♦ Always have your business card show your contact details in English on one side and Arabic on the other.

♦ If you are conducting business during Ramadan, remember the work day is short. It begins late in the morning and finishes early in the afternoon. Do not drink or eat during Ramadan meetings. Another difficult time to conduct business is during either of the feasts Eid al-Fitr and Eid al-Adha. Though the former is a three-day official holiday and the latter is four days, it takes about a week for offices to begin to get back to normal.

♦ Egyptians often mix business with friendship. If you are invited to an Egyptian's house for dinner, it is appropriate to take flowers or sweets. Learn as much as you can about the culture and some Arabic phrases. Egyptians respond warmly and encouragingly when someone speaks Arabic.

♦ Study the Egyptian economy and market, and hire a good Egyptian agent to help guide you to reliable businesses.

♦ Send the most qualified person to represent the business. Age and experience are respected more than enthusiastic youth.

Law Firms and Business Service Providers
As with finding a physician, you need to be careful about choosing a lawyer to guide you in opening a business. The firms in the box below are well recognized and established.

Work Permits
Foreign residents working in Egypt must obtain a work permit from the Ministry of Manpower and Migration. The permit is submitted to immigration, and the existing

Baker & McKenzie. In Egypt, associated with Helmy, Hamza & Partners. Address: Nile City Building, North Tower, 21st floor, 2005C, Corniche al-Nil, Ramlit Bulaq. Tel: 2461-9301. Website: http://www.bakermckenzie.com/Egypt/

British Embassy in Cairo Business Services. Website: http://ukinegypt.fco.gov.uk/en/business/contact/

Business Service Provider Directory. The directory identifies legal service providers that can assist in all areas of business financing and transactions. Website: www.buyusa.gov/egypt.

Hassouna & Abou Ali. Address: 2 Abdel Qadir Hamza St., Cairo Center, Garden City. Tel: 2792-4101/2. Website: http://www.hassouna-abouali.net

SNR Denton. Address: 9 Shagarat al-Durr St., Zamalek. Tel: 2735-0574. Website: http://www.snrdenton.com

U.S. Consular Section. For a list of attorneys in Cairo and Alexandria. Website: http://cairo.usembassy.gov/consular/acslist2.htm

tourist or residency is replaced by a work permit visa. A work permit is normally good for one year; extensions require additional fees.

Obtaining a work permit is not an easy process. You will find more information at www.amcham.org.eg. Below is a list of what you will need to apply for a work visa. For the application go to the Ministry of Manpower and Training office at the Mugamma' in Tahrir Square or to the General Authority for Investment (GAFI) and Free Zone office on Salah Salim in Nasr City. You will then need to assemble the following:

♦ Letter from the Work License of Foreigners Department approving your work in Egypt and asking for the visa to be issued, addressed to the Passport Authority and to the competent Manpower Department, the Companies' Department, or the General Authority for Investment and Free Zone.

♦ A valid passport, with valid Egyptian residence status.

♦ Seven passport-size photos.

♦ Two copies of your employer's incorporation contract.

♦ Two copies of your Tax ID card (which you will probably need to obtain from another office—officials at the Ministry of Manpower should be able to direct you to the correct location if this is the case).

♦ Two copies of your academic qualifications (such as university degrees and professional certifications; this can also include letters of reference from past employers).

♦ A copy of the commercial register (from your employer).

♦ Any licenses required for practicing your profession (have both the original and copies, just in case).

Working in Egypt   6

◆ A memorandum from your employer explaining why it is necessary to hire a foreigner rather than a qualified Egyptian citizen.

◆ Approval from the authority related to your profession (for example, investment or petroleum). You and your employer will have to obtain this through the office of that authority.

◆ A representative from your employer who will 'sponsor' your work permit.

◆ Proof of a blood test showing you are free of HIV.

◆ Approval from Egypt's State Security Service showing that you are not a threat to national security or public safety. This can be obtained through a division at the Ministry of Manpower and Training office.

◆ Finally, you will need to pay a registration fee of LE1,000 to complete the process.

(Source: http://www.justlanded.com/english/Egypt/ Egypt-Guide/Visas-Permits/Work-Visas-Permits)

What Kind of Business?

The kinds of business firms allowed in Egypt are determined by the Law of Commerce No. 17 of 1999 and the Companies Law No. 159 of 1981. Laws and regulations in a foreign country are a challenge, but Egypt is trying to streamline the process of opening your own business, bringing a business to Egypt, and importing and exporting. Registration is carried out at GAFI (contact information above). Here are the types of companies that can operate in Egypt. For the most recent information on 'Doing Business in Egypt'

(January 2010) go to http://www.uhy.com and select 'Egypt.'

The World Bank Group has prepared an easy-to-follow, step-by-step document for entrepreneurs wanting to open a business in Egypt. Website: http://www.doing business.org/data/exploreeconomies/egypt/ sub/cairo/topic/starting-a-business

Sole Proprietorship

Sole proprietorship denotes a company with a single owner, such as a small store or kiosk. To be licensed as a sole proprietor, the person should apply to the Commercial Registration Office. Foreigners cannot have a sole proprietorship unless they comply with Law No. 8 of 1997 requiring a minimum capital of LE250,000.

Simple Partnership

This is a company formed with two or more partners. There are two kinds of partnerships. First, a general partnership where all partners are jointly responsible and liable for all business obligations. Second, a limited partnership where only one partner is responsible and liable for the business while the other partners are inactive and their business liabilities are limited to what they invested in the partnership. Foreigners can engage in these types of partnership, but cannot own more than 49 percent of the capital, or sign on behalf of or manage the company.

Joint Stock Company

A joint stock company in Egypt has nearly the same description as joint stock companies everywhere else in the world. It is a "regulated company whose stock is divided into shares, the liability of each shareholder is limited to the value of his or her shares, and the shares can be traded in the stock exchange" (AmCham). The company must have at least three founders and the number of shareholders is not allowed to go below three. The shares can be traded on the Egyptian Stock Exchange (www.egyptse.com).

Limited Liability Company

"The Egyptian limited liability company is a closed company where the liability of each of its partners is limited to the value of his or her shares (called quotas) in the company. The number of partners of a limited liability company cannot be less than two persons and cannot exceed fifty. The shares or quotas of the limited liability company cannot be traded in the stock exchange. . . . If a foreign partner(s) in a limited liability company wishes to repatriate his or her capital out of Egypt, he or she has to sell his or her quotas or liquidate the company (if he or she actually owns all or most of it), deposit the proceeds of sale or liquidation in an account at one of the accredited banks in Egypt, and the bank will realize the required repatriation of the funds, free of any taxes or duties."

(Source: AmCham)

In recent years the Egyptian government has been eager to increase foreign investment in Egypt. Legislation has been passed that streamlines the system for foreign investment. According to GAFI, here are some of the recent reforms:

♦ Fast-track dispute resolution services for all investors.

♦ 100 percent foreign ownership of companies.

♦ Profit and dividend repatriation, dispute resolution, and settlement mechanisms implemented.

♦ Comprehensive corporate governance principles, anti-money laundering, anti-trust, and consumer protection laws.

♦ New commercial court system now rolling out nationwide to settle business disputes.

♦ Incorporation time slashed from an average of several months to only seventy-two hours.

♦ Minimum capital requirements for limited liability companies reduced to LE200.

♦ One-Stop Shops introduced at multiple locations throughout the country.

(Source: http://www.gafinet.org/English/Pages/FactsAboutDoingBusiness.aspx)

Egyptian Labor Law

If you start a company, you will be hiring Egyptian staff, so you must familiarize yourself with Egyptian labor laws. The labor market is regulated by Labor Law No. 12 of 2003. Each staff member must have a contract in Arabic and in triplicate with a copy for the employer, employee, and the Social Insurance Office. Ninety percent of the staff must be Egyptian for unskilled workers, 25 percent for skilled workers, and 5 percent must be of disabled status. Non-Egyptian

6 Working in Egypt

Public Authorities and Organizations

Note: Some government websites may have been changed as a result of the Egyptian Revolution. For example, the websites for the Shura Council and People's Assembly were taken down after the Revolution and at time of going to press have not been restored. However, they may be reinstated after the elections in the autumn of 2011.

Cabinet Information and Decision Support Center (IDSC). Address: 1 Maglis al-Sha'b St., Cairo. Tel: 2792-9292. Website: http://www.idsc.gov.eg/

Cairo House, The Environmental, Cultural, and Educational Center. Address: al-Khayala Road, in front of al-Fustat Houses, Fustat, Cairo. Tel/Fax: 2364-7664/7646/7033.

Cairo Stock Exchange. Address: 4A al-Sherifein St., Downtown. Tel: 2392-1402/47. Website: www.egyptse.com

Central Agency for Public Mobilization and Statistics (CAPMAS). Address: Salah Salim St., Nasr City, Cairo. Tel: 2402-0574/ 3926. Website: http://www.capmas.gov.eg/

Central Bank of Egypt. Address: 31 Qasr al-Nil St., Cairo. Tel: 2392-6108/211. Website: http://www.cbe.org.eg/

Commercial Representation Office. Address: 96 Ahmad Urabi St., Cairo. Tel: 2347-1890. Website: http://www.ameinfo.com/db-3315382.html

Customs Authority. Affiliated with the Ministry of Finance. Address: Ministry of Finance Towers, Tower 3, Imtidad Ramsis St., Nasr City. Tel: 2342-2152/3/4. E-mail: info@customs.gov.eg. Website: http://www.customs.gov.eg/ContactUs.aspx

Egypt's Information Portal. Website: http://www.eip.gov.eg/

Egypt's State Information Service. Website:http://www.sis.gov.eg/En/Default.aspx

Egyptian Cabinet. Website: http://www.cabinet.gov.eg/

Egyptian Environmental Affairs Agency (EEAA). Address: 30 Misr–Helwan Agricultural Road, behind Maadi Sofitel Hotel, Maadi. Hotline: 19808. Tel: 2525-6452. E-mail: eeaa@eeaa.gov.eg. Website: http:// www.eeaa.gov.eg/English/main/about.asp

Egyptian General Petroleum Corp. (EGPC). National oil company. Address: 270 Road 4, off Palestine St., 4th sector, New Maadi, Cairo. Tel: 2706-5345. Website: www.oilegypt.com

Egyptian Government Services. Website: http://www.egypt.gov.eg/english/default.aspx

Egyptian Ministry Directory. Website: http://www.egypt.gov.eg/english/guide/directory.aspx

Egyptian People's Assembly. Website: http://www.parliament.gov.eg/English/default.htm

Egyptian Regulatory Reform and Development Activity (ERRADA). Address: 106 Gam'at al-Duwal al-Arabiya St., 5th floor, Mohandiseen. Tel: 3749-3920/1. E-mail: errada@errada.gov.eg. Website: http://www.errada.gov.eg

Egyptian Shura Council. Website: http://www.elshoura.gov.eg/shoura_en/index.asp

General Authority for Investment and Free Zones (GAFI). Affiliated with the Ministry of Investment. Address: 3 Salah Salim St., Nasr City. Tel: 2405-5452. E-mail: investor care@gafinet.org. Website: http://www.gafinet.org/English/Pages/Default.aspx

Sales Tax Authority. Affiliated with the Ministry of Finance. Address: 26 Ubur Buildings, Salah Salim St., Nasr City. Tel: 2403-4893/6. Website: http://www.mof.gov.eg/english/Pages/ Home.aspx

Social Fund for Development. Address: 20 Muhyi al-Din Abu al-Izz St., Mohandiseen, Cairo. Tel: 3332-2333. Website: http://www.sfdegypt.org

Taxation Authority. Affiliated with the Ministry of Finance. Address: 5 Hussein Higazi St., Downtown. Tel: 2794-4719/7918. Website: http://www.mof.gov.eg/english/Pages/Home.aspx

Telecom Egypt. Website: http://www.telecomegypt.com.eg/English/index.asp

Tourism Development Authority (TDA). Address: Nile Tower, 7th floor, Murad St., Giza. Tel: 3570-3498.

Working in Egypt

6

employees cannot exceed 35 percent of the total payroll of the company.

Taxes

Taxes must be paid in every type of company, whether foreign or local. The tax rate for corporations used to be 40 percent. The government has clarified the tax code and cut the corporation tax rate to 20 percent. Personal taxes have been cut from 32 percent to 20 percent. If your business is operating in the Free Zone (Suez or Alexandria), then you are 100 percent exempt from Egyptian taxes and import duties. Because the rules that govern taxation are changing, it is important to check

144

Multilateral Institutions in Egypt
Arab League. Address: Tahrir Square, Cairo. Tel: 2575-0511. Website: http://www.arableagueonline.org/las/index_en.jsp

Delegation of the European Commission in Egypt. Address: 37 Gam'at al-Duwal al-Arabiya St., al-Fuad Office Building., Mohandiseen. Tel: 3749-4680. E-mail: delegation-egypt@ec.europa.eu. Website: http://ec.europa.eu/delegations/ egypt/index_en.htm

International Finance Corporation (IFC). Address: Nile City Towers-2005C, Corniche al-Nil, Ramlit Bulaq, North Towers, 24th floor. Tel: 2461-9140/50. Website: http://www.ifc.org/ifcext/mena.nsf/Content/Egypt

International Monetary Fund (IMF). Address: 31 Qasr al-Nil St., Central Bank, Cairo. Tel: 2392-4257. Website: http://www.imf.org/external/country/EGY/index.htm.

United Nations Development Programme (UNDP). Address: 1191 Corniche al-Nil St., Bulaq, Cairo. Tel: 2578-4840 to 4846. Website: www.undp.org.eg/

World Bank. World Trade Center, 1191 Corniche al-Nil St., Bulaq. Tel: 2574-1670/1. Website: www.worldbank.org

with the General Authority for Investment and hire a good lawyer and accountant.

Finding Employment
Foreigners in Egypt who want to live and work here have some opportunities to find employment, particularly in the fields of education, development, and writing. Egypt's unemployment is 9.4 percent, which is approximately 2.5 million of the Egyptian workforce.

Teaching, particularly for native English speakers, is often in demand, especially at local language schools. Most professional teachers are hired from overseas and come to Cairo with a package and work permit. There are tutoring opportunities; sign up at several schools and put an advertisement in the CSA magazine, *Oasis*. It never hurts to check out Cilantro's *Central* monthly magazine; it's free, so have a coffee and check out the employment opportunities.

There are two magazines on the Cairo market for employment:

♦ *The Employer* is an English monthly publication listing employment opportunities and employment fairs in Egypt and the Middle East. Address: 4 al-Marwa Buildings, Block 2, Ahmad Taysir St., Heliopolis. Tel/Fax: 2418-9939/49, 0122-322-2144/55. Website: http://www.the-employer.net

♦ *The Trainer* is a quarterly publication that gives an overview of the training courses available in Egypt and the Middle East.

Chambers of Commerce in Egypt

American Chamber of Commerce (Am Cham). Address: 33 Suleiman Abaza St., Dokki. Tel: 3338-1050. E-mail: info@am cham.org.eg. Website: www.amcham. org.eg

British Egyptian Business Association (BEBA). Address: 2 al-Misaha Square (Alkan Building), Dokki. Tel: 3749-1401/21. Website: http://www.beba.org.eg/index.asp

Canadian Chamber of Commerce (Can Cham). Address: 44 Nehru St., 10th floor, Heliopolis. Tel: 2451-0033. Email: info@cancham.org.eg. Website: http://www.cancham.org.eg/

French Chamber of Commerce in Egypt (CCFE). Address: 1 Wadi al-Nil St., Mohandiseen. Tel: 3346-9417/8, 3347-4209. Website: http://www.ccfe.org.eg/

General Federation of Egyptian Chambers of Commerce. Address: 4 al-Falaky Square, Bab al-Luq. Tel: 2796-0606/0156/0157. E-mail: info@fedcoc. org.eg. Website: www.fedcoc.org.eg

German–Arab Chamber of Industry and Commerce. Address: 21 Suleiman Abaza St., off Gam'at al-Duwal al-Arabiya St., Mohandiseen. Tel: 3336-8183. E-mail: info@ahk-mena.com. Website: www.ahk mena.com

Greek–Arab Chamber of Commerce in Egypt. Address: 17 Suleiman al-Halabi St., Downtown. Tel: 2392-1190.

Italian–Arab Chamber of Commerce in Egypt. Address: 33 Abdel Khaliq Tharwat St., Downtown Tel: 2392-2275, 2393-7944. http://www.cci-egypt.org

Netherlands Economic and Trade Division. Address: 18 Hasan Sabri St., Zamalek. Tel: 2736-8752. Website: http://www.ame info.com/db-3301533.html

Working in Egypt   6

(This magazine is difficult to find and is published sporadically.) Call for information on 2418-0594, 2322-2144/55.

Every month Cairo, and Egypt in general, hosts a good number of conferences ranging from medical to yoga to toilets. If you are looking for a job, it would be interest-

ing and maybe a career boost to participate in a conference. For a monthly listing and newsletter update, contact Egy Calendar. Address: 9 Shabab al-Mohandeseen Building, Nasr City. Tel: 2690-3053, 0100-538-5981. E-mail: info@egycalendar.com. Website: http://egycalendar.com

If you are interested in teaching English

as a foreign language, there are a number of centers that offer the RSA (Royal Society of Arts) CTEFLA (Certificate for Teaching English as a Foreign Language to Adults) certificate. If you would like further information on CELTA courses, look at the Cambridge ESOL website: http://www.cambridgeesol. org/exams/teaching-awards/celta.html. The intensive training takes four to five weeks. The cost is around LE11,000. The following institutes offer the training program:

♦ **American University in Cairo (AUC).** Website: www.aucegypt.edu

♦ **British Council.** The course is held at the British Council in Heliopolis. E-mail: CairoCELTA@britishcouncil.org.eg

♦ **Notting Hill College School of Teacher Training, Alexandria.** Teach English as a Foreign Language (TEFL). Address: 6 Syria St., Rushdi, Alexandria. Tel: 03-544-4316. Website: http://www.learn4good.com/tefl/find_tesol_certification_courses1.htm

Companies need native English speakers to work as writers, editors, and translators. English publications on the Internet, newspapers, and magazines are numerous, but the pay may not be good. Development and aid projects often have opportunities to employ foreigners who live locally, but they are highly competitive.

Scholarly Research

Arriving in Egypt to conduct research with-out a university or institution to provide sponsorship will prove difficult but not impossible. Of course, research today is so much easier and in-depth than it was even five years ago, with numerous databases and scholarly research search engines on the Internet. But if you want hands-on research, be sure to bring a letter of recommendation or introduction from your university. Have this translated into Arabic. Public lectures, field trips, and workshops are abundant. All universities offer research in many fields, so it will be a task finding the best fit.

For scholarly research at the American University in Cairo, take your introduction letter to the Office of the Dean of Graduate Studies at AUC. You can become a 'fellow without stipend,' which provides institutional affiliation with AUC and access to AUC's community and services, including the library. The research fee is equivalent to one graduate credit hour, which at writing is $855. If you already have your Ph.D., acceptance of a scholar as a 'fellow without stipend' is conditional upon the compatibility of your research interests with those of an AUC faculty member from a sponsoring department. Access to AUC's library is restricted to individuals holding a valid AUC ID. Eligibility information is available on the library's website: www.library.aucegypt.edu

The following are good places to begin:

♦ **American Research Center in Egypt (ARCE).** Address: Simón Bolívar Square, Garden City. Tel: 2794-8239. E-mail:

cairo@arce.org. Website: http://www.arce.org/ARCE

♦ **AUC Rare Books Library.** Rare Books and Special Collections Library. Website: www.aucegypt.edu

♦ **Bibliotheca Alexandrina.** The Digital Assets Repository (DAR) is a system developed at the Bibliotheca Alexandrina, the Library of Alexandria, to create and maintain the library's digital collections. Address: Port Said, al-Shatbi, Alexandria. Tel: 03-483-9999. E-mail: Secretariat@bibalex.org. Website: http://www.bibalex.org/Home/Default_EN.aspxNew.DAR Website: http:// dar.bibalex.org/webpages/dar.jsf

♦ **British Council, Egyptian Exploration Society.** 192 al-Nil St., Agouza, Cairo. Tel: 19789. E-mail for newsletter: EES.Cairo@britishcouncil.org.eg. Website: http://www.ees.ac.uk

♦ **Cairo Conservatoire.** The Cairo Conservatoire is the primary music conservatory in Egypt, established in 1959. Address: Cairo Opera House, Gezira, P.O. Box 11567 El Borg. Tel: 2739-0157/0077/0073/0088/0084.

♦ **Center for Documentation of Cultural and Natural Heritage.** Address: Smart Village, Km. 28, Cairo–Alexandria Desert Road, Giza. Tel: 3534-3222. Websites: http://www.cultnat.org, www.eternalegypt.org, www.egyptmemory.com, www.globalegyptian museum.org

♦ **Centre d'Études et de Documentation Économiques, Juridiques et Sociales (CEDEJ).** Address: 2 Sikkat al-Fadl, Qasr al-Nil. Tel: 2392- 8711/16/39. E-mail: cedej@cedej-eg.org. Website: http://www.cedej-eg.org/. Also, La Médiathèque à Mounira, 1 Madrasat al-Huquq al-Firinsiya St., Munira. Tel: 2794-7679/4095. E-mail: medcaire@cfcc-eg.org

♦ **Dar al-Kutub at Bab al-Khalq.** Rare and precious manuscripts. Address: Ahmad Mahir Square, Cairo. Tel 2398-8973/2393-8656. Website: http://www.darelkotob.gov.eg

♦ **Egyptian Center for Economics Studies (ECES).** Address: Nile City, North Tower, 8th floor, Corniche al-Nil, Cairo. Tel: 2461-9037. Website: http://www.eces.org.eg/

♦ **Egyptian Library Network.** Enables users to search the Egyptian libraries' databases via the Internet. It includes Egyptian university library networks, libraries in Egypt, union catalogs, publishers' directory, and librarians' directory. Website: http://www.egyptlib.net.eg/Site/Home.aspx

♦ **European Commission.** Address: 37 Gam'at al-Duwal al-Arabiya St., al-Fuad Office Building, 11th floor, Mohandiseen. Tel: 3749-4680. Website: http://ec.europa.eu/delegations/egypt/index_en.htm

Working in Egypt   6

♦ **Ford Foundation.** Ford Foundation in Cairo focuses on Egypt and the Middle East by funding efforts to strengthen the rule of law and human rights, public health, freedom of expression, and higher educational opportunities. Address: P.O. Box 2344, Cairo. Tel: 2795-2121. E-mail: ford-cairo@ fordfoundation.org. Website: http://www. fordfoundation.org/regions/middle-east-and-north-africa

♦ **Fulbright Commission in Egypt.** "The Binational Fulbright Commission in Egypt was established in 1949, and is the oldest and largest Fulbright program in the Arab world. Since 1949 nearly 5,000 scholars have been American Fulbrighters in Egypt or Egyptian Fulbrighters in the United States. Now in its sixth decade of operation, the Commission pursues an unchanged mandate: to cultivate mutual understanding by nourishing mutual educational exchange" (Bilateral Fulbright Commission in Egypt website). Address: 21 Amir St., al-Misaha, Dokki. Tel: 3335-9717/ 7978, 3762-6307/6305, 3797-2321/2216. Website: http://www.fulbright-egypt.org

♦ **German Archaeological Institute.** The reference library comprises some 40,000 volumes and over 300 magazines and journals. The focus is on Egyptology and associated sciences, complemented by an extensive collection of Islamic studies and a superb collection of travel literature. The entire inventory can be researched in the central online catalogue ZENON (http://

opac.dainst.org). Address: 31 Abu al-Fida St., Zamalek. Tel: 2735-1460/2321. Website: www.dainst.org/kairo

♦ **Goethe Institute.** German cultural organization. Address: 5 al-Bustan, Downtown. Tel: 2575-9877. E-mail: info@cairo.goethe.org. Website: www.goethe.de/cairo

♦ **International Center for Agricultural Research in the Dry Areas (ICARDA).** Website: http://www.icarda.org/ IntlCoop_ NVRSRP.htm

♦ **International Development Research Center (IDRC).** Website: http://publicweb site.idrc.ca/EN/Pages/default.aspx

♦ **Institut français d'archéologie orientale.** Address: 37 al-Sheikh Ali Yusuf St., Qasr al-Aini, Cairo. Tel: 2797-1600. Website: http://www.ifao.egnet.net

♦ **Institute for National Planning.** Website: http://www.inplanning.gov.eg/

♦ **Ministry of Culture.** 2 addresses: 2 Shagarat al-Durr St., Zamalek. Tel: 2736-5495; Kitkat, in front of Khalid ibn al-Walid Mosque, Imbaba. Tel: 3748-6957, 3347-6093/6092. Website: http://www.fineart. gov.eg

♦ **Ministry of Environmental Affairs.** Address: 30 Misr–Helwan Agricultural Road, behind Maadi Sofitel Hotel, Maadi. Hotline: 19808. Tel: 2525-6452. E-mail:

eeaa@eeaa.gov.eg. Website: http:// www. eeaa.gov.eg/English/main/about.asp

♦ **Ministry of Foreign Affairs.** Address: until recently this Ministry occupied the Tahrir Palace (originally Palace of Prince Kamal al-Din Hussein); see website: http:// www.mfa.gov.eg/english/ministry/Tahrir Palace/Pages/default.aspx). Call for current address. Tel : 2579-6334/6338/ 6342, 2574-6872/6871. E-mail for general inquiries: internetunit@mfa.gov.eg.Website:http:// www.mfa.gov.eg/English/Pages/default.aspx
Foreigners and Legalization Affairs: foreign.legalization@mfa.gov.eg
Citizens' Complaint Unit: Contact.Us@ mfa.gov.eg. Tel: 2574-8620.

♦ **Ministry of Tourism.** 32 Ramsis St., al-Abbasiya Square. Tel: 2261-1732. Website: http://www.egypt.gov.eg/english/guide/ directory.aspx

♦ **Mubarak City for Science and Technology.** Website: http://www.mcsrta.sci.eg/. (Name may change.)

♦ **National Archives of Folk Tradition and Egyptian Society for Folk Traditions.** Digital data library about Egyptian traditions. Address: Bayt al-Sihaymi (off Darb al-Asfar). Website: www.esft-eg.org

♦ **National Library, Dar al-Kutub.** Research of contemporary and classical titles. Address: Corniche al-Nil, next to Conrad Hotel. Tel: 2575-1078, 2575-0886.

♦ **National Research Center.** Address: Buhuth St., Dokki. Tel: 3337-1362/1433/ 1615/1933/1449. E-mail: info@nrc.sci.eg. Website: www.nrc.sci.eg

♦ **National Research Institute of Astronomy and Geophysics (NRIAG).** Located in Helwan. Tel: 2554-1100/3111, 2556-0046/0645. E-mail: info@nriag.sci.eg. Website: www.nriag.sci.eg

♦ **Nederlands–Vlaams Instituut Cairo (NVIC), Netherlands–Flemish Institute in Cairo.** Address: 1 Dr. Mahmud Azmi St., P.O. Box 50, Zamalek 11211, Cairo. Tel: 2738-2522/0. Website: http://www.insti tutes.leiden.edu/nvic

♦ **Smart Village.** Provides a high-tech environment for IT and telecommunication companies. Address: Building B19, 3rd floor, Smart Village Cairo, Km. 28, Cairo–Alexandria Desert Road, 6th October City. Tel: 3535-2000. E-mail: info@smart-villages.com

♦ **Ministry of Antiquities.** Address: 3 al-Adil Abu Bakr St., Zamalek. Website: http:// www.sca-egypt.org/.
Contact the Ministry of Antiquities:
Office of the Minister: Tel: 2736-5645.
Commercial and Event Permits Office. This office deals with commercial filming and photography permits; permits to hold special events; and special permission to visit closed sites and monuments. Go to Rules and Regulations for more details.

6   Working in Egypt

Director: Mr. Ashraf Salah. Tel: 2736-0468. E-mail: sca.permits@gmail.com

Department of Foreign Missions. Foreign missions and researchers who wish to conduct work in Egypt should contact this office. Go to Foreign Mission Resources for more details and application information and forms (Website: http://www.sca-egypt.org/eng/FMR_MP. htm). Director: Dr. Mohamed Ismail. Tel/Fax: 2735-0629. E-mail: sca_missions2@ hotmail.com.

Office of Cultural Development. Contact the Office of Cultural Development if you have questions about upcoming SCA-sponsored lectures and events. Go to Lectures and Events for more details (http://www.sca-egypt.org/eng/LE_MP.htm) or sign up for the newsletter for current lectures (sca.announcements@gmail.com). Director: Ms. Injy Fayed. Tel/Fax: 2736-0468. E-mail: injy_fayed@yahoo.com or injyfayed@gmail.com

For other inquiries, contact the Office of the Secretary General. *Townhouse Gallery.* Address: Hussein al-Mi'mar Basha St., off Mahmud Basyuni St., Downtown. Tel: 2576-8086. E-mail: info@thetownhouse gallery.com. Website: http://www.thetown housegallery.com

♦ **United Nations High Commission for Refugees (UNHCR).** Address: 17 Mecca al-Mukarrama St., 6th October City. Tel: 3835-5801/2/3. Website: http://www.unhcr. org.eg/

7

Education

ost of this chapter provides information for people who are settling in
Cairo with children and need to
know about the different educational systems available. This chapter also tells how to
find information about continuing education
and language lessons. University students
who are studying here are already affiliated
with a program, but there is a list of private
universities for convenient reference.

Choosing the Right School
The primary concern for any family moving
to a new country is what school their children will attend. The school you choose
will set the stage for your family's overall
experience in Egypt. Don't be surprised
that everything in your family's daily life
revolves around daily school activities—
cultural, academic, and social. If possible,
it is best to stay with the same system the
child is coming from. Most likely, if you
are arriving with a company or embassy,
there is a specific school that people
working there send their students to. Of
course, you will also need to consider
what school system and language your
child will continue in when you leave

Egypt. Couples who are in mixed marriages
need to discuss what cultural identity they
want the children to develop.

There are many factors to consider when
choosing a school for your child, such as
age, nationality, language, and educational
system. For a preschool-age child, being
close to home in a nurturing environment
may be a better choice than the 'best' preschool that is an hour's drive from the
house. (There are mothers who drive their
two-year-old children from 6th October
City to Maadi every morning and return
in the evening, which means hours in the
car for the sake of a rigorous program.)
For older children, consider where your
child will want to continue their higher
education and in which language and
educational system. Academics, activities,
and proximity to home are important
considerations. Carefully decide according to your child's strengths and interests

Inclusion of a school in the listings does
not imply educational superiority over
a school not included.

Education

7

which system to enter, such as British, American, French, German, Arabic, and so on. Above all, be sensitive to the considerable change and disruption in your child's life when leaving their home, their school, and their friends to come to an unknown country and begin again in a culture with different expectations.

The most important thing is to listen to your child. Nursery- and preschool-aged children cannot express why they are unhappy other than being irritable and fearful. These are important reactions to what might or not be happening at their school. Older children will become introverted and overwhelmed, and even though this might be how you are feeling yourself, it is the most important time to listen. Try to look for positive solutions in your advice and do reach out to other parents and teachers. A bit of advice (after raising my three children in Nigeria and Egypt) is that you are your child's sole protector and supporter; never dismiss your child's frustrations. There are many red flags that can signal depression—fluctuation in appetite, isolation, a dip in grades, angry outbursts, and crying, to name a few. Spend time with your child and find outside activities that you can do as a family. There are many ideas in *Cairo: The Family Guide* (AUC Press 2010) that deal with adjusting to and understanding the history and culture of Egypt, as well as an appendix, "Active in Cairo," with suggestions for all sorts of activities and programs.

Some tips to help evaluate a school

♦ Visit the school.
♦ Inquire about qualifications of the teachers, and the student/teacher ratio in a class.
♦ What is the language of instruction? Which curriculum is offered? Are there language classes other than the language of instruction?
♦ Observe the overall environment, that is, open space available, playgrounds, safety, security, medical team, healthy snacks, equipment, library, activities, and sports, music, art, and drama opportunities.
♦ School and community relations—to what extent does the school take advantage of outside events and historical venues, and provide community service activities?
♦ Is there bus service, how far is the school from home, and what is the traffic like?
♦ The American Chamber of Commerce Educational Committee has put together an excellent, in-depth guide, "Choosing the Right School." Visit the website: http://www.schoolsinegypt.com/images/banners/choosing-the-right-school.pdf

The Egyptian School System
Before the modern era, education was administered in the mosque and the madrasa, just as during the Middle Ages education

in Christian Europe was imparted in theological seminaries.

Today, there is both a religious path and a secular path to education in Egypt. The secular path is the route of primary, secondary, university, or technical education while in the religious (Islamic) path, founded at al-Azhar Mosque that was established as a university and mosque in AD 972, students study the same government-required curriculum with the addition of Islamic studies.

The education system in Egypt is divided into three parts—public education, university and higher education, and al-Azhar education. Secular education in Egypt consists of preschools and kindergartens, primary and secondary schools, and universities and technical schools. It is compulsory for Egyptian children aged six to fourteen to attend school from primary to secondary, but many do not. Children often work as an apprentice to their father's job, such as ironing or carpentry. Often young boys work in cafés or deliver groceries. Most students who follow the academic path are encouraged to study engineering, medicine, pharmacology, or commerce. Many graduates who do make it through university with a degree cannot find jobs and end up accepting employment unrelated to their studies, such as tutoring or driving taxis.

The secular Egyptian system begins at preschool and kindergarten. There are three stages of the Egyptian educational system: *al-taleem al-assasi* (primary and

preparatory stage); *al-taleem al-thanawi* (secondary education); and *al-taleem al-gammeiy* (university or post-secondary). The primary-school years are devoted to reading, writing, math, and science. In the final three years of required education, students are put on either an academic (university) or a vocational (technical) track, according to the results of standardized exams at the end of the primary stage. Test scores determine the students' educational future. A good score will award the student the 'Basic Education Certificate' and with a lower score the student will receive the 'Basic Vocational Certificate.'

The national schools are either government schools or experimental language schools. Both teach the national curriculum in Arabic and both have French as a second language. However, the experimental language schools teach science, math, and computer science in English.

International Schools in Egypt

There are nearly seventy international schools in Egypt that provide education with a variety of systems and languages—American, English, French, German, and Dutch language schools, to name a few. Each school usually runs from kindergarten to the end of secondary school. Some have nursery and preschool programs. The majority offer the American or British system and can offer more than one secondary certificate, such as the American High School Diploma, International Baccalaureate, British GCSE/IGCSE, French Baccalauréat

Listings of Schools throughout Egypt

American Chamber of Commerce. A list of American schools in Egypt. Website: http://www.schoolsinegypt.com/ images/banners/directory-of-schools.pdf

Community Service Association. Website: http://www.livinginegypt.org

*Egyptian Schools. A group of lawyers, teachers, and parents have put this website together with the aim of providing better information for parents in choosing a school for their child from nursery school to university. Website: http://egyptian-schools.com/en/

List of private universities. See: http://www.egy-mhe.gov.eg/english/private-univ-e.html

List of schools in Egypt. See: http://en.wikipedia.org/wiki/List_of_schools_in_Egypt

*MadaresEgypt. Search for all schools in Egypt—Egyptian government, integrated and language schools, boarding and private schools, as well as Egypt's international schools. MadaresEgypt also provides information about Islamic schools in Egypt, Azhar Institutes, from nursery to universities. Schools can be searched by subjects, from Qur'anic memorization to karate. Address: 6 Abdel Hamid Lutfi, behind al-Serag Mall, Nasr City. Tel: 2671-6225, 2287-3490/6959. E-mail: info@madares egypt.com. Website: http://www.madares egypt.com/en/madares-egypt

Schools Guide. Guides are available in bookstores and at On the Run shops in Mobil gas stations for LE15. Tel: 3345-8609.

Schools in Egypt website: http:// www. schools-in-egypt.com/.

* Indicates the best websites for information on schools and contacts.

Lycée, German Abitur, and the national diploma, the *Thanaweyya 'Amma*, which are recognized throughout the world. All systems are regulated by the Ministry of Education.

International schools all have an admission process with application. Students from the origin country, such as U.S. children of U.S. embassy personnel, are the first to be admitted. Transcripts from former schools and references will be requested, and possibly an interview with the admissions officer. Be sure to contact the school of your choice well before arrival in Egypt for information on their admission procedure.

Fees at international schools are high, as most of the teaching staff is hired from abroad. Tuition is not the only expense. Usually there is a one-time entrance fee, and fees for extra activities, transportation, school uniforms, sports uniforms, and books. Many companies and embassies include tuition in their overseas salary package, so this is a very important issue to check.

Nurseries, Daycare Centers, Preschools, and Montessori Schools
In the box of school listings you will find hundreds of nurseries, daycare centers, and preschools. Separation of the child from the home at this early age is traumatic for both parent and child. To help find the right match for all concerned, the best reference is from other parents. Ask parents in your company or embassy, ask parents at the school of your older children, go to the Community Service Association in Maadi. Ask and then visit. There are nurseries, preschools, and daycare centers in Cairo that teach in English and French. The operating hours are between 7:30 a.m. and 4:00 p.m., five or six days a week. If this day is too long for your child, ask the school for the hours you want. Your child's needs come first. Fees generally range between $200 and $300 per month, though some charge up to $1,000 per month.

There are only a handful of licensed Montessori schools open in Cairo, and one in Alexandria. A list follows:

◆ **Alexandria Montessori Preschool and Nursery.** Provides three schools: Baby classes for 12 to 18 months; Preschool for 1.5 to 2.5 years; Nursery for 2.5 to 5 years. Address: Villa 30, Qirdahi St., Kafr Abdu, Alexandria. Tel: 03-542-5188; Mobile:

0109-872-8899. E-mail: info@alexandria montessori.com. Website: http://www. alexandriamontessori.com

◆ **French Montessori Preschool Centre EducArt Francophonet.** Address: 6 Abdel Qawi Ahmad St., off Shihab St., Mohandiseen.

◆ **International Montessori Center.** Address: 18 Road 210, Digla, Maadi. Contact Marguerite Richardt at 2516-6407. E-mail: info@montessoriegypt.com. Website: http:// www.pmgmideast.com/imc/index.html

◆ **Montessori International Preschool.** Open: 7:30 a.m.–5:30 p.m. Closed: Friday and Saturday. Ages: 6 months to 5 years. Languages: English and French. Address: Green Heights Compound, New Cairo, First District. Tel: 0128-444-0760. Website: http://egyptian-schools.com/en/nurseries/ montessori-international-pre-school/

Special Education
For families who have the need for special education, it is important to consider the options available in Egypt well before arrival. If possible, it is a good idea to visit Cairo and the schools and centers for children with special needs beforehand. There are integrated Egyptian government schools and sometimes the programs are conducted in English. A list of recommendations to help begin gathering information follows.

If you are looking for schools, there is an extensive list of private for-profit schools

Education

7

at http://egyptian-schools.com/en/—search for 'special needs.' Here are some of the well-known establishments as a place to begin gathering information:

♦ **Advance Learning Center for Autism.** The ADVANCE Program caters its services to children, two years to twenty-one years old, with autism and other related disorders that affect their communication, physical, mental, or social development. Students are grouped according to both age and skill level. Address: 34 al-Nadi al-Gidid St., New Maadi, opposite the New Maadi Telephone Centrale. Tel: 2519-3721/3. Website: http://www.lrcegypt.org/index_files/Autism.htm

♦ **American International School in Egypt (AIS).** The Learning Support Center is dedicated to providing quality education to intelligent and motivated students, in grades one through nine, with a history of mild learning difficulties or academic underachievement due to a unique learning profile. Tel: 2618-8400 ext. 1160. Website: http://www.aisegypt.com

♦ **Baby Active Kinder Care.** Private classes for children with disabilities and special needs. Address: 65 al-Madina al-Munawwara St., off Muhyi al-Din Abu al-Izz St., Mohandiseen. Tel: 3748-8217; Mobile: 0111-765-2186. Website: www.babyactive.net

♦ **Bayty Nursery.** Certified Montessori educators. Fully equipped for children with special needs and physical disabilities. Specializes in language and speech delay, autism, learning difficulties, and Attention Deficit Disorder (ADD). An evaluation and medical consultation are available. Address: 51 Ibrahim Nawwar St., parallel to Ahmed Fakhry St., Hadikit al-Tifl, Nasr City. Tel 2690-1658, 0100-567-3840.

♦ **Center for Educational Resources and Assessment (NAS).** Address: 22 Ubur Bldgs., Salah Salim St., 13th floor, Apt. 6. Tel: 2404-9029, 2402-7047.

♦ **College des Frères de la Salle** (for boys). Has a section for special needs. Addresses: 6 Sikit al-Bishini, next to al-Saba' St., off Ramses St., al-Zahir. Tel: 2590-4740/9765; Bab al-Luq, next to AUC Downtown Campus. Tel: 2796-0300.

♦ **Continental School of Cairo.** A British-style special education school that follows the British National Curriculum; the medium of instruction is English. The school is recognized and licensed by the Egyptian Ministry of Education, and is authorized by the University of Cambridge Local Examination Syndicate (UCLES) to prepare students with special educational needs for the IGCSE examinations under the auspices of the British Council in Cairo. The CSC, wherever possible, will attempt to meet the demands of parents whose children require special education in the following categories: mild to moderate learning difficulties, specific learning difficulties, mild to moderate autism, dyslexia, hearing deficiency, speech deficiency, slow learners, Attention Deficit Disorder (ADD). Address: 7th District, al-Ubur City, Qalyubiya. Tel: 4610-2222/0428/0423. Website: http://www.continental-school.com/

♦ **Dar El Mona.** Rehabilitation center for children with special needs, particularly Down's Syndrome. Support groups and advice for parents with Down's Syndrome children. Address: Km. 20.5 on the Cairo–Alexandria Desert Road. Tel: 3799-0702/3/5/6/7/8. E-mail: darlmona@soficom.com.eg

♦ **The Egyptian Autistic Society.** The society's goal is to provide early intervention services for ages 2–11 that address autistic children's learning and development needs. The approaches, such as social-skills training and behavior-modification tecniques, are designed specifically for autism and communication disorders. They aim to provide a process of change that allows each child to integrate in the community to the extent most beneficial for them. The school is a nonprofit organization. Services offered: Head Start program; assessment and program development; individual and group sessions; integration in mainstream schools; short courses and training; The Saturday Social Club (social behavior); summer camp; The Wednesday Workshop (motor skills); meetings/conferences (new concepts and research updates); newsletter; resource room; awareness campaigns; home support program. Address: 7 Naguib Mahfouz St.,

New Nirco, Maadi. Tel: 2521-6960, 0122-217-7766. E-mail: info@egyptautism.com. Website: http://egyptautism.com

♦ **Egyptian Learning Disabilities Association.** Address: 63 al-Nadi St., Maadi. Tel: 2358-6803.

♦ **Eshraaka Center for Special Needs.** Speech and pronunciation therapy; services for speech delay, physically handicapped, autism, learning disabilities; physical therapy; behavior guidance; occupational therapy; medical consultations and evaluations available. Address: 19 Nasir al-Thawra St., beginning of Haram Rd. Tel: 0100-206-3349.

♦ **Learning Resource Center (LRC).** Provides diagnostic and consultative services for children of all ages who have a broad range of learning difficulties, developmental disorders, and/or behavior problems. They provide assessments, consultations, specialized therapies, and in-service training for schools and/or parents. Address: 9 Road 278, New Maadi. Tel: 2516-3965/3967, 0122-233-2809. E-mail: info@lrcegypt.com. Website: www.lrcegypt.com

♦ **Maadi Psychology Center.** Office hours: 9:00 a.m.–7:00 p.m., Sunday to Thursday. Address: 16 Urabi St., corner of Road 14, Old Maadi. Tel: 2359-2278, 0100-657-0691; 24 hours, call Behman Hospital: 2555-7551. E-mail: maadipc@yahoo.com

Education

7

♦ **MISR International Language School.** Has a school program for the intellectually disabled in English. Address: Beginning of Cairo–Fayoum Highway, after Rimaya Square, Haram. Tel: 2376-9421/2.

♦ **MOVE Children Center.** Specifically for children with cerebral palsy. Address: 23 Road 232, Digla, Maadi. Tel: 2521-2321. E-mail: hhelmy@movemiddleeast.com. Website: http://www.movemiddleeast.com

♦ **NIDA—Society for the Rehabilitation of Children with Communication Disorders.** Address: 30 Omar Za'afan St., off al-Tayaran St., Nasr City. Tel: 2262-6930, 2402-3636.

♦ **Psychealth Team.** Assessment and training services for children with special needs and learning disorders. Address: 13 Road 16, Maadi. Contact: Dina Soltan. Tel: 2358-5509, 0127-852-9814.

♦ **Rajac Language Schools.** Has sections for learning difficulties. Address: Km. 30 Cairo–Ismailiya Rd. Tel: 4477-1528/8, 4477-0821/2.

♦ **Toy Story Nursery School.** Speech therapy and behavior modification sessions. Address: 39 Amman St., off Shooting Club St., Dokki. Tel: 3337-6999, 0122-231-0318, 0111-150-4411.

Studying in Egypt

Study-abroad opportunities are one of the privileges of our times. Thirty years ago when this guide was first published, study abroad was less common. Now, summer programs, high schools, colleges, and universities encourage students to take a summer, semester, or year abroad and experience education from a different perspective. Most programs and schools are associated with particular institutions where students will study. If you are the independent one who is arriving in Egypt without the support of an institution and wish to study at a particular university, first visit the university of your choice and inquire about your eligibility. You will need an official certificate of graduation from a secondary school. You may be asked to have this notarized by your embassy and the Ministry of Foreign Affairs and to have transcripts sent directly to the university. Other standardized test results may be required such as ESL, an English proficiency exam, or SAT (Scholastic Aptitude Test) scores. Tuition costs vary greatly and up-to-date information is best found on the university's website or when visiting the admissions office. University housing is not as common as in the U.S., particularly for female students. Students typically look for apartments to rent and to share.

Student ID Cards

Full-time students and scholars may obtain an International Student Identity Card (ISIC). The ISIC gives 50 percent discounts on air and train tickets, and on entrance fees at museums and Egyptian antiquities. Website: www.istc.com. Cairo ISIC cards from Egyptian Student Travel Services are obtained with proof of student status, a photograph, and LE100. Address: 23 Manial St., Roda. Tel: 2531-0330. Website: www.estsegypt.com

Continuing Education

Living in another country may present the opportunity to explore a specialty or new field, or to become more proficient in your favorite pastime. Learning the basics of Arabic or studying the language of your dreams is easy to do here, with everything from private tutors to formal classes. For example, if your passion is the Italian language, get in touch with the Italian Cultural Center for a schedule of their language classes. If you have always wanted to take up the violin or other instrument, check out the Maadi Music School. Most libraries are now digital, and although in Cairo most books are in Arabic, there are many available in English, French, and German. Don't forget the cultural centers! Many of them are quite active, offering language programs and film evenings. The next chapter, "Your Leisure Time," will provide many more suggestions; the following is dedicated to formal classroom experiences.

Training Programs

♦ **AIESEC.** A student-run organization in more than 110 countries that provides an international platform to enable young people to explore and develop their leadership potential. E-mail: egypt@aiesec.net. Tel: 2520-3149. Website: http://www.aiesec.org/egypt/; or join Facebook: 'AIESEC Egypt.'

♦ **American University in Cairo's School of Continuing Education.** The areas of training are Arabic and translation, business, computers and IT, English, and a Youth and Special Studies division that includes language courses and special programs for young learners. The university welcomes learners of all ages. Working hours: 9:00 a.m.–5:00 p.m. Sunday to Thursday, and 9:00 a.m.–3:30 p.m. during Ramadan. Hotline: 16723. E-mail: sce@aucegypt.edu. Website: www.aucegypt.edu.

♦ **Cairo Music Center.** Lessons are held for all thirty-five instruments that the Associated Board of the Royal School of Music (ABRSM) includes in their practical examination, along with oriental instruments like the *'uud* and the *qanoun*. Singing lessons are included in this curriculum, too. Address: 14 al-Zuhur St., Hedico Masr Complex, off Airport Road, in front of the main gate of the Military Academy. Heliopolis. Tel: 2266-7544/8649. E-mail: cairomusiccenter@yahoo.com. Website: http://www.cairomusiccenter.com

♦ **Community Service Association (CSA).** Offers classes in art, cooking, languages, and photography. Address: 4 Road 21, Maadi. Tel: 2358-5284/0754. Website: www.livinginegypt.org

Education

7

♦ **Contemporary Image Collective (CIC).** An independent nonprofit art initiative founded in Cairo in 2004. CIC's mission spans contemporary art and educational programming that responds to and develops artistic practice, engagement, and discourse. CIC has a special interest in the many roles of the photographic image at large. They provide public projects such as exhibitions as well as courses, workshops, and technical and professional facilities aimed at sustaining strong engagement with this form both in digital and analogue. Address: 22 Abdel Khaliq Tharwat, 4th floor, Downtown. Tel: 2396-4272. For general enquiries, e-mail: info@ciccairo.com. Website: www.ciccairo.com

♦ **Symphony Maadi Music School.** Associated with Trinity Guildhall, London Music College; teaches to international standards so students can continue their musical education wherever they are. Trinity is located in sixty countries. Accredited music syllabuses and exams are available for a wide range of instruments. Adults can also fulfill their own musical ambitions: morning appointments are available for parents who have children at school and evening appointments are available for after-school lessons. Address: 4 Road 275, 9th floor, New Maadi. Tel: 2516-3278, 0100-636-2870, 0106-533-1965. E-mail: maria.harper@trinityguildhall.co.uk

♦ **Tarakeeb Training.** Training in computers and software programs, digital film editing, photoshop, and so on. Addresses (2 locations): 10 Mahmud Badr al-Din, Mohandiseen; al-Mihwar al-Markazi, above Bank Audi, 6th October City. Tel: 3344-8670, 0100-194-2115. Website: www.training. tarakeeb.com

Arabic Language Courses

♦ **Arabeya Arabic Language Center.** 13 Tahrir Square, 6th floor, above Qatar Air, Downtown. Tel: 2578-9732; Mobile: 0122-284-5140. E-mail: info@arabeya.org. Website: http://www.arabeya.org

♦ **Arabic Language Institute at the American University in Cairo.** Offers an intensive Arabic language course for students, businesspersons, diplomats, scholars, and others needing to gain a broad command of contemporary Arabic. Website: http:// catalog. aucegypt.edu/preview_program.phpca toid=15&poid=1737&returnto=475

♦ **Community Service Association (CSA).** For Arabic lessons in association with Berlitz, offering e-Berlitz. Address: 4 Road 21, Maadi. Tel: 2358-5284/0754. Website: www.livinginegypt.org

♦ **Episcopal Training Center (ETC).** Operates under Episcocare, an NGO of the Episcopal Church of Egypt; a place to study English and Arabic in Cairo. They have classes in multiple locations for the diverse needs of students of all levels. Addresses (2 locations): 18 Road 162A, Hadayik al-Maadi. Tel: 2526-7017, 0100-665-0877; All Saints' Cathedral, Michel Lutfallah St., Zamalek. Tel: 0100-665-0877. Website: www.etcegypt.org

♦ **International Language Institute (ILI).** Address: International House, Cairo, 4 Mahmud Azmi St., Madinat al-Sahafiyyin, Mohandiseen. Tel: 3346-3087, 3302-8358. E-mail: ili@arabicegypt.com. Website: http://www.arabicegypt.com

Other Language Courses

♦ **Ägyptisch–Deutsche Akademie für Wirtschaft und Technik.** German classes for all levels. Address: 5 Road 301, New Maadi. Tel: 2518-2182.

♦ **American University in Cairo's School of Continuing Education.** German, Spanish, and French language courses. Hotline: 16723. E-mail:sce@aucegypt.edu. Website: www.aurcegypt.edu

♦ **Centre Français de Culture et de Coopération.** French and Arabic courses. Address: 1 Madrasat al-Huquq al-Firinsiya St., Munira. Tel: 2794-7679/4095. E-mail: Mme Caroline Natali, caroline.natali@cfcc-eg.org. Website: www.cfcc-eg.org

♦ **German Institute (Goethe Institut).** German courses offered, and Arabic courses for Germans only. Address: 13 Hussein al-Wasit St., al-Misaha Sq., Dokki. Tel: 3748-4501/76. E-mail: info@cairo.

goethe.org. Website: http://www.goethe.de/ins/eg/kai/deindex.htm?wt_sc=kairo

♦ **Italian Cultural Institute.** Lessons in Italian for all levels. Address: 3 Sheikh al-Marsafi St., Zamalek. Tel: 2735-8791.

Egyptian Library Network
This lists all libraries and publishers in Egypt, the Librarians' Directory, the Union Catalog, and the Egyptian University Library catalog. Website: http://www.egyptlib.net.eg/Site/Home.aspx

Cultural Centers

♦ **American Research Center in Egypt (ARCE).** Address: Simón Bolívar Square, Garden City. Tel: 2794-8239. E-mail: cairo@arce.org. Website: http://www.arce.org/ARCE

♦ **Amideast Cultural Center.** Address: 23 Musaddiq St., Dokki. Tel: 19263. Website: http://www.amideast.org

♦ **Austrian Cultural Center.** Address: Riyad Tower, 5th floor, al-Nil St. Tel: 3570-2975. Website: http://www.acfc.cc

♦ **Baad al-Bahr Cultural Association.** c/o Mashrabia Gallery. Hosts exhibitions, book launches, and theater productions. Address: 8 Champollion St., Downtown. Tel: 2578-4494, 0100-170-4554. Website: http://www.baadelbahr.org

Education

7

◆ **British Council.** Addresses (2 locations): 192 al-Nil St., Agouza. Tel: 3300-1666; 4 al-Minya St., off Nazih Khalifa St., Heliopolis. Tel: 2452-3395/6/7.

◆ **Centre Français de Culture et de Coopération (French Cultural Center).** Addresses (2 locations): 1 Madrasat al-Huquq al-Firinsiya St., Munira, Downtown. Tel: 2794-1012/7679; 5 Shafiq al-Dib St., Heliopolis. Tel: 2419-3857. Website: www.cfcc-eg.org

◆ **Cervantes Institute (Spanish Cultural Center).** Addresses (2 locations): 20 Adli St., Kodak Passage, Downtown. Tel: 2395-2326; 20 Boulus Hanna St., Dokki. Tel: 3337-1962. Website: http://elcairo.cervantes.es/es/default.shtm

◆ **Chinese Cultural Center.** Address: 10 Ibn Battuta St., Giza. Tel: 3779-8203. Website: http://eg.china-embassy.org/eng/zaigx/whjl/t76287.htm

◆ **Darb 1718.** Address: Qasr al-Sham' St., al-Fakharin District, Old Cairo. Tel: 2361-0511. Website: www.darb1718.com

◆ **Egyptian Center for International Cultural Cooperation.** Address: 11 Shagarat al-Durr St. Tel: 2736-5419.

◆ **El Sawy Culture Wheel.** Address: end of 26th July St., under 15th May Bridge, Zamalek. Tel: 2736-6178. Website: www.culturewheel.com

◆ **Goethe Institute.** Addresses (2 locations): 5 al-Bustan St., Downtown. Tel: 2575-9877; 13 Hussein al-Wasit St., al-Misaha Square, Dokki. Tel: 3748-4501/76. E-mail: info@cairo.goethe.org. Website: http://www.goethe.de/ins/eg/kai/deindex.htm?wt_sc=kairo

◆ **Hellenic Foundation for Culture.** 18 Sidi al-Metwalli, Attarin, Alexandria. Tel: 03-486-1598.

◆ **Hungarian Cultural Center.** Address: 13 Gawad Husni St., Downtown. Tel: 2392-6692. Website: http://www.magyarintezet.hu/index2.jsp?lang=ENG&HomeID=7

◆ **Indian Cultural Center.** Address: 23 Tal'at Harb St., Downtown. Tel: 2396-0071. Website: http://www.indembcairo.com/Web%20Pages/MACIC.aspx

◆ **Italian Cultural Institute.** Addresses (2 locations): 3 Sheikh al-Marsafi St., Zamalek. Tel: 2735-8791/5423; 24 Gala' St., Downtown. Tel: 2576-9146. Website: http://www.iicairo.esteri.it/IIC_ilcairo

◆ **Japanese Cultural Center.** Address: 81 Corniche al-Nil, Maadi. Tel: 2528-5903/4. Website: http://www.eg.emb-japan.go.jp/e/culture_event/index.htm

◆ **Jordanian Cultural Center.** 24 Gamal Salim St., off Musaddiq St., Dokki. Tel: 3761-0145.

♦ **Makan Egyptian Center for Culture and Art (ECCA).** Its mission is to record and promote traditional music in Egypt. On Tuesday and Wednesday at 9:00 p.m. it presents Egyptian oral and traditional arts rarely practiced today. Address: 1 Sa'd Zaghloul St., Downtown. Tel: 2792-0878. E-mail: makan@egyptmusic.org. Website: http://www.egyptmusic.org/index.html

♦ **El-Mastaba Center for Egyptian Folk Music/El-Tanboura Hall.** El-Mastaba Center is located in downtown Cairo and has five regular weekly concerts, two in Cairo (el-Tan-boura Band and Rango Band) and three in the Suez Canal region (Port Said, Ismailiya, and Suez). El-Mastaba Center address: Sweqat Elsabbaeen St., Downtown, off Maglis al-Sha'b St. El-Tanboura Hall address: 30A al-Balaqsa St., Abdin. Tel: 2392-6768, 0122-322-6345. E-mail: info@elmastaba.org. Website: http://www. elmastaba.org

♦ **al-Mawrid al-Thaqafi/El-Genina Theater.** A nonprofit organization for young Egyptian and Arab artists, providing a theater space for artistic expression. Address: Al-Azhar Park. Tel: 2362-5057. Website: http://www. alazharpark.com

♦ **Netherlands–Flemish Institute in Cairo.** Address: 1 Dr. Mahmud Azmi St., Zamalek. Tel: 2738-2522. Website: http://www.insti tutes.leiden.edu/nvic

♦ **Russian Cultural Center.** Address: 127 Tahrir St., Dokki. Tel: 3760-6371. Website: http://www.rccegypt.org

♦ **South Korean Cultural Center.** Address: South Korean Embassy, 3 Boulos Hanna St., Dokki. Tel: 3761-1234/5. E-mail: egypt@mofat.go.kr

♦ **Swiss Cultural Center.** Address: Swiss Embassy, 10 Abdel Khaliq Tharwat St., Downtown. Tel: 2577-4100.

♦ **Townhouse/Rawabet Theater.** Address: 3 Hussein al-Mi'mar St., Downtown. Tel: 0122-390-3834. Website: http://www.the townhousegallery.com

♦ **Turkish Cultural Center.** Yunus Emre Turkish Cultural Center. Address: 13 al-Fardus St., off Shahin St., Agouza, Giza. Tel: 3749-9110, 3337-2357.

♦ **United Arab Emirates Cultural Center.** Address: 71 Shihab St., Mohandiseen. Tel: 3304-9808. Website: http://www.uaeinter act.com/culture/

Education

7

8

Your Leisure Time

Let the fun begin! Leisure pastimes, entertainment, and recreational sports are the small joys in life. This chapter attempts to provide well-rounded and practical information so you can try something new or continue in your passion. Getting involved is a great way to meet like-minded people and to relieve stress. Remember, times and programs change, and groups begin and end. Although we have tried to present the most up-to-date information, any of it can change without notice. From snorkeling in the Red Sea to playing softball in Cairo, from visiting an ancient archeological site to singing in the Maadi Community Choir, there is something for everyone in Egypt. Enjoy!

Where to Find Out What's On
The problem in Cairo is not a lack of activities and entertainment, but knowing when the events happen. Unfortunately, a magazine or website may begin with great promise, but within a year or two it is gone from the newsstands or languishing on the Internet. The following are magazine and newspaper listings and websites that have weathered the years. Some are

not as thorough as others, so if you *really* want to know what is happening in Cairo, consult several in the following list. Some of the sites have news-letters that provide daily updates on Twitter, such as Cairo360: www.cairo360.com; on Twitter: @Cairo360. Other sites have weekly online listings, like *al-Ahram* (http://weekly.ahram.org.eg/list.htm), and monthly online listings, such as *Egypt Today* (www.egypttoday.com) and *Community Times* (http://community timesonline.com/).

The Best Websites

♦ **www.360.com.** The best overall guide to restaurants, hotels, and shopping, with a broad interest in events in drama, art, sports, and music.

♦ **http://english.ahram.org.eg/.** The best online English language/Egyptian newspaper: Al Ahram Online

♦ **http://cairoliveeventsguide.blogspot.com.** The best music events calendar, updated daily.

◆ www.egycalendar.com. The best and only calendar for major conferences: Egycalendar

◆ http://www.ticketsmarche.com/. Ticketmarché, the best online ticketing site to find and buy tickets for concerts, sports, art, theater, family, cinema, and sightseeing. Tickets are delivered to your door.

Galleries, Theater, Music, Art, and Photography

◆ www.aucegypt.edu. A monthly calendar of events held at the American University in Cairo.

◆ www.cairoopera.org. Cairo Opera House.

◆ http://www.ciccairo.com. Contemporary Image Collective. To sign up for exhibitions, e-mail: info@ciccairo.com

◆ http://www.facebook.com/group.php? gid=18766715856. Classical music scene in Egypt. The site posts events about classical music and its news throughout Egypt. E-mail: info@classicalmusic-egypt.com

◆ www.culturewheel.com. El Sawy Culture Wheel. This is a comprehensive cultural center located under the 15th May Bridge on Zamalek island. It hosts art exhibitions, seminars, workshops, musical performances, theater, workshops, awareness campaigns, a library, a magazine, and a radio station.

◆ www.darb1718.com. Darb1718 supports contemporary art and performance.

◆ http://www.facebook.com/group.php? gid=64039919447. Jazz Society of Egypt. Advertises a plethora of jazz-related activities including workshops, lectures, and performances.

◆ www.egyptmusic.org. MAKAN and Egyptian Center for Culture and Art.

◆ www.elmastaba.org. El Mastaba Center for Egyptian Folk Music.

◆ http://www.manasterly.com. International Music Center: monthly concerts from October to June at Manasterly Palace.

◆ www.thetownhousegallery.com. Town House Gallery. The gallery promotes contemporary arts and hosts theater and experimental music performances, film screenings, public lectures, and workshops.

◆ www.yallabina.com. Online reservations at events and restaurants.

Lectures and Trips

◆ **American Research Center.** To sign up for lecture notification, e-mail: programs@ arce.org. Website: www.arce.org

◆ **Egypt Exploration Society.** E-mail for newsletter: EES.Cairo@britishcouncil.org.eg. Website: www.ees.ac.uk

Ministry of Antiquities. To sign up for lecture notification, e-mail: sca.announcements@gmail.com. Website: www.sca-egypt. org

Netherlands–Flemish Institute in Cairo. Website: http://www.institutes.leiden.edu/nvic

Community News

L'Agenda. Download pdf version from Centre Français de Culture et de Coopération. Website: www.cfcc-eg.org

The British Community Association Newsletter. Free from BCA. E-mail: bcacairo@gmail.com. Website: http://www.bcaegypt.com

G mag. An eccentric and zany guide that has been in bookstores for seven years. It comes out every two to three months. *G mag* reviews new and well-established venues, entertainment, and culture events, and has a sharp wit. However, much of it is a direct transliteration of the original Arabic, which can sometimes be tedious. You can find it for now on Facebook, but soon it will have its own website. *G book* is a new publication that comes out twice a year, starting January 2011.

Maadi Messenger. Free every month in stores in Maadi.

Oasis Magazine. Free from Community Service Association. Website: www.livinginegypt.org

Papyrus Magazin. Not free, in German. Website: www.papyrus-magazin.de.

How to Meet Other People
Ladies' Groups and Coffee Mornings
What better way to get to know people than to join a group that has similar language, nationality, and interests? Most of the groups welcome ladies who speak the same language, but they do not need to be of a particular nationality. For example, the Chinese and Turkish women's groups welcome all women who speak Chinese and Turkish respectively. There are groups that begin because of a specific need, but then may only meet for a year. You will find a changing list in *Oasis Magazine* and the *Maadi Messenger*. Below is a list of groups that intend to maintain their group through August 2013, the time of the next update of this guidebook. Coffee mornings are usually attended by women; however, unless the group is clearly labeled 'women,' there is no reason why men cannot attend. To be certain, call ahead.

Accueil Caire (French Ladies' Group). Visit the website: www.caireaccueil.org; or e-mail: caireaccueil@hotmail.com

British Community Association (BCA). Heliopolis coffee mornings held at the clubhouse every fourth Monday of the month (10:00 a.m.–noon). Clubhouse tel: 2291-8533.

♦ **Chinese-Speaking Women's Association in Cairo.** A group for all nationalities who speak Chinese. Activities include Chinese cooking lessons and tai chi martial arts classes. Chinese language lessons are offered to all nationalities. Yearly celebrations for Chinese New Year are organized. For more information, call Mary Lui at 0122-342-2935. E-mail: bam@swissmail.org.

♦ **Club de Damas de Habla Hispana (Spanish-Speaking Ladies' Club).** Founded more than forty years ago with the goal of raising funds to help the most needy in Cairo. Meetings are the first Tuesday of each month at 10:30 a.m., September through June. Contact Cecibel Elshaer at 0122-748-3993, or Rosa America Hernandez at 0100-107-1181. E-mail: Cdhhcairo@yahoo.com. Website: www.cdhh-cairo.com

♦ **Finns in Egypt Association.** E-mail: info@finnsinegypt.org. Website: www.finns inegypt.org

♦ **Heliopolis Women's Coffee Morning.** Welcomes ladies of all nationalities and meets Wednesday mornings. Call Ans Noordermeer on 0106-149-2247. E-mail: langeans@hotmail.com

♦ **Indian Community Association and Women's Club: Annapoorna Club.** The association has a register of most of the Indians living in Egypt and is active in organizing the Indian community festivals such as Dusshera, Diwali, and Holi each year. It also organizes social events and trips, and works closely with the Indian Embassy. Annapoorna Club is an informal ladies' club. Members are ladies married to Indians or ladies of Indian origin living in Egypt. Address: Road 206, Maadi, near Grand Mall. Tel: 0122-451-3434, or contact the Indian Embassy. Website: www.indiaegypt.com

♦ **Indonesian Women's Association (IWA).** Check with Community Service Association for current information on meeting place and time, or check the *Oasis* magazine from CSA (www.livinginegypt.org)

♦ **Italians in Egypt Group (GIE).** Hosts a monthly coffee morning on Sundays. For more information, contact Silvia Pietraroia (president). Tel: 0100-077-0285. E-mail: silviastangalino@hotmail.com. Website: www.giegypt.net

♦ **New Middle Eastern Wives.** Welcomes all women who are married to Middle Eastern men. Meetings are held at the BCA Heliopolis Clubhouse every second Tuesday of the month. Call Marie at 2268-9344 for more information.

♦ **Turkish-Speaking Ladies' Coffee Morning.** Open to all Turkish-speaking women. Call Feyza at 0109-159-1675 or Gamze at 0127-409-0216 for further details.

♦ **Women of the World (WOW).** A non-profit, volunteer-led organization dedicated to furthering friendship through social, cultural, and educational activities. They welcome women from all nationalities. Coffee mornings are on the fourth Wednesday of the month and held at the Maadi House. For more information, e-mail wowcairo@yahoo.com

Clubs
You will have to pay a membership fee to participate fully in club activities.

♦ **Association of Cairo Expatriates (ACE).** Social club for expatriates. Address: 2 Victoria Square, Digla, Maadi. Tel: 2519-4594.

♦ **British Community Association (BCA), Cairo.** Activities include a cricket league, a golf society, a dart league, a pool league, and a quiz night as well as formal balls in connection with special events, such as the Queen's Birthday Ball. There is a restaurant, bar, library, and DVD lending facilities as well. Mohandiseen Clubhouse: Tel: 3749-8870; Maadi Clubhouse: Tel: 2358-0889; Heliopolis Clubhouse: Tel: 2291-8533. All three clubhouses are open 10:00 a.m.–3:00 p.m. weekdays. If you are an expat and would like to receive information on BCA events, e-mail: bcacairo@gmail.com. Website: http://www.bca egypt.com

♦ **Swiss Club in Cairo.** Events, art, and sporting activities throughout the year. A German-speaking women's coffee morning is held at the Swiss Club. Address: el-Gihad St. off of Sudan St., Kitkat Square, Imbaba. Tel: 3314-2811, 3315-1455, 0100-300-9695.

E-mail: swissclb@link.net.   Website: www.swissclubcairo.com

♦ **Women's Association (WA).** Welcomes all English-speaking women. Activities include lectures, trips, tennis, bridge, art and dance classes, and language lessons. Address: 11 Yehia Ibrahim St., Zamalek. Tel: 2736-4187. E-mail: WAC@intouch.com

Hobbies, Interests, Pastimes
Archaeology
Egypt is one of the most exciting and prolific countries in which to study archaeology. There is an extensive list of archaeology groups in the Scholarly Research section in chapter 6. However, if you wish to take in some lectures, put your name on the circulation lists of the newsletters of the Supreme Council of Antiquities (sca.announcements@gmail.com) and the American Research Center in Egypt (programs@arce.org). Both groups have monthly lectures, for free and usually in English. The Egypt Exploration Society (EES.Cairo@britishcouncil.org.eg), and Netherlands Institute (info@nvic.leidenuniv.nl) also have lectures. Both also have libraries.

Architecture
As with archaeology, there are many opportunities to learn about architecture in Egypt. All the groups listed in "Scholarly Research" in chapter 6 have lectures and libraries on the many varieties of architecture in Egypt. *Magez Design* is a monthly publication in English and Arabic dedicated to architecture.

Your Leisure Time

8

Art Classes

Opportunities are increasingly available for art classes of every kind. The only drawback is that many of them are not offered consistently. Two good places to begin looking are the Community Service Association and the Women's Association. For children, there is an extensive list of art classes in *Cairo: The Family Guide* (AUC Press 2010).

Art Galleries

For a list of art galleries in Cairo, refer to the Cairo360 website (www.cairo360.com) which is an excellent place to read reviews and keep up with all the art exhibitions and events throughout Cairo. Also, you will find a comprehensive list of art galleries in *Egypt Today* and *al-Ahram Weekly*.

Arts and Crafts

From calligraphy to pottery, from leatherwork to jewelry making, there are many classes that are offered across Cairo. Check with the Community Service Association and women's groups. Here are a few:

♦ **Art Café.** Offers classes in drawing, painting, candle making, découpage, quilting, scrapbooks, mosaic, jewelry, flower arranging, photography, cake decoration, and sculpture. Address: 62 Road 13, Maadi. Tel: 0122-705-0753. E-mail: info@artcafe-egypt.com. Website: www.artcafe-egypt.com

♦ **Art Zone.** An emerging art center whose mission is to spread awareness, appreciation, and love of art by encouraging cross-cultural artistic interactions and exchange. Adult classes are offered in sculpture, printmaking, studio lighting, abstract art, oil painting, and painting and drawing. Address: 35 Misr–Helwan Agricultural Road, Maadi. Tel: 2526-2319, 0127-604-0293. E-mail: info@egyptartzone.com. Website: http://www.egyptartzone.com

♦ **Cairo Art Village (CAV).** Located in Fustat, Cairo. It offers workshops and classes in pottery, abstract, concept and documentary photography, jewelry design, silver- and coppersmithing, sculpture, traditional Egyptian patchwork *(khayameya)*, traditional Egyptian shell work, wood carving, ceramic clay, wire sculpture, candle making, stained glass, mosaic, hieroglyphic and Arabic calligraphy, illustration, painting, and eco-art and recycling. Tel: 0122-459-5425. E-mail: info@cairoartvillage.com. Website: http://www.cairoartvillage.com

♦ **Community Service Association.** A community center that supports Cairo's international community by providing an array of art activities, language and cooking classes, a wellness and fitness center, bazaars, trips, and tours, as well as newcomer programs. Address: 4 Road 21, Maadi. Tel: 2358-5284/0754. Website: www.livinginegypt.org

♦ **Decoree's Craft Center.** Offers courses in Arabic calligraphy, beadwork and jewelry, leatherwork, photography, painting and drawing, and appreciating Arabic music/percussion. Address: 48 Muhammad Mazhar St., Zamalek. Tel: 2735-4429, 0128-149-0013. E-mail: Decoree.c.c@gmail.com

♦ **Fagnoon.** Offers pottery, carpentry, jewelry making, welding, gardening, baking in a mud-brick oven, and other activities. Address: Saqqara Road, 12.5 km from Pyramids Road, Mariutiya. Tel: 0100-158-6715.

♦ **The Mud Factory.** Offers pottery classes. Address: 261 Sudan St., Dokki. Tel: 3347-3445.

♦ **Wissa Wassef.** Pottery classes. Address: Saqqara, Harraniya. Tel: 3385-0746.

Backgammon
Pick up a rousing game of backgammon at any of the cafés throughout Cairo. However, most of these places are male-dominated and women are not particularly welcome.

Balls
Contact the British Community Association, which sponsors formal balls throughout the year. Website: http://www.bcaegypt.com/. Contact Community Service Association about their annual ball. Website: www.livinginegypt.org

Birdwatching
This hobby will take you out of Cairo to bird sanctuaries near al-Arish, Lake Qarun near Fayoum, Dakhla, and Sinai. Read Richard Hoath's monthly articles, "Nature Notes," in *Egypt Today*. Visit the website about birdwatching in Egypt: www.birdinginegypt.com

Boating on the Nile
Gather some friends and spend an afternoon sailing in a yacht down the Nile. Some yachts have a set price per person that covers food, or you can bring your own and they serve it for you. Reservations need to be made at least five days in advance.

♦ **Christina Yacht.** Maximum twenty-five people. Bring your own food and music. The boat provides water only. Address: 110 al-Nil St., in front of Cairo Sheraton Hotel. Tel: 0122-211-8533.

♦ **El Marquise Nile Cruise.** Run by the Grand Hyatt Hotel; capacity 200 people. This is a more formal arrangement with belly dancer, live band, and open buffet. Tel: 2365-1234.

♦ **Nile City Boat, Zamalek.** A stationary boat which has a private boat to rent for thirty people. You can order from any of the restaurants on the Nile City Boat. Tel: 2735-3122, 2738-8065. No reservations needed, just show up!

♦ **Valentine's Yacht.** Two sizes: thirty and seventy people. They can provide food at LE50–80 per person. Address: in front of Sofitel Hotel in Gezira. Tel: 0122-157-2434.

Your Leisure Time   8

For a longer journey, gather a group and take an all-day trip to Qanater on a government-run double-decker boat. It leaves every day around 10:00 a.m. from the jetty on the Corniche in front of the Radio and Television Union building and costs LE10 for a round trip. You will spend several hours on an island in Qanater where you can walk or ride bicycles and horses. Women should not go alone, but with a group there is no problem. The boat can be "rented" for a group by going the day before and purchasing all the tickets for that trip. There is a 10-person minimum for the boat to sail.

Bridge

The Bridge Group meets every Monday at 9:30 a.m. at the Women's Association Center at 11 Yehia Ibrahim St., Zamalek. Tel: 2736-4187, 0100-631-9888. E-mail: wac@intouch.com

Gezira Sporting Club, Zamalek. Contact Mr. Ashraf Wanas, Bridge Director at Gezira Club, through the Women's Association. Tel: 2736-0328.

Cafés and Shisha

A favorite Cairo pastime is to spend a couple of hours sipping tea and smoking shisha. Cairo360 has put out "The Shisha Lovers' Guide to the Capital" (http:// www.cairo 360.com/article/cafés/180/the-shisha-lovers-guide-to-cairo/). They also suggest that al-Borsa Café, Downtown, offers good shisha for a reasonable price. There are many varieties of exotic tobacco. Be aware: smoking shisha is dangerous to your health.

Calligraphy

International Language Institute (ILI) gives calligraphy lessons from time to time. Address: 4 Mahmud Azmi St., Madinat al-Sahafiyyin, Mohandiseen. Tel: 3346-3087, 3302-8358. E-mail: ili@arabicegypt.com. Website: http://www.arabicegypt.com

Mohammed Hassan and Osman Young can arrange a calligraphy workshop or lessons. Address: Kitkat Studio, al-Alamein St., Building C, 3rd floor, Apt. 39, Kitkat Square, Imbaba. Text Osman for information: 0100-619-9327.

Car and Motorcycle Rallies

The annual Pharaoh's Rally is held in October for eleven days. It includes cars, 4-wheel-drives, and motorcycles over Egypt's tough terrains. Website: http://www.rallyedespharaons.it

For the less adventuresome, there is the Radio Auto Club of Egypt that meets at Victory College Field twice a month. Tel: 0100-169-0402. E-mail: jeklingler@hotmail.com. Website: http://www.racegypt.org

Choir

If you are a singer and enjoy singing in a choir, there are several opportunities to satisfy your passion—the Cairo Choral Society and the Maadi Community Choir.

The Cairo Choral Society is a group of 60 to 70 singers, both Egyptians and expats, that performs great choral-orchestral works of the western tradition. It is affiliated with the American University in Cairo. The current director, John Baboukis, is the Director of the Music Program at AUC. Rehearsals are Tuesday nights, 7:30–10:00 p.m., at Ewart Hall on AUC's Downtown campus, in English. They perform two or three concerts every December and May, usually with the Cairo Festival Orchestra. Contact Catharine Moustafa (membership): butchaya@yahoo.co.uk, or John Baboukis (director), baboukis@aucegypt.edu. Website: http://www.aucegypt.edu/huss/pva/music/choral/Pages/Home.aspx

The Maadi Community Choir, under the direction of Barbara Comar, is a lively group of singers who practice on Wednesday nights in preparation for concerts in the late fall and spring. It is a volunteer community group that has a diverse membership. Since it began in the mid-1980s it has attracted many fine singers from many nations. Contact Nancy at nliou@hotmail.com, Judy at judithvivian2@gmail.com, or Jeanette at jhwill123@gmail.com

Church Activities

Many denominations are represented in Cairo. The best way to find out about English-speaking church services is to contact the Maadi Community Church (http://www.maadicommunitychurch.com/) and/or All Saints Cathedral (http://www.diocese ofegypt.org/english/allsaintscathedral) in Zamalek, or to pick up a copy of the *Maadi Messenger* at stores in Maadi.

Cinemas

Movies are released in Egypt at the same time they are released worldwide. For list-

ings of movie theaters, go to the Cairo Cinema Guide at Cairo360 (www.cairo 360.com), *al-Ahram Weekly* (http://weekly. ahram.org.eg/list.htm), or the "Listing Guide" in *Egypt Today* (www.egypttoday. com). Note that some cinemas charge less for morning shows.

Cooking Classes

From time to time, five-star hotels offer cooking classes along with their advertised food promotions.

♦ **Community Service Organization.** Has cooking classes which are by observation, not hands-on. There are classes offered in many international cuisines, including Egyptian, Thai, and Indian.

♦ **Dina Sarhan.** Cooking classes for professionals or those who just want to learn more about food and cooking. Address: 103 Mirghani St., 1st floor, Suite 2, Heliopolis. Tel/Fax: 2290-3343. E-mail: info@dinasarhan. com. Website: www.dinasarhan.com

♦ **The Four Seasons** and **Grand Hyatt** provide cooking classes at random times.

Couch Potato

Having a quiet night in and watching your favorite movie couldn't be easier than ordering a DVD online and having it delivered to your door.

EGDVD First Online DVD Rental Service in Egypt. Tel: 0122-123-4569. E-mail: sales@egdvd.com. Website: www.egdvd.com

Your Leisure Time

8

Cultural Salon

Cairo Cultural Salon is a group of like-minded expats and locals who appreciate culture. They organize dinners and outings to attend events together. If you are interested you can visit their Facebook page.

Felucca Rides

A felucca ride to end a day or on a Saturday afternoon is one of the joys of living by the Nile. The best felucca spots are on the Corniche in Garden City, across from the Four Seasons Nile Plaza, and in Maadi near TGI Friday. Take a picnic and a guitar; it's a great activity for a group of friends. Negotiate the price before you begin the ride. The driver will expect a tip at the end of the trip. If you decide to go with your lover, do not show overt affection. Consider the felucca as public transportation: the boatman will be very stern if there are any romantic tendencies. Alcohol is not welcome, and if you do bring some, do not offer it to the boatman.

Films and Film Festivals

Egypt's film industry has had a glorious past. For decades Egyptian films dominated the Arab world. The Cairo Film Festival is the first and oldest in the Middle East, begun in 1976. This paved the way for many other film festivals, such as the Children's Film Festival and the Egyptian Film Festival, both held in the spring, or the Animation Film Festival at El Sawy Culture Wheel, to name but a few. Besides this, art galleries often have showings of artists at work and cultural centers present films of specific countries. The Bibliotheca Alexandrina has a dynamic program of films each month. Contact Ahmed Nabil, Film Program Coordinator, Art Center, Bibliotheca Alexandrina. Tel: 03-483-9999 extension 2312. E-mail: ahmed.nabil@bibalex.org. The screenings are free and often there is a panel discussion after the film is shown.

Garden Show

The springtime Flower Festival is the annual gathering of flowers, plants, and garden shops. It is held at the Orman Botanical Gardens in Giza every year from late March to early April, for two to three weeks. This is a great time to buy some new plants and walk around a beautiful city garden.

Motorcycles

Pharoahz Riders of Egypt Harley Davidson Chapter was established in 2003 and has over two hundred members. They ride all over Egypt. E-mail: admin@hog-egypt.com

Music—Instruments and Singing Lessons

♦ **Cairo Music Center.** Lessons are held for all thirty-five instruments that the Associated Board of Royal School of Music (ABRSM) includes in its practical examination, along with oriental instruments like the 'uud and the qanuun. Singing lessons are included in this curriculum, too. Address: 14 al-Zuhur St., Hedico Masr Complex, off Airport Road, in front of the main gate of the Military Academy, Heliopolis. Tel: 2266-7544/8649.

♦ **Music Center.** Lessons for all ages in ancient and modern instruments, as well as courses in singing and music theory. Address: 27 Shagarat al-Durr St., Zamalek. Tel: 2735-2010/3750.

♦ **Sonata Music Center.** Classes in guitar: classic, electric, oriental, flamenco; piano (classical and jazz); oriental lute *('uud)*; vocal training. All ages. Address: 34 Road 9, 3rd floor, Maadi. Tel: 2378-2448, 0122-086-2451.

♦ **Symphony Maadi Music School.** Associated with Trinity Guildhall, London Music College, teaching to international standards, so students can continue their musical education wherever they are. Trinity is located in sixty countries. Accredited music syllabuses and exams are available for a wide range of instruments. Adults can also fulfill their musical ambitions: morning appointments are available for parents who have children at school, and evening appointments are available for after-school lessons. Address: 4 Road 275, 9th floor, New Maadi. Tel: 2516-3278, 0100-636-2870, 0106-533-1965. E-mail: maria.harper@trinityguildhall.co.uk

Music stores selling instruments:

♦ **Distingo Music Stores.** Addresses: 70 Road 9, Maadi. Tel: 2378-0897; 114 26th July St., Zamalek. Tel: 3737-0336.

♦ **El Shams Musical Instruments.** Addresses: 1/4 al-Lasilki St., above Gas Misr, New Maadi. Tel: 2970-1796, 0122-340-9850; 154 Muhammad Ali St., Downtown. Tel: 2393-1758; 14 Shihab St., Mohandiseen. Tel: 3338-8743. Website: http://www.elshamsmusic.net

For music stage sound and lighting, and technical production services for live performances, contact Nando Music Center. Address: 36a Bahgat Ali St., Zamalek. Tel: 2735-0417/1972, 2736-0841. Website: http://www.nandomusic.com/Nando

Needlework
Ans Noordermeer in Heliopolis supports groups who would like to get together to knit, crochet, and quilt. Tel: 0106-149-2247. E-mail: langeans@hotmail.com

Open Mic
Since December 2009 Project Yourself has been organizing monthly 'Open Mic' events where youth from around Cairo come to perform and to see and hear something new. Attendance at these events has increased from sixty people at the first event to 250 by only the third event, all through Facebook and by word of mouth. If you are interested in performing, send an e-mail to Linda Cleary at lindawildfire@hotmail.com. Addresses: Cairo Art Village. Tel: 0122-459-5425; al-Waha (al-Waha al-Nayruziya) al-Muqattam, Middle Hill, 2nd District. Tel: 2792-0878; Darb 1718. Tel: 2361-0511. E-mail: itsyou@nahdetmasr.org

Your Leisure Time

8

Orchestra

The Maadi Community Orchestra has performed for many years under a series of conductors and thus has had the privilege of experiencing many different conducting and musical styles. The last three years have been under the direction of Gary Brand. Since Brand's unexpected death in April 2011, Graeme Abernethy has been the Orchestra's new director.

The Orchestra normally meets on Monday nights at CAC (Cairo American College) to rehearse classical favorites for string orchestra. They perform twice a year, in December and in May, when they join students of the CAC Strings After-school Program at the CAC Theater. Their performances of classic standards, like the *1812 Overture*, have thrilled audiences and inspired young musicians. Contact Nancy at nliou@hotmail.com, Judy at judithvivian2@gmail.com, or Jeanette at jhwill123@gmail.com

Photography

With digital cameras and editing software, everyone can be a professional photographer. Many arts and crafts studios also give lessons in digital photography. Below are two that are specifically dedicated to all aspects of photography. Also, if you need your camera repaired, each group will give reliable suggestions.

♦ **Contemporary Image Collective (CIC).** Address: 22 Abdel Khaliq Tharwat St., 4th floor, Downtown. Tel: 2396-4272. For general inquiries, e-mail: info@ciccairo.com. Website: www.ciccairo.com

♦ **Expert Studios.** Photography and art courses. Address: 11 Road 204, Digla, Maadi. Tel: 2521-3777, 0122-464-3330. E-mail: info@Expert-Studios.com

Film processing:

♦ **Antar Photo Stores.** Address: 180 al-Tahrir St., Downtown. Tel: 2794-0786, 2795-4449.

♦ **Hany Foto Quick.** Professional photographic services, camera cleaning, and repair. Address: 71 Road 9, Maadi. Tel: 2349-4695.

Pool Party

Why not throw a pool party? No pool? Here are places you can rent for the day.

♦ **Plein Air.** Address: Km. 28 on Cairo–Ismailiya Road. Tel: 0100-498-7169. Website: www.pleinaireg.com

♦ **La Villa.** Address: Cairo–Ismailiya Rd., in front of al-Watanya gas station.

♦ **Villa Urabi.** Address: Gam'at Ahmad Urabi area. Tel: 0100-123-3440, 0122-214-8122.

Public Speaking

Cairo Toastmasters Club is a group interested in improving their public speaking abilities. For more information, visit their website: http://www.cairotoastmasters.com

Puppetry
Aragoz Workshop and Puppet Shadow teaches courses in the art of puppetry at Bayt al-Suhaymi. Tel: 2591-3391.

Sightseeing
Egypt is the 'mother lode' for sightseeing. Almost every civilization has passed through Egypt and left its mark. Clubs, groups, and community and cultural centers organize trips for their members. Museums and monumental sites are minutes away from your doorway. All you will need is time!

Sports and Fitness
Belly Dancing
Community Service Association and Gold's Gym have belly-dancing lessons from time to time.

A website is dedicated to belly dancing lessons in Cairo: http://www.bellydance classes.net/egypt

Body Building and Training
For a list, see chapter 5, "Health."

Bowling

♦ **Bandar Mall Bowling Center.** Address: inside Bandar Mall, New Maadi. Tel: 2516-6837/8.

♦ **International Bowling Center.** Address: behind October Panorama, Nasr City. Tel: 2261-2120/2.

♦ **Maadi Family Land.** Address: 11 Osman Towers, Corniche al-Maadi. Tel: 2524-3200/300.

♦ **MG Bowling.** Address: Genina Mall, al-Batrawi St., Nasr City. Tel: 2404-6261.

♦ **Serag City Bowling Center.** Address: inside Serag City Mall, Nasr City. Tel: 2276-0500.

Camping in the Desert
Wadi Digla Protectorate, Maadi. Directions: From Autostrade Highway, go to Wadi Degla Country Club. Facing the entrance, turn left and continue to the fork in the road at the Nissan factory; take the right fork. There is a Wadi Digla Protectorate sign. Continue slowly as the road is unpaved. The entrance is beyond the rock wall. Tel: 2524-8792, 2527-1391. Fees: Non-Egyptians per person LE5, car LE5, overnight LE10; Egyptians per person LE3, car LE3, overnight LE10.

If you are a novice at desert travel, one of the best guides in the business is Hany Amr, founder of Desert Adventures Egypt. Amr is an expert in desert travel and offers short trips to Fayoum, the White Desert, and Sinai. His meals are nutritious and you are sure to have a safe and enjoyable outing. He also offers sandboarding day trips.

♦ **Desert Adventures Egypt.** Address: 23 Road 233, Digla, Maadi. Tel: 0100-190-5999. E-mail: desertadventures@gmail.com. Website: www.desertadventuresegypt.com. Facebook: http://www.facebook.com/n/? group. php&gid=7555251273

Climbing in Sinai

Desert Divers in Dahab organize groups to go 'bouldering'—climbing on short, low rocks without the use of safety ropes. Tel: 069-364-0500. E-mail: info@desert-divers.com

Cricket Leagues

Contact British Community Association. Website: http://www.bcaegypt.com

Croquet

For a rousing game of croquet, go to the Gezira Sporting Club, Zamalek. Tel: 2736-0328, 2735-6000/6.

Cycling

There is rapidly growing interest in cycling in the city.

♦ **Cairo Cycler's Club (CCC).** E-mail: cairo cyclersclub@gmail.com. Website: http://cairocyclists.wordpress.com

♦ **Cycle Egypt.** Website: http://egyptiancyc ling.wordpress.com/

♦ **Cycle Egypt Club.** Tel: 0109-914-4142, 0122-574-5034. E-mail: Cec@cycle-egypt. com. Website: www.cycle-egypt.com. Facebook: cycle egypt

♦ **MTB Egypt.** Website: MTBEgypt.com. For mountain-bike enthusiasts. The website has extensive information, from what tires are best to ride in Egypt's desert terrain to how to get to Wadi Digla. Great information and tips. Website: http://mtbegypt.com

On Facebook there are several groups:

♦ **Alexandria Cycling** (several groups).

♦ **Cairo Night Cyclists.**

♦ **Cycling Tours.**

A safe area for cycling is Wadi Digla Protectorate, Maadi. Directions: From Autostrade Highway, go to Wadi Degla Country Club. Facing the entrance, turn left and continue to the fork in the road at the Nissan factory; take the right fork. There is a Wadi Digla Protectorate sign. Continue slowly as the road is unpaved. The entrance is beyond the rock wall. Tel: 2524-8792, 2527-1391. Fees: Non-Egyptians per person LE5, car LE5, overnight LE10; Egyptians per person LE3, car LE3, overnight LE10.

Bike stores to buy a bicycle:

♦ **Abou El Goukh.** Carries Orbea bicycles. Addresses: 76 al-Gomhoreya St., Downtown. Tel: 2593-2087; Central Spine, al-Madina Center, 4th District, in front of Police Station, 6th October City. Tel: 3832-0945, 0122-414-8004; numerous other stores all over Cairo. Website: http://www. abouelgoukh.com/index.html

♦ **Bescletta** (3 locations). Addresses: 20a al-Khaleefa al-Maamoun St., Heliopolis. Tel: 2453-6664/89; 37 Ahmad Urabi St., Mohandiseen. Tel: 3305-2649; al-Rehab City, Mall 2, beside Casino door, New

Cairo. Tel: 0100-216-8006/8003. Customer service: 0100-120-0094, 0100-120-0093. E-mail: info@bescletta.com

Dance

♦ **Arthur Murray Dance Studio Cairo.** Ballroom dancing. Address: 1 al-Mahatta Square, Maadi Palace, Maadi Sarayat. Tel: 2751-5006. Website: http://arthurmurray cairo.com.

♦ **Scottish Country Dancers.** Every Wednesday evening at the British Embassy in Garden City. 7:30 p.m. to 9:30 p.m. For information call Nelle at 0122-424-8004, 0100-120-0557.

Many of the health clubs and women's groups offer salsa and zumba classes from time to time. Watch for notification. The Community Service Association is also a good place for dance classes.

Dart Leagues
Contact the British Community Association (website: http://www.bcaegypt.com) and the Association of Cairo Expatriates (ACE), a social club for expatriates. Address: 2 Victoria Square, Digla, Maadi. Tel: 2519-4594.

Diving and Snorkeling
The Red Sea has a reputation for magnificent coral reefs for divers and snorkelers. Professional and amateur divers rave about the spectacular underwater scenery. You need to be certified before diving. Sharm

al-Sheikh is the best-known spot, with a coast surrounded by barrier reefs. You will see hard and soft corals, an 800-meter reef wall, mantas, moray eels, hammerheads, barracudas, and so much more. Sharm al-Sheikh has three national parks: Ras Muhammad, Tiran, and Nabq.

Hurghada is the next most popular place for diving and where you will see many varieties of coral and fish. Marsa Alam, Dahab, and Taba are all diving destinations with stunning surroundings.

♦ **British Sub-Aqua Club Diving School.** A club for divers around the world. Divers can join dive trips and enroll in free training courses. The British Sub-Aqua Club certificate is recognized worldwide. Members meet every other Tuesday at the British Embassy for discussions and dive-related entertainment. Call ahead to check or inquire at BCA (contact information under Clubs, above).

♦ **Nautilus Diving.** Address: 4 Omar Sha'ban St., Heliopolis. Tel: 2417-6515.

♦ **Scuba.** Address: 21 Mecca St., Dokki. Tel: 3748-0818, 3749-5717.

♦ **Scuba Fun.** Address: Road 233, Maadi. Website: www.scuba4fun.net

♦ **Scubatec Egypt.** Address: 3 Dr. Hasan Aflatun St., Heliopolis. Tel: 2290-3420.

Your Leisure Time

8

Fencing

International Fencing Academy, Olympic Center, Hall One (fencing hall), Maadi. You will need equipment: fencer's steel-mesh mask, strong protective clothing, and foil. Equipment is provided by the academy only for your first two weeks. Contact Dr. Sameh Magdi. Tel: 2700-3424, 0122-370-4949, 0100-758-3544. E-mail: i_f_academy@hotmail.com. Website: www.internationalfencingacademy. blogspot.com

Golf

♦ **British Community Association**, Golf Society. Website: http://www.bcaegypt.com

♦ **Dreamland Golf and Tennis Resort**, 6th October City. Eighteen holes. Tel: 3855-3164/2.

♦ **Gezira Club**, Gezira. Eighteen holes. Tel: 2736-0328/19/07.

♦ **Hilton Pyramids Golf Resort**, Dreamland, al-Wahat Road, 6th October City. Eighteen holes. Tel: 3855-3164.

♦ **JW Marriott**, Mirage City, Maadi Ring Road. Eighteen holes. Tel: 2411-5588.

♦ **Katameya Heights Golf and Tennis Resort**, Qattamiya. Twenty-seven holes. Tel: 2758-0512/05.

♦ **Mena House Oberoi**, Mena House Hotel, Giza. Eighteen holes. Tel: 3376-6644, 3377-3222.

♦ **Pyramids Golf and Country Club** (al-Suleimaniya). Ninety-nine holes. Tel: 3910-2000.

Gyms and Health Clubs

For a list see chapter 5, "Health."

Horseback Riding

♦ **FB Stables and Amina Stables, Pyramids.** Tel: 3385-0406. Website: http://www. fbstables.com

♦ **MG Stables, Pyramids.** Tel: 0122-311-2582.

♦ **Nadi al-Furusiya.** Membership required to use the riding grounds, but provides riding lessons for non-members. Address: Gezira Club, Gezira. Tel: 2738-1719.

♦ **Zinc Club.** Address: Concorde El Salam Hotel, Heliopolis. Tel: 2622-4000, 2293-1085.

Over the last five years, horse care products and support have become more popular. A new, free publication, *Horse Times: Egypt's Official Equestrian Magazine*, can be found on newsstands or through their website: www.horsetimesegypt.com

Equicare Company carries horse para-phernalia, such as saddles, jump helmets, snaffles, gag bits, breast plates, stirrups, rubber boots, and Chester Boots (sole agent in Egypt). Address: 2 Bahgat Ali St., Zamalek. Tel: 2735-6939. Website: www. equicareproducts.com

Mud Wrestling

Fagnoon provides the mud and you provide the fun. Take extra clothes and go as a group. Call for reservations. Address: Saqqara Road, 12.5 km from Pyramids Road, Mariutiya. Tel: 0100-158-6715.

Paintball Games

Fun for groups, parties, and birthday parties:

♦ **Kee Action Sports.** With obstacle course. One hundred paintball bullets cost LE85, 150 bullets cost LE110, 200 bullets cost LE130. Address: al-Rehab Club, Gate 5. Tel: 0111-307-2722/2723.

♦ **Sodfa Pasha Country Club.** In Mansuriya. Offers a paintball arena that has an obstacle course. Tel: 0106-333-3389. Website: www. sodfapasha.com

♦ **Xmania.** Will come to the place of your choice and organize paintball-related games like 'Capture the Flag.' Requirements are at least eight people and one hundred paint bullets that cost LE100 per person and LE50 for a refill. Tel: 0106-155-3582.

Parkour Training

♦ **Parkour Egypt.** Bouncing off of walls. Website: www.parkouregypt.com (in Arabic).

Pilates

♦ **Community Service Association, Fitness Studio.** Website: www.livinginegypt.org.

♦ **Reform Pilates Studio.** Stott method of Pilates, as well as yoga classes. Open 8:00 a.m.–9:00 p.m. Address: 15 Taha Hussein St., 2nd floor, Zamalek. Tel: 0122-220-7669.

Rowing

♦ **Egyptian Rowing Canoe Federation.** Address: 3 al-Shawarbi St., Downtown. Tel: 2393-4350.

♦ **Egyptian Rowing Club.** Address: 115 al-Nil St., near Cairo Sheraton. Tel: 3748-9639, 3335-9029.

Rugby

♦ **The Rugby Club.** Address: 10 Road 104/161, Maadi. Website: www.cairo rugby.com

Running

♦ **Hash House Harriers.** Website: www. cairohash.com

♦ **Maadi Running Club.** Meets every Friday morning about 7:00 a.m. at Community Service Association for a long run. All ages and abilities are welcome. For times and details call Mohsen on 0100-155-8352 or e-mail: mohsen.a@internetegypt.com

A safe area for runners is Wadi Digla Protectorate, Maadi. Directions: From Autostrade Highway, go to Wadi Degla Country Club. Facing the entrance, turn left and continue to the fork in the road at the Nissan factory; take the right fork. There is a Wadi Digla Protectorate sign. Continue slowly as the road is unpaved. The entrance is beyond the rock wall. Tel: 2524-8792, 2527-1391. Fees: Non-Egyptians per person LE5, car LE5, overnight LE10; Egyptians per person LE3, car LE3, overnight LE10.

Sailing

With the Nile at your feet, learn to sail at the Sailing Academy. Conveniently located at the Maadi Yacht Club, the Sailing Academy provides instruction on beautiful Nile Class boats (this type of sailboat was developed in the 1930s by the British). For ten lessons, the price is LE1,500; for two lessons, the price is LE350. For first-time entrance into the Maadi Yacht Club there is a fee. After joining the Sailing Academy there is no entrance fee to the club. The manager of the Academy is Mohammed Essam.

Or, if you are already a sailor, you can rent Nile Class sailing boats by the hour. The boat holds one to four people. Renting prices per hour range from LE40 to LE80, depending on the day of the week. If you like to race, join tournaments. Check out Nile Crocodiles on Facebook for more information. Tel: 0111-281-8663. E-mail: nilesailing@gmail.com

Sandboarding

This board sport is gaining popularity in Egypt. It is similar to snowboarding, but instead of launching oneself down a snow-covered mountain, one climbs to the top of a sand dune, and down you go. The drawbacks are that dunes give just one descent and after a couple of falls there is sand in every crevice of the body. The good news is that you don't have to spend a fortune on clothing. There are a couple of sandboarding companies: see Cairo360, "Cairo's Weekend Warriors" (www.cairo360.com). Dune Raiders Egypt is to host the World Sandboarding Championships in 2011. Website: http://www.duneraideregypt.com

♦ **Desert Adventures Egypt.** Hany Amr specializes in sandboarding excursions. Address: 23 Road 233, Digla, Maadi. Tel: 0100-190-5999. E-mail: desertadventures@ gmail.com. Website: www.desertadventures egypt.com

To buy sandboards:
Tel: 0100-144-5702. E-mail: surf@surfshop egypt.com or info@surfshopegypt.com. Website: www.surfshopegypt.com. Orders are placed online only.

Softball

Cairo American Softball League. Men's and women's leagues and a chance to be an umpire or scorekeeper. Also Maadi Little Leagues. The Cairo American Softball League Fields are located at Midan Victoria in Maadi, on the campus of Victory College. Playground hours: Daily 3:00 p.m. to 8:00 p.m.; Saturday 8:00 a.m. to 8:00 p.m. E-mail: seatac24@live.com. Website: http://www.caslegypt.com

Sporting Clubs

Egyptian sporting clubs offer soccer, swimming, basketball, volleyball, and tennis. Some have areas designated for roller skating, croquet, gymnastics, billiards, and table tennis. All have areas for children to run and playground equipment. Most have exercise rooms and tracks for walking and running. Although the clubs have membership quotas for Egyptians with a one-time membership joining fee and inexpensive yearly fees thereafter, all clubs do offer membership to foreigners. Yearly fees for foreigners are quite high and, depending on the number of family members, can reach $2,500 a year. Daily use is around LE30 to enter, with extra fees for use of swimming pools and courts. Many clubs have monthly membership fees, so if you are interested in a particular club it is best to call or visit. Be aware that many administrators do not speak English. Most clubs require a residency permit or recommendation letter from work to obtain membership. Below are some membership prices that are current in 2011.

♦ **Al-Ahly Sporting Club.** Two locations in Zamalek and Nasr City. Membership for foreign residents is a one-time fee of LE125,000 and LE300 each year afterwards. Membership for one month is $100 per person. Tel. Zamalek: 2735-2113/4; Nasr City: 2472-5771/6731. Website: http://www.el-ahly.com/english

♦ **Gezira Sporting Club,** Zamalek. Membership for Egyptians is LE140,000, after which the yearly dues are nominal. Single membership for foreign residents for three months: $400; six months: $650; one year: $1,250. Tel: 2736-0328, 2735-6000/6.

♦ **Heliopolis Sporting Club,** Heliopolis. Tel: 2417-0061/2/3/4. Call for membership information.

♦ **Katameya Sporting Club,** Qattamiya. Membership for foreign residents is LE80,000. Membership for six months: LE6,000. Tel: 19714, 2521-8140/1. Website: http://www.petrosport.com/EN/

♦ **Maadi Sporting Club,** Maadi. Membership for foreign residents is LE75,000. For three months: $405; six months: $705; one year $1,200. Tel: 2380-2066, 2358-5455.

♦ **Nasr City Sporting Club,** Nasr City. Tel: 2263-3001/2. Call for membership information.

♦ **Shams Sporting Club,** Heliopolis. Tel: 2623-6460. Call for membership information.

♦ **Shooting Club,** Dokki. Tel: 3337-4333/4464. Call for membership information.

♦ **Swiss Club in Cairo.** Tel: 3314-2811, 3315-1455, 0100-300-9695. Call for membership information. Website: http://www. swissclubcairo.com

♦ **El Tersana Sporting Club,** Mohandiseen. Tel: 3345-0160. Call for membership information.

♦ **Wadi Degla Club,** Maadi and New Cairo. Single membership is LE72,725. Short-term membership for foreigners only. Six months single: $600; six months family: $800; one year single: $1,200; one year family: $1,500. Tel: 19917. Website: http://www.wadidegla.com

♦ **Zamalek Sporting Club,** Mohandiseen. One-time membership fee for foreign residents is LE64,000. There is a membership for foreigners for one year or less; you can call and check. Tel: 3302-6300/33, 3346-6655.

There are opportunities for hotel memberships at JW Marriott, Grand Hyatt, Four Seasons, and Fairmont. The average membership fee for three months is LE3,000; six months is LE4,900; one year is LE7,500. For day use, the cost is around LE650 to LE700. This includes pool, gym, sauna, steam room, and Jacuzzi. The typical opening hours are from 11:00 a.m. till 8:00 p.m.

Swimming
For a list of hotel swimming pools that have daily to yearly membership fees, see chapter 5, "Health." Also, see Sporting Clubs above. If competitive swimming is your sport and you are in training to shave off a second or two in a race, contact the Swimming Academy at Tel: 19734.

Tennis

♦ **Dreamland Golf and Tennis Resort,** 6th October City. Eight courts and school. Tel: 3855-3164/2.

♦ **Katameya Heights Golf and Tennis Resort,** Qattamiya. Ten courts. Tel: 2758-0512/05.

♦ **Smash Tennis Academy,** behind Novotel Airport Hotel, Heliopolis. Tel: 2267-0467/0779.

Walking

♦ **Cairo Walking Group.** Usually meets on Friday mornings when the streets are empty. They also meet in the evening at least twice in Ramadan. For more information and a schedule, contact Muhammad Farag. E-mail: MuhammadFarag@gmail.com

♦ **Tree Lovers Association.** Holds an annual Maadi tree walk. Tel: 2519-5240, 2358-0099. E-mail: ZeitounS@mac.com

Windsurfing
Egypt has sun, wind, and water, which are the three ingredients for this sport. The best place is Dahab, which is on the Red Sea coast, eighty kilometers from Sharm al-Sheikh. Al-Gouna is located twenty-two kilometers north of Hurghada. This is a city

that specializes in water sports! About two hours outside of Cairo is Zaafarana where you can find windsurfing courses and plenty of wind.

To purchase surfboards, skimboards, kite-surfs: Tel: 0100-144-5702. E-mail: surf@surf-shopegypt.com or info@surf shopegypt. com. Website: www.surfshop egypt.com

Yoga

Yoga is spreading rapidly in Cairo. There are private classes and yoga is offered in various gyms. Yoga has a wide range of different practices and different levels, so inquire first and ask to take a complimentary class to see if it is the yoga for you. First look on http://www.yogafinder.com, a website that lists yoga studios in Cairo, Alexandria, and the Sinai.

♦ **Bodyworks.** Address: 29 al-Shahid Ishaq Ya'qub St., Heliopolis. Tel: 2291-6484.

♦ **The Breathing Room.** Address: 10 Road 216, Maadi. Tel: 0127-852-9798 for weekly schedule; 0100-629-2684 for general questions. Website: http://www.the-breathing roomcairo.blogspot.com

♦ **Egypt Yoga Art Studio.** Dokki. Tel: 0122-222-9016. Website: http://www.egyptyoga art.com

♦ **Ki Studio.** Dokki. Yoga and Jin Shin Yitzu. Sessions by appointment. Tel: 3336-3930, 0122-219-8131. E-mail: kshawki@google mail.com

♦ **Maulana Azad Center.** Address: Indian Cultural Center, 23 Tal'at Harb St., Downtown. Tel: 2393-3396, 2396-0071. E-mail: macic@indembcairo.com. Website: www. indembcairo.com

♦ **Mira Shihadeh in Zamalek.** Teaches ashtanga yoga. Location: behind Beanos on Sheikh al-Marsafi St., across from the Italian Cultural Center, Zamalek. Tel: 0122-275-8625.

♦ **Reform Pilates Studio.** Stott method of Pilates, as well as yoga classes. Open 8:00 a.m.–9:00 p.m. Address: 15 Taha Hussein St., 2nd floor, Zamalek. Tel: 0122-220-7669.

♦ **STEP Center.** Offers yoga, Pilates, and a wellness center. They often invite international professionals to lead yoga classes. The SAFE Academy claims to be the first International Fitness Education academy in the Middle East and offers certification classes in yoga and Pilates. The managing director and founder is Karim Strougo. Address: 8 Dr. Hanim Muhammad St., Rimaya Square, behind Le Meridien Pyramids Hotel, Giza. Tel: 0100-511-1752. Website: http://www.step-center.com

Fun Parks and Gardens

♦ **Andalusya Garden.** Open: lower garden 9:00 a.m.–10:00 p.m. and upper garden 9:00 a.m.–5:00 p.m. Tickets: lower garden LE2; upper garden LE10 foreigners, LE5

Opera House and Theaters

More listings in *Egypt Today* and *al-Ahram Weekly*:

♦ **Arab Music Institute.** Address: Ramsis St., between 26th July St. and Nadi al-Musica St. Tel: 2574-3373.

♦ **Balloon Theater and al-Gad Theater.** Address: al-Nil St., next to 26th July and 15th May Bridge, Agouza. The theaters share the same entrance, separated by a café.

♦ **Cairo Opera House.** Holds events ainthe Main Hall, Small Hall, Open Air Theater, Gomhouria Theater, Arab Music Institute. Tel: 2737-0603. Website: www.cairoopera.org

♦ **al-Geneina Theater.** An open-air amphitheater situated inside the al-Azhar Park on Salah Salim Road.

♦ **al-Gomhouria Theater.** Address: 12 al-Gumhuriya St., Abdin, Downtown. Tel: 2390-7707.

♦ **Manasterly Palace** and **Prince Muhammad Ali Palace,** International Center for Music. Manasterly Palace is at the furthest southern point of Roda Island. Prince Muhammad Ali Palace is Manial Palace, off of University Bridge, Manial. Website: www.manasterly.com

♦ **National Theater,** Ataba Square. Currently under renovation.

♦ **Puppet Theater** or **al-Arayes Theater.** Address: in front of Azbakiya Park, next to the Ataba car park. Tel: 2591-0954.

♦ **Rawabet Theater.** Location: near Townhouse Gallery at 3 Hussein al-Mi'mar St., Downtown. Tel: 0122-390-3834, 0100-145-4617.

♦ **Sama' Khana** (Hall of Listening), also known as Sufi Theater. Address: 31 al-Siyufiah St., Helmia al-Gidida. Tel: 2510-7806.

♦ **El Tanbura Hall.** Address: 30a al-Balaqsa St., Abdin, Downtown. Tel: 0100-317-1762. E-mail: info@elmastaba.org. Website: www.elmastaba.org

Egyptians. Address: Sa'd Zaghloul Square, across from the Novotel Hotel, Gezira.

♦ **Aqua Park.** Open: 10:00 a.m.–10:00 p.m., summer only. Tickets: Adults LE60, children LE45. Address: Cairo–Ismailiya Road, near al-Sherouk City.

♦ **al-Azhar Park,** Salah Salim Road. Open: 9:00 a.m.–10:00 p.m. (winter), 9:00 a.m.–midnight (summer). Tel: 19135.

♦ **Crazy Water.** Open: 10:00 a.m.–10:00 p.m., summer only. Tickets: Adults LE70, children LE55. Address: Cairo–Alexandria

Desert Road, Giza, next to 6th October City. Tel: 3781-4564.

♦ **Dream Park.** Tickets: LE50. Address: Fayoum–Oasis Road, 6th October City. Tel: 19355.

♦ **Fish Garden.** Tickets: adults LE2, children LE1. Address: Corniche al-Nil, Zamalek. Tel: 2735-1606.

♦ **Geroland, al-Ubur City** (40 minutes from Downtown). Tel: 4610-3601.

♦ **Giza Zoo.** Address: Murad St., Giza. Tel: 3570-8895/1552.

♦ **Helwan Japanese Garden.** Directions: Take the metro to Helwan. At the exit, turn left, walk four blocks.

♦ **Hurriya Garden.** Open: 9:00 a.m.–10:00 p.m. Tickets: LE2. Address: Entrance at Sa'd Zaghloul Square, Gezira.

♦ **International Garden.** Open 9:00 a.m.–10:00 p.m. Tickets: adults LE2. Address: Abbas al-Aqqad St., Nasr City. Tel: 2263-3033.

♦ **Magic Galaxy Park, City Stars Mall.** Open: 3:00 p.m.–midnight. Tickets: LE2 plus game ticket. Tel: 2480-2031.

♦ **Media Production City (Magic Land).** Open: 10:00 a.m.–midnight (summer); 10:00 a.m.–7:00 p.m. (winter). Tickets: LE50. Address: Fayoum–Oasis Road, 6th

October City. Tel: 3855-5064/094.

♦ **Merryland Park,** Heliopolis. Tel: 2451-2313/5/6.

♦ **Wadi Digla Protectorate,** Maadi. Directions: From Autostrade Highway, go to Wadi Degla Country Club. Facing the entrance, turn left and continue to the fork in the road at the Nissan factory; take the right fork. There is a Wadi Digla Protectorate sign. Continue slowly as the road is unpaved. The entrance is beyond the rock wall. Tel: 2524-8792, 2527-1391. Fees: Non-Egyptians per person LE5, car LE5 , overnight LE10. Egyptians per person LE3, car LE3, overnight LE10.

Entertainment, Restaurants, and Nightlife

Cairo has a vibrant nightlife. The diversity of choice is truly amazing. One evening you can see the opera *Aida* at the Pyramids and on the next night take in Sudanese *zaar* music at Makan. There is an abundance of opportunities to experience every kind of genre from classical to folk to jazz, with local and internationally renowned performers. Many events are free or charge a nominal entry fee. All you have to do is show up!

In 1959 the Ministry of Culture established the Academy of Arts, composed of three institutions—film, music, and ballet. The Higher Institute of Dramatic Arts had opened in 1944 and later became a part of the Cairo Conservatoire. It was then

Your Leisure Time

8

merged with the Higher Institute of Arabic Music and the Institute of Cinema to form the Academy of Arts. In 1981 the Institute of Folk Art was created to include Troupes for Folk Music, the Academy of Arts Symphonic Orchestra, the Children and Youth Chorale, the Academic Troupe for Ballet, and the Academic Troupe for Theater. It is no wonder we have a wealth of opportunities to take in a superb repertoire of world-class performances in all classical fields.

For musical entertainment there is no place in the world like the Cairo Opera House (www.cairoopera.org). It hosts international groups in all genres as well as supporting its own symphony, ballet, opera, modern dance troupe, and choir. If your passion is classical music, join an informal group on Facebook called "Classical Music Scene in Egypt." This group welcomes all classical music lovers and keeps an updated posting about where classical music events take place in Egypt. For more information, e-mail info@classicalmusic-egypt.com.

Another little-known group is the European-Egyptian Contemporary Music Society (http://www.eecms.eu/). The group promotes contemporary music in Egypt and coordinates activities at various cultural institutions. The International Center for Music (www.manasterly.com) invites an internationally renowned classical performer every month. For Egyptian folk music and dance, the places to go are Makan (http://www.egyptmusic.org), El Mastaba (www.elmastaba.org), Bayt al-Suhaymi, and

the famous Tannura Sufi Troupe at Wakalat al-Ghuri. El Sawy Culture Wheel (http://www.culturewheel.com) hosts international as well as local groups. For lovers of jazz, not only is Cairo Jazz Club (www.cairojazzclub.com/) rocking every night of the week, but there is also a yearly Jazz Festival that brings international greats to Egypt. The Jazz Society of Egypt (http://www.facebook.com/group.php?gid=640399 19447 promotes jazz in Egypt by providing activities that include workshops, lectures, and performances. Tel: 0122-218-3335, 0111-490-7744. E-mail: jsegypt@gmail.com

Music on Ramadan evenings is shared by all, free of charge, and in Cairo's historic surroundings. Troupes from all over the Middle East as well as local musicians serenade the city's inhabitants after long days of fasting. The performances differ nightly and the venues are held in ancient monuments, public gardens, and cultural centers.

All schedules, performances, and venues are listed in *al-Ahram Weekly*, and online at http://weekly.ahram.org.eg/list.htm, Cairo360 (www.cairo360.com), and Cairo Live Events (http://cairolive eventsguide.blogspot.com).

Then there are the restaurants, clubs, and gallery exhibitions. Check out Cairo360 (www.cairo360.com), updated weekly, and even daily on Twitter, with new restaurants, places to go, and things to do. The reviews are honest and in-depth. There is a thorough section on "Restaurants, Nightlife, and City Life," which rates each place that is reviewed. However, if you need a hand-held guide to restaurants, buy *The Ultimate Dining Guide* (available at most bookstores and newsstands). The *Ultimate Dining Guide* is updated yearly and lists all restaurants and fast-food outlets in each area of Cairo as well as outdoor and floating restaurants. Don't forget that Cairo is the delivery capital of the world. Whether it is fast food or fine dining, everything can be delivered to your door.

Your Leisure Time

8

9

Making a House Your Home

"My home is my palace," as the saying goes, so whether you will live in a hotel for six months or intend to stay in Egypt for many years, your living space is a welcome respite from the outside world. Ask yourself this question: "Am I a minimalist or a collector?" Before furnishing a home think of what is important to you and your family members. When returning from a busy day, how do you like to relax or entertain friends? In a hotel room or furnished apartment you might like a cup of tea or a soft bed, so buy a kettle and a foam mat. (If you don't want to return to your home country with these articles, give them to Reception. They will find a charity that will appreciate any extra item.) However, in an apartment or villa you face many more decisions, and this chapter is here to help. In this section you will find suggestions for companies, stores, and individuals to help in your search for furnishings, repairs, and home accessories. Continuing the shopping spree, chapter 10 broadens the Cairo shopping experience. Alongside this book, do consult two excellent websites for specific shops and products: Cairo 360,

www.cairo360.com and Yellow Pages Egypt, http://www.yellow pages.com.eg/.

When the Egyptian Revolution erupted, some foreign governments advised their nationals to evacuate the country. The exodus occurred over a forty-eight-hour period. Each person was allowed only one suitcase. A word to the wise: leave your heirlooms and precious mementos in your home country, if possible. In furnishing a home in Egypt, particularly if it is temporary, buy items that you won't regret leaving behind should you be forced to evacuate. In the appendix, you will find an emergency evacuation checklist that will help sort out the most important issues when confusion is all around.

Your Household Needs
Appliances

Most major international brands of large appliances are found in Egypt. Appliances that are made in Egypt are reasonably priced compared to imported brands. Phillips and National, though international brand names, manufacture appliances in Egypt, while Fresh and Kiriazi are Egyptian-owned companies that manufacture locally. They will certainly have a lifespan of at least three to five years. All appliances come with a one-year warranty, but the store where an appliance was purchased will not repair it. You will be directed to another company for repairs and spare parts.

Air conditioners/heaters are either window units or split units. If you have a choice, the latter is the better option, as they are more efficient, quieter, and more powerful. Carrier, Trane, and Unionaire are the most popular brands. New air conditioners usually have reusable filters but the older models need replacement filters. If you move into an apartment with existing air-conditioning units, be sure to have each one serviced and cleaned. Ask your landlord where to buy filters. All filters need to be changed or washed at least once a year so the air conditioner can function most efficiently. In summer months, high usage of air conditioners means excruciatingly high electric bills, and a filthy filter causes an air conditioner to use more energy to suck air through its cooling system.

When selecting a vacuum cleaner, check that the filter is washable and reusable. If you bring your vacuum cleaner from another country and it uses disposable filter bags, be sure to bring plenty of bags as it will be difficult to find the exact fit here. Also, a 110V vacuum cleaner will need a transformer, so it is smarter to buy a 220V vacuum cleaner in Egypt. (Tip: When leaving Egypt, donate your vacuum cleaner to a mosque. They have lots of rugs to clean daily and the gift will be highly appreciated.)

Appliance Stores

♦ **B. Tech.** Comes highly recommended as an electronics store with small to large appliances at reasonable prices. They have a good array of brands and colors with different finishes. The staff is knowledgeable and helpful. Payments can be made on an installment plan. Available are water heaters, fridges, washing machines, stoves, and other equipment of local and international brands. Address: 194 al-Nuzha St., Heliopolis. Branches in al-Rehab City, Downtown, Haram, Hadayik al-Qubba, Helwan, Maadi, Mohandiseen, Muqattam, New Cairo, Shubra. Tel: 19966. Website: http://b.tech.com.eg

♦ **Carrefour.** Three megastores in Cairo with small and large appliances. Addresses: inside Dandy Mega Mall, Km. 28, Cairo–Alexandria Desert Road, Giza, Tel: 16061, 3539-2613; inside Maadi City Center, Ring Road, Maadi, Tel: 16061; inside Golf City Mall, Cairo–Isamilia Desert Road, al-Ubur City, Tel: 16061; al-Gazyer St., New Maadi, Tel: 16061; Road 90, Fifth Settlement, Qattamiya, New Cairo, Tel: 16061. Website: www.carrefour.com.eg/stores.aspx

♦ **Electric Center.** Local and imported appliances. Addresses: Road 9, Maadi. Tel: 2525-4835; 58 Sur Nadi al-Terssana, Mohandiseen. Tel: 3305-8974, 3345-6805.

♦ **Electric House.** Satellite receivers, local and imported appliances. Address: 3 Wahib

Doss St., al-Mahatta Square, Maadi. Tel: 2359-1018/0559, 2358-7029.

♦ **El Ogeil.** A good selection of small appliances. Addresses: 159 26th July St., Zamalek. Tel: 2735-4368/6/7; Ubur Buildings, Salah Salim St., Nasr City. Tel: 2401-0852.

♦ **Samsung–Mantronix.** Samsung is a leading consumer electronics powerhouse guaranteed by Mansur. The products are LCD and Plasma TVs, home theaters, DVDs, air conditioners, washing machines, micro-wave ovens, and vacuum cleaners. Address: 13 Road 294, New Maadi. Tel: 16690, 2704-9274, 2706-9525.

♦ **United Engineering Establishment– Whirlpool** has brand-name refrigerators, washing machines, dryers, microwave ovens, freezers, and air conditioners: Whirlpool, Admiral, Ariston, General Electric, Westinghouse, Kelvinator, Maytag, Magic Chef, Frigidaire, and Samsung. They provide after-sales appliance service, in-home repair, and maintenance. Address: 37 Muhammad Yusuf Musa St., Nasr City. Tel: 19032, 2261-0394, 2261-6921. Website: www.westinghouse-ueo. com/ar/home.php

♦ **Universal Group Co.** Began manufacturing gas cookers in 1994. Since then the company has evolved rapidly to become the biggest manufacturer of gas cookers in the Middle East. Also available are built-in ovens, dishwashers, heaters, LCDs, micro-waves, refrigerators, televisions, vacuum cleaners, washing machines, and water heaters. Address: 20 Syria St., Mohandiseen. Tel: 19933, 19797, 3338-2003/6. Website: www.universalgroup.org

♦ **Zanussi.** An excellent reputation for washing machines and refrigerators in Egypt. They deliver all over the country. The appliances carry a one-year warranty on maintenance and spare parts, which must be replaced at one of their authorized service centers. The company is not responsible for equipment fixed outside its service centers and the warranty will not be honored. Address: 56 al-Salam St., off al-Maryutiya St., beside Future School, Faisal, Giza. Tel: 19160, 3772-1251/1252/1336.

Bath and Bed
Bathrooms
Most bathrooms have individual, external water heaters. At first, the presence of a tank on the bathroom wall may seem like an eyesore, but over time it blends into the bathroom ambiance. The good news with individual water heaters is control of the water temperature, which saves on the electricity bill. Turn off the water heater when a bathroom is used infrequently or when traveling. Before moving into an apartment, check carefully for possible leaks around the pipes or a running toilet. A slow drip can cause massive damage to walls and floors, and create an unhealthy environment.

Making a House Your Home   9

Aquatop. Luxury bathrooms and jacuzzis. Addresses: 10 Suleiman Abaza St., Mohandiseen; al-Nuzha St., Heliopolis. Tel: 3336-4712/3. E-mail: marketing@ aquatop.net. Website: www.aquatop.net

Duravit. Bathroom furnishings, wall-mounted toilets, mirror cabinets. Showrooms: al-Mushir Ahmad Ismail St. (off Salah Salim St., behind Fairmont Hotel), Sheraton Heliopolis, and Designopolis, Cairo–Alexandria Desert Rd. Tel: 19219.

Ideal Standard. Has bathroom fittings, toilets, sinks, and so on. Service on all products is honored by Ideal Standard stores, all of which have a good reputation for promptness and customer satisfaction. Tel: 19696. Addresses: 136 al-Bahr al-Azem St., Giza. Tel: 3774-0374; 102 Gam'at al-Duwal al-Arabiya, Mohandiseen. Tel: 3337-9078; 2 Idris Ragheb St., off Port Said St., Daher, Tel: 2591-6042; 117 al-Thawra St., Heliopolis. Tel: 2418-9068. Website: http://www.idealstandard-egypt.com

Mahgoub. Has bathroom fittings, toilets, sinks, and so on. Address: al-Nil St., Giza, just past Abbas Bridge going south. Tel: 3571-3465/2562; 1 Makram Ebeid St., Nasr City. Tel: 2287-9991. Website: www.mahgoubgroup.com

Al-Faggala Street, off Ramsis Square, has a number of stores with less expensive fixtures.

Bath Accessories

Bath towels made of Egyptian cotton can be found in a variety of qualities. Be sure to inspect the towel for irregularities.

Fairtrade Egypt. All items in this shop support traditional Egyptian handmade crafts and artisans. Handmade bath rugs, Egyptian cotton bath towels, and natural beige mats made from kattan plants are a few of the beautifully crafter accessories for bathrooms. Address: 27 Yehia Ibrahim St., Zamalek. Tel: 2736-5123. Website: www. fairtradeegypt.org

Halawa. Addresses: 165 Muhammad Farid St., Downtown. Tel: 2391-2744/2013; 34 Syria St., Mohandiseen. Tel: 3760-1023, 3761-1692.

al-Hammam. A fine array of soaps and bath products using the finest virgin olive oil. Hours: 11:00 a.m.–8:00 p.m., daily except Friday and Sunday when the hours are 11:00 a.m.–2:00 p.m. and 5:00 p.m.–8:00 p.m. Address: 2 Taha Hussein St., Zamalek. Tel: 2735-8026, 0100-524-2643. E-mail: sales@domainehorus.com

al-Haramlek. Address: 1/1 al-Zahra' al-Maadi (off Road 216), Digla, Maadi. Tel: 2517-1462. E-mail: alharamlek.egypt@yahoo.com

La Prince Bathroom Accessories. Hours: 10:00 a.m.–10:00 p.m., closed on Sundays. Address: 5 Ibn Maysser St., Sheikh al-Marsafi Square, Zamalek. Tel: 2736-8934.

✦ **Nefertari.** Egyptian cotton towels, bathrobes and bath slippers, soaps free from preservatives and coloring agents, loofahs and sponges, linens and bath products. One hundred percent natural body care products. Address: 26A al-Gezira al-Wusta St., Zamalek. Tel: 2735-9667. Website: http://www.nefertaribodycare.com

✦ **Sidi.** Address: 159 26th July St., Zamalek. Tel: 2734-9142.

Bed Linen and Bedding
Egyptian cotton sheets with a high thread count can cost a fortune in Europe and the U.S., so buy sheets and pillow cases while in Egypt. Your only problem is making sure of your bed size, as bed sizes vary from standard U.S. sizes, even if the labels say 'twin,', 'full,' 'queen,' and 'king.' Fitted and flat sheets are sometimes sold separately and a fitted sheet may have a duvet as a top sheet. Also, the sheets wrinkle and some might shrink slightly.

Caring for Cotton Sheets
Wash in warm water with a mild detergent that is dissolved completely before putting the linens in the machine. Do not use bleach or softener. Air dry or put machine dryer on low and dry for about ten minutes to avoid shrinkage. Remove linens when damp and smooth while folding or iron.

✦ **& Company.** Divine bed linens made with Egyptian cotton, but pricey; bath towels and sleepwear. Hours: 10:00 a.m.–11:00 p.m. Addresses: 3A Bahgat Ali St., Zamalek. Tel: 2736-3689; 15 Road 216, Digla, Maadi. Tel: 2754-2104. Website: www.andcompanyonline.com

✦ **Branka Design.** Natural products using 100 percent silk, linen, and cotton for bed linens. Address: 75 Abdel Mun'im Riyad St., al-Mutamayyiz District, 6th October City. Tel: 0100-345-7500. E-mail: f.branka@ brankadesign.com. Website: www.branka design.com

✦ **Fairtrade.** Akhmim bedspreads, curtain material, table linens, cushion covers, and cotton. Open from Monday to Saturday. Address: 27 Yehia Ibrahim St., Zamalek. Tel: 2736-5123. Website: www.fairtrade egypt.org

✦ **al-Haramlek.** Bed linens, bedspreads, pillow covers. Address: 1/1 al-Zahra' al-Maadi (off Road 216), Digla, Maadi. Tel: 2517-1462. E-mail: alharamlek.egypt@yahoo.com

✦ **Malaika.** Has exquisite sheets made with a 200- and 400-thread count of Egyptian cotton. Sleeping on Malaika's bed linens is a delight, but also, by supporting the company, you are supporting underprivileged women. Malaika trains village women in embroidery, enabling them to work from their homes and make money. Address of main office/factory: 66 Abul Mahasin al-Shazli St., Agouza. Tel:

3304-1592, 0122-143-0509. E-mail: ahmed@malaikalinens.com. Send an e-mail to find shops that carry Malaika products, or check out The Factory in Mohandiseen (Tel: 3336-7276), Beymen in Garden City (Tel: 2792-6679), or Mounaya in Zamalek (http://www.mounaya.com).

♦ **Malek.** Luxurious bed linens made in Egypt. Address: 2/1 al-Lasilki St., Maadi. Tel: 2517-4818, 0122-321-2154. E-mail: info@maleklinen.com. Website: www.maleklinen.com

♦ **Oum El Dounia.** Bedspreads and curtains from India, carpets, pillow covers. Hours: Daily 10:00 a.m.–9:00 p.m. Addresses: 3 Tal'at Harb St., 1st floor, Downtown. Tel: 2393-8273; Road 23 (off al-Nadi St.), Golf Area, Maadi. Tel: 2753-0483.

Beds and Mattresses

You spend one-third of your life sleeping, so you might as well find the mattress that gives you the best possible rest. A good night's sleep is the key to a productive day and it begins with a mattress that is suitable for your body. There are three companies in Cairo that sell mattresses and they are listed below. Taki was the only mattress company in Egypt for years. Masterbed opened in Egypt several years ago and has a large range of different kinds of mattresses. They also sell thin foam pads to put on top of a hard mattress to provide more comfort.

♦ **Habitat.** La Casa Habitat Mattress Distributors. Address: Hurriya Sq., Road 216, Maadi. Tel: 2521-0323, 0122-735-1133. Website: http://www.lacasa-habitat.com/index.html

♦ **Masterbed.** Has mattresses of all sizes, pillows, bedroom furniture, bedhead boards, and accessories. Masterbed is also distributed through more than 650 furniture galleries throughout Cairo, Alexandria, and various provinces. Website: www.masterbedsae.com Contact information by area:

Haram. 188 al-Haram St. Tel: 3586-6659.

Heliopolis. 5 al-Mamalik St., off Ibrahim al-Lakani St.. Tel: 2257-9309.

Heliopolis. Sheraton Residences, 88 Saqr Quraysh St. Tel: 2267-5825.

Maadi (Digla). 199 Digla St. Tel: 2519-5928.

Maadi. Suweiris Square. Tel: 2380-2240.

Matariya. In front of *al-shahr al-'aqaari* office. Tel: 2282-9315.

Mohandiseen. 17 Lebanon St., off Lebanon Square. Tel: 3346-2317.

Mohandiseen. 45 Shihab St. Tel: 3304-7273; showroom: 3344-4715.

Nasr City. 47 Abbas al-Aqqad St. Tel: 2402-0391.

Nasr City. 25 Makram Ebeid St. Tel: 2275-4142.

al-Rehab. Suuq al-Hirafiyyin. Tel: 3607-7148.

Zamalek. 10 Bahgat Ali St. Tel: 2735-6716.

♦ **Taki.** Address: 483 Hadayik al-Qubba Square, Hadayik al-Qubba, Cairo. Tel: 2601-0743, 0122-587-3185.

♦ **El Watany Factory.** For sponge mattresses, medical pillows, and mattresses for allergies. A leader in the manufacture of spring and sponge mattresses in all sizes. Sponge mattresses are available in all thicknesses, sizes, and compressions. Address: Industrial Zone, Asafra al-Manzala, al-Dakahliya. Tel: 050-788-0035, 0100-297-0692, 0100-579-4112.

Carpets and Floor Coverings
Egypt is the country to buy carpets, rugs, and kilims. You can find these handmade, colorful floor coverings to suit any home. Drive along the Saqqara Road from the Ring Road toward the Saqqara Pyramids and you will find many stores to visit. Or browse through Khan al-Khalili. Always bargain when purchasing oriental carpets. It is expected.

Oriental and Handmade Carpets

♦ **El Kahhal.** Originally from Syria, the family has passed its carpet traditions from generation to generation. They are known for repairing, trading, and weaving fine handmade rugs. Addresses: Khan al-Khalili: 5 Sikit Badistan, Khal al-Khalili. Tel: 2590-9128. Mohandiseen: 5 Sphinx Square, Mohandiseen. Tel: 2305-8032. Heliopolis: 24 Ibrahim al-Lakani St.,

---

What You Should Know before Buying an Oriental Rug
Handmade rugs, including kilims and tapestries, are chosen for their luxurious look and long-term use. A pile rug, which may take months or even years to complete, differs from other handmade floor coverings in that the knots are individually inserted into the foundation and then cut one at a time.

Before setting out to buy an oriental carpet, the questions to ask yourself are: What color and size meet your needs? Does the carpet look beautiful? Does the cost fit within your budget?

Tips:
♦ Check the overall structure of the carpet. Closely examine the knotted pile, warp and weft threads, fringe, and selvages or sides of the carpet. In every square inch there can be as many as 1,000 knots or as few as 50. Usually, a rug with a high knot count indicates a more valuable rug, but not always.
♦ Look at the back of the rug. Check for breaks or cuts in the warp and weft threads.
♦ Check the pile for holes, stains, and moth damage (particularly in old rugs).
♦ Inspect the fringe to check whether it is in good shape and original. The selvages should be fairly straight.
♦ Test the color for running by wiping a damp cloth firmly over the rug.
♦ The pile should be even and consistent in all areas. The lay of the rug is important.
♦ The most important factor is to find a reputable dealer.

Making a House Your Home

9

Heliopolis. Tel: 2415-9754, 2419-9557. Website: http:// www.elkahhal.com

♦ **El Kattan.** Handmade Egyptian carpets since 1930. 'El Kattan Carpets' were legally registered by the Ministry of Labor as the only training center in Egypt for handmade rug weaving. They also wash and mend carpets. Address: Incha Palace, P.O. Box 36, Hadayik al-Qubba. Tel: 2257-8066, 2452-6467, 0128-245-5110. E-mail: carpets@elkattan-eg.com. Website: http://www.elkattan-eg.com

♦ **Mamdouh El Assiouty.** Mamdouh El Assiouty's family began in the carpet business in 1956 and has built a good reputation over the years for excellence. Assiouty also provides special services for carpet maintenance, repair, and cleaning. Addresses: Hotel Sofitel al-Maadi. Tel: 2525-9191, 0122-776-6210; and 30 Misr–Helwan Agricultural Rd., in the Ministry of Environmental Affairs Building, Maadi. Tel: 2525-6018, 0122-776-6210. E-mail: info@mamdouhel assiouty.com. Website: http://www.mam douhelassiouty.com

♦ **Mustafa Oriental Carpets** (The Egyptian Factory for Oriental Rugs). Mamluk-design carpets. Address: 5 Almaza Square, Heliopolis. Tel: 2291-6683, 0100-166-9913.

Modern and Factory-made Carpets

Oriental Weavers has a vast selection of styles ranging from area rugs to wall-to-wall carpeting. You can choose the type of fabric, pile, and design to have a carpet specially made for a particular room. Addresses: 8 al-Shahid Zakariya Khalil St., Sheraton Heliopolis, behind Fairmont Hotel, Heliopolis. Tel: 2267-2121, 2266-9191; al-Zamalek Club Wall, 26th July St., Shop No. 5, Mohandiseen. Customer Service: 0800-888-8666. E-mail: customer service@orienalweavers.com. Website: www. orientalweavers.com

Doormats

A doormat with a rough surface is a MUST to set outside every entry door to your home: it limits tracking in all sorts of dirt and crud from the streets. People spit on sidewalks and pet owners do not pick up their animals' waste; therefore, shoes can track in filth and germs. Doormats are called *mashshaaya* and are available at most large stores like Alfa and Carrefour.

♦ **Egypt Craft Center/Fairtrade.** Has doormats from al-Beheira. Address: 27 Yehia Ibrahim St., Zamalek. Open from Monday to Saturday. Tel: 2736-5123. Website: www.fairtradeegypt.org

Factory-made Tile Flooring

♦ **Ceramica Cleopatra Group.** An Egyptian-owned company that began in the 1980s. Today, they have four state-of-the art ceramics and porcelain manufacturing factories in Egypt. For a listing of showrooms, visit the website. Main showroom address: 36 al-Battal Ahmad Abdel Aziz St., Mohan-

diseen. Tel: 3761-4000. Website: www.
cleopatraceramics.com

♦ **Crys-Tile Products.** Crystal mosaic tiles
made of pure lead crystal, scratch resistant
and tightly sealed. Address: Kulliyit al-Zira'a
St., Corniche al-Nil, Industrial Zone Shubra
al-Khayma, Qalyubiya. Tel: 16218, 4220-
1032; Mobile: 0100-534-0063. Website:
www.asfourcrystal.com/Crystal/index.asp

♦ **Gemma Ceramic and Porcelain Tiles.**
Check website for the store nearest you. Tel:
16757. Website: http://www.gemma.com.eg

♦ **Royal Ceramica.** Offers a vast and varied
array of ceramic and stone tiles. On their
website you can find the nearest location
and search for the availability of tiles at
that location. Head office/factory address:
al-Ubur City, First Industrial Zone, Block
13034, Helwan. Tel: 2610-2080/81, 2610-
2940/41, 19968. E-mail: info@royalceram
ica.com. Website: http://www.royalceram
ica.com

The largest outlet in Cairo that supplies
Royal Ceramica products is Ahmed El Sallab
Mall. Address: Autostrad Road, intersection of
Ring Road, beginning of Muqattam.
Tel: 19075, 0100-839-3664, 0100-162-2886.

Handmade Tile Flooring
Tile-makers at Darb al-Ahmar can repro-
duce tiles from an old tile or a picture of a
pattern or old floor that you wish to repro-
duce. They produce a diagram which will
be the plan for the construction of a metal
mold of the pattern. Colors for the pattern
are poured into the grooves to make the
pattern and the metal outline is swiftly
removed. Tiles are set with a sprinkling of
cement and placed in a press for twelve
hours, then in a pool of water for a day or
until the cement hardens. About 2.5 meters
of tiling can be made per day. Contact:
Mahmud Rashid in Darb al-Ahmar Street,
to the right of Qijmas al-Ishaqi (Abu Hu-
rayba Mosque).

Wood Flooring

♦ **Decorama.** Parquet floors. Kulliyit al-
Zira'a St., Corniche al-Nil, Industrial Zone,
Shubra al-Khayma, Qalyubiya. Tel: 16218,
4220-1/670, 0100-534-0063. Website:
www.decoramaegypt.com

Stone and Marble Flooring
Egypt is known for its granite and stone.

♦ **AFID.** Natural stone, marble, limestone,
granite, slate, onyx, and sandstone. Address: 2 al-Sobki St., al-Dahabi Square,
Roxy. Tel: 2419-9138, 2290-6889, 0122-
784-5257. Website: www.afiddesigns.net

♦ **Zahran Marble Works.** Has numerous
products such as mosaics, rock-face, chis-
eled, antique, polished, sandblasted.
Address: Building 2009, Ring Road, in front
of al-Zahra' entrance of police academy,
ground floor. Tel: 2409-4033. Website:
www.zahranmarbleworks.com

Carpet Care

Carpets and rugs need special care to ensure a long life. The first step is to vacuum frequently to lift dirt and dust and prevent soil buildup. Pile rugs need to be vacuumed with the brush bar to loosen the pile and free the dirt, whereas looped rugs need to be vacuumed without the brush and need frequent vacuuming. Change the storage bag before it is completely full, as dust can escape from the vacuum cleaner.

Oil buildup causes matting and discoloration. Use warm water and a mild detergent such as Woolite to clean the rug and towel dry. For spills, immediately absorb it with paper or cloth towels before it dries. Apply warm water and mild detergent and blot up the excess water and residue. When completely dry, vacuum the area.

Tip for a cleaner house: If you have pets, keep animal hair off the carpets and furniture by wiping down cats and dogs with a microfiber dusting cloth. This cuts down on the amount of hair and dander. The electrostatic properties of microfiber cloths attracts the hair, dander, and dust.

Carpet Cleaning and Repair

♦ **al-Assiouty Carpets.** Addresses: Hotel Sofitel al-Maadi. Tel: 2525-9191; Mobile: 0122-776-6210; and 30 Misr–Helwan Agricultural Rd., in the Ministry of Environmental Affairs Building, Maadi. Tel: 2525-6018, 0122-776-6210. E-mail: info@mamdouhel-assiouty.com. Website: http://www.mam douhelassiouty.com

♦ **El Kattan.** Address: Incha Palace, Hadayik al-Qubba. Tel: 2257-8066, 2452-6467, 0128-245-5110. E-mail: carpets@elkattan-eg.com. Website: http://www.elkattan-eg.com

♦ **Panorama Group.** Opened in 1999 in Cairo and now have three branches in Cairo and one in Alexandria. They specialize in suction and shampooing carpets, wall-to-wall carpets, upholstered furniture, and mattresses. Address: 47 Road 7, Maadi. Tel: 2359-5818, 0100-783-3430. E-mail: panoramagroup_2008@yahoo.com or nagla_77@yahoo.com

♦ **al-Sisi Carpet Co.** Oriental carpet repair and cleaning. Address: 11 al-Kamil Muhammad St., Zamalek, in front of Officers' Club. Tel: 2735-0996.

♦ **El Zayat.** Address: 4 Brazil St., Zamalek. Tel: 2735-1046.

Designers and Decorators

Designopolis shopping plaza (http:// www. designopolis.com/) is a new center dedicated to all types of interior decorating. Most shops sell imported international furniture brands for the home and office. CityStars mega-mall (http://www.citystars. com.eg/citystars/index.asp) has a variety of stores for household items. Before you go to either mall, visit their website first to check the stores and products; verifying product availability prior to a visit will save time. You will find what you want—if you have patience. If you just don't know where to begin, it is a good idea to consult an expert. A couple of people who come highly recommended are Heba Shunbo (heba_shunbo @yahoo.com) at The Factory and Lamia Hassanein (lamia_hassanein@ yahoo.com) at Tanis. At the Design Emporium, Aziza Tanani will help you with interior design that is innovative and meets your budget. Address: 41 al-Ansar St., Dokki. Tel: 3478-3848, 3338-9910, 3761-7187. E-mail: sales@designemporiumegypt.com. Website: www.designemporiumegypt.com.

There are numerous furniture exhibitions throughout the year (for conferences and exhibitions, consult Egycalendar at http://www.egycalendar.com/, or Egyptian Furniture Export Council at www.efecfurniture.com/WebPages/Common/Home. aspx). At newsstands and bookstores you can find a wide selection of interior decorating books and magazines. These advertise stores for furniture, fabrics, floor coverings, kitchens, and bathrooms as well as miscellaneous items such as hot tubs, glass fittings, and home accessories. *Obelisque* and *Magez Design* are two popular English magazines that highlight interior decoration and architecture in Egypt.

Electronics and Entertainment

Radios, televisions, satellite dishes and receivers, audio and video equipment, vacuum cleaners, and microwaves are plentiful on the local market. Please note that television sets manufactured for use in the United States (NTSC system) will not work in Egypt (PAL-SECAM system). Likewise, videotapes made for NTSC will only play on an American or multisystem machine. With access to videos from the Internet, watching movies on DVDs and videos is dying out. Electronics like 'Apple TV' hook your computer to the TV so iTune movies can be uploaded for viewing on the TV. Most electronics have dual voltage, 110/220, but be SURE to check before plugging your American electronic equipment into the electric socket in Egypt.

Electronics Stores

♦ **Apple Center Showroom.** Address: 7 al-Thawra Square, Mohandiseen. Tel: 3762-8391.

♦ **B.Tech.** Comes highly recommended as an electronics store with reasonably priced appliances. They have a good array of brands. The staff is knowledgeable and helpful. Payments can be made on an installment plan. Address: 194 al-Nuzha St., Heliopolis. Branches in al-Rehab City, Downtown, Haram, Hadayik al-Qubba, Helwan, Maadi, Mohandiseen, Muqattam, New Cairo, Shubra. Website: http://www.b.tech.com.eg

♦ **Compu Me.** Home electronics, computer gadgets, laptops, mobile accessories, digital cameras. Address: CityStars, Phase 1, Shop #4-125, Heliopolis. Tel: 2480-2330.

Making a House Your Home

9

♦ **Digital Living.** Everything on your wish list for home entertainment systems and audio/visual equipment. Address: 32 Dr. Michel Bakhum St., Dokki. Tel: 3336-5602/8.

♦ **Hyper 1.** Video and digital cameras, mobile phones, PCs, and laptops. Address: al-Sheikh Zayed City, 6th October City. Tel: 16404.

♦ **IntelliTech Home Entertainment Solutions.** Offers security solutions and home entertainment, which includes automation, home cinema, audio systems, light control, motorized curtains, and climate control. Address: 8 Ahmad al-Rashidi St., Ard al-Golf, Heliopolis. Tel: 2415-5531/27. Website: www.2intellitech.com

♦ **Panasonic.** A variety of home entertainment systems and digital cameras. Address: CityStars, Phase 2, Shop #7-004, Heliopolis. Tel: 19363.

♦ **Radio Shack.** The first place to go for electronic components and equipment. There are branches in every area of the city. If you are looking for something specific, any Radio Shack store can check the inventory of all Radio Shack stores in Cairo. To find the store nearest you, call 19419 or check the website: http://www.radioshackegypt.com

♦ **Sony.** LCD and Plasma TVs. Address: 44 Higaz St., off Wadi al-Nil, Mohandiseen. Tel: 19966.

Electronic Parts to Make Your Own Components

If you or someone in your family enjoys constructing entertainment systems, electrical components, or even computers, these are the places to find the parts and pieces.

♦ **Connectors City.** All kinds of cables, connectors, terminals, and ready-made internal and external computer cables. Address: 20 Yusuf al-Gindi St., Bab al-Luq. Tel: 2393-0717, 2395-6920, 2392-3500, 2390-0014. E-mail: connectorscity@nekhely.com

♦ **Electronic Components City.** All types of fixed and variable resistors, paper and chemical capacitors, transistors, integrated circuits, and diodes. Hours: 10:00 a.m.–7:00 p.m., closed Friday. Address: 176 Tahrir St., Bab al-Luq. Tel: 2393-6301, 2390-9916, 2391-7592. E-mail: mainbranch@nekhely.com. Website: http://www.nekhely.com

♦ **Instruments City and Supplies Office.** Electronic measuring and scientific instruments, such as multimeters, oscilloscopes, power-meters, insulation testers, temperature and humidity meters, air speed meters, cable fault detectors, panels production equipment, electronic trainer kits. Address: 4 al-Daramalli Passage, off Mustafa Abu Heif St., Bab al-Luq. Tel: 2393-6373. E-mail: suppliesbranch@nekhely.com

♦ **Kits City.** Mini kits and light effects, alarms and car applications, audio/HiFi and household applications, power supplies, and controllers. Address: 20 Yusuf al-Gindi St., Bab al-Luq. Tel: 2393-0717, 2395-6920, 2392-3500, 2390-0014. E-mail: kitscity@nekhely.com

♦ **Power City Electrical.** Transformers of all powers from 2VA to 500KVA. All powers of stabilizers, all powers of UPS Powerbanks for laptops, all powers of desk adapters for notebook computers. Switch mode power supplies for electronic projects. Address: 4 al-Daramalli Passage, off Mustafa Abu Heif St., Bab al-Luq. Tel: 2393-6373. E-mail: powercity@nekhely.com

♦ **Tools City.** Hand tools for installing, stripping, and cutting cables, and crimping tools for cable terminals. All kinds of soldering and desoldering stations. Electrical and electronic tool sets. Address: 3 al-Daramalli Passage, off Mustafa Abu Heif St., Bab al-Luq. Tel: 2393-6373. E-mail: suppliesbranch@nekhely.com

♦ **Wireless City.** All kinds of wireless LAN internal and external cards, hot spots, access points, bridges, high speed wireless LAN 108mb/s. Address: 20 Yusuf al-Gindi St., Bab al-Luq. Tel: 2393-0717, 2395-6920, 2392-3500, 2390-0014. E-mail: lancity@nekhely.com

Fabrics, Drapery, and Upholstery

If you like handwoven and unique textiles, there is an array of fabric choices in Cairo that will not disappoint. Of course, there are imported fabrics from Europe, Asia, and the Middle East but some of the most interesting and unique textiles are created right here in Cairo. For an experience in fabric shopping, take a trip to Wakalat al-Balah market on the Nile Corniche just before the World Trade Center. This is a huge, vibrant market where tailors and designers go to buy quality material at low prices. Note that it is closed on Sundays.

If you prefer a more traditional shopping experience, there are fabric stores in every area of Cairo that carry Egyptian-made fabrics.

♦ **Alef.** Creative and inventive designs. You can order a specialized color and amount in any fabric. Hours: Monday–Saturday 10:30 a.m.–2:00 p.m. and 5:00 p.m.–8:00 p.m. Address: 14 Muhammad Anis St., Zamalek. Tel: 2735-3690, 0100-145-9338. E-mail: monagrieche@alefgallery.com. Website: www.alefgallery.com

♦ **El Patio Interiors.** For Egyptian-inspired printed textiles for upholstery and curtains. Address: 4 Road 77, Maadi. Tel: 2359-6654/43, 0100-106-4025.

♦ **Print Shop.** Simple designs at reasonable prices. Address: 11/2 al-Nasr St., New Maadi. Tel: 2754-7452. Website: http://printshopeg.com

♦ **Shatex.** Addresses: 7/2 al-Nasr St., New Maadi. Tel: 2754-6783; 27 Lebanon St., Mohandiseen. Tel: 3305-3813/4; and Designopolis. Website: http://www.shatexhome.com

Making a House Your Home

9

♦ **Tanis.** The sister company of El Patio. Addresses: 35 Giza St., inside First Mall, Giza. Tel: 3573-0609; 9 Muhammad Anis St., Zamalek. Tel: 2737-2555.

♦ **Texmar.** Addresses: 73 Omar ibn al-Khattab St., Heliopolis; 29 Yathrib St., Dokki. Tel: 3761-0250.

Flowers
We all love to give and receive a bouquet or arrangement of flowers. In Egypt, flowers are popular to give for a birthday, the arrival of a new baby, or on return from a trip. Many Egyptians take flowers when invited to a dinner party at home. For your convenience, flower shops deliver, but be sure to provide them with the exact name, address, and telephone number of the recipient.

Before the importation of flowers to Cairo, it was possible to enjoy flowers in every room of the house and not hurt your budget. Even when flowers are only shipped in from the Nile Delta, prices are outrageous. *Baladi* roses (roses from the farm that are usually pink and red, sometimes yellow) are still a reasonable price during the winter months. They are found at the small flower kiosks or sold by children on 26th July Street in Zamalek for LE10 a dozen. *Baladi* roses are leafy and thorny, and often dusty, so you will have to go through some pain and mess to prepare them for the vase. Place the bouquet in sugar water and in a cool place. You will enjoy, each day, the delicate blossoms and delightful fragrance. Dry the petals for potpourri. Flower Power

is still the best florist in Cairo for exotic and creative arrangements, though it is expensive. Flower Power asks for your budget, gives their clients the best possible service, and stays within the budget.

♦ **Flower Power.** Addresses: 21 Abdel Mun'im Riyad St., Mohandiseen. Tel: 3337-8380; 14 Wadi al-Nil St., Mohandiseen. Tel: 3304-8000. In Alexandria, Tel: 0128-716-6679, 0128-163-3394. E-mail: info@flowerpowerdesign.com. Website: http://www.flowerpowerdesign.com

Fresh Water and Water Filters
The question of drinking tap water or bottled water has only arisen in the last fifteen years or so. Before that time, people drank tap water. Water was boiled and filtered. Usually people did not like ice in their drink for fear the ice was contaminated. Along came bottled water . . . convenient, yes . . . environmentally friendly, no! The problems of water in plastic bottles are many. Questions have been raised as to the origin of the water and marketing practices. It has been proven that some companies pump water from bore holes rather than from 'springs.' Also, of serious concern is the chemical seepage from plastic bottles, particularly when the plastic expands and contracts. Imagine millions of chemical-seeping plastic bottles in landfills!

However, if bottled water or a water cooler is your choice, the bottled water that passed all the tests was Nestlé. They deliver water-cooler refills.

♦ **Nestlé Egypt.** Address: Zamalek. Customer Service Tel: 19800.

Refrigerator and sink water filters are not a luxury item in Cairo, they are a necessity. Install a water filter and you will save money and protect the environment by not buying bottled water.

♦ **Purity Water Treatment Systems.** Address: 27a Baghdad St., al-Korba Square, Heliopolis. Tel: 2290-6636/9468, 0111-119-2452, 0100-002-2132.

♦ **Soul Water.** Specializes in water purification and desalination units, and state-of-the-art filters for home use. Address: 11 Sibawayh al-Masry St., Rab'a al-Adawiya, Nasr City. Tel: 2260-6085. Website: http://www.soulwaterfilter.com

♦ **Water World International.** Sole agent for Pure Pro (U.S.) in Egypt, providing the latest drinking water filters and treatment/ purification systems to substitute bottled water. Address: 39 Hamuda Mahmud St., off Makram Ebied St., Nasr City. Tel: 2670-3062, 2287-0192, 0100-733-3007, 0100-240-5735. Website: www.waterworldusa.com

Furniture

Household Furniture

Al-Mansura furniture market in Ataba is one of the oldest markets in town. All types of furniture are available—bedroom sets, dining rooms, kitchens, living rooms, and accessories. Interestingly, furniture at wholesale stores in the al-Mansura area can be found at expensive furniture stores. At this market you need to bargain, but can come away paying half the original asking price for a bedroom set. If you are worried about the quality of wood, buy the wooden frames and then pay for the upholstery. To get there, take the metro, exiting at Ataba metro station, or park your car in the Opera Square multistory garage and walk to al-Mansura on Muhammad Ali Street.

Damietta is where 60 percent of all Egyptian furniture is designed, crafted, and manufactured. For centuries, Egyptian furniture manufacturing had a long tradition of exceptional craftsmanship, creating styles influenced by Islamic, Coptic, French, and British designs. In the early twentieth century, a foreign influx of French and Italian manufacturing companies opened factories in Egypt as the demand grew for furniture in European classical styles which were the decorating rage in the homes of the foreign community and élite Egyptians. In 1952 furniture imports ended and companies were nationalized. The quality of Egyptian furniture began to deteriorate in the 1980s, particularly with the importation of poor quality wood and with improper drying techniques. In the last ten years the governor of Damietta made progress in improving the quality of imported wood and drying techniques, and was instrumental in revitalizing the Egyptian furniture market here and abroad. It might be well worth a trip to Damietta to visit the manufacturers. If you want custom-made furniture, visit a few.

Making a House Your Home

9

The Egyptian Furniture Export Council oversees the exportation of Egyptian furniture. There are 131 companies listed on their website, organized by production specialty. This council is responsible for the very successful Furnex exhibitions each year, usually held at the Convention Center in Nasr City. In 2010, Furnex opened a groundbreaking exhibition that juxtaposed tradition and innovation brand-name furniture in three historical Cairo houses—Bayt al-Suhaymi, Bayt Kharazati, and Mustafa Ga'far—all along the pedestrian street, al-Mu'izz. You can find out about the council and its exhibitions at the EFEC website: www.efecfurniture.com/WebPages/Common/Home.aspx

Damietta furniture manufacturers:

♦ **Amir El Baz Co.** Design and manufacture classic furniture such as chairs, couches, chaises longues, tables, consoles, vitrines, and natural wood frames. Export to the EU, U.S., and Arab countries. Address: al-Madaris St., al-Sinaniya, Damietta. Tel: 057-232-1222: Mobile: 0100-505-1444. Website: http://www.amirelbaz.com

♦ **Asal Furniture Co.** One of the biggest manufacturers of high-quality furniture in Egypt for over fifty years, including a factory producing upholstery. Address: Plot 82/8 Industrial Zone, New Damietta, Damietta. Tel: 057-240-4855, 057-240-5256, 0100-678-6111, 0122-223-3760. Website: http://www.asalfurniture.net

♦ **Al Kasem Furniture.** Uses the best natural woods, well-dried, and carving is done by very specialized craftsmen. Address: al-Sinaniya Ard al-'Itr St., Damietta.Tel: 057-235-2772, 0100-604-1457, 0100-944-4497. Website: http://www.alkasemfurniture.com

Al-Mansura sells furniture made in Damietta, Egypt, at wholesale prices. The nearest metro stop is Ataba station. By car, park at Opera Square's multistory garage. Entrance to al-Mansura is on Muhammad Ali Street.

Furniture stores in Cairo for home, office, and garden furniture:

♦ **Abaza's Divan.** Handmade wooden furniture designed with beautiful Arabic calligraphy by Mohamed Abaza. Egyptian-designed furniture and motifs. A few antique door-knocks and various other items. Hours: Open daily from 11:00 a.m. to 8:00 p.m. Address: 27 Road 231, Digla, Maadi. Tel: 0106-932-4907.

♦ **Alamein.** There are four stores that comprise Alamein: Caravanserai for antique reproductions; Geneena for garden furniture; Funtime for playground and recreational equipment; and Nile Class for sailing boats. Head Office address: 28 Hasan Asim St., Apt. 17, Zamalek. Tel: 2736-3835, 2738-4179, 0100-577-7283. Factory address: Shabramant, Km. 8, Saqqara Road, Giza. Stores: Caravanserai (brass chandeliers, lighting, antique reproductions). Address: 16 Mar'ashli St., Zamalek. Tel: 2735-0517,

0100-167-5851; Geneena (garden furniture and accessories) Tel: 2736-3835. Website: www.geneena.com; Funtime (playground equipment, ping-pong tables, trampolines, and billiards) Tel: 2736-3835. Website: www.alameinegypt.com/funtime; Nile Class (wooden sailing boats developed in 1930 by the British; take six weeks for delivery). E-mail: sales@alameinegypt.com.

For all stores: E-mail: info@alamein egypt.com. Website: www.alameinegypt.com

♦ **Baron Center.** Home and office furniture, local and international brands. Address: Ring Road, Qattamiya. Tel: 16234. Website: www.oud.com.eg.

♦ **Black Welders.** Wrought-iron furniture. Main office address: 33 Road 231, Digla, Maadi. Tel: 0122-230-9301. Branch addresses: 37 Ahmad Hishmat St. Tel: 0128-553-0088; Villa 4, Abdel Mun'im Riyad Mosque, beside Karnak EgyptAir Office. Tel: 0122-257-2919, 0122-230-9301. Factories: Basatin Industrial Zone. E-mail: saft2030@hotmail.com

♦ **Cavalli Corner Gallery.** Also customizes its furniture: wooden furniture takes between ten days and two weeks to be made, while curtains and other fabrics take an average of two days. Hours: 10:00 a.m.–10:00 p.m. Address: 9 Road 151, off Hurriya Square, next to Bank of Abu Dhabi, Maadi.

♦ **Decorama.** Furniture for home and office, and wooden flooring. Addresses: 5 Sudan St., 1st floor, Apt. 1, beside al-Marwa Hospital, Dokki. Tel: 3761-7662/1/3, 0100-943-8333; 52 Muhammad Farid St., Heliopolis. Tel: 2635-4485, 2633-7617; Mobile: 0100-176-3008. Website: http://www.decorama egypt.com

♦ **Design Emporium Ltd.** Has been in the interior decorating business since 1991. The company boasts that it "is the largest sole agent and distributor of European and American fabrics, soft furnishings, wall-coverings, furniture, lighting, and accessories in Egypt." Address: 41 al-Ansar St., Dokki. Tel: 3478-3848, 3338-9910, 3761-7187. E-mail: sales@designemporiumegypt.com. Website: www.designemporiumegypt.com

♦ **Designopolis.** Stretched along 850 meters directly on the Cairo–Alexandria Desert Road. Going to Alexandria, the mall is located on the left side of the road, six kilometers after the toll station. Hours: 10:00 a.m.–10:00 p.m., seven days a week. Address: Sheikh Zayed City, Km. 38, Cairo–Alexandria Desert Road. Tel: 3303-9421/6. E-mail: info@designopolis.com. Website: http://www.designopolis.com

♦ **Ebony & Ivory.** Furniture for home, office, and garden. Addresses: 45 Road 6, Maadi. Tel: 2753-0022; and Designopolis.

♦ **Eklego Design.** A firm specializing in contemporary interior and furniture design, as well as home accessories. Hours: 10:00 a.m.–10:00 p.m., seven days a week. Address: 8 Sheikh al-Marsafi Square, 1st floor (above Beanos), Zamalek. Tel: 2736-6353. Website: http://www.eklegodesign.net

♦ **Fayek.** Fine and decorative furniture. Address for Factory 1 and Headquarters: Merghem, Km. 23 Cairo–Alexandria Desert Road. Tel: 03-470-3098. Address for Factory 2: 25 al-Farrabi St., Labban, Alexandria. Tel: 03-393-5872/4906. Address for Showroom 1: 31 Salah Salim St., Attarin, Alexandria. Tel: 03-487-6878. Address for Showroom 2: 49 al-Hurriya St., Heliopolis. Tel: 2418-4233. Address for Showroom 3: 27 Abdel Mun'im Riyad St., Mohandiseen. Tel: 3337-6062. E-mail: mfayek@fayek.net. Website: www.fayek.net

♦ **El Helow Style.** For office furniture. Address: 14 Fuad Badwan St., Nasr City. Tel: 2275-9234/7939/9318/9272.

♦ **IDdesign Cairo.** Imported Scandinavian furniture for home, office, and garden. Address: 35 Corniche al-Nil, Sara Tower, Maadi. Tel: 2751-3155.

♦ **In and Out Furniture.** Has a variety of affordable furniture as well as pullout beds (magic sofa-bed, Product 806), pillows, sheets, and towels. There are nine branches in five locations—Cairo, Alexandria, North Coast, Hurghada, Giza. Check the website for the exact addresses. Their delivery service is free of charge if you live below the third floor. Above the third floor there is a charge of LE15 for each floor—for the entire order, not per piece. Staff are helpful but not pushy. Tel: 16663. Website: http://www.inoutfurniture.com

♦ **Istikbal.** A Turkish company that offers a reasonably priced variety of styles of furniture—steel, classic, modern, office, and garden furniture, also lighting and mattresses. Address: 16b Ubur Bldgs., off Salah Salim St., Nasr City. Tel: 2480-2134, 0100-259-4533.

♦ **Mashrabiyya Workshop.** Furniture, room screens, doors, mirrors. Three workshops together produce beautiful handmade *mashrabiyya* furniture. The furniture is displayed on the sidewalk. Craftsmen will custom design the furniture to fit your requirements. Bargain down by 10–20 percent of the asking price; once the price is agreed upon, a down payment is required. Finishing dates are honored. Address: Road 9, next to Café Greco, Maadi.

♦ **Meubles Bamboo Anto.** Rattan and cane manufacturers since 1948. Address: 195 Ramsis St., Cairo. Tel: 2590-0738/2049.

♦ **Miac Fine Furniture.** Branch addresses: Designopolis. Tel: 2520-2586; 24 Gam'at al-Duwal al-Arabiya St., Mohandiseen. Tel: 3344-1813; Abu Ghali Center, al-Ubur City. Tel: 4477-0846. Website: www.miac-eg.com

♦ **Mit Rehan.** Fine furniture. Address: 13 al-Mar'ashli St., Zamalek. Tel: 2735-4378, 2738-1447.

♦ **Nadim.** Besides a wide selection of contemporary furniture, there is a range of traditional products including ceilings, flooring, furniture, doors and windows, handmade carpets, handmade brass lamps, and small decorative items like mirrors and picture frames. Address: Abu Rawash Industrial Zone, Cairo–Alexandria Desert Road, Giza. Behind Smart Village. Tel: 3539-1601/8. E-mail: nadiminfo@nadim.org. Website: http://www.nadim.org

♦ **Noon.** Wooden furniture designed with hand-carved Arabic calligraphy. Address: 29 Sheraton Housing Zone, (behind Fairmont Hotel, formerly the Sheraton Hotel), Heliopolis, Airport Road, Cairo. Tel: 0122-171-6951, 0100-147-6560. Email: info@noon-designs.com. Website: www.noon-designs.com

♦ **Philosophy.** European- and Japanese-style furniture. Address: 40B Muhammad Mazhar St., Zamalek. Tel: 2738-0163.

♦ **White House.** Ultra-modern furniture imported from the Netherlands. Address: Omar ibn al-Khattab St., CityStars, Shop No. 160, Heliopolis. Tel: 16566, 2480-2230, 0128-188-8818, 0109-001-1120.

♦ **Zimmer.** A well-stocked showroom of household furniture (indoor and outdoor), rugs, lighting, wallpaper, and accessories. Zimmer carries international brands of contemporary furniture and fabrics for upholstery. They carry modern rugs by El Kahhal, a famous name in rug weavers in Egypt. The store accepts payment in U.S. dollars and Egyptian pounds. Hours: Saturday–Thursday 10:00 a.m.–10:00 p.m., Friday 2:00 p.m.–10:00 p.m. Addresses: 23A Ismail Muhammad St., Zamalek. Tel: 2736-0420. Designopolis, Shop S-136, Sahara Cluster, Km. 38, Cairo–Alexandria Road. Tel: 3857-1991. Website: http://zimmershowroom.com

Antique Furniture

There are well-known areas to shop for antiques: Zamalek, Downtown, and Khan al-Khalili in Cairo, and the Attarin district in Alexandria. Antiques are as expensive as imported furniture, plus you need to know about them to be able to spot the difference between a genuine antique and a reproduction. Be informed that anything over one hundred years old requires an export permit and may not be allowed out of Egypt.

Downtown:

♦ **Gallery Baha.** Address: 28 Bustan St.

♦ **Louvre Meuble.** Address: 14 Mustafa Abu Heif St. Tel: 2392-3048.

♦ **Osiris Auction House.** Address: 15–17 Sherif St., in front of National Bank. Tel: 2392-6609, 0122-379-7217, 0100-144-2036.

Downtown on Hoda Shaarawy Street:

Hoda Shaarawy Street is full of shops selling antiques. Some shops have no name.

Making a House Your Home

9

Take someone who is familiar with prices and able to bargain.

♦ **Ahmed Zeinhoum.**

♦ **Gallery El Hag Hamdi El Araby.** Antique masterpieces and furniture. Tel: 2392-3550, 0122-736-3469.

♦ **Gallery El Shark.** Address: 16 Hoda Shaarawy St. Tel: 2392-0259, 0122-878-1709.

♦ **Hassan & Ali.**

♦ **Mahrous Mohamed El Assal.** Address: 21 Hoda Shaarawy St. Tel: 2393-8852, 2390-4263, 0122-211-0216.

Zamalek:
The best way to look for antiques in Zamalek is to begin walking on 26th July Street. Stroll through the small streets and alleys; there are treasures to be found around every corner. Here are a few suggestions:

♦ **Atrium.** Address: 4 Muhammad Mazhar St. Tel: 2735-6869.

♦ **Caravanserai.** Antiques and reproductions. Address: 16 Mar'ashli St. Tel: 2735-0517, 0100-167-5851.

♦ **Le Souk.** Antique furniture, carpets, paintings, and silver. A beautiful store and very friendly staff. They host monthly exhibitions of Egyptian artists. Definitely a store to visit and enjoy the beautiful collection. Address: 6 Salah al-Din St. Tel: 2736-5772, 0100-041-2525. Website: www.lesoukegypt.com

♦ **Nostalgia.** Address: 6 Zakariya Rizq St. Tel: 2737-0880.

♦ **The Loft.** Address: 12 al-Sayyid al-Bakri St. Tel: 2736-6931. Website: http://www.loftegypt.com

Maadi:

♦ **Anni Z Antiques.** Address: At the beginning of the main bridge into Maadi on the left. 38 Road 6, Maadi. Tel: 0100-109-1468.

♦ **Morgana.** Address: 57 Road 9. Tel: 2380-2370, 0122-983-3336.

♦ **Old House Antique Gallery.** Soud Roushdy specializes in wooden windows and doors. Address: 28D Road 232, Nirco Buildings, Digla, Maadi. Tel: 2521-2562, 0100-527-3280.

Antiques: Restoration and Repair
Art and antiques restorer: A few meters down the narrow Mirghani alleyway in Downtown, close to the American University in Cairo campus, there is an old brass door leading to a staircase. On the top floor there are four small rooms, decorated with paintings. This is the atelier of Mohamed Modar, one of the few art restorers in Egypt. He repairs damaged parts of antique

surfaces (paintings, boxes) to restore and preserve their original image. Hours: after 5:00 p.m. Address: 15 Mirghani Alleyway (Harat al-Mirghani), off Muhammad Mahmud St., Downtown. Tel: 2794-8642, 0100-143-2574.

Antique furniture restoration: Ayman el-Azabawi at Morgana. Address: 57 Road 9, Maadi. Tel: 2380-2370.

Children's Bedrooms and Furniture

♦ **Bon Bon.** Address: 34 Michel Bakhum St., Dokki. Tel: 3335-2663, 0100-101-3303.

♦ **Paper Airplane.** For children's bedroom wall designs. Tel: 0100-455-5568. E-mail: paperairplane@chadisalama.com

♦ **Sia Home Fashion.** Head Office address: 11 Suleiman Abaza St., Mohandiseen. Tel: 3761-7248. E-mail: info@singe-eg.com. Website: www.singe-eg.com

Gardens and Shade
When one thinks of Cairo's environment one rarely thinks green, yet Cairo has many beautiful gardens to enjoy. Plant nurseries are along sidewalks and tucked away under bridges. Most apartments have balconies, which are the perfect places to enjoy a little garden in your own home. You will need to assess the shade and sunlight before buying plants. Summer heat can dry up a potted plant within days, so it is important to select plants that can survive the environment. Plants have one goal and that is to grow. They will try adapting to any environment to survive, so with an appreciative plant owner, a gorgeous garden balcony can be created.

Another reason to decorate with potted plants is to detox your home from airborne pollutants and to create a buffer to absorb noise. Research has proven that certain plants revitalize the air and clean up toxins, such as formaldehyde and carbon monoxide, that are found in Cairo's air. NASA has conducted an official study of the top ten air-purifying plants. Top of the list is the areca palm tree, which removes chemical toxins and is an air humidifier. The lady palm *(Rhapis excelsa)* and bamboo palm are top-ranked purifying plants. The rubber plant *(Ficus robusta)* requires less light and removes formaldehyde from indoor air. The spider plant (Boston fern or *Nephrolepis exalta*) is called the "most efficient filtering plant." The mother-in-law's-tongue plant (snake plant or *S. trifsciata laurentii*) also filters chemical toxins, but beware: If you have pets or babies, the leaves are poisonous (as are poinsettias).

Potted Plants
Pots come in all shapes and sizes and are either earthenware or terra-cotta. They can be bought in quantity and cheaply on the main road leading to Fustat in Old Cairo. Buy plastic pots and rectangular plastic planters for hanging on balcony railings at nurseries and large supermarkets. Buy soil and peat moss from flower stores or plant stores. Carrefour carries 1–2 kilogram bags of peat moss.

Making a House Your Home

9

Plants and Gardening Accessories
If you want a varied selection, take a day and visit greenhouses: Website: http://www. egypt-green.com

♦ **Centech.** Address: 6 Zakariya Rizq St., Zamalek. Tel: 2737-0371. Contact: Dr. Mohamed Adel El Ghandour. Tel: 0122-214-0031.

♦ **Safwat Habib Greenhouses.** Address: al-Mansuria–Imbaba–Giza. Tel: 3890-0506/7, 0100-639-4558, 0100-160-1276.

♦ **El Shourouk Farm.** Km 72, Cairo–Alexandria Desert Road. Tel: 0100-663-8272, 0100-341-1530, 0100-160-1276.

Nurseries in the city are along the Nile banks in Roda Island, Giza, and Zamalek. In Digla, Maadi, there are nurseries on both sides of the railroad tracks.

There is a Garden and Flower Show that brings together nurseries from across Egypt for three weeks in March at Orman Botanical Garden in Giza. Here you can buy anything from the smallest cactus plant to a massive bougainvillea tree. Investigate the various garden stores and their products.

Inexpensive garden supplies are in Taht al-Rab'a market along Ahmad Mahir Street. There you can find tools, fertilizers, garden hoses, and seeds. Along the street there are shops that sell canvas for umbrellas and ready-made garden umbrellas. Across from the entrance of Bab Zuwayla, fabric for upholstering outdoor furniture is on the Khayamiya, Tentmakers' Street.

Date-palm chairs and tables are the best choice for outdoor furniture. They are inexpensive, comfortable, environmentally friendly, weather well, and look great. Add colorful cushions. Bamboo and cane furniture is more expensive; go to Ahmad al-Gindi St., Downtown, and Meubles Bamboo Anto (rattan and cane manufacturers since 1948) 195 Ramsis St., Cairo. Tel: 2590-0738/2049.

For outdoor garden paraphernalia, take a trip to Old Cairo, cross al-Salih Bridge from the Corniche, and along the road driving toward Fustat there are potters and plaster artisans. From fountains to plaster medallions, the perfect decoration to grace a garden or balcony is to be found here. Be sure to bargain.

Tagoury's House specializes in outdoor furniture that is durable and colorful, lighting, flooring, outdoor chaises, decor, tables, chairs, benches, fountains, fire pits, and gardening supplies. Tagoury uses materials that range from teak, aluminum, wood, wicker, and cedar to wrought iron. Also, they have a shade solution that comes as a multifunctional umbrella of various shapes and materials to fit the space needed. Tel: 2417-8914, 2290-8491. Web-site: www.tagouryshouse.com. To locate a showroom, go to the website.

Shading

◆ **Daghash.** Outdoor shading solutions. Address: Ring Road, New al-Marg, 23rd July Village. Tel: 4463-1264. E-mail: daghash@link.net. Website:www.daghash group.com

At **Taht al-Rab'a**, along Ahmad Mahir Street near Bab Zuwalya, you can find small shops selling patio umbrellas. Tagoury's House (see above) has a shade solution in the form of a multifunctional umbrella.

Hardware Stores, Locks, and Keys
Ataba market is the area to investigate for all hardware items, paints, and electrical fittings. One store leads to another. It is almost like going on a scavenger hunt; you will find some unusual and interesting items. All this takes time and a working knowledge of Arabic, so if you just want to buy the item without a cultural experience, try Carrefour, Spinneys at CityStars, or Hyper 1 in 6th October City. In Zamalek there is a small hardware store on 26th July Street with helpful staff. Sidi Contractor, Lotfy H. Sheta. Address: 159 26th July St., Zamalek. Tel: 2735-9142.

Household Services, Maintenance, and Repairs
A reliable and knowledgeable carpenter, plumber, or electrician is not easy to find. When you do, thank your lucky stars!

◆ **T.G. General Services.** Plumbing, electrical, painting, carpentry, air conditioners, appliance repair, and local moves. Address: 13 Road 314, New Maadi, behind GUPCO Company. Tel: 2702-5432, 0122-221-0432. E-mail: info@generalser viceson line.com. Website: www.general services online.com

◆ **Osman Group Services.** Offers services and repairs in electronics and appliance repairs, flooring (wood, tile, stone), painting, plumbing, car rentals, and local moving. Hours: Saturday to Thursday 9:30 a.m.–10:00 p.m. Address: 4 and 23 Road 205, Maadi. Tel: 2754-3575, 2520-1669, 0100-400-0409, 0122-212-8914. E-mail: info@osmangroupservices.com. Website: www.osmangroupservices.com

Professional Upholstery and Carpet Cleaner
Panorama Group opened in 1999 in Cairo and now has three branches in Cairo and one in Alexandria. They specialize in suction and shampooing carpets, wall-to-wall carpets, upholstered furniture, and mattresses. Address: 47 Road 7, Maadi. Tel: 2359-5818, 0100-783-3430. E-mail: panoramagroup_2008@yahoo.com or nagla_77@yahoo.com.

Kitchens

◆ **Amr Helmy Designs.** Ultramodern and custom-design kitchens. Addresses: 34 Ahmad Urabi St., Mohandiseen. Tel: 2358-0133, 2378-3914, 2359-0540; Maadi Classics: 46 Road 9. Tel: 2359-4098; 2

Making a House Your Home

9

Saudia Bldg., al-Nuzha St. Tel: 2690-8578. E-mail: info@amrhelmydesigns.com. Website: http://www.amrhelmydesigns.com

♦ **Contistahl.** Address: 42 Ahmad Urabi St., Mohandiseen. Tel: 3344-2835, 3305-0544. E-mail: orabi@contistahlgroup.com. Website: www.contistahlgroup.com

♦ **Dupont Products SA.** Dupont developed different types of materials to use on countertops, such as Corian. Corian lends itself to any style of kitchen design. It permits the assembly of sinks, counters, or wall panels without visible seams. It is seamless, nonporous, repairable, stain-resistant, and hygienic, and has a 10-year warranty. Contact: Antoine Rizkallah. Address: 106 Markaz al-Madina al-Tugari St., First Settlement, New Cairo. Tel: 2754-6580, 0127-138-5678, 0122-783-2815. E-mail: Antoine.n.rizkallah@egy.dupont.com. For information on Dupont science and innovations, go to these sites: www.corian.com, www.zodiaq.com, www.buildingonscience.dupont.com

♦ **Häcker.** German-made kitchens. Showroom addresses: 1007 Corniche al-Nil. Tel: 2364-5916; and Designopolis. Website: www.hacker.com.eg

♦ **Ossama El Shahed Group, La Poupée Décor.** Address: 36 Gam'at al-Duwal al-Arabiya St., Mohandiseen. Tel: 3302-3397, 3303-0966. E-mail: hofashion@link.net

Kitchen Accessories

Hyper 1 and Carrefour have inexpensive kitchenware. Alfa Market branches have kitchenware, but they are pricier. If you are looking for cheap goods (not quality), go to El Tawheed wal Nour. There are stores in every area of Cairo; to find out where, check out www.yellowpages.com.eg

♦ **Bouri Center–Moulinex.** A wide variety of kitchen equipment featuring blenders, choppers, coffee makers, mixers, vacuum cleaners, irons, and food processors. Address: Multi-trade Bldg., Road 17, Fifth Settlement Service Area, New Cairo. Tel: 2618-2333.

♦ **Gourmet Egypt.** Sells Weber charcoal and gas BBQs. Tel: 19339. Website: www.gourmetegypt.com

Lighting—Chandeliers

In every area of Cairo there are small stores selling a range of styles of lamps and ceiling lights. For oriental styles, Khan al-Khalili is the place to look, but be prepared to bargain.

♦ **Alef.** Decorative and expensive chandeliers and lamps, but all pieces are one of a kind. Hours: Monday to Saturday 10:30 a.m.–2:00 p.m. and 5:00 p.m.–8:00 p.m. Address: 14 Muhammad Anis St., Zamalek. Tel: 2735-3690, 0100-145-9338. E-mail: monagrieche@alefgallery.com. Website: www.alefgallery.com

♦ **Atelier 87.** Stained-glass lamps and chandeliers. Address: 18 Jeddah St., off Muhyi al-Din Abu al-Izz St., Mohandiseen. Tel: 0100-153-8113.

♦ **Crystal Asfour.** Crystal lamps and chandeliers. Address: Kulliyit al-Zira'a St., Corniche al-Nil, Industrial Zone, Shubra al-Khayma, Qalyubiya. Tel: 16218, 4220-1032/1670, 0100-534-0063. Website: www.asfourcrystal.com/Crystal/index.asp

♦ **Luxor Co. Alabaster Products.** Alabaster chandeliers and accent lamps. The showroom and factory in Muqattam encourages visits to watch artisans make these beautiful objects. Customized items can be made on request. Main showroom: First left on

Controlling Pests

Where there is one cockroach, there are many more! Proteins called allergens are found in cockroach feces and saliva that cause allergic reactions and asthma in some people. Cockroaches have been around for millions of years and love crowded cities, so they are not going to go away. Cockroaches and ants are the most common household pests in Cairo. Here are some tips to keep pests under control.

1. Clean your house regularly. Cockroaches feed on crumbs and are attracted to sugar. Clean up spilled beverages immediately, clean out cabinets regularly, and cover containers. Eliminate cockroaches' food sources and keep surfaces clean.
2. Wash dishes as soon as you use them; keep counters and sinks clean.
3. Fix leaks immediately and replace rotten wooden cupboards or baseboards.
4. Seal cracks in tiles and cabinets.
5. Remove boxes and newspaper where pests hide.

6. Keep kitchen and bathroom garbage bins clean.

Home remedies against cockroaches:
1. Boric acid powder is safe for humans and pets and kills cockroaches. Mix equal parts of boric acid powder with cane sugar, and pour the mixture in dark places—under sinks, under the refrigerator and stove, and in dark cabinets.
2. Clean areas well and spray with a bottle of water and capful of bleach, and air dry overnight.
3. Take a thin slice of cucumber or bay leaf, put it on a paper towel and place it in corners of kitchen and bathroom cabinets. Cockroaches hate the smell of cucumbers and bay leaves, but they need to be replaced every two weeks.
4. If sprays are used, only spray the infested area. Do not spray near food or where children play, crawl, or sleep. Read the directions carefully. Make sure the area is well ventilated.

Making a House Your Home

9

the road to A.P.E. Recycling Plant, Muqattam; Branch 1: 23 Road 231, Digla, Maadi; Branch 2: Mustafa Kamil St., in front of Metro Market, Road 9, Maadi. Tel: 0122-354-1403, 0122-976-0900. E-mail: elgelany 2000@yahoo.com

Pest Control and Cockroaches
It is advisable to have your apartment or villa sprayed for pests before you move furniture into your home. Once you are living in your home, be extremely cautious when making the decision to bring in a pest control company to fumigate. If there is an infestation of cockroaches and ants that you cannot get rid of by the usual hand-held sprays or home remedies, you might need a professional company. The sprays that the companies use are toxic to humans and pets, and leave a residue on surfaces, dishes, and furniture that can cause illness and, in some cases, death. Most companies ask the residents to leave their home for forty-eight hours so the chemicals can settle. So leave this approach till the last resort. Below are two companies that have been mentioned as being reliable, but it is good to ask your employer or Egyptian friends for their recommendations.

♦ **Insectox for Pest Control.** Address: 20 Abdel Hafiz Salama St., Faisal, Giza. Tel: 3568-0700, 0122-317-3400, 0122-799-2943. E-mail: info@insectox.com or insectox@hotmail.com. Website: http://www. insectox.com/index.htm

♦ **Kaltex International Group.** This group advertises the opposite of the warning above: "is the only company with ISO 90001 & Ministry of Health certification. Safe & health-friendly pesticides that are odorless, non-toxic & doesn't require leaving home." Address: 50 al-Nasr Road, Nasr City. Tel: 2409-4488, 0100-457-3157. Website: http://www.kaltex-eg.com

Picture Framers
There are many shops that frame pictures. Here are two that come highly recommended:

♦ **Riad Soliman.** Excellent framers, limited choice of frames. Address: 32A Yehia Ibrahim St., Zamalek. Tel: 2736-4365, 0122-312-4196.

♦ **Readers Corner.** Well-known framers. Address: 33 Abdel Khaliq Tharwat St., Downtown. Tel: 2392-8801.

Silver Plating, Polishing, and Silvering
There are many silver shops around Cairo, but Saad of Egypt is probably the most well-known. You can take your silver to their shops for polishing. Saad of Egypt also re-silvers antiques, silverware, and silver pieces. Pieces are sent to the Khan al-Khalili workshop for re-silvering and polishing. Ask the shop which day of the week a polisher visits; then your silver can be polished on the same day.

♦ **Saad of Egypt.** Addresses: 7 Suleiman Abaza St., Mohandiseen. Tel: 3761-3796/8,

0100-190-0415; inside Ramses Hilton, Downtown. Tel: 2574-6980, 0100-190-0414; 95B al-Mirghani St., Heliopolis. Tel: 2290-9466, 2291-4154, 0100-190-0412; Khan al-Khalili. Tel: 2589-3992/3, 0100-190-0413; 71 Road 9, Maadi. Tel: 2358-5065, 0100-667-0058.

Tableware and Glassware
Porcelain china and stoneware factories produce a rather small quantity compared to demand. Most large supermarkets such as Carrefour, Alfa, and Spinneys carry imported tableware, usually from China. Lu'lu'at al-Zamalek carries Egyptian-made tableware, though sets are not consistently the same quantity. Royal Home also carries made-in-Egypt tableware and glassware as well as inexpensive kitchen items. For something different, beautifully crafted onyx and alabaster goblets and tableware are made in Muqattam from alabaster slabs brought from Luxor. In Khan al-Khalili there are still shops that sell hand-blown glassware. For inexpensive, handmade ceramic tagines, tea sets, plates, bowls, and cups in floral and abstract designs, take a trip to Fustat and visit the Abdeen Factory for Ceramics.

♦ **Abdeen Factory for Ceramics.** Hours: 10:00 a.m.–10:00 p.m. Address: Fustat al-Gidida Market Shop No. 1, near Amr ibn al-'As Mosque, Old Cairo. Tel: 2365-1677.

♦ **The Factory.** Imported glassware, reasonably priced. Addresses: 46 al-Thawra St.,

Mohandiseen. Tel: 3336-7276; 8 Sisostris St., Korba, Heliopolis. Tel: 2415-2237, 2414-1233.

♦ **Lu'lu'at al-Zamalek.** Address: 171 26th July St., Zamalek. Tel: 2736-1188, 0100-310-3310, 0100-515-4440.

♦ **Luxor Co. Alabaster Products.** The showroom and factory in Muqattam encourages visits to watch artisans make these beautiful objects. Customized items can be made on request. Main Showroom: First left on the road to A.P.E. Recycling Plant, Muqattam; Branch 1: 23 Road 231, Digla, Maadi; Branch 2: Mustafa Kamil St., in front of Metro Market, Road 9, Maadi. Tel: 0122-354-1403, 0122-976-0900. E-mail: elgelany2000@yahoo.com

♦ **Nashat Mohamed Hasan Co.** Hand-decorated wine glasses and tea sets. Address: Way 12, Khan al-Khalili. Tel: 2592-7510, 0100-108-4950. E-mail: nashatmohamed@link.net. Website: www.NashatOfEgypt.com

♦ **Royal Home.** Addresses: 45 Gam'at al-Duwal al-Arabiya St., Mohandiseen. Tel: 3760-7432; 18 Shagarat al-Durr, Zamalek. Tel: 2736-1660.

Traditional Egyptian Food
What better way to end a chapter about a house becoming your home than to talk about food! Food brings people together, so invite your neighbors and prepare, pick up, or get delivered some mouth-

Making a House Your Home

9

Traditional Drinks

'Ahwa. Thick, sugary coffee served in a small coffee cup. *'Ahwa saada* has no sugar, *'ahwa 'arriiHa* has a little sugar, *'ahwa mazboot* is medium sweet, and *'ahwa ziyaada* is very sweet. *'Ahwa* is never served with milk.

'Asiir, meaning juice. In Egypt enjoy freshly squeezed, seasonal juices: mango, pomegranate, orange, carrot, and *asab* (sugar cane), served cold.

Herbal teas. Mint, cinnamon, ginger, anise, *karkadeeh*, served hot.

Irfa. A cinnamon drink, served cold or hot.

'Irq sus. A chilled licorice drink.

Karkadeeh. An infusion made from the calyces of the *Hibiscus sabdariffa* flower, served hot or cold.

Limoon. A cold drink made with lime and (sometimes) mint. The drink can be heavy with sugar, served cold.

Mango lassi. A yogurt, milk, and mango drink, served cold.

Sahlab. A drink made of milk and sesame seeds, served hot and topped with nuts. (*Sahlab* is a thickening agent like flour made from grinding the dried tubers of *Orchis mascula*.)

Shayy. A black tea, served hot, usually thick with sugar but no milk. It is traditionally served in a glass. *Kushari* (loose) tea leaves are sometimes replaced by tea bags. Traditional *shayy kushari* is sweetened with cane sugar and flavored with mint.

Tamar hindi. A sour, chilled drink made from tamarind seed that is mainly found in the summer months. A Ramadan favorite.

watering Egyptian dishes to celebrate your move to Egypt. In chapter 10 there are plenty of suggestions for carrying on the shopping experience . . . and one needs sustenance to take on the vast shopping choices in Cairo!

Bread, legumes, fruits, and vegetables are the staples of an Egyptian diet. From these ingredients comes a diverse range of dishes that define the Egyptian kitchen. From Turkey to Egypt, over the centuries, there has been a diffusion of the Middle Eastern cuisines, so, in each country, you will find similarities in ingredients and dishes. Bread and beans provide lasting sustenance throughout the day. *'Eesh baladi* or *'eesh masri* (local bread or Egyptian bread) is a flat, whole-wheat bread baked in fired ovens. *'Aish'* literally means 'life' or 'to sustain life' in Arabic. There is nothing more satisfying and sustaining than a hot loaf of *'eesh baladi* filled with *fuul* (*fuul medammes*—mashed fava beans), chopped parsley, onion and garlic, lemon juice, and olive oil. (Tip: If you love Mexican burritos and cannot find a can of refried beans, substitute a can of *fuul medammes*.)

Egyptian cuisine is a combination of fresh meats and vegetables that go together to make a variety of stews, usually served with sticky rice. Often vegetables such as squash and eggplant *(mahshi)* or grape leaves *(wara' 'inab)* are stuffed with rice and meat. *Mulukhiyya* (Jew's mallow or jute leaves) is a leafy vegetable that looks like mint, but has a distinct taste. This traditional dish is served with rice and poultry. (Legend has it that the third Fatimid ruler, al-Hakim, 996–1021, had a dire hatred of *mulukhiyya* and banned it from the Egyptian diet!) *Kufta* and *kabab* are ground meat and chunks, respectively, that are charcoal grilled. Pigeon *(Hamaam)* is a national delicacy served grilled or stuffed with green wheat *(firiik)*, which is one of the steps when processing this grain.

Cheeses native to Egypt's cuisine are two: *gibna ruumi* is a hard, sharp cheese that is an excellent substitute for Parmesan cheese, and *gibna beeDa* is similar to feta cheese. Fruit is usually served after a meal, but there are plenty of syrupy sweets like *basbuusa* to satisfy any sweet tooth. *Umm Ali* is a hot dessert similar to bread pudding. A pudding called *mahalabiyya* is made with milk, sugar, vanilla, and starch.

Fitir is the Egyptian pancake and is served with sweet or savory fillings. *Ta'miyya* is a larger variety of the well-known Levantine treat, falafel, made from mashed chickpeas or fava beans and fried. *Ta'miyya* is usually eaten with bread, *taHina* (sesame) sauce, and pickles. *Fisiikh* is a fermented, salted, and dried fish that is served at *Shamm al-Nisim* (spring celebrations) as the traditional dish. (Beware of eating *fisiikh*, as every year there are out-

Kushari: **Egypt's national dish—food of revolutionaries!**
Kushari, a dish of rice, macaroni, and lentils, is considered the national dish of Egypt and played an important part in nourishing the demonstrators during the 25 January Revolution. Two of the most famous *kushari* restaurants are Abou Tarek and Koshary El Tahrir.

♦ **Abou Tarek.** Established in 1950 and recently featured on CNN. Hours: 7:00 a.m.–midnight. Address: 16 Champollion St., Downtown. Tel: 2577-5935. Website: http://www.aboutarek.com

♦ **Alex Top.** Address: 2 Taha Hussein St., Zamalek. Tel: 2735-7601.

♦ **Kushari al-Tahrir.** Address: 12 Yusuf al-Gindi St., off Bab al-Luq St., Downtown. Tel: 2795-8418.

♦ **Kushari Hind.** Address: 5 al-Thawra St., Heliopolis. Tel: 2418-3946.

♦ **Lux Kushari.** Address: 1 al-Suuq Bldgs., al-Falaki Square, Downtown. Tel: 2794-5178.

breaks of salmonella due to improperly treated and dried fish.)

One dish that is almost always included in an Egyptian *mezza* (hors d'oeuvre) is a plate of *babaghannuug*. Eggplant (aubergine) is the major ingredient that gives this

Babaghannuug

1 large or 3 small eggplants
2–3 tablespoons of taHina (sesame seed paste)
2–3 tablespoons lemon juice
Salt to taste

If you have a gas stove (not an electric stove), char the skin of the eggplant over the gas flame, turning the eggplant to blacken the skin. Place on a tin-foil-lined oven dish in a hot oven (200°C) and roast until the eggplant collapses. Remove from the oven and slit it open (careful of the steam), removing the flesh and discarding the seeds. Cool. Pound the flesh using a pestle and mortar or a food processor. Add remaining ingredients. According to your preference, the food processor makes a smooth consistency or you can leave it chunky. Adjust seasonings. Chill a few hours or overnight. If you wish, pour a tablespoon of olive oil on top and decorate with chopped parsley.

starter its slightly bitter, smoky flavor. The difference between a good babaghannuug and a fabulous babaghannuug is the eggplant itself and the preparation of it.

The eggplant should be firm and heavy, and the skin a shiny deep purple in color. An eggplant that has deep grooves or wrinkles is the best, as it has less water, fewer seeds, and the flesh is darker in color. It is essential to 'smoke' your eggplant. If you have a gas stove-top burner, grill the eggplant directly over the fire to char the skin. Do not prick the eggplant. If you have an oven, turn it to maximum heat and bake the eggplant for about thirty minutes until it smokes, or wrap it in tin foil to grill.

Catering

If, after all the shopping, cleaning, and organizing, what you really need is for someone else to do the cooking, here are two groups that come with top recommendations:

♦ **House 2 House Catering Co.** Offers customized catering and event planning for all occasions. No event too small or too large. They have a talented team, dedicated to making each celebration distinctive. The decoration, menu, and music are designed to meet your needs. Call Osman Ghaleb at 0100-110-2516. E-mail: osmang@house2housecatering.com

♦ **Kitchen Moves.** Caters particularly for businesses and events, but also for cocktail receptions, birthdays, and buffets. They deliver boxed lunches. The food is fresh and homemade, either delivered or served at the client's request. Tel: 0114-777-7187. E-mail: info@kitchenmoves.com

10
Shopping

Shopping—the final chapter! If you are like me, you hate to shop. Did you know that 28 percent of American women hate to shop? For them, shopping produces stress and anxiety any time they think about hitting the mall. For those of you who find this emotion inconceivable, have mercy. As shopping enthusiasts who enjoy the challenge of the hunt you will always find the specials, the bargains, the sales, and the most interesting shops. However, this chapter does not exclude you! We salute you and need your expert advice to reduce the pain of shopping, so, while you are in Egypt and wish to share your expertise, please do send an e-mail: aucpress@aucegypt.edu.

It has been over a decade since the ban was lifted on the importation of goods into Egypt. The ban was in place to protect the Egyptian textile, clothing, and furniture industries. Free-trade regulations opened the Egyptian market to worldwide competition. International brands flooded in. Malls grew up throughout the city to showcase these well-known and popular commodities. Now, there is no need to buy an airplane ticket to Europe to bring back your favorite type of underwear from Marks and Spencer or a pair of Ferragamo shoes from Paris, or to bring corn tortillas back in your suitcase. It's all in Cairo!

Well-known international and luxury brands are sold here, but are no less expensive than they are in the country of origin. With freight, customs, and general markup, prices can be the same and often higher. To sort out the different types of shopping experiences Cairo has to offer, this chapter begins with an overview of the old *suuqs*: the traditional shopping areas of Egyptians where they have shopped for centuries. Then there is a short description of the modern *suuq*s: malls and supermarkets. At this point the chapter takes a turn off the beaten path, providing information about stores that sell specialty foods, books, traditional crafts, and Egyptian goods. These stores support entrepreneurs and local crafts without which we may lose traditional techniques of beautiful handmade articles such as *mashrabiyya* and tally embroidery.

As this chapter only scratches the surface of the multitude of shopping experiences in Cairo, an excellent source of information is Cairo360: www.cairo360.com, which carries weekly reviews on everything, so

Shopping

10

sign up for the newsletter. The Yellow Pages (www.yellow-pagesegypt.com) is a directory that is a good place to check for businesses, with the advantage of a map to locate any address.

Consumers Unite!
One of the reasons that people avoid shopping is the worry of getting ripped off. Bargaining is time-consuming, and although some love the game, others find it a waste of time and just want a fair price for the goods. Another reason for anxiety is that, once a purchase is made, it usually cannot be returned. Most stores in Egypt have a policy of no returns, no exchanges, and all sales are final. This can be exasperating if it is your first post from the U.S. or Europe, where everything is returnable. However, there is help on the way through the Consumer Protection Agency as well as a private Egyptian citizens' initiative—Going Local.

Consumer Protection Agency
The following information has been taken from the website: http://www.cpa.gov.eg/english/services.htm.

Consumer Complaint Service: Helps consumers know about their rights and obligations. Hotline: 19588. The hotline service was first activated for experimental purposes in certain districts. It was then gradually extended to all Cairo districts. Now the hotline serves Cairo, Giza, and Qaliubiya.

Services offered through the Egyptian National Postal Authority: A joint cooperation protocol has been signed by the CPA and the Egyptian National Postal Authority (ENPA) to offer free-of-charge complaint forms to consumers who wish to report any problems they face when buying a product. Consumers can write their complaints and send the form, free of postal charges, to the CPA.

Consumer complaints are being received at the Mohandiseen Operations headquarters:

Walk-in consumers can file their complaints in person at the consumer protection office located at 96 Ahmad Urabi St., Mohandiseen.

Website Complaint Filing System: The purpose of this service is to facilitate complaint filing. Complaints received through the website are checked and examined daily so that a procedure may be taken in accordance with the Consumer Protection Law and its Executive Regulations that were mainly enacted to protect consumers. Further consumer protection services will be offered through our constantly updated website: http://www.cpa.gov.eg/english/services.htm. Select 'Contact' to submit your complaint. E-mail address: info@cpa.gov.eg. Head office in Mohandiseen. Tel: 3305-5762/5/8, 3305-5795/6/7. Fax: 3305-5753. Complaints Department in Smart Village, Tel: 3538-0380/1/2/3. Fax: 3538-0384.

Going Local
A group of Egyptians has put together an initiative, Going Local, to fight back and demand consumer rights. The following is from their website:

Mission:

1. Expose all the shops/businesses that have a reputation for putting many people through disturbing or humiliating shopping experiences.

2. Become a well-established reference for all the shops that everyone living in/visiting Egypt should NOT shop at.

How to interpret information from this group:

1. A business with one bad mention on the group's list does not necessarily mean a bad business. Most probably it's a single bad employee. So please help the business to eliminate him, and name him!

2. A business with several bad experiences probably means that the shop's management sucks! You should be careful before choosing to deal with them.

3. A business with a huge list of horrible customer experiences probably means you should never ever enter the shop, even if they are the only shop in Egypt selling that product.

Going Local operates from 9:00 a.m. to 5:00 p.m. every day except Friday. They will only take action after receiving a fax with your story and a copy of your receipt. Always keep your receipts, and call within fourteen days of purchase.

(Source: http://buyegypt.blogspot.com/2009/03/getting-ripped-off.html)

Suuqs or Traditional Markets

♦ **Khan al-Khalili.** A fourteenth-century bazaar and, today, a tourist attraction with many of the trinkets 'made in China.' Beware of the hype (unless you want the experience) to coax you into a shop. If you do agree, remember that bargaining is a must; prices given are set up for bargaining as merchants expect this. Busloads of tourists crowd the narrow alleys every day like locusts, sweeping up cheap memorabilia of their trip. Keep in mind that merchants are aware that the tourists need to buy quickly, so they know all the marketing tricks. If you are a resident of Cairo, go for the experience and be discerning.

♦ **Taht al-Raba'.** An area on the other side of Khan al-Khalili, from al-Ghuri complex to Bab Zuwayla. Along Ahmad Mahir Street you will find an authentic marketplace where Egyptians have done their household shopping for centuries. Prices are less expensive than in stores if one speaks Arabic and knows the going price for things.

♦ **Suuq al-Khayamiya.** The Tentmakers' Bazaar at the entrance of Bab Zuwayla.

♦ **al-Muski** (Ataba Square to Khan al-Khalili). Electrical and hardware shops, paper products, buttons, sewing notions, bridal supplies, and so on. A real treasure of everything!

♦ **Suuq al-Futuh.** At the northern end of al-Mu'izz li-Din Illah St. It is not the market it

Shopping

10

Bargaining Tips

The ancient game called bargaining has been honed for centuries. Like any game, it takes practice to become an expert and get the price that you want or, at the very least, a fair price. Merchants raise prices as they expect the buyer to bargain. If you don't, you are the loser. Don't expect the merchant to come running after you and give you your money back. Bargaining is time-consuming and exhausting, and this is what the merchant hopes will make you give up and pay more for what you desire.

Here are the rules of the game:
♦ Show disinterest in what you want by looking at several items, casually asking for the price of each item. Realize that the correct price is probably half of the asking price. (It helps if you have some idea of the item's worth before engaging in the bargaining process.)
♦ Walk around, show disinterest, return to another item (not the one you want), discuss the price, go to the article you want, discuss that price.
♦ If you have not succeeded in getting the price to what you feel is fair, walk out of the shop.
♦ If you REALLY want the item, and the merchant does not call you back, you might return and offer a little more.

Bargaining is all about patience and perseverance. You can be sure that for all the sob stories a shopkeeper throws out, no matter what he/she says, once the price is agreed upon, the shopkeeper has gotten the price he/she wants. Remember, a vendor will NEVER let you leave with an item unless they have a margin of profit.

used to be, particularly in the spring when a wholesale market of green onions and garlic brought the pungent fragrance of springtime in the Egyptian countryside. Today al-Mu'izz is a pedestrian street rather than a neighborhood market. Still, there are shops with *shisha* pipes and metal workshops still scattered throughout.

♦ **Perfume and Spice Market.** An area in the Khan where al-Mu'izz and al-Azhar Streets meet.

♦ **Ataba Market.** A food market with household goods.

♦ **Wakalat al-Balah.** A daily flea market, closed Sundays, located on the Nile Corniche just before the World Trade Center. Wakalat al-Balah is known for its fabric market, with affordable upholstery and clothing fabric.

♦ **Suuq al-Azbakiya.** A second-hand book market. It is organized, with its own Arabic language website: http://www.sourelazbakia.

com/. If you enjoy a treasure hunt, there are books in Arabic, English, French, and sometimes German. It is located near the Ataba Garage, in front of the Puppet Theater.

♦ **Bab al-Luq.** A covered food market off Falaki Square.

♦ **Dokki Market.** A street with fruit, vegetables, butcher, and hardware stores, along Suleiman Guhar Street.

♦ **Manial Market.** Off of Manial Rd. on Roda Island. It is a small outdoor market with fruits, vegetables, meat, poultry, and bread.

♦ **Tawfiqiya Market.** An outdoor food market in Downtown.

Specific Kinds of Stores

Every area has its own mall, shopping streets, and traditional market. Take time to get to know the shops and supermarkets in the neighborhood, before you branch out to other areas. For an overview of shopping throughout Cairo, this section is separated into shopping categories—by malls, by supermarket, and by specialty stores. An effort has been made to provide shopping information in a variety of areas of the city. Some supermarkets are in malls, as are some cinemas. For a directory of cinemas and an up-to-date listing of movies, check weekly on www.Cairo360.com and http://english.ahram.org.eg/.

Malls

♦ **Bandar Mall.** An entertainment complex more than a mall, with movie centers, billiards, and a bowling center. Hours: 10:00 a.m.–midnight. Address: 1 Palestine St., Maadi. Tel: 2519-8855/44.

♦ **City Center.** Usually visited by locals. A retail haven, with brand names both international and local, the shopping mall is also home to City Center Cinema, a cinema complex with four screens. Hours: 10:00 a.m.–midnight. Address: 3 Makram Ebeid St., Nasr City. Tel: 2273-8855.

♦ **CityStars.** To date, this is Cairo's most grandiose mall: 750,000 square meters of shopping and eating pleasure. It has 645 stores (and counting). There are six levels in the grand atrium with every level housing local and international luxury brands. There is no need to go to Khan al-Khalili for traditional trinkets; CityStars has its own shops in addition to a Khan al-Khalili walk-through area. It contains Spinney's Supermarket, Virgin Mega Store, an international exhibition area, two indoor theme parks (Magic Galaxy Park for kids and E-zone), twenty-two wide-screen cinemas, coffee shops galore to keep you caffeinated to continue shopping, and food, food, and more food. Hours: 10:00 a.m.–midnight. Address: Omar ibn al-Khattab St., Heliopolis. Tel: 2480-0500. Website: www.citystars.com.eg

♦ **Dandy Mega Mall.** Built by the French company Chabot, this complex occupies

Shopping

10

82,000 square meters of land and includes Carrefour, a hypermarket, a three-screen cinema, and seventy shops including Marks and Spencer, IKEA, and Gourmet Egypt. Hours: 11:00 a.m.–1:00 a.m. Address: Km 28, Cairo–Alexandria Desert Road, 6th October City. Tel: 3539-0932/4/6. Website: www.dandyonlinemall.com

♦ **Designopolis.** Stretched along 850 meters directly on the Cairo–Alexandria Desert Road, it is a new center dedicated to all types of interior decorating. Going to Alexandria, the mall is located on the left side of the road, six kilometers after the toll station. Hours: 10:00 a.m.–10:00 p.m., seven days a week. Address: Sheikh Zayed City, Km. 38, Cairo–Alexandria Desert Road. Tel: 3303-9421/6. E-mail: info@de signopolis.com. Website: http://www.de signopolis.com

♦ **First Mall.** Three floors of exclusive shops that include jewelry, clothing, bags, and shoes of international luxury brands. First Mall is connected with the Four Seasons at the First Residence, Giza. Hours: 11:00 a.m.–midnight. Tel: 3571-3639.

♦ **Galleria.** Offers a shopping and entertainment experience on seven floors that include retail outlets and cinemas. Hours: 11:00 a.m.–11:00 p.m. Address: Grand Hyatt Cairo, Corniche, Garden City. Tel: 2365-1234.

♦ **Genena Mall.** Offers all basic elements, over three hundred diverse shops, six

cinemas, and ice skating arena, video games, and billiards. Hours: 11:00 a.m.– midnight. Address: al-Batrawi St. (off Abbas al-Aqqad St.), Nasr City. Tel: 2404-7901/ 6261. E-mail: info@genena.com. Website: http://www.genena.com

♦ **Maadi City Center.** A prestigious shopping center built on the Ring Road leading to Qattamiya, and occupies an area of about 65,000 square meters. Built outside the city periphery, it provides many hours of entertaining activities, including Magic Planet for young kids, over forty-two stores, and Carrefour, Egypt's biggest hypermarket. Hours: 10:00 a.m.–midnight, Fridays 2:00 p.m.–midnight. Address: Ring Road, Maadi. Tel: 16061, 2520-4300, 2520-4000/1. Website: www.carrefouregypt.com

♦ **Nile City Mall.** A beautiful shopping center, but not easy to access as the Corniche is often crowded and blocked. There are two first-class cinemas. Hours: 11:00 a.m.–midnight. Address: Corniche al-Nil, Downtown. Tel: 2461-9000/2. Website: http://nilecitytowers.com

Supermarkets and Grocers
Supermarkets . . . grocers . . . kiosks . . . vegetable stands . . . hypermarkets, where to start? It can be difficult to know where to begin shopping. Neighborhood small grocers are an integral part of the city's fabric. Vegetable and fruit carts and stands that sell seasonal produce have been typically how Egyptians have shopped over

the centuries. Every area has traditional markets, except Zamalek. In these markets one can buy meat, poultry, fish, and fruits and vegetables.

Abu Zekry was the first to offer customers wholesale foodstuffs. Imported products are found at major chains—Alfa, Metro, Seoudi. Alfa offers more of a department store experience with garden furniture, tableware, clothing, kitchenware, and a variety of goods, whereas Metro and Seoudi maintain a purely grocery shopping experience. Most stores deliver.

Have you ever decided to bake a cake and found you didn't have enough eggs? This is when the nearby neighborhood store can save the day! Just call and they will deliver immediately. Of course, this requires prior knowledge of your area, so check out your nearest neighborhood grocer and their shelf stock such as boxes of water, yogurt, tomato paste, fresh oranges, bread, and eggs. Don't forget the telephone number—they will know your preference and will deliver within a few minutes.

In the last five years Egypt has allowed wholesale companies to open mega-superstores in the outskirts of Cairo. With plenty of parking and wholesale prices, these shops are very popular with Egyptians. Carrefour, Hyper 1, and Spinneys are the equivalent of Walmart. Do not shop on Thursday nights or Friday afternoons, which are peak shopping hours for Egyptians with families. If you want to beat the crowds, the best time is during the morning on a weekday.

♦ **Abu Zekry.** The pioneer wholesale-goods store. Outlets are in Abbasiya: Tel: 2483-0295; Giza: 4 Izz al-Din Omar St. Tel: 3771-9103; Heliopolis: 33 al-Higaz St. Tel: 2451-5811, and 9 Farid Simika St. Tel: 2636-9436; Maadi: Road 9. Tel: 2358-4281; Mohandiseen: 79 Ahmad Urabi St. Tel: 3304-3898, and 9 Muhyi al-Din Abu al-Izz St. Tel: 3335-3020; Nasr City: 35 Abbas al-Aqqad St. Tel: 2405-0694, and in front of Ahly Club. Tel: 2272-3124; Zamalek: 17 Bahgat Ali St. Tel: 2735-2924.

♦ **Alfa Market.** Supermarket and small department store where you'll find everything from food to stationery items, kitchen supplies, and even sporting goods. Home delivery hotline: 19299. Stores are in Dokki: 7 al-Sadd al-Ali St. Tel: 3338-2280; Heliopolis: 7 al-Zahabi Square (off Khalifa al-Ma'moun St.), Roxy. Tel: 2690-3125; Maadi: 7A Corniche al-Nil. Tel: 2525-6400; Zamalek: 4 al-Malik al-Afdal St. Tel: 2737-0804. Website: http://www.alfa.com.eg

♦ **Carrefour.** Mega-market that carries wholesale appliances, clothing, household goods, and groceries with a bakery, butcher, and spice center. Three outlets: Cairo–Alexandria Desert Road. Tel: 3539-2606; Maadi: Ring Road. Tel: 16061; al-Ubur City: Golf City Mall, Mubarak St. Tel: 2520-4200. Call Center: 16061.

♦ **Hyper 1.** Another mega-market shopping experience with a massive selection of groceries and cleaning supplies, also a bakery, butcher, and spice center. The second floor has toiletries, cosmetics, power tools, kitchenware, and appliances. There is indoor and outdoor furniture for sale as well. Hours: 10:00 a.m.–1:00 a.m. Address: 6th October City. Tel: 16404, 3850-4778.

♦ **Kimo Market.** One of the two best markets to find American products that are expensive, but, at least, available, such as Karo syrup, old-fashioned oatmeal, pumpkin pie filling, flour tortillas. Address: 1 Road 210, Victoria Square, Maadi. Tel: 2516-1788.

♦ **Mariam Market.** Caters to the expat community with a large selection of international and American foods. Expensive, but worth it when looking for comfort foods from 'home.' Hours: 9:00 a.m.–10:00 p.m. Address: 7B, intersection of Road 205 with Road 253, Digla, Maadi. Tel: 2519-6499/6488, 2516-5833.

♦ **Metro.** Has over twenty stores throughout Cairo. Metro is one of the few grocery stores that has an already-prepared food section: grilled chicken, *kufta*, brown rice and almonds, hommos, macaroni, *babaghannuug* are on the regular menu. Fresh breads—whole wheat and white—as well as mini hors d'œuvres and croissants are freshly baked, daily. Delivery number: 19619.

♦ **Seoudi.** Well-stocked Egyptian market. Stores are located in Dokki: 25 al-Misaha St. Tel: 3748-8440; Heliopolis: Khalid ibn al-Walid St. Tel: 2266-1155; Maadi: 4 Road 205. Tel: 2516-3627, and intersection of Road 153 with Road 214, Digla. Tel: 2754-6777; Mohandiseen: 68 al-Higaz St. Tel: 3346-0391; Zamalek: 20 Mar'ashli St. Tel: 2735-9596.

♦ **Spinneys.** Address: Omar ibn al-Khattab St., 1st floor, CityStars, Nasr City. Tel: 2480-2547/2341/2340/2342.

Organic, Gourmet, and Specialty Stores

Organic food specialist, Isis Company, one of the Sekem group of companies, was established in 1977. They are a leading producer of natural organic fruits, vegetables, herbal teas, and a variety of foodstuffs. Organic foods were not popular in Cairo's supermarkets until the beginning of this century. Then, after a decade, many produce groups entered the organic foods market. There were no regulations to ensure authenticity for the consumer. Consumers began to question if food labels that touted 'organic' or 'biodynamic' were a ruse to charge higher prices. The Ministry of Trade and Industry responded to complaints and introduced certification regulations. The Egyptian Organization for Standardization and Quality (EOSQ) was formed and requires producers to be accredited and registered with them. If inspection reveals standards have not been met, the producer will be shut down.

Organic

♦ **Bio Shop.** Carries top organic brands in foodstuffs, clothing, and accessories. Address: 27 Road 231, Maadi (behind Green Mill restaurant). Tel: 2521-2103.

♦ **Farmer's Market.** Held at Community Service Association. Every week small farmers bring their fresh organic fruits, herbs, and vegetables to CSA. Every Thursday from 9:00 a.m.–2:00 p.m. Address: 4 Road 21, Maadi. Tel: 2358-5284. Website: www.livinginegypt.org

♦ **Isis Company.** One of the Sekem group. Foods are free from pesticides, artificial additives, and preservatives. Their products are all organic: juices and drinks, herbal teas and coffee, fresh fruits and vegetables, cereals, flakes and muesli, sweeteners, sesame energy bars, rice and legumes, pasta, honey, jams, dates, nuts, dried fruits, dried herbs and spices, oil seeds, and edible oils. Sekem companies support social institutions of education, hospitals, and research. Tel: 0800-444-8444.

♦ **Organic & More Supermarket.** Organic fruits and vegetables, free of preservatives, genetically modified organisms, chemicals, or artificial colors. For home delivery call one of the branches. Addresses: 3 Cairo–Bilbeis Desert Road, al-Salam. Tel: 2656-4124/5; 8 Ahmad Sabri St., Zamalek. Tel: 2738-2747; 18 Road 218, Digla, Maadi. Tel: 2519-8325.

♦ **The Tree.** Organic vegetables and fruits. Home delivery. Open every day 7:00 a.m.–11:00 p.m. Address: 76 Road 9, Maadi. Tel (mobile): 0100-144-8241, 0100-567-9687.

♦ **The Veg Box.** The main service is to deliver boxes of fresh, high-quality fruits and vegetables twice a week, or according to the customers' requirements, in Maadi, Qattamiya, and New Cairo. Standard boxes of the best seasonal produce are prepared for customers or a box is prepared according to the customer's preferences. Free delivery times in Qattamiya and New Cairo are every Monday and Thursday. Free delivery times in Maadi and Digla are every Sunday and Wednesday. Customers can choose to receive a small, medium, or large box of their preferred selection. Every item is carefully packed in a plastic crate and then in one big box. A deliveryman delivers the box and collects the empty ones to be recycled. Plastic bags are rarely used. Call Nasr at 0100-073-1411. E-mail: thevegbox@hotmail.com, info@vegbox.net. Order from the website. There is a complete description of available choices. Website: www.thevegbox.net

Gourmet

Gourmet and specialty food shops have found a market niche. From designer cupcakes to bee pollen products, there is an assortment of clever, unique shops that are worth at least one visit. The most popular and successful shop for gourmet food is Gourmet Egypt. They rarely close. (Usually open on holidays.) They deliver within two hours of any order, anywhere in Cairo. They are reliable and the imported food is top quality.

♦ Cook's Day Off at Community Service Association. Cooks and bakers bring their goodies for sale every Thursday from 9:00 a.m. to 2:00 p.m. You will find soups, salads, desserts, and Egyptian food! Something new every week. Address: 4 Road 21, Maadi. Tel: 2358-5284. Website: www.livinginegypt.org

♦ El Fahd. Fresh exotic and familiar spices in bulk. Although most supermarkets carry spices, the variety and freshness is lacking. If you aren't up for a trip to the Spice Market in Khan al-Khalili, there is an alternative solution in Zamalek. El Fahd carries a vast array of fresh spices. The only problem is that the signs are in Arabic and the staff only speaks Arabic. So, if you know your spices, this store is convenient. Address: 2 Taha Hussein St., across from the Yamama Center. Home delivery. Tel: 2735-3700.

♦ Gourmet Egypt. Qattamiya Store: Hours: 9:00 a.m.–10:00 p.m. seven days a week. Address: 3 Badr Bldgs., Qattamiya Ring Road, just after Carrefour entrance, next to Ceramica Cleopatra showroom, Qattamiya. Dandy Store. Hours: 9:30 a.m.–midnight seven days a week. Address: Dandy Mega Mall, Cairo–Alexandria Desert Road. Tel: 19339. E-mail: Customer.

Relations@gourmetegypt.com. Twitter: @Gourmet_Egypt. Website: http://www.gourmetegypt.com

♦ Imtenan Health Shop. Organic food products. The Egyptian honey brand, Imtenan, carries a variety of honey, bee pollen products, herbal teas, and packaged nutritious snacks. Honey infused with peppermint, lavender, or eucalyptus as well as honeycomb and crystallized bee pollen are just a few to taste before deciding on a honey treat. Address: Road 9, Maadi. Tel: 16246.

♦ Voila Luxury Foods. Imports fine luxury food and beverages and delivers to your door. Try foie gras, Mobier cheese, Häagen-Dazs ice cream, Beluga caviar, and much more. Tel: 19853. Website: www.voilaluxuryfoods.com.

♦ Wadi Foods. Has a full selection of gourmet olives, pickles, and virgin olive oil without additives or preservatives. Products are in major supermarkets and their own stores. Home Delivery. Addresses: 47 Baghdad St., behind Beirut Hotel, Korba, Heliopolis. Tel: 2419-1193; 29 Mustafa Kamil St., off Road 9, Tawfiq Tower, Maadi. Tel: 2380-4005. Website: http://www.wadifood.com/home/

Specialty Stores
The delight of eating something only found in one city and not replicated throughout the world is like carrying a secret in your pocket . . . you know where to go for the

best hamburger or the best ice cream or the best croissant, but ONLY found in your city . . . not Paris, London, or New York. So here are some 'bests' and favorites in Cairo.

Cheesy Delights:
Cheese Quiche. Delicate cheese quiche with a white cheese filling that melts in your mouth. The crust is light with a tender, light pastry. This quiche has graced many a buffet table with not a crumb left behind. (The double layer coffee shortbread cookies filled with coffee butter cream are decadent but worth the calories.) Call to order as they are made per order which ensures freshness. Le Bec Sucré. Hours: 9:00 a.m.–10:00 p.m. Address: President Hotel, next to Euro Deli, 22a Taha Hussein St., Zamalek. Tel: 2735-0652.

The cheeses are exquisite at La Fromagerie, which has a superior selection. Address: 9 Road 231, Digla, Maadi. Tel: 2521-0406. Delivery number: 2521-0407. In Sharm al-Sheikh: Gazya Mall, al-Hadaba. E-mail: info@lafromagerie. Website: http://www.lafromagerie-egypt.com

Cold, sweet treats:

♦ **Abdel Rahim Koueider.** The most scrumptious ice cream in Cairo, second only to Bakdash in Damascus. The ice cream is chewy due to pounding and *sahlab*. (*Sahlab* is a thickening agent like flour made from grinding the dried tubers of *Orchis mascula*.) The Downtown parlor is the original patisserie and it is a necessity

to go and try the ice cream at least once in your life. Open 9:00 a.m.–11:00 p.m. Home delivery available from any of its branches. Address: 42 Tal'at Harb St., Downtown. Tel: 2575-5189. Website: http://www.ar-koueider.com

♦ **Mandarine Koueider.** Opened its doors in 1928. The best frozen yogurt cake with blackberry sauce that literally melts in your mouth. Hours: 9:00 a.m.–1:00 a.m. Addresses: 17 Shagarat al-Durr St., Zamalek. Tel: 2735-5010; 33 Abu Simbel Tower, Corniche al-Nil, Maadi. Tel: 2359-8000; 5 Baghdad St., Korba, Heliopolis. Tel: 2418-6555.

♦ **Rigoletto.** Frozen cheesecake (say no more!). Hours: 9:00 a.m.–11:00 p.m. Address: al-Yamama Center, 1st floor, 3 Taha Hussein St., Zamalek. Tel: 2735-8684.

Croissants:
Everyone knows the difference between an 'okay' croissant and one that is airy, buttery, crunchy, and soft. One bite and you know! Well, at TBS you will come back for many bites and many croissants. People describe them as "like the croissants in France." Croissants are baked fresh all day long, seven days a week. The only problem is a growing waistline! They also offer a healthy choice of breads enriched with grains, Pan-O-Col bread that has oats and oat bran to manage cholesterol levels, and bread with Omega 3. Addresses: 4D Gezira Street, next to Fauchon behind the Gezira

Shopping

10

Club. Tel: 2736-0071/0073; 22 Baghdad St., Korba, Heliopolis. Tel: 2290-8388/9018.

Granola, homemade:

It is not easy to give out this secret, but, for the common good, here it is . . . homemade, baked granola in Maadi! At Jared's Bagels you can buy half-kilo (LE22) or kilo bags (LE40) of the crunchy fibrous delight made of baked oats, toasted sesame and sunflower seeds, and sweet yellow raisins. It's like eating an oatmeal-raisin cookie without the sugar and fat! Address: 82 Road 9, Maadi (200 meters south of the Maadi metro station). Immediate delivery: order by phone from 6:30 a.m. to 4:00 p.m. daily. Tel: 2359-6255; Mobile: 0122-788-8702. Website: www.jaredsbagels.com. (Click the STORE tab to order online.)

Juices:

Juice shops have been on the streets of Cairo for decades. The most famous is Farghali in Mohandiseen. If you are driving, no need to leave your car. Waiters rush over to the window to take your order and to deliver the healthy treat. Head over to Farghali's on a summer night to enjoy a cold, freshly squeezed mango juice. It is one of the joys of life! Fruits and vegetables are seasonal in Egypt, so you will have a different treat every three to four months. You can take containers of freshly squeezed juice home, too. Address: 71 Gam'at al-Duwal al-Arabiya St., Mohandiseen. Tel: 3338-4375.

Al Rahmani in Sayyida Zeynab is a standing-room-only juice shop. The reason you go there is for *sobya*, made from coconut and rice milk. It is sweet, creamy, and delicious. Hours: 2:00 p.m.–11:00 p.m. Address: 2 al-Mubtadayan St., Sayyida Zeynab (located at the intersection between Mubtadayan and al-Komi St.). Tel: 2362-5216.

Pasta:

La Bottega Italiana has all varieties of Italian pasta, cheeses, and coffee. Address: 27 Road 231, Digla, Maadi (between Bio Shop and Muhammad Abaza Diwan). Tel: 0122-223-8476.

Alcohol, Ice, and Sparkling Water
Alcohol

Alcohol is not sold in supermarkets or grocery stores; however, there are two liquor stores that carry wine, beer, and a selection of other spirits. Both stores have a fast delivery service. If you are arriving in Egypt, you can go to the Duty Free shop. There are Duty Free stores in several areas of Cairo—Downtown, Mohandiseen, Maadi, Salah Salim—as well as at the airport. In addition to the one liter of alcohol with which you can arrive in Egypt, you can purchase three more liters of alcohol (or a case of beer) within forty-eight hours of your arrival at a Duty Free Store. (Be sure to take your passport!)

♦ **Cheers.** Hours: 10:00 a.m.–11:00 p.m. Addresses: 25 Champollion St., Downtown; 112 Road 9, Maadi; Gouna Industrial Zone, al-Gouna, Red Sea. Tel: 19131.

♦ **Drinkies.** Addresses: 157 26th July St., Zamalek; 10 al-Higaz St., al-Mahkama Square, Heliopolis; 55 Ramsis St., corner of Demashq St., Heliopolis. Tel: 19330. Website: www.alahrambeverages.com

Ice

Rock Ice. You will NEVER have to make ice again! Buy a bag and put it in your freezer. A time saver and rest assured the ice is safe: it is made with pure hygienic water, free from impurities, odors, taste, and bacteria using multi-filter and UV stations. The Rocks Egypt Co. Tel: 3761-2610; Mobile: 0122-216-0897. At Metro and Alfa supermarkets.

Sparkling Water

For those who love sparkling water, there are choices. Baraka has a sparkling water produced locally, while other brands, like San Pellegrino, are imported. It all comes down to price because the taste is the same. My advice is to buy local. However, if imported sparkling water is the only kind that pleases you, it is worth going directly to the distributor and getting a discount. The bad news for whatever brand you choose is that there is no recycling for the lovely green glass bottles!

Baraka Sparkling Water (local) vs. Perrier and San Pellegrino Sparkling Water (imported): A 240-ml bottle of Baraka Sparking Water is guaranteed for quality by Vittel laboratory. It comes from a deep well source in Kafr Arbeen, Egypt, and sells for LE2 at Alfa Supermarkets. A 330 ml bottle of Perrier sells for LE11 and a 1000 ml bottle of San Pellegrino sells for LE17, both imported from Europe. Baraka Sparkling Water is excellent, so why support global warming by buying imported bottles of water? But if you must, below is the distributor for San Pellegrino to allow you to pay less than at supermarkets.

To have San Pellegrino delivered, call ABO International Supplies. Representative: Waleed Shawky. Address: 4 Muhammad Mazlum St., Anwar Wagdy Building, 4th floor, Bab al-Luq. Tel: 2396-0055; Mobile: 0106-663-9442. E-mail abooffice@abo egypt.com

Egyptian Clothing

Egypt is known for its cotton. Goods made with Egyptian cotton carry a high price in the west. For many years, Egyptian clothing was for export and only the 'seconds' were on sale here. Egyptian consumers did not regard their own products highly and preferred imported clothes. In the last decade all this has changed. Even though imported clothes and famous fashion designs have hit the Egyptian market, local brands are in the competition again, which has resulted in affordable, fashionable, and high-quality textile designs.

Egyptian clothing companies with chains throughout Cairo, Alexandria, and large cities throughout Egypt, to name a few, are Concrete, Mobaco (famous for camel polo shirts), &Company, Dalydress (has large sizes), Fabulous, and On Safari. All these stores sell men's and women's

Shopping

10

clothing for sport and daily wear. In the winter, sweaters and light jackets are also available at Mobaco and Concrete.

For handmade Egyptian *gallabiyyas* and *abaayas* from Egyptian fabric and embroidered to personal taste, visit:

♦ **Abbas Higazi.** Address: 5 Khan al-Khalili St., parallel to Sikit Badistan, around the corner from the Naguib Mahfouz Café. Tel: 2592-4730.

For sleepwear and underwear for men, women, and children, made with Egyptian cotton in Egypt:

♦ **Charmaine.** No need to leave your home—shop through their catalogue on-line. They deliver to your door. (Minimum home delivery order is LE200.) If you wish to change the color or size of your purchase, visit the nearest Charmaine store with your receipt within seventy-two hours from the date of delivery. They have over twenty stores in Cairo and branches in other major Egyptian cities. Tel: 3563-2260. For the address of the store nearest you, visit the website: http://www.charmaine.com.eg

♦ **Halawa.** Has traditional sleepwear in winter and summer fabrics. So comfortable! Addresses: 165 Muhammad Farid St., Downtown. Tel: 2391-2744/2013; 34 Syria St., Mohandiseen. Tel: 3760-1023, 3761-1692.

Tailors

There are still tailors in Cairo who can make an old dress look like new or copy your favorite pair of trousers to perfection. The prices are reasonable and the frustration minimal.

♦ **Atelier Mr. Abdel Hamed Mohamed.** Handmade and designed shirts and blouses of superior quality for men and women. Address: 3 Mustafa Abu Heif St., off al-Bustan, Bab al-Luq, Downtown. Tel: 2392-7335.

♦ **Atelier Hamdy.** Address: 50 Qasr al-Nil St., Downtown. Tel: 2392-0434.

♦ **Atelier Mr. Mahmoud Abo Zarifa.** Highly recommended by the expatriate community; an excellent tailor for men and women. Mr. Mahmoud speaks Arabic and French and a little English. Hours: 11:00 a.m.–7:00 p.m., closed Sunday. Address: 11 Gawad Husni St., Downtown. Tel: 2393-9079, 0128-052-4189.

♦ **Salem Ahmad Osman.** Tailor for men's handmade suits. Address: 20 Adli St., Kodak Alley (Harat al-Kodak), Downtown. Tel: 2392-6771.

Shoes

Drive through the Downtown streets and you will see windows filled with shoes, shoes, shoes. Some look gorgeous, but most, though inexpensive, are not well made and your feet will let you know it!

What Is a Sebu'?

The *sebu'* is the traditional celebration of an Egyptian baby's seventh day. *Sebu'* means 'seventh,' and it is on the seventh day after the birth of a baby that the family gathers. The celebration is observed throughout Egyptian society, by both Coptic and Muslim families. There are specific items that symbolize this day: a mortar, a large round sieve, pottery candle holders, and a set of candles. They are decorated in special colors for a boy or girl. On the seventh day, the celebration begins with baby being given a bath and dressed in new clothing. Salt is scattered on the mother and around the house to keep away the evil eye. Then the baby is placed in a decorated sieve from which he or she is shown the home, followed by members of the family carrying decorated candles. During this ceremony, the mother steps over the baby seven times without touching it, while older women pound the mortar noisily, so the baby is aware of sounds. The grandparents shake the baby gently and give the baby orders to obey the family. After a family meal, bags of candy, nuts, and sweets are distributed. Traditionally, the seventh day was also for circumcising boys and piercing the ears of girls, but these are now often done in hospitals separately from the *sebu'* ceremony.

To buy a decorated *sebu'* set, go to Antopola. Addresses: Heliopolis: 14 Samir Mukhtar St., off Nabil al-Waqqad St., beside Cortigiano Restaurant, Golf Area. Tel: 2417-7376. Nasr City: 27 Abdel Mun'im Sanad St., off Abbas al-Aqqad St., in front of St. Mary's Church. Tel: 2262-9763. E-mail: info@antopola.com

It is a pity because excellent leather is available and creativity is abundant; the problem is comfort and sizing. Years ago you had to bring your shoes from abroad, but now there are imported brands in all price ranges available in every mall, as well as Nike and Adidas sports stores. There are a few shoemakers that have been recommended among the expatriate community:

♦ **Babel Shoe Factory.** Expert in handmade shoes for any size foot. Exceptional leather quality. They also make orthopedic shoes. Engineer Mahmoud Abdel Tawab. Address: 20 Adli St., Kodak Alley (Harat al-Kodak), Downtown. Tel: 2393-6645. E-mail: babelshoes@yahoo.com

♦ **M.A.R. Group International Koenings Leather Products.** Address: 165 Muhammad Farid St., City Center, Nasr City. Tel: 2391-4265, 3347-6561; Mobile: 0122-232-3058.

Maternity, Newborn, and Children's Clothes

Stylish maternity clothes have never been easy to find in Egypt. Of course, there are loose-fitting clothes available

Shopping

10

like *gallabiyya*s. If you want western design, you will need to buy from abroad or go to the mall for imported maternity clothes. For the first trimester, you may not need to buy any maternity clothes, though you might need a 'belly button band,' which is a simple device consisting of elastic with buttons. You can widen jeans and skirts as your waist grows. Cover with a long top and no one will know the difference. Shop at maternity clothing stores. Staff should be knowledgeable on appropriate sizes.

Maternity and children's clothing stores:

♦ **Brand Names.** For children. Addresses: CityStars: Store 428, Phase 1, 4th floor; City Center: Makram Ebeid, Store 13D, 2nd floor; Geneina Mall: Store 61C, 2nd floor; Heliopolis: 45 Cleopatra St.

♦ **Mother and Child Magazine.** This magazine has extensive listings for maternity wear, children's clothes, toys, and shoes. Available at Diwan or at website: http:// mother-and-child.net

♦ **Mothercare.** UK retailer of maternity clothes as well as baby furniture, newborn clothing, and baby products. Expensive, but they do have sales. Address: CityStars, Omar ibn al-Khattab St., Phase 2, Shop 2170, Nasr City. Tel: 2480-2471.

♦ **Occasions.** For maternity clothes and formal wear for children. Address: 35 Mu'izz al-Dawla St., off Makram Ebeid St., Nasr City. Tel: 2671-5745, 0122-360-5262. E-mail: occasions@occasionsegypt.com. Website: www.occasionsegypt.com

Books, Books, Books
Cairo boasts bookstores galore, so where do you start? The following bookstores have a good selection of books about Egypt and children's books in different languages. Wireless Internet is available at most stores now and also usually a place to sit and drink coffee to enjoy a few hours of quiet time. Don't forget, once a year in the last two weeks of January, Cairo hosts the largest book fair in the Middle East: the Cairo International Book Fair at the International Fair Grounds in Nasr City. This is an experience not to be missed!

The 25th January Revolution began as the 2011 International Book Fair was due to open. Of course, it had to be canceled. Post-Revolution, in March, the AUC Press answered the call, organized the Tahrir Book Fair, and invited all bookstores to participate. The event was such a success that it will be held twice a year. The next date is expected to be in November 2011 at the AUC downtown campus on Tahrir Square.

♦ **Abdel-Zaher Atelier.** For bookbinding: take all your old books to be re-bound at very reasonable prices. Address: 31 al-Sheikh Muhammad Abdu St. (behind Al-Azhar Mosque). Tel: 2511-8041. E-mail: hossam@abdelzaherbinding.com. Website: www.abdelzaherbinding.com

♦ **Academic Bookshop.** Online orders and home delivery. Addresses: 7 Tag al-Din al-Subki St., Ard al-Golf, Heliopolis. Tel: 2419-3436; 12 al-Tahrir St., Dokki. Tel: 3336-2342, 3748-5282. E-mail: sales.h@abcacademic.com. Website: http://www.abcacademic.com

♦ **American University in Cairo Bookstores.** AUC New Cairo: Hours: 9:00 a.m.–6:00 p.m., Saturday–Thursday (Ramadan hours 9:00 a.m.–2:00 p.m.). Address: AUC New Cairo Campus. Tel: 2615-1303; AUC Downtown: Hours: 9:00 a.m.–6:00 p.m., Saturday–Thursday. Address: corner of Tahrir Square and Sheikh Rihan St., Tahrir Campus. Tel: 2797-5929; Zamalek: Hours: 10:00 a.m.–7:00 p.m., Saturday–Thursday, 1:00 p.m.–7:00 p.m. Friday (Ramadan hours 9:00 a.m.–2:00 p.m.). Address: AUC Hostel, 16 Muhammad Thaqib St., Zamalek. Tel: 2739-7045. Website: www.aucpress.com/t-aucbookstores.aspx

♦ **al-Balad.** Address: 31 Muhammad Mahmud St., Downtown. Tel: 2792-2768.

♦ **Bikya Book Café.** An entirely different experience in book shopping. Secondhand books at reasonable prices in a fun environment. You can browse their wide selection of books, relax, and read an afternoon away in a place so cozy you'll never want to leave. Have a coffee, tea, or sandwich while you are there and be sure to take in their many wonderful events! Hours: 10:30 a.m.–11:00 p.m. Address: 23 Dr. Zaki Hasan St., off al-Nasr St., Nasr City. Tel: 2404-6688. E-mail: Info@Bikya bookcafe.com. Stay updated as to the exact schedule of events announced on both Facebook and twitter: http://www.facebook.com/pages/Bikya/19275505406932, http://twitter.com/#!/bikyabookcafe

♦ **Book Spot.** For used books. Address: 71 Road 9, Maadi. Tel: 2378-1006.

♦ **Books & Books.** Address: Intersection of Roads 233 and 199, Digla, Maadi. Tel: 0100-237-2345

♦ **Diwan Bookstores.** The first bookstore in Cairo to offer a coffee and pastry while you browse. Addresses: Cairo Marriott Hotel. Tel: 2735-1125; Cairo University: Faculty of Urban Planning, near the main library faculty entrance. Tel: 0122-150-3493; City View: Km. 19, Cairo–Alexandria Road. Tel: 0122-861-1022; Heliopolis: 105 Abu Bakr al-Siddiq St. Tel: 2690-8184/85; Maadi: 45 Road 9. Tel: 0109-888-7326; Oasis Mall: Uruba Road, near Cairo Airport Bridge. Tel: 0122-150-6947; Zamalek: 159 26th July St. Tel: 2736-2582/98; Zamalek: Gezira Sporting Club, Children's Garden. Tel: 0109-888-7325. Home delivery: 2690-8185, 0122-600-0168. E-mail: info@diwanegypt.com. Website: www.diwanegypt.com

♦ **International Language Bookshop (ILB).** Founded in 1975 with the aim of supplying institutions with superior material using a dedicated and helpful staff. Since its formation, ILB has become a top provider of educational material for schools in Egypt, as well as expanding its strong presence within the Middle East. It deals with the best publishers to supply the finest educational materials. Whether your institution is using the Egyptian national system, a semi-international system, the IGSCE, or the American system, whether you require material for university, adult education, or you are simply looking for a good book to read, ILB has the solution for you. Place personal orders or orders for your company. Visit the website or call the head office. Head office address: 16 al-Badya St., off al-Thawra St., Heliopolis. Tel: 2417-8623. E-mail: ilb@ilbegypt.com. Website: http://www.ilbegypt.com/index.php/home

♦ **al-Kotob Khan Bookshop.** A quiet, well-stocked store that offers coffee and sweets, too. Book signings and lectures are scheduled throughout the year. Address: 3/1 al-Lasilki St., New Maadi. Tel: 2519-4807. Website: www.kotobkhan.com

♦ **Labib Ghobrial.** A private seller of old books. Address: 94 Road 105, Maadi. Tel: 2525-0744, 0122-777-1911. E-mail: labib_ ghobrial@yahoo.fr

♦ **Oum El Dounia.** A good selection of French-language books. Hours: 10:00 a.m.–8:00 p.m, seven days a week. Address: 3 Tal'at Harb St., 1st floor. Tel: 2393-8273.

♦ **Shorouk Bookstore.** Sells imported books and Arabic-language books. Addresses: Downtown: 1 Tal'at Harb Square. Tel: 2391-2480; Giza: First Mall, 35 Giza St. Tel: 3573-5035; Heliopolis: 15 Baghdad St., Korba. Tel: 2417-1944; Mohandiseen: 26 Muhammad Kamil Mursi St. Tel: 3336-1774; Nasr City: CityStars Mall, 1st floor. Tel: 2480-2544; Zamalek: 17 Hasan Sabri St. Tel: 2735-9418. Website: www.shorouk.com.

♦ **Suuq el-Azbakiya** is a second-hand book market. If you enjoy a treasure hunt, there are books in Arabic, English, French, and sometimes German. It is located near the Ataba Garage in front of the Puppet Theater. Website: http://www.sourelazbakia.com

♦ **Volume One.** One of the older bookstores that sells mainly English language books and has a good selection of children's books. Addresses: Maadi: 17 Road 216/206. Tel: 2519-8831; Mohandiseen: 3 Abd al-Halim Hussein St. Tel: 3338-0168.

Useful websites:

♦ www.egyptianbook.org.eg/en/Internsalepoints.aspx
♦ www.ilbegypt.com/index.php/contact-us
♦ www.osirisbookshop.com/Default_en.aspx

Arabic only:
♦ www.madboulybooks.com
♦ www.anglo-egyptian.com

Buy Local

Help others by frequenting stores and community bazaars that help others help themselves. At Christmas and in the spring, many organizations bring together individuals, craft groups, and stores that support local artisans and crafts. All profits go to charities. Check with your women's group, embassy, or school to find out about bazaars. Every week Community Service Association in Maadi holds a farmer's market and garden market for growers, artists, and cooks to sell their products.

The following shops support local artisans and traditional crafts. Without your support and with the constant threat of imports (cheap and otherwise), techniques and materials for traditional crafts are on the endangered list. Indigenous and handmade goods have been hard hit by massive industrialization and globalization. Quality of local products fell off and the consumer turned to imports, but in the past decade a revival of homemade products has taken place. It is good to remember that your Egyptian pounds go directly to groups and individuals for the purchase of more materials, thereby sustaining development and supporting families. It is more likely that a youth will become an apprentice of a craft and carry on the trade if it provides sustainability and growth. Please add to this list!

♦ **Abaza's Divan.** Atelier of Muhammad Abaza. Beautifully hand-carved wooden objects with Arabic calligraphy, unusual antiques, and handcrafted items. Address: 29 Road 231, Maadi (behind Green Mill restaurant, next to Bio Store).

♦ **Abdel-Zaher Atelier.** For bookbinding and exquisite handmade notebooks and journals. Take all your old books to be rebound at very reasonable prices. Address: 31 Sheikh Muhammad Abdu St. (behind al-Azhar Mosque). Tel: 2511-8041. E-mail: hossam@abdelzaherbinding.com. Website: www.abdelzaherbinding.com.

♦ **Akhmim.** The Association of Upper Egypt for Education and Development sponsors an annual exhibit of weaving, embroidery, and art by more than 120 women from Akhmim. Based on a program founded forty-eight years ago, this women's cooperative provides income for young women. Known in antiquity for its textile production, Akhmim is the perfect spot for such a creative center. The range of products is unique—from bedspreads, tablecloths, napkins, cushions, and wall hangings in vivid colors and striking patterns to hand-embroidered scenes of life in Upper Egypt. The exhibit is held in the early spring at the Association's headquarters. For more information e-mail: upperegypt@link.net, or visit the headquarters at 65 Ubaysi St., al-Zahir, 11271, Cairo, or call 2589-8364/2588-4243. A large selection of woodwork from the neighboring town of Hagazi is also on display.

Shopping

10

◆ **Atelier 87.** Specialty is stained and fused glass. Offers glassmaking and glass art workshops. Address: 18 Jeddah St., off Muhyi al-Din Abu al-Izz St, Mohandiseen. Contact: Fatma Al Tanani. Tel: 0100-153-8113.

◆ **Charisma.** Profits go directly to the group or individual that made the merchandise. Address: 25B Ismail Muhammad St. (in front of the Music College), Zamalek. Tel: 0100-529-1838. E-mail: vivian@charisma-arts.net. Website: www.charisma-arts.net

◆ **Diocesan Craft Shop.** Traditional crafts that support refugees and special needs. Hours: Daily 9:30 a.m.–5:00 p.m. winter, 9:30 a.m.–6:00 p.m. summer, Sundays and Fridays 11:00 a.m.–4:00 p.m. Address: All Saints' Cathedral, Zamalek. Tel: 2735-4350.

◆ **Egypt Crafts Center/Fair Trade Egypt.** Traditional crafts that support economically disadvantaged producers which have been hard-hit by massive industrialization and globalization. Just a few of the products are Akhmim textiles from Sohag such as silk and cotton scarves, shawls, cotton bed linens, and curtains; from al-Arish, embroidered cushion covers, wallets, and bags; from Siwa, organic dates, silver jewelry, and embroidered clothes; from Fayoum, glazed pottery, Quta and el Karia el Tania olive oil soaps, and baskets; from al-Beheira, buffalo horn sculptures, wool carpets and kilims, and doormats. Address: 27 Yehia Ibrahim (off 26th July St.), 1st floor,

Apt 8, Zamalek. Tel: 2736-5123. Website: www.fairtradeegypt.org

◆ **Graffiti Artistoys.** Unique toys made by artists rediscovering classical toys and those that have long been part of the cultural memory of people. Eduardo Ortiz and El Hamy Naguib are the artists who create toys from wire, papier maché, and recycled objects. Piñatas and puppets can be made to your specification. Classes for children aged 4–15 and adults give the child a chance to explore and make a toy that works with different scientific principles such as levers, catapults, gears, and electricity. Address: 28D Road 232, Nirco Buildings, Digla, Maadi. E-mail: graffitiartistoys@gmail.com. Website: www.graffitiartistoys.webs.com

◆ **El Horreya.** Funky and fun purses, accessories, and clothing that use traditional crafts in creative designs. Designer: Hana Elawadi. Address: 14 Muntazah St., Zamalek. Tel: 0106-022-2246. E-mail: el7orreya@gmail.com. Website: www.elhorreya.com

◆ **Kaf Fatima.** Traditional crafts and interesting decoupage of famous Egyptian celebrities. Address: al-Shurta (Police) Building, 15 Road 233, Maadi. Tel: 0122-233-3426.

◆ **Khan Misr Tulun.** This wonderful shop opposite the Ibn Tulun Mosque contains a large selection of handcrafted Egyptian products. There are pottery and glass items and hand-woven products from projects that sustain women's communities. Sells handmade Egyptian crafts at fixed prices. Hours: 10:00 a.m.–5:00 p.m. daily, closed Sundays. Address: across the street from Ibn Tulun Mosque. Tel: 2365-2227.

♦ **Mahmoud Farag.** Original appliqué for pillows, bedcovers, wall hangings, and Christmas stockings. Addresses: 29 Mustafa Kamil St., intersection of Road 9 and Mahatta Square, in front of Metro Market. First floor, upstairs on balcony, Shop 7. Tel: 2380-8827, 0122-330-5492, 0111-135-0166; 19 Khayamiya St., Bab Zuwayla, Darb al-Ahmar. Tel: 2511-7580. E-mail: mfarag cairo@yahoo.com

♦ **La Maison de Miriette T.** Specializes in personalized découpage. Address: 7 Ahmad Hishmat St., Zamalek. Tel: 2735-1925/9698.

♦ **al-Mansura.** Sells furniture made in Damietta at wholesale prices. Address: al-Ataba metro station. By car, park at Opera Square's multistory garage. Entrance to al-Mansura market is on Muhammad Ali St.

♦ **Markaz Craft Revival and Development Center.** Traditional handicrafts. Hours: Saturday to Thursday 10:00 a.m.–7:00 p.m., Fridays and holidays 1:00 p.m.–7:00 p.m. Address: 1B Road 199 (entrance on Road 233), Digla, Maadi. Tel: 2754-7026, 0100-240-5858.

♦ **Al Nafeza.** Sells paper products made in the tradition of the pharaohs from rice straw and banana leaves. Hours: Saturday to Thursday 9:30 a.m.–3:30 p.m. Address: Qasr al-Sham' St., behind the Coptic Museum (next to Darb 1718 art gallery), Old Cairo. Tel: 0122-934-7716. Website: www.elnafeza.com

♦ **Oum El Dounia.** Traditional crafts from Egypt and India. Hours: Daily 9:30 a.m.–8:30 p.m. Addresses: Downtown: 3 Tal'at Harb St., 1st floor. Tel: 2393-8273; Maadi: Road 23 (off al-Nadi St.), Golf Area, Maadi. Tel: 2753-0483.

♦ **Al Qahira.** Locally made home accessories. Hours: 11:00 a.m.–9:00 p.m. Next to Masterbed, 6 Bahgat Ali St., Zamalek.

♦ **Suuq al Fustat.** Store after store in this *suuq* carries traditional crafts and supports local artisans. The opening times vary according to shop owner. Address: next to Amr ibn al-'As Mosque, Old Cairo.

♦ **Tally traditional embroidery.** Tally embroidery is done by women in Sohag. The art of tally is in the use of metallic threads sewn onto net material. The patterns symbolize village life and the technique dates back to the eighteenth century. Orders can be placed through NADIM. Tel: 3539-1603/8. Website: www.nadim.org.

Shopping

10

◆ **Traditional Crafts Co.** Noura Mossallem supports traditional handwork sewn by Egyptian women. Address: 3 Wazarat al-Zira'a Street, Dokki. Tel: 3762-3764

◆ **Wady Craft Shop.** Crafts are made by the deaf, blind, disabled, refugees, prisoners, widows, and the disadvantaged. Every time you shop at Wady Craft Shop you support these people. Hours: Wednesday to Sunday 2:00 p.m.–7:00 p.m., Friday 9:30 a.m.–7:30 p.m. Address: St. John's Church, corner of Port Said Road and Road 17, Maadi. Tel: 0122-844-6220. E-mail: wadycraftshop@yahoo.com. Website: www. wadycrafts.com/shop

Ten Things to Love about Cairo:
1. Anything can be made to order.
2. Doctors and veterinarians make house calls.
3. *Everything* is delivered to your door (www.otlob.com for restaurant delivery).
4. Ironed sheets by the neighborhood *makwagi* (ironer).
5. Strings of *full* flowers sold in the middle of traffic on a summer's evening.
6. Inexpensive taxi fares.
7. Wedding celebrations on bridges.
8. *Tannura* troupe at al-Ghuri complex.
9. Owning or renting and boarding an Arabian horse at a reasonable price.
10. Verdi's opera *Aïda* at the Giza pyramids.

NAWWARTU MASR

Appendix

Cairo Arabic: The Basics
From the Arabic . . .

Orange (naranj: bitter orange, and in Spanish *naranja* means orange), cipher (Sifr: zero), giraffe (zaraafa), sugar (sukkar), admiral (amir al-baHr: commander of the sea), camel (gamal), algebra (al-jabr: reduction), cotton (quTn), coffee (qahwa), guitar (qithara): These are just a few of the hundreds of words from the Arabic that color and enrich everyday English.

Short-term visitors limiting themselves to upscale hotels and tourist haunts can get by with no Arabic whatsoever in Cairo. But for foreign residents dealing with 'real life,' a minimal vocabulary is vital. Upperclass and professional Egyptians speak English, and often French as well, as do tourist-oriented shopkeepers, but the vast mass of Cairenes do not. So if you plan to travel independently, shop, and meet your neighbors, you can sally forth with this very brief introduction. We hope it will whet your appetite for more.

There are hundreds of Arabic classes and tutors in Cairo (see Language Classes in the Directory). You're bound to find one that suits your needs and interests. Learning Modern Standard Arabic, the language of literature, newspapers, and formal discourse, requires a serious commitment. But picking up a useful vocabulary of colloquial spoken Arabic is relatively easy. The various guttural sounds may throw off native English speakers initially, but the pronunciation guide below will help demystify these. To expand upon the brief vocabulary given here, check the "Shopping and Other Lists" at the end of this chapter for all sorts of shopping and household terminology. There is even a list of "Words for a Revolution." Next, try Stevens and Salib's *A Pocket Dictionary of the Spoken Arabic of Cairo* (The American University in Cairo Press, 2004); if you are put off by phonetic transcription symbols, though, use *Say It in Arabic* (Egyptian) by Farouk al-Baz from Dover Publications.

So plunge in. Ask questions, make mistakes, and use this great tip from our Research Editor: label everything in the house as you learn its name, using whatever transcription system works best for you. Then photocopy the lists at the end of this chapter and post them in the kitchen; using these words will earn you much credit with your local shopkeepers.

Pronunciation and Very Limited Grammar

1) Gender variants are indicated by a slash: male version/female version.

2) Alternatives and explanations are preceded by a semicolon.

Consonants

Distinctly lengthen any consonant that is doubled, e.g., pronounce "kk" as the "k" sound in bookcase, and don't ignore the oft-cited difference between Hamaam (pigeon) and Hammaam (toilet).

Capital letters anywhere in a word indicate a stronger emphasis on the sound than their lower-case counterparts; D, S, T, Z, H require a Heavier, Harder Hit than d, s, t, z, h.

g   is always pronounced hard, as in English 'go'

j   is pronounced "zh," as in the English 'measure'

kh is equivalant to "ch" in the Scottish 'loch' or the German 'Buch'

gh is similar to "kh," but with the vocal cords vibrating

q   sounds like a softer English "k" uttered from further back in the mouth

r   is a trilled r, as in Italian and Spanish

s   is pronounced as in 'its,' never as in 'his' or 'hers'

'   (apostrophe): glottal stop, like "tt" in American 'Manhattan' or Cockney 'matter'

'   (reversed apostrophe): the 'ain, a forcing of the air through a constriction in the throat, a kind of backward gulp. If you find it impossible, substitute 'a' as in 'cat.'

Vowels

a   as in 'back'

aa as in 'car' if near an emphatic consonant (S, T, D, Z), otherwise as in 'care'

ee as in 'cane'

i   as in 'win'

ii as in 'clean'

oo as in 'bowl'

u   as in 'put'

uu as in 'cool'

Minimalist's Grammar

The Arabic verb 'to be' is rarely used in the present tense; instead, one uses the personal pronoun plus the adjective for statements which describe a condition, e.g., ana 'ayyaan/a, meaning 'I [am] sick.'

Nouns have gender, as in French and Spanish. Those ending in -a are usually feminine; the rest are masculine, with a few exceptions.

Sex further complicates matters as follows: In speaking to males, -ak is added to certain phrases; to females, -ik is added, e.g., min faDlak ('please') to a male, min faDlik to a female. We indicate this by showing -ak/ik where appropriate. Another version of this same general principal is the addition of -i to a verb, e.g., law samaHt ('if you please') to a male, but law samaHti to a female.

There are also linguistic differences between male and female speakers: in referring to themselves, men use the masculine (m) adjective form and women the feminine (f), e.g., ana aasif (m) and ana asfa (f) ('I [am] sorry'). We indicate this with a slash, with the masculine first, the feminine following.

Adjectives generally follow the noun they modify and agree in gender and number.

Verb conjugations are less irregular than in English; nevertheless, we're skipping the whole subject here.

Mish in front of a word negates it, e.g., mish mumkin: 'impossible.'

General Vocabulary
Courtesy
hi/hello: ahlan; ahlan wa sahlan
goodbye: salaamu 'aleekum; ma'a-s-salaama; salaam
how are you?: izzayak/ik
fine, thanks: kwayyis/a il-Hamdulillaah
my name is ____: ismi ____
thank you: shukran
please: law samaHt/i; min faDlak/ik
excuse me, pardon me: 'an iznak/ik
I'm sorry: ana aasif / asfa
I don't know Arabic: ana mish 'aarif / 'arfa 'arabi
I don't understand: mish faahim / fahma
I understand: faahim / fahma
to your health: fi SaHHitak/ik

Questions
what's your name?: ismak/ik eeh?
do you speak English?/French?: bititkallim/i ingiliizi / faransaawi?
who is that?: miin da / di?
what is this?: eeh da / di?
what are these / those?; eeh dool?
where (is) ____?: feen ____?
when?: imta?

how?: izzaay?
how much (money)?: bi kaam?
how many?: kaam?
why?: leeh?
which (one)?: anhi?
who knows?: miin 'aarif?

Urgencies and Emergencies
where is the toilet?: feen il-Hammaam?
now: dilwa'ti
it's not working: 'aTlaan/a; bayZ/a
help me! (emergency): ilHa'uuni!
help me (less urgent): saa'idni/saa'diini
emergency: Taari'
police: shurTa; buliis
fire: Harii'a
water: mayya
hospital: mustashfa
call a doctor: 'ayziin duktuur ('we want a doctor')
help! thief!: ilHa'uuni! Haraami!

Common Expressions
Given in the approximate descending order in which you will hear them.
thanks be to God: il-Hamdulillaah
God willing: insha'allah
yes: aywa; aah
no: la'; la'a (more emphatic)
and: wa; u
don't worry; no problem: ma'lish
I mean: ya'ni
so / then: fa
again: kamaan
also: barDu
don't: balaash
okay, can do: maashi (lit. 'it goes')

sure, no problem: mish mushkila
can do, possible: mumkin
finished, done, okay: khalaaS
isn't it? n'est-ce pas?: mish kida?
impossible: mish mumkin
not bad, okay, so-so: mish baTaal
okay, fine: Tayyib; Tab
connections, influence: wasTa; koosa
nonsense, empty talk: kalaam faaDi
exactly: miyya miyya, (lit. 'a hundred
   percent'); biZZabt
so-so, okay: nuSS u nuSS (lit. 'half
   and half')
only, quit it, enough: bass
bit by bit: shwaya shwaya
almost never: fi-l-mishmish (lit. 'in the
   time of apricots')

Directions
Especially handy with taxi drivers.
straight ahead: 'ala Tuul
right: yamiin
left: shimaal
next to: gamb
across from, in front of: 'uddaam
facing: fi-wishsh
behind: wara
before: 'abl
after: ba'd
near, close to: 'urayyib min
far from: ba'iid 'an
corner (of a street): naSya
this corner: in-naSya di
between ____and ____ :
   been ____wa ____
**at ____ : fi ____
stop here: hina kwayyis (lit. 'here is good')

go slowly: bi-shweesh
go quickly: bi-sur'a
how many kilometers?: kaam kiilu? (better
   by far than 'How far?')

Places
Just say the word, and add law samaHt/i for
'please.'
airport: maTaar
bridge: kubri
cathedral: ik-katidra'iyya
church: kiniisa
embassy: sifaara
floating restaurant: resturan 'aayim
home: beet
hotel: fundu'
market: suu'
____mosque: gaama'____ ; masgid____ ,
   e.g., gaama' SulTaan Hasan
museum: matHaf
office: maktab
post office: busta
school: madrasa
square: midaan
street: shaari'
train station: maHaTTit il-'atr
university: gam'a
For names of landmarks, see the chart at
the front of the book.

Money (and Polite Bargaining)
pounds: gineeh
piasters: 'irsh
and a half: u nuSS, e.g., itneen gineeh u
   nuSS: two and a half pounds
and a quarter: u rub', e.g., talaata gineeh
   u rub': three and a quarter pounds

small change: fakka
change (back from transaction): baa'i (literally 'the rest')
do you have change?: ma'ak fakka?
no change: mafiish fakka
I'm broke: ana mifallis
how much?: bi kaam; kaam?
too much / unreasonable: kitiir; mish ma''uul
my last word / offer: aakhir kalaam
congratulations: mabruuk; response: allah yibaarik fiik/i; depending on tone of voice, this exchange concluding a bargaining session indicates genuine or sarcastic admiration of the opponent's bargaining skill

Family, Friends, and Other People
people: naas
(my) mother: umm(i); waldit(i) (formal)
(my) father:abu(ya); waalid (waldi) (formal)
(my) brother: akhu(ya)
(my) sister: ukht(i)
(my) son: ibn(i)
(my) daughter: bint(i)
(my) children: awlaad(i)
(my) husband: gooz(i)
(my) wife: maraat(i), il-madaam (formal)
man: raagil
woman: sitt
child: Tifl
children, kids: aTfaal; 'iyaal (slang)
baby: beebi; Tifl
boy: walad
girl: bint
my friend: SaHbi (m) / SaHbiti (f)
my sweetheart: Habiibi (m) / Habiibti (f)

my fiancé/e: khaTiibi (m) /khaTibti (f)
stranger: ghariib/a
foreigner: agnabi (m) / agnabiyya (f)
westerner: khawaaga (m) / khawagaaya (f) (can be friendly, derogatory, or deferential)

Time (wa't)
now: dilwa'ti
later: ba'deen
today: innaharda
tonight: innaharda bil-leel
tomorrow: bukra
day after tomorrow: ba'da bukra
yesterday: imbaariH
morning: iS-Subh
afternoon / evening: ba'd iD-Duhr
evening / night: bil-leel
on time: fi-l-ma'aad
(five) o'clock: is-saa'a (khamsa)
half past five: khamsa u nuSS
five fifteen: khamsa u rub'
five forty-five (quarter to six): sitta illa rub'
Sunday: il-Hadd
Monday: il-itneen
Tuesday: it-talaat
Wednesday: il-arba'
Thursday: il-khamiis
Friday: il-gum'a
Saturday: is-sabt

Personal Pronouns and Demonstrative Adjectives
I: ana
you (s): inta (m) / inti (f)
he: huwwa
she: hiyya

Appendix

we: iHna
you: (pl): intu
they: humma
this, that: da (m) / di (f)
those: dool

Adjectives
To add emphasis indicating 'very' or 'too,' add 'awi after the adjective; to negate, precede it with mish. Feminine endings are shown as /a; if not shown, the adjective is invariant.
big: kibiir/a
small: Sughayyar/a
more: aktar
nice / good / fine: kwayyis/a, Tayyib/a
beautiful / pretty: gamiil/a; Hilw/a (sweet)
ugly: wiHish/wiHsha
bad: wiHish/wiHsha; mish kwayyis/a
broken, not working: bayZ/a
interesting: kwayyis/a
boring: mumill/a
important: muhimm/a
crowded, busy: zaHma
tall: Tawiil/a
short: 'uSayyar/a
fat: tikhiin/a
thin: rufayya'/a
funny: muDHik/a
generous: kariim/a
greedy: Tammaa'/a
happy: mabsuuT/a
honest: amiin/a; shariif/a
hot; cold: Harr; bard (for weather)
hot; cold: sukhn/a; saa'i' / sa''a (for temperature of things and food)
polite: mu'addab/a

sick: 'ayaan/a
spicy: bi-shaTTa; Haami/Hamya
strange: ghariib/a
terrible: faaZii'/a
tired: ta'baan/a
wonderful: haayil/hayla

Adverbs
slowly: bi-shweesh
quickly: bi-sur'a
immediately: Haalan
later / next: ba'deen
soon: 'urayyib
often / a lot: kitiir
here: hina
there: hinaak

Prepositions
in: fi
inside: guwwa
outside: barra
up / on top of: foo'
down / under: taHt
around / about: ta'riiban; Hawaali
after: ba'd
before: 'abl
with: ma'
without: bi-duun; min gheer

Deterrents
Women may experience unwanted attention from men in the street—from polite attempts at conversation to coarse language or gestures to (rarely) physical assault. Talking to other foreign women about their experiences here and how they've dealt with them can be an enormous help and

Appendix

comfort. At first it is daunting and can even be frustrating and upsetting, but soon you will devise your own methods of dealing with street harassment. Carrying a shawl or light jacket to cover yourself, walking with purpose, looking like you know exactly where you're going, not making eye contact with men on the street, and avoiding conversation with taxi drivers (bring a book to read instead) are all helpful ways of deterring harassment. If you're someone who enjoys a walk or run through the streets at home, do it early in the morning (and cover up) or join a local gym.

If harassment does occur, depending on the situation, some of the following deterrents may be useful. And remember that if you raise your voice (in any language) you will immediately attract a crowd, who will probably deal swiftly and efficiently with your aggressor.

ana mitgawwiza: I'm married
'eeb: shame on you, for shame!
iHtirim nafsak: have respect! (lit. 'respect yourself')
inta magnuun?: are you crazy?
bass kifaaya: enough! leave me alone!

For situations in which you feel threatened, do not hesitate to say: hagiib al-buliis (I'll call the police). This works wonders, as the last thing any Egyptian male wants is to go near a police station.

Food
Egyptian Specialties
babaghannuug: smoked mashed eggplant / oil / garlic dip
baTaarikh: semi-dry, pressed Egyptian fish roe; an acquired taste
fuul: stewed broad beans; the Egyptian breakfast of champions
kufta: spiced, grilled meatball fingers
kushari: lentils, macaroni, and rice topped with dry-fried onion and spicy tomato sauce—delicious
mazza: mixed appetizers
mulukhiyya: Jew's mallow, a slightly bitter, spinach-like green used in soup of the same name
'ul'aas: taro-like starchy root vegetable used alone or in soup
Umm Ali (lit. 'Mother of Ali'): rich bread pudding with coconut, cream, nuts (for dessert or breakfast)
TaHiina: dip of ground sesame seed paste with mild spices
Ta'miyya: fried patties of ground broad beans, onion, herbs, and (sometimes) egg; felafel is similar but made with ground chickpeas instead of broad beans
wara' 'inab: stuffed vine leaves

Breads and Pastries
'eesh: bread in general
'eesh baladi: whole-wheat pita-like bread
'eesh shaami: white-flour version of 'eesh baladi
'eesh shamsi: Egypt's answer to pain poilane; superb, but so far available only in Upper Egypt

[pastries] all sweeter than sweet; try kunaafa (thread-like cake), ba'laawa, basbuusa, rumuush

fiTiir a versatile puff-pastry; great for home-made pizza crust, or top with sweet fruit topping

[baguettes, croissants, etc.] use the same words for these and other khawaaga (foreigner) foods

Dairy Products
butter: zibda
clotted cream: ishTa
eggs: beeD
ghee: samna
milk: laban; Haliib
sour cream: ishTa fallaaHi; ishTa miziz
whipping cream/heavy cream: krem labbaani
yogurt: zabaadi
yogurt, Middle Eastern: labna (used to make dips with lemon and olive oil)

Cheese (gibna)
Egyptian cheeses are listed by their very approximate English equivalents.
cheddar: sheedar; much less sharp than foreign brands; a good all-purpose cheese
feta: gibna beeDa; available hard or soft, spiced or plain, dry or runny
mozzarella: mutsarilla; look for wet plastic bags marked "for pizza"
parmesan: barmizaan (old gibna ruumi will do)
ricotta: rikutta; sold in plastic bags
romano: gibna ruumi

Swiss: gibna swisri; usually imported

Fruit
For ripe fruit, say mistiwi; for juice, ask for 'aSiir ('juice') followed by the fruit's name; for dried fruit, add naashif ('dried') after the fruit.
apples: tuffaaH
apricots: mishmish; dried in sheets: 'amar id-diin
avocado: abukaadu
bananas: mooz
cantaloupe: kantalubb
cherries: kireez
coconut: gooz il-hind ('India nut')
dates: balaH
figs: tiin
gooseberries: Harankash
grapefruit: gribfruut
grapes: 'inab
guavas: gawaafa
kiwi: kiiwi
limes, lemons: lamuun
mango: manga
mulberries: tuut
olives, black: zatun iswid
olives, green: zatun akhDar
oranges: burtu'aan
peaches: khookh
pears: kummitra
persimmon: kaaka
pineapple: ananaas
pomegranates: rummaan
prickly pear: tiin shooki
raisins: zibiib
strawberries: farawla
sweet melons: shammaam
tamarind: tamr hindi

tangerines: yustafandi
watermelon: baTTiikh

Vegetables (khuDaar)
artichoke: kharshuuf
asparagus: kishkalmaaZ
aubergine: bidingaan
beets (beetroot): bangar
broad beans: fuul
broccoli: brukli
carrots: gazar
cauliflower: 'arnabiiT
celery: karafs ifrangi
corn (maize): dura
courgettes: koosa
cucumber: khiyaar
eggplant: bidingaan
fennel: shamar
fenugreek: Hilba
french beans: lubya
green beens: fuSuulya khadra
Jew's mallow: mulukhiyya
leeks: kurraaT
lentils, brown: 'ads bi-gibba
lentils, yellow: 'ads aSfar
lettuce: khass; salata (greens in general)
lupine: tirmis
mushrooms: 'ish ghuraab; shampinyoon
okra: bamya
onions: baSal
onions, pearl: 'awirma
peas: bisilla
peas, black-eyed: lubya
peas, sweet: bisillit iz-zuhuur
peppers, sweet: filfil ruumi
potatoes, sweet: baTaaTa
potatoes, white: baTaaTis

pumpkin: 'ar' 'asali
radish, red: figl ruumi
radish, white: figl abyaD
scallions: baSal akhDar
spinach: sabaanikh
taro: 'ul'aas
tomatoes: 'uuTa; TamaaTim
turnips: lift
zucchini: koosa

Poultry (Tuyur)
breast: Sidr
chicken: firaakh
duck: baTT
gizzards: 'awaaniS
goose: wizz
leg: wirk
pigeon: Hamaam
quail: simmaan
turkey: diik ruumi

Meat (laHma)
bacon: beekan
beef: kanduuz
brains: mukhkh
chitterlings: mumbaar
escalope: iskalubb
feet: ruguul
filet: filittu
ham: jamboon
heart: 'alb
kidney: kalaawi
lamb: Daani; 'uuzi
liver: kibda
pastrami: bastirma (not always beef)
pork: khanziir
rabbit: arnab

roast: rustu
roast beef: ruzbiif
sausage: sugu'
shanks: kawaari'
steak: bufteek
tongue: lisaan
tripe: kirsha
veal: bitillu

Fish (samak) and Seafood
anchovies: anshuuga
calamari; squid: kalamaari; subeeT
clams: gandufli
crabs: kaburya
grouper (sea bass): wa'aar
herring: ringa
lobster: istakooza
mullet, grey: buuri
mullet, red: barbuuni; murgaan
mussels: balaH il-baHr
salmon: salamun
sardines: sardiin
shrimp / prawns: gambari
sole: muusa
tuna: tuuna

Nuts, Seeds, and Grains
almonds: looz
barley: shi'iir
bulghur: burghul
carob: kharruub
chickpeas: Hummus
couscous: kuskusi
filberts (hazelnuts): bundu'
lentils: 'ads
peanuts: fuul sudaani
pecans: bikaan

pinenuts: sineebar
pistachios: fuzdu'
popcorn: fishaar
pumpkin seeds: libb abyaD
sunflower seeds: libb suuri
walnuts: 'een gamal

Herbs (a'shaab) and Spices (tawaabil; buharaat)
ground: maTHuun
whole: SiHiiH
allspice: buharaat
anise seed: yansuun
basil: riHaan
bayleaf: wara' lawra
capers: abu khangar
caraway: karawya
cardamom: Habbahaan
cayenne: shaTTa
celery seeds: bizr karafs
chard (leaves): sal'
chicory: shikurya
chili powder: filfil aHmar amrikaani
cinnamon: 'irfa
cloves: 'urunfil
coriander: kuzbara
coriander, fresh: kuzbara khaDra
cumin: kammuun
curry powder: kaari
dill: shabat
fennel: shamar
fennel seeds: Habbit il-baraka
fenugreek: Hilba
garlic: toom
ginger: ganzabiil
green mixed spices: khuDra (dill, parsley, coriander, and/or chard)

horseradish: figl baladi
mace: bisbaasa
marjoram: barda'uush
mint: na'naa'
mixed spices: buharaat (nutmeg, cinnamon, sweet pepper)
nutmeg: guzt it-tiib
oregano: za'tar
paprika: paprika; filfil ruumi
parsley: ba'duunis
pepper: filfil
pepper, black: filfil iswid
pepper, hot: shaTTa
pepper, white: filfil abyaD
peppercorns: 'arn filfil
rosemary: HaSalbaan
saffron: 'uSfur; za'faraan (usually not
  genuine)
sage: maryamiyya; marmariyya
salt: malH
savory: stoorya
sesame seeds: simsim
spring onion: baSal akhDar
tarragon: Tarkhuun
thyme: za'tar
turmeric: kurkum
vanilla: vanilya

Food Staples
baking powder: bakinbawdar
baking soda: bikarbunaat
candy: bunboon
chocolate: shukalaaTa
cookies (biscuits): baskoot
cornstarch: nisha
flour: di'ii'
gelatin: jelatiin

honey: 'asal abyaD
hot sauce: hut soos; shaTTa
ketchup: katshab
mayonnaise: mayuneez
molasses: 'asal iswid
mustard: mustarda
oil: zeet
oil, corn: zeet dura
oil, olive: zeet zatuun
oil, safflower: zeet 'uSfur
oil, sunflower: zeet suuri
rice: ruzz
salt: malH
sugar: sukkar
sugar, icing: sukkar budra
vinegar: khall
wine vinegar: khall 'inab
Worcestershire sauce: lii an birinz
yeast: khamiira

Beverages
alcohol: kuHuul; khamra
alcoholic beverages: khumuur
beer: biira
cocoa: kakaw
coffee: 'awha
hibiscus tea: karkadeeh
juice: 'aSiir
soft drinks: [use brand name]; haaga sa''a
tea: shayy
water: mayya
water, mineral: mayya ma'daniyya
wine: nibiit

Clothing (huduum)
do you have ____?: 'andak/ik ____?
my size: ma'aasi

I need size _____: 'ayz/a ma'aas_____
medium: mutawassiT
large, larger: kibiir/a, akbar
small, smaller: Sughayyar/a, aSghar
same style, different color: nafs il-stayl
bass loon taani
bathing suit: mayooh
bathrobe: burnuus
blouse: biluuza
brassiere: sutyaan
cardigan: biluuvar maftuuH
coat: balTu
dress: fustaan
jacket: jaakit
nightgown: 'amiiS noom
pajamas: bijaama
panties: kilutt
pantihose: kuloon
pants (trousers): bantaloon
scarf: isharb
scarf, wool: kufiyya
shawl: shaal
shirt: 'amiiS
shoelaces: rubaaT
shoes: gazma
skirt: jiiba; juup
slip / underskirt: 'amiiS taHtaani
slippers: shibshib
socks: shuraab
suit: badla
suit jacket: jakitta
suit, women's: tayiir
sweater: swiitar; biluuvar
undershirt: fanilla
underwear, men's: slibb

Colors
light: faatiH/fatHa
dark: ghaami'/gham'a
plain: saada
patterned: man'uush/a
striped: mi'allim/a
beige: beej
black: iswid / suda
blue: azra' / zar'a
blue, pale: labani
blue, navy: kuHli
brown: bunni
gold: dahabi
gray: rumaadi
green: akhDar / khaDra
maroon: nibiiti
orange: burtu'aani
pink: bamba
purple: moov
purple, violet: banafsigi
purple, royal: bidingaani
red: aHmar / Hamra
silver: faDDi
violet: banafsigi
white: abyaD / beeDa
yellow: aSfar / Safra

Fabrics ('umaash)
canvas: kheesh; 'umaash khiyam
corduroy: 'aTiifa
cotton: 'uTn
flannel: kastuur
leather: gild
linen: tiil; kittaan
silk: Hariir
suede: shamwaa
velvet: 'atiifa

wool: Suuf

Very Important People
I need a/an ____ who is excellent,
  honest, and reasonably priced: 'ayz/a
  ____mumtaaz, amiin, wa mish ghaali
barber: hallaa'
cabinetmaker: naggaar
carpenter: naggaar
doorkeeper: bawwaab
dressmaker: khayaaT/a
driver: sawwaa'
drycleaner: tanturleeh
dyer: maSbagha
electrician: kahrabaa'i
exterminator: raagil yurushsh il-beet
gardener: ganayni
hairdresser: kwafeer
ironer: makwagi
maid: shaghghaala
mailman: bustagi
nanny: naani
painter: na"aash; mibayyaD
plumber: sabbaak
servant: sufragi
tailor (men's): tarzi rigaali
tailor (women's): tarzi Hariimi
translator: mutargim

Furnishings (farsh) and Furniture (mubiliya)
used furniture: mubiliya musta'mal
awning: tanda
bed: siriir
blanket: baTTaniyya
bookcase: maktaba
chair: kursi

crib / cradle: mahd
cupboard: dulaab
curtain: sitaara
desk: maktab
file cabinet: shaanun
lamp: abajuura
lampshade: burneetit abajuura
mirror: miraaya
picture frame: birwaaz
pillow (bed): makhadda
pillow (floor): shalta
pillow (sofa): khudadiyya
sheet: milaaya
shelf: raff
shutters: shiish
sofa: kanaba
table: tarabeeza
table, dining: sufra
tent: khiima
tentmaker: khayyaam
towel: fuuTa
towel, large: bashkiir
toys: li'b aTfal

Handy Household Terms and Items
this ____ doesn't work / is broken: il
  ____ da / di bayZ/a
this chair is broken: il-kursi da bayZ
this table is broken: il-tarabeeza di bayZa
clean (adj.): niDiif/a
dirty: mish niDiif/a
air conditioner: mukayyif; takiif
air filter: filtar hawa
bathroom: Hammaam
bathtub: banyu
batteries: Higaara
bedroom: oodit noom

bucket: gardal
butagaz tank: anbuuba
candles: sham'
dining room: oodit sufra
door: baab
drawer: durg
drill: shanyuur
electrical outlet: bariiza
electrical switch: muftaaH nuur
elevator (lift): asanseer
extension cord: waSla; silk
faucet (tap): Hanafiyya
flashlight (torch): baTTariyya
floor: arD
flowerpot: 'asriyya
flowers: ward
freezer: friizar
garden hose: kharTuum gineena
hammer: shakuush
heater: daffaaya
ice: talg
key: muftaaH
kitchen: maTbakh
living room: oodit saloon
lock: kaloon
mop: mamsaHa
multiplug socket: mushtarak
newspaper: gurnaal
oven: furn
padlock: 'ifl
rat(s): faar (firaan)
receipt: faTuura
recipe: waSfa
refrigerator: tallaaga
roaches: SaraSiir
scissors: ma'aSS
screwdriver: mifakk

shower: dushsh
sink: HooD
sponge: safinga
stairs: sillim
stove / cooker (butane): butagaaz
subscription: ishtiraak
toilet: twalitt
towel rack: fawwaaTa
transformer: tarans
voltage stabilizer: stibilayzar
washing machine: ghassaala
water heater: sakhkhaan
water pressure: DaghT il-mayya
window: shibbaak
window screen: silk shibbaak

Cars and Car Trouble
fill it up: fawwilha
I'm having trouble with my car: fii
  mushkila ma' 'arabiiti
I think it's the ____: aftikir hiyya fi-l ____
battery: baTTariyya
car: 'arabiyya
carburetor: karbiriteer
engine: mutoor
fuel line: sikkit il-banziin
gas (petrol): banziin
gas (petrol) station: maHattit banziin
gasket: juwaan
headlight: fanuus
ignition: marsh / kuntakt
oil: zeet
shock absorber: musaa'id
spark plugs: bujihaat
steering: diriksyoon
tire: kawitsh
wheel: 'agala

Appendix

Words for a Revolution

army: geesh
constitution: dustuur
curfew: Hazr tagawwul
democracy: dimuqraTiya
demonstration: muZahra
elections: intikhabaat
freedom: Hurriya
government: Hukuuma
minister: waziir
police: shurTa
president: ra'iis
referendum: istiftaa'
revolution: sawra
state security: amn il-dawla
thugs: balTagiya

Arabic Numbers

0	٠	Sifr
1	١	waaHid / waHda
2	٢	itneen
3	٣	talaata
4	٤	arba'a
5	٥	khamsa
6	٦	sitta
7	٧	sab'a
8	٨	tamanya
9	٩	tis'a
10	١٠	'ashara
11	١١	Hidaashar
12	١٢	itnaashar
13	١٣	talattaashar
14	١٤	arba'taashar
15	١٥	khamastaashar
16	١٦	sittaashar
17	١٧	sab'ataashar

18	١٨	tamantaashar
19	١٩	tis'ataashar
20	٢٠	'ishriin
21	٢١	waaHid wi 'ishriin
22	٢٢	itneen wi 'ishriin
30	٣٠	talatiin
40	٤٠	arba'iin
50	٥٠	khamsiin
60	٦٠	sittiin
70	٧٠	sab'iin
80	٨٠	tamaniin
90	٩٠	tis'iin
100	١٠٠	miyya
101	١٠١	miyya wi waaHid
120	١٢٠	miyya wi 'ishriin
125	١٢٥	miyya khamsa wi 'ishriin
200	٢٠٠	miteen
273	٢٧٣	miteen talaata wi sab'iin
300	٣٠٠	tultumiyya
356	٣٥٦	tultumiyya sitta wi khamsiin
400	٤٠٠	rub'umiyya
500	٥٠٠	khumsumiyya
600	٦٠٠	suttumiyya
700	٧٠٠	sub'umiyya
800	٨٠٠	tumnumiyya
900	٩٠٠	tus'umiyya
1,000	١٠٠٠	alf
2,000	٢٠٠٠	alfeen
3,000	٣٠٠٠	talattalaaf
10,000	١٠٠٠٠	'ashartalaaf
100,000	١٠٠٠٠٠	miit alf
1,000,000	١٠٠٠٠٠٠	milyoon

Conversion Tables

Temperature

To convert degrees Celsius to Fahrenheit, multiply by 9, divide by 5, then add 32,

e.g.:

$20°C \times 9 = 180$, $180 \div 5 = 36$, and $36 + 32 = 68°F$

To convert degrees Fahrenheit to Celsius, subtract 32, multiply by 5, then divide by 9,

e.g.:

$68°F - 32 = 36$, $36 \times 5 = 180$, and $180 \div 9 = 20°C$

Imperial Measures and Equivalents

Distance

1 inch = 2.54 centimeters

1 centimeter = 0.394 inches

1 foot (12 inches) = 0.3048 meters

1 meter = 3.28 feet

1 yard (3 feet) = 0.9144 meters

1 meter = 1.094 yards

1 mile (1,760 yards) = 1.609 kilometers

1 kilometer = 0.621 miles

Weight

1 ounce = 28.35 grams

1 pound (16 ounces) = 0.454 kilograms

1 kilogram = 2.2 pounds

Liquid Measure

British

1 pint (20 fluid ounces) = 0.568 liters

1 liter = 1.76 pints

1 gallon (8 pints) = 4.456 liters

1 liter = 0.22 gallons

Cooking Temperatures

Oven Description	Temperature in °F and °C		Gas
Very Cool	225°F	110°C	1/4
	250°F	120/130°C	1/2
Cool	275°F	140°C	1
	300°F	150°C	2
Warm	325°F	160/170°C	3
	350°F	180°C	4
	375°F	190°C	5
	400°F	200°C	6
Hot	425°F	220°C	7
	450°F	230°C	8
	475°F	240°C	9

In thermostatically controlled electric ovens, the thermostat scale is usually marked either in degrees Fahrenheit, or in serial numbers (1, 2, 3 etc.) corresponding with 100°F, 200°F, 300°F (38°C, 93°C, 150°C), etc.

American

1 pint (16 fluid ounces) = 0.473 liters

1 liter = 2.11 pints

1 quart (2 pints) = 0.946 liters

1 liter = 1.05 quart

1 gallon (4 quarts) = 3.785 liters

1 liter = 0.26 gallons

Emergency Evacuation Preparedness

Emergency Numbers

Ambulance—123

Cairo Water Utility—125

Child Helpline—16000

Electricity Information
and Emergency—121

Fire Brigade—180

Highway Emergency
Service—0122-111-0000

Police Help—122

Railway Police—145

Traffic Police—128

Tourism Police—126

Your Embassy Emergency Contact

You do not need to go through a revolution to have an emergency evacuation checklist! You may never need to use it, but emergencies such as a natural disaster or fire come without warning. Those who are prepared will save precious time if required to leave a house on short notice. Taking time to organize and to inventory your valuables will facilitate insurance claims and income tax returns. Being prepared is the best way to make sure you and your family come out of a displacement, disaster, or emergency in the best possible condition. If you have just minutes to gather your family and important papers, and get out of your house, are you prepared? Where would you go? What would you take?

Whether you are at home or traveling, keep your most important documents together and in an accessible area, so if, at a moment's notice, you need to evacuate, the folder can immediately be collected before leaving a room, home, or building. In this folder, put an extra hotel room key or a house key so if you are required to leave immediately and the door locks behind you, you will be able to reenter without inconvenience. (People have spent hours in the hotel lobby after a false fire alarm trying to get another key to their room because they had no identification.)

Planning ahead is crucial.

1. Arrange Your Evacuation Ahead of Time

♦ Identify where you can go if you must leave your home. Be sure to have the emergency number of your embassy in an easily accessible place, for example in your mobile phone address book. Create a landline telephone tree. Identify a 'warden' in your company who gathers information and is the person to call in case of separation or for relevant information. Inquire at your child's school as to whether they have a policy in place in case of an emergency.

Try to have more than one option of a place to go: the home of a friend, a hotel, or a shelter. Have phone numbers and addresses accessible. Map out your primary route and a backup route in case roads are blocked or impassable. Make sure you have a map of the area available.
◆ Identify a specific place to meet and a contact person in case your family members are separated before or during the evacuation. Be clear that everyone must meet in one place, preferably at home, and you agree to wait for them to arrive. Children must be met at school and escorted home.
◆ Listen to the local radio or TV stations.

2. If you must stay in your home, organize a cupboard with extra food, restocking every six to eight months. Have a jerry can for water storage. Always fill your car's gas tank when it becomes half empty. Keep a battery-operated light in case the electricity goes out. Make sure to have an extra gas canister for your gas stove. Keep flashlights and batteries charged. Prepare a first-aid kit and include medications for diarrhea, vomiting, fever, and cough.
3. Create a home inventory of your personal property. Take photos or videos of all possessions along with receipts, and leave it with a family member or in a safety deposit box in your home country.
4. Plan what to take (see checklist)
5. Keep important documents in a safe place that you can access easily.
6. Have a plan for your pet. If your embassy

evacuates its personnel, animals are not allowed. With this knowledge you will need to have a friend or shelter willing to care for the animal. Consult with local veterinarians about your options for the appropriate facilities if a pet must be left behind. In all cases, be prepared. Have the animal's vaccinations, records, and health certificates current. Consider a chip implant. Stockpile pet food and medication. Have a hand-held animal cage (carrier) available and check with the airlines about transportation regulations.
7. Take ten minutes to do a ten-minute test in real time to gather your family, pets, and important items and put them in a car or in a suitcase.

What to Take Checklist
Decide what items to gather, depending upon the time given to evacuate.

Documents
Passports, picture IDs
Recent photograph of all family members
Birth certificates
Social Security cards
Recent tax returns
Employment information
Wills, deeds
Stocks, bonds, and other negotiable
  certificates
Bank, savings, and retirement account
  numbers
Home inventory
Car insurance card
Computer backup disks

Computers
Drivers' licenses
Health insurance card
House deed
Insurance papers
Legal documents
Marriage certificate

Valuables
Decorations, pins, awards
Family heirlooms
Gold, silver, and other valuable jewelry
Mobile phone(s)
Cash
Checkbooks
Credit cards
Purse and wallet

Medical Items
Prescription dentures
Prescription glasses
Prescription hearing aids
Prescription medicines

Sentimental
Irreplaceable keepsakes
Original paintings
Photos and albums, slides, movies, home
    videos

*Food and Water (for three to seven
    days—if time permits)*
Manual can opener
Non-perishable, ready-to-eat food
Pet food

Water (at least one gallon per person and
    pet per day)

*Clothing (appropriate for the season—
    if time permits)*
Change of clothing for each person (for
    one to seven days)
Change of underwear
Coats and jackets
Gloves and scarves
Hats and caps
Infant supplies and toys
Shoes and boots
Sleepwear

Toiletries (if time permits)
Sanitary devices
Shaving articles
Soap and towels
Toothbrushes and toothpaste

Additional Items
Cameras and extra batteries
Covered container to use as an
    emergency toilet
Flashlights and extra batteries
Portable radio and extra batteries

Pets
Pets (if advance warning, take to a shelter)
Pet ID tags
Pet leashes
Pet medications and medical/inoculations
    records
Pet water bowls

Index